Kant and Artificial Intelligence

Kant and Artificial Intelligence

Edited by
Hyeongjoo Kim and Dieter Schönecker

DE GRUYTER

This work was supported by the Ministry of Education of the Republic of Korea and the National Research Foundation of Korea (NRF-2017S1A6A3A01078538).

ISBN 978-3-11-135569-6
e-ISBN (PDF) 978-3-11-070661-1
e-ISBN (EPUB) 978-3-11-070666-6
DOI https://doi.org/10.1515/9783110706611

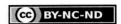
Library of Congress Control Number: 2021951180

Bibliographic information published by the Deutsche Nationalbibliothek
The Deutsche Nationalbibliothek lists this publication in the Deutsche Nationalbibliografie; detailed bibliographic data are available on the Internet at http://dnb.dnb.de.

© 2023 with the authors, editing © 2022 Hyeongjoo Kim and Dieter Schönecker, published by Walter de Gruyter GmbH, Berlin/Boston.
This volume is text- and page-identical with the hardback published in 2022.
The book is published open access at www.degruyter.com.

Cover image: Just_Super/E+/Getty Images
Typesetting: Integra Software Services Pvt. Ltd.
Printing and binding: CPI books GmbH, Leck

www.degruyter.com

Contents

Aesthetics

Preface

What we now call *Artificial Intelligence* did not yet exist in Kant's time, or at least only in an extremely rudimentary form. However, this does not preclude the question of what Kant would have thought about Artificial Intelligence or, more generally, how one can judge the claims and limits of Artificial Intelligence on the basis of Kantian philosophy. And it certainly does not preclude pursuing the question, conversely, of how one can evaluate the claims of Kant and Kantian philosophy from the perspective of Artificial Intelligence.

The contributions in this volume deal with both questions. We thank the authors and Walter de Gruyter publisher, and we are grateful to the HK + Artificial Intelligence Humanities Project team at the Humanities Research Institute, Chung-Ang University, for their support as well as to Ji Hyun Choi, Kwang Young Park, and Seon Ah Jung for their help with compiling the index.

Hyeongjoo Kim
Dieter Schönecker

Theoretical Philosophy

Tobias Schlicht

1 Minds, Brains, and Deep Learning: The Development of Cognitive Science Through the Lens of Kant's Approach to Cognition

Abstract: This paper reviews several ways in which Kant's approach to cognition has been influential and relevant for the development of various paradigms in cognitive science, such as functionalism, enactivism, and the predictive processing model of the mind. In the second part, it discusses philosophical issues arising from recent developments in artificial intelligence in relation to Kant's conception of cognition and understanding. More precisely, it investigates questions about perception, cognition, learning, understanding, and about the age-old debate between empiricists and rationalists in the context of so-called deep neural network architectures as well as the relevance of Kant's conception of cognition and understanding for these issues.

1 Introduction

If you follow the headlines, you can easily get the impression that much of contemporary cognitive science is heavily influenced by Kant's philosophy. Philosopher Andrew Brook (1994) called him the "intellectual godfather" of cognitive science, since Kant allegedly already defended a functionalist theory of mind, arguably the philosophical foundation of artificial intelligence. Neuroscientist Georg Northoff (2018, viii) reports that rereading Kant's *Critique of Pure Reason* has awakened him from his dogmatic slumbers, just like reading Hume had awakened Kant. Impressed by empirical evidence about self-generated brain activity, Northoff and others speak of the "Kantian brain" and associate this activity with Kant's notion of spontaneity (Fazelpour/Thompson 2015). Francisco Varela (Weber/Varela 2002) acknowledged Kant's enormous influence on his own autopoietic approach to life and cognition, and more recently Link Swanson (2016) has traced the popular predictive processing paradigm back to Kant's general project. This is striking, given that Kant's project was not primarily concerned with issues in the philosophy of mind but driven rather by epistemological

Tobias Schlicht, Ruhr-University Bochum

concerns. But although Kant may not have subscribed to all these views attributed to him, such writings present various ideas from his theoretical philosophy as having had or still having an enormous influence on contemporary philosophy of mind and cognitive science.

In this review paper, I will first sketch several ways in which Kant's approach to cognition has been influential and relevant for the development of cognitive science. Kant's relevance goes well beyond some vapid and superficial similarity of certain concepts; many philosophers claim that Kant already anticipated several tenets of classical cognitivism, enactivism, and the predictive processing model of the mind. In the second part, I will add one more piece to this story by discussing philosophical issues arising from recent developments in artificial intelligence. More precisely, I want to sketch some of the philosophical issues associated with so-called deep neural network architectures and the relevance of Kant's conception of cognition and understanding for these issues. As will become clear, the performance of deep neural networks (DNNs) raises important questions about perception, cognition, learning, understanding, and about the age-old debate between empiricists and rationalists; this has led some researchers in machine learning to revive some of Kant's core ideas regarding cognition, developing a Kantian cognitive architecture to overcome the shortcomings of existing deep learning architectures.

2 Cognitive Science Through the Lens of Kant's Theoretical Philosophy

Kant's general influence on contemporary thinking is unquestioned and familiar. Gomes (2017) lists an impressive number of mental phenomena for which Kant's philosophy has been and still is very influential, e.g., the connection between consciousness and self-consciousness (Schlicht 2016/2017) or the debate about conceptual and non-conceptual perceptual content (McDowell 1994, Hanna 2008).[1] Brook (1994) already considered several of Kant's central claims

---

1 Moreover, Gomes (2017) emphasizes the strong influence on specific philosophers in the 20th century, like Strawson and Sellars, who have then shaped the development of analytic philosophy. Most recently, a special issue of *Synthese* (198, Suppl. 13, 2021) brings together several authors discussing the relevance of various Kantian ideas, most notably his method of transcendental argument, for issues in the metaphysics of grounding, the use of the imagination and modal knowledge, virtue epistemology, ethics, and others.

about the mind as having fueled cognitive science more directly; most notably the claim that "most representations require concepts as well as percepts", and Kant's method of transcendental argument, understood as the attempt to "reveal the conditions necessary for some phenomenon to occur" (Brook 1994, p. 12). Based on this initial familiarity of Kant's stance on issues in the philosophy of mind, cognitive science and contemporary debates, one can reconstruct the historical changes that cognitive science underwent through the lens of various aspects of Kant's theoretical philosophy and find traces of some specific ideas of his thinking in the works of cognitive scientists.

2.1 Kant and Functionalism

When John McCarthy coined the term 'artificial intelligence' (AI) in the context of the famous Dartmouth conference in 1956, he described the goal of this project as "that of making a machine behave in ways that would be called intelligent if a human were so behaving" (McCarthy et al. 1955). In a similar vein, Margaret Boden describes the overarching goal of research in AI as "to make computers do the sorts of things that minds can do" (Boden 2016, p. 1). The focus in the first research phase that followed was already set by McCarthy et al. They intended to "attempt [. . .] to find how to make machines use language, form abstractions and concepts, solve kinds of problems now reserved for humans, and improve themselves" (McCarthy et al. 1955, p. 12). While this has been achieved in some areas like speech production and chess computers, in which AI systems sometimes even outperform humans in very specialized problem-solving tasks, the "holy grail" (Boden 2016, p. 18) of AI research has always been the development of an AI system that exhibits "general intelligence", understood "as the ability to perform tasks and attain goals in a wide variety of environments" (Shanahan 2019, p. 91, cf. Legg/Hutter 2007). This broad-stroke characterization of intelligence bypasses the apparent vagueness of the notion which may otherwise yield "terminological quibbles" (Walmsley 2012, p. 3). Walmsley does not regard the terminological choice of "intelligence" as significant but thinks that – echoing McCarthy's goal – "the central issue of AI [. . .] is a comparative one: whatever *we* (humans) have, whether we call it intelligence', 'thinking', 'cognition', 'mind', or something else, can machines have it too?" (Walmsley 2012, p. 3).[2]

---

2 The notion of intelligence is of course vague and difficult to operationalize, let alone compare across very different kinds of philosophical systems. Kant's notion of (an) intelligence is not very helpful for the present project, since calling a creature "intelligent", in his view, amounts to

Boden's and Walmsley's characterizations put *computers* and *machines* into focus. But, as Boden observes, computers or machines themselves aren't what matters. AI is not about hardware, but about what artificial hardware can *do*. Therefore, the focus is not on machines, but on *virtual machines* (Boden 2016, p. 3), which are nothing but *information-processing systems* that can be implemented in a variety of hardware. Consequently, the favored philosophical background theory supporting the possibility of AI has been functionalism, according to which mental states in general are conceived in terms of their functions (or causal roles). Every mental state is identified by its set of causal relations to system inputs and outputs as well as other system states (Putnam 1965). The realization of this causal network of functions is taken to be contingent because the functions are considered to be multiply realizable (Polger/ Shapiro 2016). Thus, *Classical Cognitivism*, the first paradigm in cognitive science, conceived of cognition as information processing along the lines of that present in digital computers. In particular, cognition was understood as constituted by syntactically driven manipulations of symbolic representational structures in the brain that are "sandwiched" (Hurley 1998) between sensory inputs and motor outputs (Fodor 1975, Pylyshyn 1984). For example, when I look at the coffee mug in front of me, sensory information hitting my retina is processed in specialized modules that eventually produce a detailed three-dimensional image of the mug that can guide actions like grasping it. Marr (1982) has provided an exemplary theory of perception in this regard.

One claim relevant for thinking about artificial intelligence is that Kant allegedly defended a functionalist conception of the mind. In *Kant and the Mind*, Andrew Brook (1994) interprets Kant's agnosticism about the underlying substrate of the mind in this way. Despite Kant's "implacably hostile" attitude towards materialism, Brook argues that "materialism fits remarkably easily into his overall theory" (Brook 1994, p. 15). Impressed by Kant's position that "so far as the real nature of the mind is concerned, strict neutrality has to be the order of the day", Brook takes this agnosticism to be an instance of the contemporary functionalist idea of the "multiple realizability" of mental functions; as do Sellars (1974) and Meerbote (1989).

However, this functionalist interpretation of Kant's philosophy of mind faces some problems: Firstly, it ignores Kant's peculiar conception of matter as mere appearance, which leads Ameriks (2000) to interpret Kant's position as a

---

considering it free and capable of self-determination, i.e., as belonging to the world of noumena rather than phenomena (GMS, p. 452, p. 458). Therefore, I suggest moving from *intelligent* to *cognitive* capacities for the purposes of this paper.

form of "mere immaterialism". He arrives at this interpretation by allowing for a minimal knowledge about substrates of appearances, i.e., that they are not material. But this presupposition of knowledge of things in themselves, strictly rejected by Kant, makes Ameriks' interpretation itself problematic. Secondly and relatedly, the functionalist interpretation of Kant's philosophy of mind collides with the fact that contemporary functionalism is typically formulated as entirely ontologically neutral, but rather put forward as a stepping stone to materialist reductionism, since the analysis of mental phenomena in terms of their causal roles is usually complemented by an additional claim about (possibly multiple) *physical* realizations of these mental functions (Chalmers 1996/Kim 1998/Levine 2001/Block 2015). Interpreted this way, Kant would clearly oppose functionalism. Thirdly, it is questionable whether Kant would have taken all "functions" of the mind (KrV: A78f/B103f) to be 'functionalizable' in the sense required for being "realized" by a physical mechanism. For example, what Kant calls the "spontaneity" of mind, properly understood and characteristic of the understanding, seems incompatible with materialism.[3] Allison, for example, is less optimistic than Brook and argues that Brook's functionalist-materialist interpretation of Kant's theory of mind cannot be right, since, in Kant's view (or, rather Allison's interpretation of it), "cognition must be conceived as more than an elaborate information processing procedure, one which begins with raw sensible input and ends with the relatively reliable products of the understanding (cognitions). [. . .] What is missing in such a picture of cognition (at least from the Kantian perspective) is precisely its self-conscious, apperceptive character" (Allison 1996, p. 63).

Whether there is a way of incorporating the notion of spontaneity (with or without its alleged intrinsic self-conscious aspect) and the unity of apperception within a broadly naturalist framework, is an interesting further question that I cannot pursue in depth here. Hanna and Thompson (2003), Northoff (2012), and Fazelpour and Thompson (2015) consider the brain's self-generated activity as a candidate for a neural correlate of the function that Kant calls spontaneity, but this interpretation has not been justified in any detail (for a critical discussion see Schlicht & Newen 2015, cf. Northoff 2013/2014 for further connections to neuroscience).[4]

---

3 Indeed, 'spontaneity' is characteristic of 'freedom', which is typically contrasted to 'nature' and 'mechanism' in Kant's works. Regarding the nature of the understanding, there is a debate about its absolute or merely relative spontaneity which raises the issue of whether cognition in general or acts of understanding in particular can be conceived as being caused by prior events. Grüne (2013) discusses these issues further.
4 Given such problems with a genuinely functionalist interpretation of Kant's stance on mental phenomena, it is not surprising that a number of alternative interpretations of Kant's view

2.2 Kant and the Cartesian Theatre in the Brain

Whether functionalism provides us with an accurate portrayal of the mind depends partly on the features of the biological implementation of mental functions in human (and animal) brains. Can cognition be conceived of as a set of causal functions in abstraction of the biological features of its realization, such that this set of functions could in principle be realized by a machine using a non-biological realization? Or is cognition a biological phenomenon whose realization depends on the presence of a complex dynamical biological system, namely, an organism (with a brain and nervous system), exhibiting crucially biochemical means of information processing? For example, might mental representational states be "aspects" of neural computations, i.e., biological, rather than being abstract functions enjoying some independence from their realizers (Piccinini 2020)?[5]

In the 1980s, new imaging techniques in neuroscience initiated a research focus on the brain, resulting in *connectionist neural network models* of cognitive phenomena. They still remained computational and representational, but information (about the coffee mug in front of me, say) was now supposed to be processed subsymbolically; representations were proposed to have a non-linguistic structure (Smolensky 1988, Clark 1991, Sejnowski 1992, Churchland 1997). This turn was accompanied by new developments in robotics and artificial intelligence, since some researchers now rejected the need for full-fledged models of the world in favor of much sparser "subsumption architectures" that do not rely on a detailed representation of the world (Brooks 1991). As we will see in the second part of the paper, this turn towards brain architecture also inspired the more recent machine-learning techniques, with deep learning being the most prominent one.

Against the background of this controversy over functionalist and biological approaches to cognition, it is striking that on the one hand, Kant anticipated certain problems with the precursor to functionalism, namely the identity theory of mind and brain (Place 1956/Smart 1959), which later resurfaced as Dennett's

---

of the mind-body problem have been put forward in addition to Ameriks' (2000) mere immaterialism, e.g., dual-aspect theory (Sturma 1985), and epistemological dualism (Schlicht 2007), each of them highlighting different aspects of Kant's epistemology. Whichever way we evaluate these interpretations, we should keep in mind Kant's more fundamental transcendental idealism, which he himself calls "a dualism" (Kant 1781/1998, A370).

5 Block's (2002) paper on *The Harder Problem of Consciousness* contains a relevant and interesting discussion of the relation between functionalism and physicalism as metaphysical views on the mind.

'Cartesian Theatre' objection against materialism about consciousness, while on the other hand Kant was also impressed by the brain's features that might explain certain cognitive phenomena. This tension can be brought to light by having a look at his exchange with the physician Samuel Thomas von Sömmerring.

In 1796, Samuel Sömmerring published a short book, *On the Organ of the Soul*, in which he speculated about the possible function of the liquid contained in the brain's ventricles with respect to the unification and separation (synthesis and analysis) of sensory data. Prior to publication, he had an exchange with Kant about his ideas, specifically that of a sensory organ or seat of the soul in the brain. In one of his letters, Kant respects Sömmerring's position but expresses his explicit doubts about the general approach, since "it is the concept of a *seat of the soul* that occasions the disagreement of the faculties concerning the common sensory organ and this concept therefore had better be left entirely out of the picture, which is all the more justified since the concept of a seat of the soul requires *local presence*" (AA 12, 31–32). In contrast to this approach, Kant suggests taking seriously the idea of a mere "*virtual presence*" of the mind in the brain, which makes the whole question of what could serve as a 'seat of the soul' disappear, or so he claims. Sadly, he does not clarify what he means by virtual presence here. A further striking passage in this regard can be found in his *Lectures on Metaphysics* (V-Met) where he stresses that "*the location of the soul in the body* [. . .] *cannot be determined* [his emphasis] [. . .] I cannot feel the place in the body where the soul resides." (AA 28, 281) Yet, despite this epistemological restriction, Kant puts forward an argument that sounds like he is alluding to the contemporary idea of supervenience, which posits the ground of all sensations in the brain. It is worth quoting this passage in full (Kant's emphases):

> But the cause of all sensations is the nervous system. Without nerves we cannot sense anything outer. But the root of all nerves is the brain; the brain is accordingly aroused with each sensation because all nerves concentrate themselves in the brain; accordingly, all sensations concentrate themselves in the brain. Thus the soul must put the *seat of its sensations* in the brain, as the *location of all conditions* of the sensations. *But that is not the location of the soul itself*, but rather the location from which all nerves, consequently all sensations as well, arise. [. . .] When, e.g., I hold a finger to the fire, then I experience pain in it; but in the end all sensations from every particular part of the body are concentrated in the brain, the stem of all nerves; for if the nerves from one part of the body are cut, then of course we feel nothing from that part. Accordingly, the principle of all sensations must be in the brain. [. . .] When we imagine a position in the brain which is the first principle of the stem of the nerves where all nerves run together and end in one point, which is called the seat of the senses <*sensorium commune*>, but which no physician <*medicus*> has seen, then the question arises, does the soul reside in this seat of the senses <*sensorio communi*>? Has it taken up a little spot there from which it directs the

whole body, somewhat like an organist can direct the whole organ from one location; or does it have no location at all in the body, so that the body itself is its location? Granted, if the soul took up a little spot in the brain where it plays on our nerves as on an organ, then we could believe that if we had gone through all the parts of the body we ultimately would have to come upon this little spot where the soul resides. Now, if one took away this little spot, the whole human being might still be there, but the location would be lacking where the organist is supposed to play, as though on an organ: but this is thought very materialistically. (V-Met, AA 28, 281–282)

I want to highlight two impressive features of this passage and of Kant's engagement with Sömmerring's proposal in the present context. Firstly, these passages in effect anticipate Dennett's (1991) objection against what he calls 'Cartesian materialism', a position allegedly shared by many contemporary neuroscientists who try to identify certain brain areas or processes as being causally responsible for (or identical with) consciousness.[6] The terminological contrast between a local and a merely virtual presence of the mind in the brain has a very modern ring to it, considering Dennett's characterization of the mind as a "virtual machine implemented in the parallel architecture of a brain" (Dennett 1991, p. 210), indeed anticipating the functionalist view of the mind. It is difficult to determine, though, whether Kant's use of "virtual" in his discussion of Sömmerring's proposal is akin to Dennett's.

Secondly, Kant even engages with Sömmerring's specific proposal concerning the liquid contained in the brain's ventricles, expressing his "great scruple" that this candidate substrate is not *organized*. Only something having some sort of organization or "purposive disposition of its parts" could serve to locate the mind. This is reminiscent of Kant's own groundbreaking and very influential discussion of organisms as natural purposes, i.e., self-producing and self-organizing beings in his *Critique of the Power of Judgment*. In contrast to a mere *mechanical* organization, Kant considers what he calls a "*dynamical* organization" to be crucial for the mind. Again, what he means by this is not specified any further in the passage quoted, but it can be illuminated by his discussion of the contrast between mechanistic and teleological explanation in the third *Critique*. This discussion of the immanent purposiveness of living organisms has inspired generations of philosophers, leading up to the present-day development of so-called "enactive" approaches to the mind (Varela et al. 1991, Weber/Varela 2002, Thompson 2007).

---

6 For a recent installment of this controversy see the exchange between neuroscientists Alan Hobson and Karl Friston on the one hand and philosophers Krzysztof Dolega and Joe Dewhurst on the other (Hobson/Friston 2014, Dolega/Dewhurst 2015, Hobson/Friston 2016). Schlicht/Dolega (2021) discuss the prospects of the predictive processing framework as a guide of this search for neural correlates.

2.3 Kant and Enactivism

In one of his last texts, Francisco Varela acknowledges his debt to Kant's ground-breaking discussion of organisms for the development of the 'autopoietic' or 'enactive' conception of cognition in the early 1990s (Weber/Varela 2002). Together with Brooks' (1991) work in robotics, the *enactive-embodied* approach to cognition challenged both the representationalist paradigm and its explicit separation of perception from action in the traditional 'sandwich conception' (Hurley 1998) of cognition in favor of a dynamic view. In contrast to a traditional linear progression from sensory input via cognitive computation to action, enactivism conceives of perception and cognition not simply as functional brain states but as entangled and intertwined embodied activities of whole organisms (agents, systems) that can be explained without appeal to mental representations (e.g., Varela et al. 1991, Noë 2004, Chemero 2009, Hutto/Myin 2013, Gallagher 2017). Indeed, in this framework, the equivalence of intentionality and mental representation is no longer taken for granted (Schlicht 2018). Applied to our example used above, perceiving a coffee mug not only requires multiple actions like eye-, head- and body-movements (gaze turning etc.); perceiving is *in the service* of detecting action possibilities (like grasping) from the start (Gibson 1979).

All enactivists subscribe to what Thompson (2007, p. 128) calls the "deep continuity of life and mind", i.e., the claim that the organizational features of mind are an enriched version of those of life (Noë 2009, p. 41; Colombetti 2013, p. xvi; Gallagher 2017, p. 102; Di Paolo et al. 2017, p. 3, 178). In an evaluation of Kant's influence on current cognitive science, this is the crucial aspect of enactivism. At the heart of this conception is the notion of autopoiesis (Maturana/Varela 1980). An autopoietic system – the minimal living organization – is one that continuously produces the components that specify it, while at the same time realizing it (the system) as a concrete unity in space and time, which makes the network of component production possible (Weber/Varela 2002, 115). In his second *Critique*, Kant conceives of organisms as 'self-organized' and 'self-producing', i.e., autopoietic, systems that cannot be explained in purely mechanistic terms, but which we have to 'make intelligible' to us by relying on teleological principles that are not part of natural science but *borrowed* from practical contexts. Impressed by certain animals' (e.g., zebra fish, salamanders) ability to regrow damaged or even severed body-parts (Simon 2012), Kant discusses examples to demonstrate that animals exhibit a certain *form* or *organization* that, if conceived *merely* as the result of blind mechanistic causal processes, appears completely contingent. Yet, "since reason must be able to cognize the *necessity* in every form of a natural product if it would understand the conditions connected with its generation", our understanding must borrow the concept of final cause to make sense of this organization.

This leads Kant to his conception of organisms as "natural ends", i.e., as natural products *and* as ends at the same time. This looks like a contradiction, since the notion of an 'end' or 'purpose' – being a "stranger" (KU, AA 05: A390) in natural science – must be projected into nature for the sake of an understanding of (some of) its products. Unlike a watch, the parts of an organism, its organs, must be taken to *produce themselves* rather than being produced by an external power, and they *arrange themselves* in relation and mutual dependence to each other. Analogously, unlike a watchmaker, in the case of organisms the guiding *idea* is not to be found outside the product (the watch), but within it (the organism itself). "An organized being is thus not a mere machine, for that has only a *motive* power, while the organized being possesses in itself a *formative* power, and indeed one that it communicates to the matter, which does not have it (it organizes the latter)" (KU, AA 05: A374). Thompson (2007, p. 62) refers to this formative power as "circular causality", i.e., a causal dependence which goes two ways: on the one hand, the features of the whole (organism) are determined by its parts (organs); on the other hand, the local interactions of the parts (organs) are determined by the whole (organism). But as Kant makes explicit in the third *Critique*, this assumption is to be taken only in an epistemological sense, i.e., we only regard it *as if* organisms were possible only through reason, since as natural products they must come about through purely mechanistic causes, and thus be amenable to a mechanistic explanation. We cannot *prove* that organisms indeed exhibit this formative power, since we cannot acquire an intuition of it.[7]

Francisco Varela regarded Kant's position as important, because he took Kant to have "developed the possibility of a third way between a strong teleology and a brute materialism" (Weber/Varela 2002, p. 99). Varela acknowledges Kant's insight but considers his position "unstable" and in need of revision "on the basis of modern developments of biological research and thinking". According to Weber and Varela, Kant's conception of an organism as a self-organized and self-producing being is closely analogous to the definition of an organism in Varela's own theory of "autopoiesis". In this view, biological autonomy and individuality warrant the assumption of an "intrinsic teleology", to the effect that "*organisms are subjects having purposes according to values encountered in*

---

7 At this point it is important to emphasize that Kant, unlike some of the idealist philosophers after him, does not regard humans to be capable of an intellectual intuition in contrast or in addition to a merely sensory intuition. See Grüne (2009) for more detailed discussion on Kant's theory of intuition.

the making of their living" (Weber/Varela, p. 102). The theory of autopoiesis as a theory of living systems is supposed to help *naturalize* Kant's original theory of organisms. The question of whether Kant's epistemic and critical position on this issue of teleology or Varela's naturalistic theory of autopoiesis is warranted, is beyond the scope of this review.[8] But this illustrates how Kant's philosophy of biology left a footprint with wide-ranging implications in the historical development of cognitive science.

One particular implication of the autopoietic approach to cognition and the mind-life continuity thesis is that *all* organisms may exhibit at least some basic form of cognition, whereas such views have a problem allowing for genuine cognition in artificial systems. In contrast to more traditional cognitivist approaches, the possibility of cognition in 'simple' biological systems has recently been taken seriously with respect to organisms such as bacteria (Ben Jacob et al. 2006), plants (Calvo/Keijzer 2011, Calvo et al. 2020, Mancuso 2018, Sims 2019), and slime molds (Vallverdú et al. 2018), for example. Whether Kant would have regarded the life-mind continuity thesis as credible must be left open here, although Nunez (forthcoming), drawing on the *Critique of the Power of Judgement* (§65), argues that Kant would have had to at least ascribe desires to plants on the basis of how they move and on how Kant himself treated the notion of being alive.

Developmental biologist Michael Levin somehow takes this story full circle by arguing that we should apply the computational approach not only to animals with brains and nervous systems, but also to simple organisms without a brain. Rather than continuing to contrast the brain with the rest of the body (even in the so-called embodied cognition research program, see Shapiro 2011), Levin invites us to consider the body as performing calculations as well, so as to overcome the traditional life vs. machine dichotomy and according to an updated notion of 'machine' (Bongard/Levin 2021). Puzzled by an organism's formative power, Levin speculates that cells and tissue may exhibit some basic forms of memory and action, using bioelectricity to communicate and decide or plan development (Levin et al. 2021, Pezzulo et al. 2021). For example, he succeeded in 'reprogramming' a planarian worm to grow a second head in place of its tail which he had cut off. What he'd done was to change the bioelectrical signals or 'code' which would normally have led to the growth of a new tail. Levin's work suggests a convergence between biology and computer science and is thus highly relevant for the future of artificial intelligence.

---

[8] For further details and discussion see Thompson (2007); cf. Schlicht (2011) for a critical evaluation of Thompson's account.

2.4 Kant and Predictive Processing

Major developments in machine learning also heavily inspired recently popular *predictive processing* models of the brain which are taken to provide "the first truly unifying account of perception, cognition and action" (Clark 2016, p. 2) by conceiving of the brain as a prediction machine. This view implicates a delicate balance between bottom-up and top-down processing, in contrast to traditional serial bottom-up processing accounts: Perception and cognition are defined in terms of the brain testing hypotheses about the (sources or causes of) incoming sensory stimulation; hypotheses are generated by a hierarchical generative model of the world and constantly updated in response to prediction error signals (Friston 2010, Hohwy 2013, Clark 2016, Metzinger/Wiese 2017). To return to our example, perceiving the coffee mug is a process already informed by underlying brain processes that constitute a set of more or less likely expectations about sensory input and its causes. These expectations are constantly compared to the actual incoming sensory information, resulting in prediction errors (deviations) that are processed in the brain. The traditional picture of the brain using incoming sensory information to build up a representation of the world is thus turned upside down, since the new picture holds that "the rich representation of worldly states of affairs is signaled in the top-down predictions of sensory input, maintained by the perceptual hierarchy in the brain" (Hohwy 2013, p. 47).

Link Swanson (2016) argues that this most recent paradigm in cognitive science also has roots in Kant's philosophy and tells a convincing story tracing back this influence via Helmholtz's thesis of perception as unconscious inference, which in turn was a primary source for Friston's (2005; 2010) original proposal regarding predictive processing as a unified brain theory. The radical reversal of processing (top-down hypothesis-testing rather than bottom-up model-building) characteristic of predictive processing finds an analogue in Kant's so-called Copernican revolution with its combination of intuition (providing the material) and concepts (generating an understanding of what's perceived), presenting "us with a view of perception as a Kantian in spirit, 'spontaneous' interpretative activity, and not a process of passively building up percepts from inputs" (Gładziejewski 2016, p. 574). But Swanson also links more specific concepts from the predictive processing story to specific analogues in Kant's theory – e.g., generative models and schemata, which are both heavily informed by intuitions as well as concepts in the process of object recognition. Indeed, it's striking that both Clark and Hohwy choose a starting point that sounds very familiar to Kantians, only formulated from the perspective of the brain whose task, "when viewed from a certain distance, can seem impossible: it must discover information about the likely causes of impinging signals without any form of direct access to their source"

(Clark 2013, p. 183). Put this way, the central issue is understanding causation, i.e., understanding relations between worldly causes and sensory inputs. Assuming a Humean framework, this is impossible according to Kant, who posits an innate conceptual machinery (the categories) that must be applied to sensory input in order to enable such understanding.

But only Hohwy's interpretation of the predictive processing framework is internalist like Kant's. Indeed, Hohwy argues that the prediction error minimization theory "reveals the mind to be inferentially secluded from the world", showing that strong embodied views of cognition and mind should be rejected in favor of "a more old-fashioned, skepticism-prone view of the mind-world-relation" (Hohwy 2014, pp. 259–260). Thus, Beni (2018) complains that Swanson's reconstruction only holds true for Hohwy's version of predictive processing, while it ignores the dominant embodied and action-oriented versions put forward by Clark (2016) and Bruineberg and Rietveld (2014) or Bruineberg, Kiverstein and Rietveld (2016), which are much more inspired by Gibson's (1979) ecological psychology than by Kant's transcendental idealism. Whether the embodied variety of predictive processing is tenable and coherent, given the epistemic starting point it shares with Hohwy's version, cannot be pursued further in this paper. In any case, the view that predictive processing is rooted in Kant's view of the mind must thus be taken with a grain of salt, just like the idea that assimilates Kant's view of the mind to functionalism.[9]

With respect to the alleged roots of functionalism, enactivism, and predictive processing in Kant's philosophy, it is important to keep in mind that these different paradigmatic backgrounds take different stances towards the relation between cognition, intentionality, and representation, and propose different explanatory strategies in cognitive science. It seems unlikely that Kant would have subscribed to all of these views at once, given the opposition (and genuine incompatibility) of some of the contemporary stances.[10] While classical cognitivism alludes to mental representations, embodied enactivism eschews them (Gallagher 2017, p. 7). While the former is based on functionalism and explicitly allows for the possibility of cognition in artificial systems, the latter is based on a strong continuity of life and mind, making this possibility problematic.

---

9 Anderson & Chemero (2019) indeed criticize Clark for trying to embrace *both* an embodied-enactive view of the mind *and* the predictive processing architecture, simply because it seems to be somewhat rooted in Kant's framework, which they take to have been overcome by an embodied perspective on the mind.

10 See Di Paolo, Thompson, and Beer (2021) for a statement on the incompatibilities between the free-energy approach (underlying the predictive processing framework developed by Hohwy and Clark) and enactivism.

2.5 Interlude: Aspects of Kant's Account of Cognition

As we saw, at the heart of the predictive processing approach is the project of understanding causal relations. This is also the recurrent theme linking Hume's empiricism with Kant's transcendental idealism and his 'Copernican Revolution'. Hume recognized that an understanding of a causal relation between A and B cannot be grounded in sensory input alone, since this does not provide us with a connection between events A and B but only with their temporal succession, yielding his skepticism about an understanding of causation. Kant followed Hume in his assessment of the inadequacy of sensory experience in accounting for an understanding of causal relations; at the same time, he was willing to borrow a priori concepts from the rationalists and claim that it is the faculty of understanding itself which is the source of a system of concepts that provide the necessary unification. It is now worth reminding the reader of the core of Kant's theory of cognition, prior to the discussion presented in the second part of the paper.

In two very instructive papers, Marcus Willaschek and Eric Watkins (Watkins/Willaschek 2017, Willaschek/Watkins 2020) outline the complex usage of the notion of cognition in Kant's works. The most prominent usage is what they call *cognition in the narrow sense*, which requires a unification of intuition and concept, i.e., the combination of sensory receptivity and spontaneity of the understanding. *Cognition in the broad sense*, by contrast, allows for several "degrees of cognition", sketched in different, yet not necessarily incompatible, ways in the so-called *Jäsche Logik* (AA 16: 64–65) and in the *Critique of Pure Reason* (KrV: A320/B376). In the latter, they are presented as more or less demanding cases of "representing something", be it unconsciously, consciously, through perception, understanding or reason, with or without concepts or intuition being involved. The most basic degree of cognition is "to represent something", without any further conditions; the highest or most complex degree is to "comprehend something" through reason and a priori. Importantly, in Kant's taxonomy, *cognition* does not imply truth or assent, and is therefore to be distinguished from the notion of *knowledge* (Willaschek/Watkins 2020). Taken in the broad sense, any conscious representation that represents an object counts as a case of cognition, even if the object does not exist (or if it cannot be given in experience).

But despite the variety of dimensions of the concept of cognition, as used by Kant, cognition in the narrow sense is singled out as "cognition in the proper sense" (KrV: A78/B103) and this is the notion that will concern us here. Cognition in this sense can be described as a "conscious representation of a given object and of (at least some of) its general features" (Watkins/Willaschek 2017, p. 86). For cognition of an object to obtain, this must be given and a concept must be applied to it. The former is the task of sensibility, the latter is performed by the understanding. And such cognition is actively achieved rather than simply happening by chance, since it is a product – "the mere effect" – of the synthesis performed by the imagination, "without which we would have no cognition at all", at least not in this crucial narrow sense. This passage places great emphasis on the function of synthesis, which is conceived as "the action of putting different representations together with each other and comprehending their manifoldness in one cognition" (Watkins/Willaschek 2017, p. 86). An act of synthesis, as such the beginning of an answer to the problem posed by Hume, "collects the elements for cognitions and unifies them into a certain content". Without such a unificatory process of concept application to a given object, intuitions remain "blind" and thoughts "empty" (KrV: A51/B75-76). Kant therefore stresses that if we are interested in "the first origin of our cognition", we have to focus on synthesis.

What the conception of degrees of cognition in the *Jäsche Logik* and the "progression" passage in the *Critique of Pure Reason* have in common is the idea that cognition in the narrow sense presupposes consciousness. In the *Jäsche Logik*, where Kant outlines a gradual concept of cognition, *this idea is* found in the fourth degree, defined as "to be acquainted with something *with consciousness*, i.e., to *cognize* it" (AA 16: 65), whereas in the "progression" Kant develops it as follows: "The genus is representation in general (*repraesentatio*). Under it stands the representation with consciousness (*perceptio*). A perception that refers to the subject as a modification of its state is a sensation (*sensatio*); an objective perception is a cognition (*cognitio*)" (KrV: A320/B376). Taking the progression seriously, Tolley (2020) argues that Kant classifies sensing, intuiting, perceiving and mere thinking as "lying earlier" than, and providing conditions for, cognition, while still considering cognition as being placed on a "psychologically elementary level" compared to knowledge, understanding, and explaining. In contrast to Watkins and Willaschek, Tolley argues that Kant's concept of cognition is unified rather than equivocal.

Without intending to settle this dispute with respect to Kant's use of "cognition", all sides agree that he emphasized cognition in the narrow sense, where the other candidates fall under the umbrella of the concept of cognition as it is used in contemporary cognitive science. And since cognition in the narrow sense, in Kant's view, is a "distinctive form of consciousness of a real object by way of a specific kind of combination of representations" (Tolley 2020, p. 3217), consciousness is a condition of cognition in this proper sense (I will return to this point in the last section of this paper). By Kant's lights then, for an artificial system to be capable of cognition in the narrow sense, it would have to be capable of consciousness as well. This is certainly not a view of cognition that is widespread among contemporary cognitive scientists. Proponents of the predictive processing approach to perception and cognition also do not hold that these processes require consciousness, although they often claim that the framework can also be applied to explain consciousness (Hohwy/Seth 2020, Clark 2019). But even if an artificial system may not be conscious in the relevant sense, it may still be capable of cognition in the broad sense. That is, it may be said – minimally – to have representations of something or other.

With these reminders of Kant's view of cognition, we can now turn, in the second part of this paper, to more recent developments in artificial intelligence, namely, the ascent and success story of deep learning architectures that led to the recent AI spring. As I will try to show, this fascinating development raises interesting philosophical issues about the nature of perception, learning and understanding and about the more general question of empiricist vs. rationalist approaches.

3 The Potential and Limitations of Deep Learning

After a series of dark winters, AI research has made considerable progress, pushed forward by the advent of so-called "deep learning architectures" (LeCun/Bengio/Hinton 2015; Buckner 2018/2019, Sejnowski 2018). This has been – so far – the result of a development in which the connectionist approach to AI superseded the "Good Old-fashioned AI" (or GOFAI-) approach. Current discussions of AI often focus on software that does not only process fixed *programmed* algorithms, but can be *trained* using algorithms, such that part of the process can be developed by the software itself. This machine-learning approach to AI is one among many and includes supervised, unsupervised and reinforcement learning. Deep Learning on the basis of artificial neural networks is currently the most promising and most widely discussed (and used) approach, which is why we will focus on it here.

The crucial difference compared to traditional GOFAI-approaches is that these neural networks are inspired by the organization of the human brain – more specifically, the layered architecture of the visual cortex – while the main difference compared to their historical precursors, the connectionist networks from the 1980s and 1990s, is the number of layers of simulated neurons. Whereas classical networks only consisted of an input layer, one hidden layer and an output layer, *deep* neural networks are deep in the sense that there are many more than one hidden layer, indeed there are numbers reaching hundreds of layers. This increases their computational power exponentially, enables them to represent even abstract features of the environment and is taken to be largely responsible for their recent success in many applications. Thus, although this new phase already started in the 1980s, researchers only developed computers with the necessary computational power in the late 2000s. The nodes of the network are connected – just as real neurons are connected via dendrites – and the connections between them have different weights. The larger the weight between A and B, the greater the influence of A on B, and vice versa (since weights are symmetric).

Using cats, neuroscientists and Nobel laureates David Hubel and Torsten Wiesel (1962) discovered that light of different wavelengths activates cells in the back of the eye and that this activation is then processed via the optic nerves into the brain, ending up in the hierarchically organized series of layers of neurons in the visual cortex. Neurons in different layers have specific preferences (or receptive fields) and thus detect increasingly complex features, from edges via simple and complex shapes to whole objects, like faces.[11] The *nodes* of the network are like simplified, formal neurons. The input layer provides the data for the network – images, spoken words, hand-written digits, games –, whereas the output layer produces the desired results, e.g., a classification of an image or object, a number or word. In between, multiple hidden layers perform calculations that produce this result:

> An image, for example, comes in the form of an array of pixel values, and the learned features in the first layer of representation typically represent the presence or absence of edges at particular orientations and locations in the image. The second layer typically detects motifs by spotting particular arrangements of edges, regardless of small variations in the edge positions. The third layer may assemble motifs into larger combinations that correspond to parts of familiar objects, and subsequent layers would detect objects as combinations of these parts. The key aspect of deep learning is that these layers of features are not designed by human engineers: they are learned from data using a general-purpose learning procedure. (LeCun/Bengio/Hinton 2015, p. 436)

Several major factors are important for their performance:
(1) First, as the name suggests, these networks are able to *learn* and can therefore be *trained* on the input data; they are not pre-programmed (although the programmer chooses the input data). Learning takes place by adjusting the weights

---

11 Hubel and Wiesel dubbed them "simple" and "complex" cell types respectively. This inspired Fukushima (1980) to develop a new kind of network, the "Neocognitron" which was supposed to demonstrate this stronger computational power.

according to sensory feedback. These networks start with arbitrary weights and adjust them in the course of a training phase in which they are bombarded with data. If the goal is to learn recognizing objects, the inputs will be images; if the goal is to learn playing games, the input will be games of this sort. And so on.

(2) This is the second important factor: Using internet databases such as image-net, the training set for a given network can consist of millions of examples, e.g., millions of images of dogs and cats, or millions of games of Go – many more dogs and cats and games than any human being could encounter or play in their lifetime. Note well: the point is not that since DNNs *can* rely on so much data, they have a significant computational advantage when compared with humans; the point is that they *must* rely on so much data to achieve this significant level of performance. Children, by contrast, can learn very quickly from just a few examples (Carey 2009). That's an important difference. Since the real world does not come as neatly labeled as suggested by a supervised learning training set for networks, this cannot be the route to *mimic* human learning or understanding. It is different from the very start. But that does not preclude us from considering the procedure "intelligent" or as an instance of "cognition", since these phenomena may allow for multiple realizations.[12]

Yet, if the images come already labeled (this is a dog, this is a cat) – which is the most common method of machine learning – the network will eventually learn to produce confident results (outputs) in recognizing dogs and cats. In general, the output does not consist of a single answer, but comes as a "vector of scores, one for each category" where the goal is to get the machine to give the desired category the highest score (LeCun et al. 2015, p. 436). For example, if the input is an image of a dog, the network might spit out 70% dog, 20% fox, 10% cat, i.e., outputs with different confidence ratings. Eventually, after initially making many errors, performance increases because these errors are processed using so-called 'backpropagation': it calculates the difference between the intended and the actual output and sends this error signal (this is not a dog) back through the hidden layers of the network. By adjusting the weights along the way, the network can perform better the next time it encounters this image.

Although it isn't clear whether there is a biological analogue to this process of backpropagation, it works well for these networks. Since what a network can 'recognize' on each layer is not pre-programmed, it must find out about the most salient and characteristic features that are central for the task (of recognizing dogs, say). This is important for the test phase in which the network is

---

12 See Buckner (2020) for rebuttals to similar criticisms against deep learning networks.

supposed to classify and recognize with high confidence new objects (more cats and dogs) which weren't in the training set. So far, DNNs do not make it intelligible to us how they reach a decision when they recognize an object with high confidence, for example, 60% dog, 30% cat, 10% fox. The most prominent artificial neural networks today – convolutional neural networks, or ConvNets (Mitchell 2020, pp. 73–88) are named after the operation leading the DNN to yield a certain output: convolution.[13] Convolution is a mathematical procedure that works like a filter that slides across an image and creates a layer of features across this image (Sejnowski 2018, p. 130–131). It thereby determines whether a certain portion of an image, say, a set of pixels in a grid, contains or signifies a certain feature and then assigns a certain numeral to that part of the grid. Repeating this procedure for several layers covers ever increasing portions of the image and detects ever more abstract features, thus corresponding to Hubel and Wiesel's 'simple cells.'

The network is still relying on human expertise in the form of feedback (labels) about its results. That makes the learning process "supervised". The inputs are fixed and the results are determined; the network must learn to get from A to B using only its own resources, simulated neurons in multiple layers connected by different weights. After having received the input image, the network performs its layer-by-layer calculations and finally produces an output. This can be formulated as a certain degree of confidence (between 0 and 100%) regarding every image and category. Some networks have already achieved more than 90% accuracy in the image-net competition (Mitchell 2020, p. 101). Nevertheless, their performance is limited, since they can only succeed or fail in categorizing an input-picture (or word) correctly but they cannot produce any new insights. This seems possible in unsupervised learning when the result (the label "dog", say) is not given but found by the network by associating and clustering certain patterns with each other. For example, the network might be able to detect words in social media feeds which are used more frequently than others or might recognize that customers who bought product A also often bought product B, which can then be recommended to new customers who bought A.

(3) A third and peculiar aspect of DNNs concerns the kinds of errors they make and how different these errors are from the kinds of errors humans make.

---

[13] According to LeCun, Bengio and Hinton (2015, p. 439), ConvNets (or DCNNs) proved to be easier to train and "generalized much better" than other networks, cf. LeCun et al. (1990). 'Pooling' is a procedure that is seen as corresponding to convolution and similar to Hubel and Wiesel's 'complex cells', since it aggregates each feature over a region and guarantees for invariance.

Since humans also make mistakes – being subject to visual illusions, for example –, such networks need not be perfect in their performance. But it is instructive how easily they can be fooled:

> While they also get confused by images containing multiple objects, unlike humans they tend to miss objects that are small in the image, objects that have been distorted by color or contrast filters the photographer applied to the image, and "abstract representations" of objects, such as a painting or statue of a dog, or a stuffed toy dog.
>
> (Mitchell 2020, p. 105)

Moreover, and most disconcertingly, DNNs are easily duped and fooled, both by intentional manipulation of the input data and by new situations in the real world that the network is not sufficiently prepared for. Thus, a self-driving car's autopilot mode got confused by salt lines which had been laid out on a road in anticipation of a storm, since they looked just like lane markings – an unlikely yet possible situation. Mitchell (2020, p. 120) reports results from her colleague Will Landecker who had trained a network in classifying images into "contains an animal" and "does not contain an animal". But the test phase revealed that the network had classified all photos with a blurry background as containing an animal since there was a high correlation between a macroscopic picture taken of an animal and the photo having an otherwise blurry background. That is, the network 'overfitted' to its training set and thus failed to accurately predict future data that are slightly dissimilar but nevertheless belong to the same relevant category. Another, rather embarrassing and inexcusable because discriminatory, mistake happened to the Google Photos App when it labeled a selfie taken by an African-American couple as "Gorillas" (Vincent 2018).

DNNs can be fooled more systematically using so-called "adversarial examples". These are images which have been intentionally distorted by making very small changes that the human eye cannot detect but lead a DNN to classify the object depicted on it in an arbitrary manner, even though it had correctly classified the original image before. For example, a lion was now classified as a library, both times with high confidence (Szegedy et al. 2015). Subsequently, Nguyen, Yosinski and Clune (2015) showed that it is possible to produce copies of images showing an object A where the copy contains differences which are unrecognizable to the human eye and yet allegedly recognized as showing another object B with 99% confidence by a DNN. This seems to show that not only do DNNs learn very differently than humans – "at the most specific grain of detail, DCNNs [*Deep Convolutional Neural Networks*, T.S.] and human perceptual cortex do not produce exactly the same phenomena" (Buckner 2018, p. 28)[14] – they also cannot be

---

14 Generative Adversarial Networks (GANs) can be seen as a reaction to this problem. Here, one network's task is to recognize and classify images correctly, while another one generates

trusted. Thus, it remains obscure why ConvNets work as well as they do.[15] This opacity of the learning and decision-making process makes it difficult to understand *what* and *how* such networks learn. Mitchell (2020, p. 132) concludes that "something very different from human perception is going on".

3.1 Philosophical Interpretations of Deep Neural Networks

As we saw in the first part, one crucial aspect of Kant's theory of cognition is that he posits a balanced interaction between bottom-up and top-down processing, in his terminology between intuition and concept. A second, yet different, aspect of his approach is the positing of a priori contributions to cognition, i.e., contributions that are independent and systematically prior to experience or learning. With respect to our understanding of causal relations, for example, Kant shared the same starting point with Hume, stressing that it cannot be conceived as a "direct consequence of data-driven learning" (Butterfill 2020, p. 93). However, contrary to Hume's skepticism, Kant concluded that there must be a contribution to understanding that is not learned which is often identified with being "innate".[16]

Considering the preceding paragraphs, DNNs also raise a number of interesting issues concerning perception, classification, abstraction, conceptual learning, and understanding, and also concerning the debate about innate vs. learned against the background of the controversy between empiricists and rationalists. Buckner argues that in today's debates, the question is no longer whether the mind starts out as an unstructured 'blank slate' but whether categorical representations "are due mostly to domain-specific or domain-general cognitive mechanisms" (Buckner 2018, p. 3). A typical example for a domain-specific cognitive mechanism is Chomsky's universal grammar, which constitutes a language acquisition device underlying our learning of all natural languages; it is domain-specific since it only pertains to language. By contrast, one may posit only one domain-general all-purpose learning device allowing one to acquire knowledge across domains (as done, for example, in Skinner 1957, the book criticized by Chomsky 1959). Crucially, opponents in the debate would not count the

---

data like those in the training set. In this competitive way, the two networks can improve on their performance.

15 This feature of DNNs gives rise to the research program of "explainable AI" which aims at making such networks intelligible (see also Sejnowski 2020).

16 Samuels (2004, p. 139) criticizes this characterization for being uninformative.

latter as evidence for a nativist position, since, as Long (ms., p. 3) argues, every-one agrees that learning requires that *something* be innate. He proposes, following Margolis and Laurence (2013), to frame the controversy in terms of this contrast, with nativism holding that cognition (in a given domain) requires domain-specific mechanisms, and empiricism holding that (for any domain) domain-general mechanisms are sufficient. The questions we are facing then are the following: Given that DNNs do not start from scratch, do they require domain-specific mechanisms or can they make do with domain-general ones in order to achieve general intelligence? (2) Does Kant's system of categories constitute a domain-general or a domain-specific cognitive mechanism?

Regarding question (1), Long (ms.) has usefully framed the development of artificial intelligence in terms of this opposition and formulated more fine-grained theoretical options. To keep things as simple as possible, we will focus on only two of them: "*Necessity Nativism* is the claim that necessarily, a human-level AI system will be a nativist system" (Long, ms., p. 6). That is, in this view general intelligence requires nativist (domain-specific) mechanisms. By contrast, *Possibility Empiricism* "is the claim that it is possible for a human-level AI system to be an empiricist system" (Long ms., p. 6); i.e., general intelligence, in this view, does not require domain-specific mechanisms but can be acquired by relying on domain-general mechanisms alone. Long argues that "empiricist human-level AI is at the very least possible" (Long, ms., p. 1). That is, Long belongs to a group which we may dub "optimists". Optimists claim that developers may overcome the obstacles that current AI systems face compared to human-level understanding without having to rely on domain-specific mechanisms. Pessimists, by contrast, claim that developers will not succeed in building AI systems that can achieve human-level understanding solely by relying on domain-general mechanisms. Domain-specific, i.e., innate mechanisms are necessary for this feat.

(a) Optimists

In a seminal article, LeCun, Bengio and Hinton (2015, p. 436) claim that DNNs are able to "learn representations of data with multiple levels of abstraction". If that were so, this would be fantastic, since – according to Mitchell (2020, p. 319) – "abstraction, in some form, underlies *all* of our concepts, even from earliest infancy" and it would therefore open the door for the possibility that DCNNs may acquire concepts and understanding simply from being exposed to data. That is, LeCun, Bengio and Hinton are optimists. So is Buckner (2018), who is impressed by the success of ConvNets and discusses them in the context of an empiricist philosophy of mind, claiming that they "model a distinctive kind of abstraction from experience", and thereby "one crucially important component of intelligence – a form of categorial abstraction", among other components necessary for general intelligence (Buckner 2018, p. 3). He also highlights several core features of DNNs – multiple layers, convolutional filters, and pooling – and argues that "they jointly implement a form of hierarchical abstraction that reduces the complexity of a problems feature space [. . .] by iteratively transforming it into a simplified representational format that preserves and accentuates task-relevant features while controlling for nuisance variation", i.e., variations that are irrelevant for categorization (size, location etc.). He calls this process "transformational abstraction" (Buckner 2018, p. 18). In his rich and densely argued paper, Buckner nicely presents both Locke's as well as Berkeley's and Hume's somewhat mysterious and unsatisfactory accounts of abstraction, culminating in the puzzle of how the mind can get from specific exemplars to abstract categories (Locke) or from abstract categories to exemplars (Hume). Where does the knowledge come from which details should be left out (Locke) or added (Berkeley, Hume) along the way? While at one point he acknowledges that what he is developing "begins to look more like the theory of abstraction provided by Kant (and contemporary Kantians like Barsalou [. . .] who emphasized the need for rules of synthesis to generate a range of specific possible exemplars corresponding to an abstract category" (Buckner 2018, p. 12), he nevertheless argues, along the lines of *possibility empiricism*, that this challenge may be met by an empiricist account. He is content to have shown that DNNs perform abstractions that vindicate "elements of the Lockean, Berkeleyan and Kantian views", without committing himself neither to any one of these historical interpretations, nor to the crucial differences between these accounts.

(b) Pessimists

At the time being, it is fair to say that the group of pessimists pointing out several limitations of Deep Neural Networks is larger, or at least louder than the group of optimists (depending on whom you talk to). As Buckner (2018) notes, contemporary rationalists are skeptical about domain-general mechanisms being sufficient. Indeed, Mitchell (2020, p. 132) argues that the main problem of deep neural networks is "one of understanding". The networks lack the rich background knowledge – about functions of objects (affordances), memories, and context dependent cognition – which informs human perception. She suggests that "humans are endowed with an essential body of core knowledge" (Mitchell 2020, p. 309), appealing to the influential work by Spelke and Carey (1996) which posits domain-specific core knowledge systems enabling the recognition of objects, agents, numbers, and so on – i.e., concepts like cause, number, object, and agent. The list of features of these systems typically contains "innateness".

An even more dismissive assessment of what deep neural networks can achieve is that given by Marcus and Davis (2019, p. 145). They agree with Mitchell but go further, objecting that what DNNs provide is just more of the same that was already possible with their precursors. They complain that "machine learning people, for the most part, emphasize learning, but fail to consider innate knowledge" (Marcus/Davis 2019, p. 144). Also appealing to Spelke's work, they submit that

> humans are likely born understanding that the world consists of enduring objects that travel on connected paths in space and time, with a sense of geometry and quantity, and the underpinnings of an intuitive psychology. Or, as Kant argued [. . .], an innate 'spatio-temporal manifold' is indispensable if one is to properly conceive of the world.
>
> (Marcus/Davis 2019, p. 145)

Leaving Kant and the question of whether Marcus and Davis' charge against machine-learning researchers is justified aside for the moment, it should be emphasized that innateness is not a necessary feature of the core systems identified by Spelke and Carey. As Butterfill (2020, pp. 93–103) shows, the evidence for such systems being innate is far from clear, and "poverty of stimulus arguments" have been provided only in the case of syntax (Chomsky 1959), whereas other works in developmental psychology suggest an agnostic position on innateness of core systems. Thus, one may accept the evidence mentioned in favor of a distinction between a limited number of core knowledge systems but nevertheless reject the claim that they can be cited in favor of *necessity nativism*.

In a similar vein, and with a focus on the goal of developing an artificial system exhibiting general intelligence, computer scientist and philosopher Judea Pearl (2018, p. 10) considers "machines' lack of understanding of causal relations" as being "perhaps the biggest roadblock to giving them human-level intelligence [. . .] I believe that strong AI is an achievable goal and one not to be feared precisely because causality is part of the solution."[17] "A causal reasoning module will give machines the ability to reflect on their mistakes, to pinpoint weaknesses in their software, to function as moral entities, and to converse naturally with humans about their own choices and intentions." Yet, despite his optimism, he considers present-day learning machines still only as "sharing the wisdom of an owl". Despite regular news about rapid advances in machine-learning systems – self-driving cars, speech and face

---

[17] For Pearl, strong AI is the claim that an AI system exhibits general human-level intelligence.

recognition systems, and the like – even recent deep learning networks have only "given us machines with truly impressive abilities but no intelligence. The difference is profound and lies in the absence of a model of reality" (Pearl 2018, p. 30).

In order to illustrate what's missing compared to the human level of understanding, Pearl sketches a threefold "ladder of causation" (Pearl 2018, pp. 23–52), specifying three levels of cognitive ability that a learner must achieve for a true understanding of causal relations. The first and most basic level, which we share with many animals, consists in detecting regularities through observation. An owl may observe a rat and figure out where it will be next, for example. Such reasoning proceeds merely by association and seeing such regularities enables a cognitive agent to make predictions guided by the question '*What if I see* [. . .]?'. Only some of such observations may actually discover causal relations, and the data themselves do not disclose cause and effect. The second cognitive level is characterized by action which enables a cognitive agent to bring about changes in the world. Actions are interventions into the physical causal order. To use Pearl's example, "seeing smoke tells us a totally different story about the likelihood of fire than making smoke" (Pearl 2019, p. 31). Humans use such interventions all the time, e.g., when taking an aspirin to cure a headache. Tool use in the animal kingdom is an illustration of the range of creatures capable of this cognitive level. The guiding question on this level is: '*What if I do* [. . .]?' The final cognitive ability, enabling a human-level understanding of causal relations, is counterfactual reasoning. Once the headache is gone, we can ask why and consider the probabilities of different causes, asking, in effect, '*What if I had done* [. . .]?' An instance of this question is, e.g., 'What would have happened if I had not taken the aspirin?'. Such thinking opens up new possibilities, taking us beyond data into an imaginary world where some facts, obtaining in the real world, do not hold, or are even contradicted. This hallmark of human intelligence enables the development of scientific theories, art, and improving on our past actions.

The point of all this is that, in Pearl's view, present-day AI has not yet progressed beyond level one because even DNNs operate entirely in association mode, being fully driven by a stream of data. Recall that being a direct consequence of data-driven learning was how we identified the empiricist position. According to Pearl then, this empiricism is limited. Even the successful computer program Alpha Go only churns through accumulated data, its database consisting of millions of Go games, "so that it can figure out which moves are associated with a higher percentage of wins" (Pearl 2018, p. 29). But this is all that it is capable of, obviously exceeding human memory by far, but not achieving any understanding. By contrast, humans make use of a mental "model of reality" (Pearl 2018, p. 30, see also Mitchell 2020, ch. 14) which Pearl considers as a necessary ingredient to achieve our level of understanding. While many researchers in AI attempt to solely rely on data for all cognitive tasks, Pearl emphasizes "how profoundly dumb data are about causes and effects" (Pearl 2019, p. 16).

Whether optimists or pessimists may turn out to be correct is an empirical question, and not one to be settled in this paper. At least, the limitations and challenges are more or less known. Cremer (2021) presents a survey of expert interviews on the potential and limitations of deep learning wherein such experts list forty limitations. Success in this area depends on whether the question is if AI systems are supposed to exhibit cognition and intelligence that is like cognition and intelligence in humans or if we would be content with such systems being successful in a sufficiently high number of tasks or in a sufficiently high number of domains, regardless of whether the way they achieved this resembles the way humans do. I highlighted the potential connections to (and relevance of) Kant's theory of cognition in this context as well as to its borderline position between empiricism and nativism. This was the second question we posed above. On the one hand, given that his system of categories is characterized as being a priori (and thus systematically prior to any experience), his position would be classified as nativist. On the other hand, given that his system of categories can be considered domain-general, his position would be classified as empiricist. Thus, given the different terminological systems used by Kant and contemporary cognitive scientists, it is challenging to formulate a clear statement on this issue that is both true to Kant's writings and to the way dichotomies are characterized in todays' debates. As a final remark in this review, it is worth introducing a very recent approach to machine learning that specifically alludes to Kant's view of cognition in its formulation of a cognitive architecture, namely the position developed by Richard Evans (2022, this volume 39–103).

3.2 Start Making Sense!

Like Pearl and Mitchell, Richard Evans and his colleagues – computer scientists at *Deep Mind*, one of the leading companies developing state-of-the-art AI – allude to mental models and add specifications about its ingredients and constraints (Evans et al. 2021). Concerned with the problem of how to make sense of a sensory sequence, they allude to Kant's theory, since "Kant defines exactly what it means to make sense of a sequence: to reinterpret that sequence as a *representation of an external world composed of objects, persisting over time, with attributes that change over time, according to general laws*" (Evans 2022, this volume, p. 40). This "involves constructing a symbolic causal theory that both explains the sensory sequence and also satisfies a set of unity conditions" (Evans et al. 2021, p. 1). More specifically, they postulate the "requirement that our theory exhibits a particular form of *unity*: the constituents of our theory – objects, properties, and atoms – must be integrated into a coherent whole [. . .] This extra unity condition is necessary, we argue, for the theory to achieve good accuracy at prediction, retrodiction, and imputation" (Evans et al. 2021, p. 2). To meet these unity requirements on sense-making, Evans suggests interpreting Kant's first *Critique* as providing a cognitive architecture, specifically "as a precise computationally-implementable description of what is involved in making sense of the sensory stream" (Evans 2022, this volume, p. 40). That is, according to Evans, it is possible to capture Kant's cognitive architecture in rigorous algorithmic form and implement it in a machine in order to test it in experiments.[18] Although not all details of Kant's account can thereby be captured, the gain is a detailed and precise description on the level of a computer algorithm. That is, Kant's a priori psychology here forms the template for a machine-learning system which requires translating the various faculties that are involved in cognition in the narrow sense and their interaction into one program. In terms of concrete results, these are the *understanding* – with its capacity to form judgements – corresponds to an unsupervised learning program, the *power of judgement*, which subsumes intuitions under concepts, is implemented as a binary neural network, and the *imagination* which is responsible (and indispensable) for the connections between intuitions (productive synthesis) in terms of a set of non-deterministic choice rules (Evans 2022, this volume, p. 95). The fourth and final condition is sensory intuition, which provides the input for the cognitive architecture.

In a more recent article, Evans et al. (2021) describe a particular computer system they call "Apperception Engine", designed to perform an "*unsupervised program synthesis*" (Evans et al. 2021., p. 2) and to implement the various

---

18 Moreover, he takes this to yield original rather than merely derived intentionality. The latter presupposes another system with original intentionality (a human being) that can confer its intentionality on the system in question (by interpreting its symbols, for example). Notoriously, Searle (1980) postulates that only a biological system is capable of original intentionality, while all artificial systems will always remain capable only of derived intentionality. Evans (2017, p. 43) argues, by contrast, "that a computational agent built to satisfy a Kant-inspired cognitive architecture is capable of achieving original intentionality. It doesn't matter what it is made of as long as it achieves the necessary structural organization."

faculties in one unified system.[19] Delving into the rich details of this implementation is beyond the scope of this review and must be left for another occasion, but the readers may consult Evans' contribution to this volume themselves (Evans 2022, this volume, ch. 2). This requirement explicitly exceeds the typical empiricist approaches that are purely data-driven, as criticized by the "pessimists" such as Pearl, Mitchell and Marcus & Davis (see above). But it does not mean that Evans thereby takes his Apperception Engine to constitute a nativist system, as demanded by Marcus and Davis. With respect to the debate between optimists and pessimists, Evans objects to Marcus' interpretation of Kant as a nativist, because it is important what is taken to be innate. That is, it makes a difference whether one claims that concepts are innate or faculties (capacities) whose application produces such concepts. Kant allegedly did not conceive of the categories as innate concepts: "The pure unary concepts are not 'baked in' as primitive unary predicates in the language of thought. The only things that are baked in are the fundamental capacities (sensibility, imagination, power of judgement, and the capacity to judge) [. . .]. The categories themselves are *acquired* – derived from the pure relations *in concreto* when making sense of a particular sensory sequence" (Evans 2022, this volume, p. 74). Evans follows Longuenesse (2001), who grounds her interpretation in a letter Kant wrote to his contemporary Eberhard; in it, he distinguishes an "empirical acquisition" from an "original acquisition", the latter applying to the forms of intuition and to the categories. Evans is right in saying that, as far as the cognition of an object is concerned – like the "I think" – the categories come into play only by being actively (spontaneously) applied through the understanding, and can thus be derived, if you will, through a process of reverse engineering which reveals that they have to be presupposed in the first place, being a transcendental condition of experience. But this is compatible with the claim that, given their a priori status (and given that they can be applied also in the absence of sensory input, though not to yield cognition in the narrow sense but still cognition in the broad sense, as characterized above), "they have their ground in an a priori (intellectual, spontaneous) capacity of the mind" (Longuenesse 2001, p. 253). In contrast to Evans, Barsalou (1999, p. 581) firmly categorizes Kant as a nativist, arguing that Kant "assumed that native mechanisms interpret and organize images". If such mechanisms are supposed to be the categories, then this interpretation speaks against Kant's elaboration in his letter to Eberhard, but we need not settle this issue here.

---

19 They formulated the unity conditions and chose the name for the computer program in honor of Kant's background theory in the *Critique of pure reason* (Evans et al. 2021, p. 8, n. 17).

One way the categories are applied is described in the schematism chapter of the first *Critique*. Thus, when the question is how we "form the general idea of a triangle when we have only been exposed to a series of particular and idiosyncratic exemplars" which we are forced to "unify" (Buckner 2018, 8), then Kant's answer can be framed in terms of the combination of sensory and conceptual representations, arguing that unificatory concepts (categories) are "schematized" when combined with a series of exemplars. A schema, in Kant's parlance, is a third kind of representation which can mediate between an intuition and a concept and can thus enable the application of a concept to a given intuition. Analogously, the schematism is the process of applying the concepts of the understanding to appearances. Kant distinguished between schemata for empirical concepts like "chair" and schemata for pure sensory concepts from geometry like "triangle", which is Buckner's example. In Kant's theory, which can only be hinted at, schemata result as an effect of the imagination's task to produce a given concept's image (KrV, AA: A140/B179). While the understanding produces a concept that acts like a rule, the imagination produces a general *Gestalt* (the schema of that concept) and a concrete image, either in free association or based on sensory input. Schemata are sensory by being imagistic representations, and yet general rather than merely particular, guided by the rule provided by the concept. I will leave it at these brief remarks on schemata, as there are many interpretative problems to do with this important notion (see Pippin 1976, Pendlebury 1995 and Matherne 2014 for further discussion).[20] The upshot is, of course, that this consideration leads us away from a purely empiricist account towards a mixed account that incorporates rationalist elements. It is an area of research that deserves a closer look on another occasion.

Another way in which Kant's theory of cognition is quite different from the typical empiricist approaches has to do with the central notion of spontaneity. As Evans notes, apart from the passive sensibility which only receives information, all other faculties involved in cognition in the narrow sense contain a spontaneous element. It is crucial for Evans' interpretation that spontaneity is free of any constraints, such that the cognitive agent is "continually constructing the program" that she can execute, being "free to construct *any rules whatsoever* – as long as they satisfy the unity conditions" (Evans 2021). Yet, Evans is well aware that a number of features that are important for Kant are either not represented in the Apperception Engine or represented differently, for example, space, time, and

---

20 In addition to interpretative difficulties, it may be problematic that Kant did not rewrite the chapter on schematism from the first to the second edition, although many of his reconceptualizations, including that of the place of the imagination, might have effects on this overall view.

self-consciousness. Thus, while Kant takes the spontaneity of the understanding to be typically a self-conscious activity – i.e., an activity being conscious of itself (B 153) which allows the subject performing the spontaneous synthesis to become conscious of "the identity of the consciousness in [. . .] conjoined [. . .] representations (B 133) –, this has as yet not been implemented in Evans' program. Evans himself acknowledges that there is still much more work to be done in order for the Apperception Engine to be fair to Kant's original theory. But what's more important for his practical purposes is whether the resulting performance of the program is in need of further elements. It is of course an empirical question of whether Evans' Kantian machine-learning approach is superior to competing deep-learning architectures or whether alternative routes are sufficient or yield better results. But given the purpose of this paper, which was to present an overview of where Kant's conception of cognition has been and still is influential, it is fascinating to see that many of his ideas are still very much alive and relevant.

4 Conclusion

In this paper I presented a survey intended to outline various approaches developed by researchers in cognitive science and artificial intelligence with an eye on the influence of Kant's theory of cognition on these respective approaches. As it turned out, many elements of Kant's philosophy have been influential and are still relevant in the search for the right paradigm to explain and experimentally approach cognition. It was not the purpose of this paper to remain faithful to all of Kant's texts and engage in Kant-exegesis. Rather, this text was an exercise to see what cognitive scientists and contemporary philosophers of mind can take from Kant's philosophy and apply it usefully to address open questions such as what's needed for an artificial system to make sense of sensory input, or to develop cognitive models such as the predictive processing paradigm to capture neural processing in the brain. This is a fascinating area of study. Time will tell what elements of Kant's philosophy of mind will remain fruitful and necessary in the best theories of cognition and the development of artificial systems exhibiting general intelligence.[21]

---

21 I am grateful for funding from the Volkswagen-Foundation of my Lichtenberg-Professorship and the associated research project on Situated Cognition. Thanks also for helpful feedback and comments on an earlier draft by Cameron Buckner, Richard Evans and Dieter Schönecker and my team members Krzysztof Dolega, Marco Facchin, Paola Gega, François Kammerer, Firuze Mullaoglu, Nina Poth, Bartosz Radomski, Caroline Stankozi, Tobias Starzak, and Elmarie Venter.

References

All references to Kant's works follow the German original, *Gesammelte Schriften*, ed. by the Königliche Preussische Akademie der Wissenschaften, 29 Volumes. De Gruyter et al. 1902. Where available, English citations follow the *Cambridge Edition of the Work of Immanuel Kant in Translation*.

GMS Grundlegung zur Metaphysik der Sitten/*Groundwork of the Metaphysics of Morals*
KrV Kritik der reinen Vernunft/*Critique of Pure Reason*
KU Kritik der Urteilskraft/*Critique of the Power of Judgement*
V-Met Metaphysik-Vorlesungen (*Lectures on Metaphysics*)

Allison, Henry E. (1996): "On naturalizing Kant's transcendental psychology". In: *Idealism and Freedom. Essays on Kant's Theoretical and Practical Philosophy.* pp. 53–66.

Ameriks, Karl (2000): *Kant's Theory of Mind. An Analysis of the Paralogisms of Pure Reason.* 2nd Ed. Oxford: Clarendon Press.

Anderson, Michael/Chemero, Anthony (2019): "The world well gained. On the epistemic implications of ecological information". In: Matteo Colombo/Elizabeth Irvine/Mog Stapleton (Eds.) *Andy Clark and his Critics.* pp. 161–173.

Barsalou, Lawrence (1999): "Perceptual symbol systems". In: *Behavioral and Brain Sciences* 22. pp. 577–660.

Ben-Jacob, E., Y. Shapira, and A. Tauber (2006). Seeking the Foundations of Cognition in Bacteria: From Schrödinger's Negative Entropy to Latent Information. Physica A 359, 495–524.

Beni, Majid D. (2018): "Commentary: The Predictive Processing Paradigm has roots in Kant". In: *Frontiers in Systems Neuroscience* 11. DOI: 10.3389/fnsys.2017.00098.

Block, Ned (2002): "The harder problem of consciousness". In: *The Journal of Philosophy* 101. pp. 1–35.

Block, Ned (2015): "The Canberra plan neglects ground". In: *Qualia and mental causation in a physical world. Themes from the philosophy of Jaegwon Kim.* pp. 105–133.

Boden, Margaret A. (2016): *Artificial intelligence. A very short introduction.* Oxford: Oxford University Press.

Bongard, Joshua/Levin, Michael (2021): "Living Things Are Not (20th Century) Machines: Updating Mechanism Metaphors in Light of the Modern Science of Machine Behavior". In: *Frontiers in Ecology and Evolution* 9. DOI: 10.3389/fevo.2021.650726.

Brook, Andrew (1994): *Kant and the Mind.* Cambridge: Cambridge Univ. Press.

Brooks, Rodney A. (1991): "Intelligence without Representation". In: *Artificial Intelligence* 47. Nr. 1–3, pp. 139–159.

Bruineberg, Jelle/Rietveld, Erik (2014): "Self-organization, free energy minimization and optimal grip on a field of affordances". In: *Frontiers in Human Neuroscience* 8. pp. 599.

Bruineberg, Jelle/Kiverstein, Julian/Rietveld, Erik (2016): "The anticipating brain is not a scientist: the free-energy principle from an ecological-enactive perspective". In: *Synthese* 195. Nr. 6, pp. 2417–2444.

Buckner, Cameron (2018): "Empiricism without magic: transformational abstraction in deep convolutional neural networks". In: *Synthese SI: Neuroscience and its Philosophy.* DOI: 10.1007/s11229-018-01949-1.

Buckner, Cameron (2019): "Deep Learning: A philosophical introduction". In: *Philosophy Compass* 14.

Buckner, Cameron (2020): "Black Boxes or Unflattering Mirrors? Comparative Bias in the Science of Machine Behavior". In: *The British Journal for the Philosophy of Science*. DOI: 10.1086/714960.

Butterfill, Stephen A. (2020): *The developing mind. A philosophical introduction*. London: Routledge.

Calvo, Paco/Keijzer, Fred (2011): "Plants: Adaptive behavior, root brains, and minimal cognition". In: *Adaptive behavior* 19. Nr. 3, p. 155.

Calvo, Paco/Gagliano, Monica/Souza, Gustavo/Trewavas, Anthony (2020): "Plants are intelligent, and here is how". In: *Annals of Botany* 125. Nr. 1, pp. 11–28.

Carey, Susan (2009): *The origin of concepts*. Oxford: Oxford University Press.

Chalmers, David J. (1996): *The conscious mind*. Oxford University Press.

Chemero, Anthony (2009): *Radical embodied cognitive science*. Cambridge, MA: MIT Press.

Chomsky, Noam (1959): "A review of B. F. Skinner's verbal behavior". In: *Language* 35. pp. 26–57.

Churchland, Paul M. (1997): *The Engine of Reason, the Seat of the Soul. A Philosophical Journey into the Brain*. Cambridge, Mass.: MIT Press.

Churchland, Patricia S./Sejnowski, Terrence J. (1992): *The Computational Brain*. MIT Press.

Clark, Andy (1991): *Microcognition*. Cambridge, Mass.: MIT press.

Clark, Andy (2013): "Whatever next? Predictive Brains, Situated Agents, and the Future Of Cognitive Science". In: *Behavioral and Brain Sciences* 36. Nr. 3, pp. 181–204.

Clark, Andy (2016): *Surfing Uncertainty* Oxford: Oxford University Press.

Clark, Andy (2019): "Consciousness as Generative Entanglement". In: *Journal of Philosophy* 116. Nr. 12. 645–662. DOI: https://doi.org/10.5840/jphil20191161241, visited on:

Colombetti, Giovanna (2013): *The Feeling Body Affective Science Meets the Enactive Mind*. Cambridge, Mass.: MIT Press.

Cremer, Carla Z. (2021): "Deep limitations? Examining expert disagreement over deep learning". In: *Progress in Artificial Intelligence*. pp. 1–6. DOI: 10.1007/s13748-021-00239-1.

Dennett, Daniel C. (1991): *Consciousness Explained*. New York: Basic Books.

Di Paolo, Ezequiel/Buhrmann, Thomas/Barandiaran, Xabier (2017): *Sensorimotor Life. An Enactive Proposal*. Oxford: Oxford University Press.

Di Paolo, Ezequiel/Thompson, Evan/Beer, Randall D. (2021): "Laying down a forking path: Incompatibilities between enaction and the free energy principle". In: *PsyArXiv Preprints* 10.31234/osf.io/d9v8f.

Dolega, Krzysztof/Dewhurst, Joe (2015): "Curtain call at the Cartesian theatre". In: *Journal of Consciousness Studies* 22. Nr. 9–10, pp. 109–128.

Evans, Richard (2017): "Kant on constituted mental activity". In: *APA Newsletter: Philosophy and Computers* 16. pp. 41–53.

Evans, Richard (2019): "A Kantian cognitive architecture". In: Don Berkich/Matteo V. D'Alfonso (Eds.) *On the Cognitive, Ethical, and Scientific Dimensions of Artificial Intelligence*. pp. 233–262.

Evans, Richard (2022): "The Apperception Engine". In: Dieter Schönecker/Hyeongjoo Kim (Eds.) *Kant and Artificial Intelligence*. pp. 39–103.

Evans, Richard/Hernández-Orallo, Jose/Welbl, Johannes/Kohli, Pushmeet/Sergot, Marek (2021): "Making sense of sensory input". In: *Artificial Intelligence* 293.

Fazelpour, Sina/Thompson, Evan (2015): "The Kantian brain: brain dynamics from a neurophenomenological perspective". In: *Current Opinion in Neurobiology* 31. pp. 223–229.

Fodor, Jerry A. (1975): *The Language of Thought*. New York: HUP.

Friston, Karl (2005): "A theory of cortical responses". In: *Philosophical Transactions of the Royal Society* B: Biological Sciences 360. Nr. 1456, pp. 815–836.

Friston, Karl (2010): "The free-energy principle: A unified brain theory?" In: *Nature Reviews Neuroscience* 11. pp. 127–138.

Fukushima, Kunihiko (1980): "Neocognitron: A Self-Organizing Neural Network Model for a Mechanism of Pattern Recognition Unaffected by Shift in Position". In: *Biological Cybernetics* 36. Nr. 4, pp. 193–202.

Gallagher, Shaun (2017): *Enactivist Interventions*. Oxford: Oxford University Press.

Gava, Gabriele (Ed.) (2018): "Special Issue on The Current Relevance of Kant's Method in Philosophy". In: *Synthese* 198. pp. 3107–3111.

Gibson, James J. (1979): *The Ecological Approach to Visual Perception*. Houghton Mifflin.

Gładziejewski, Pawel (2016): "Predictive coding and representationalism". In: *Synthese* 193. Nr. 2, pp. 559–582.

Gomes, Anil (2017): "Kant, the Philosophy of Mind, and Twentieth Century Analytic Philosophy". In: Anil Gomes/Andrew Stephenson (Eds.) *Kant and the Philosophy of Mind*. Oxford: Oxford University Press.

Grüne, Stefanie (2013): "Kant and the spontaneity of the understanding". In: Dina Emundts (Ed.) *Self, World, and Art*.

Grüne, Stefanie (2009): *Blinde Anschauung*. Frankfurt/M.: Klostermann.

Hanna, Robert (2008): "Kantian non-conceptualism". In: *Philosophical Studies* 137. Nr. 1, pp. 41–64.

Hanna, Robert/Thompson, Evan (2003): "Neurophenomenology and the Spontaneity of Consciousness". In: *Canadian Journal of Philosophy* 33. Nr. 29, pp. 133–162.

Hobson, Allan J./Friston, Karl J. (2014): "Consciousness, Dreams, and Inference: The Cartesian Theatre revisited". In: *Journal of Consciousness Studies* 21. Nr. 1–2, pp. 6–32.

Hobson, Allan J./Friston, Karl J. (2016): "A response to our theatre critics". In: *Journal of Consciousness Studies* 23. Nr. 3–4, pp. 245–254.

Hohwy, Jakob (2013): *The Predictive Mind*. Oxford: Oxford University Press.

Hohwy, Jakob (2014): "The self-evidencing brain". In: *Noûs* 50. Nr. 2, pp. 259–285.

Hohwy, Jakob/Seth, Anil (2020): "Predictive processing as a systematic basis for identifying the neural correlates of consciousness". In: *Philosophy and the Mind Sciences* 1. Nr. 2. DOI: https://doi.org/10.33735/phimisci.2020.ii.64.

Hubel, David/Wiesel, Torsten (1962): "Receptive fields, binocular interaction, and functional architecture in the cat's striate cortex". In: *The Journal of Physiology* 160. pp. 106–154.

Hurley, Susan L. (1998): *Consciousness in Action*. Cambridge: Cambridge University Press.

Hutto, Daniel D./Myin, Erik (2013): *Radicalizing Enactivism*. Cambridge, Mass: MIT Press.

Kim, Jaegwon (1998): *Mind in a physical world*. Cambridge, Mass: MIT Press.

LeCun, Yann/Boser, Bernhard/Denker, John S./Henderson, Donnie/Howard, Richard E./ Hubbard, Wayne E./Jackel, Lawrence D. (1990): "Handwritten digit recognition with a back-propagation network". In: *Proc. Advances in Neural Information Processing Systems*. Nr. 2, pp. 396–404.

LeCun, Yann/Bengio, Yoshua/Hinton, Geoffrey (2015): "Deep Learning". In: *Nature* 521. pp. 436–444.

Legg, Shane/Hutter, Marcus (2007): "Universal intelligence: a definition of machine intelligence". In: *Minds and Machines*. Nr. 17, pp. 391–444.

Levin, Michael/Keijzer, Fred/Lyon, Pamela/Arend, Detlev (2021): "Uncovering cognitive similarities and differences, conservation and innovation". In: *Philosophical Transactions of the Royal Society B* 375. Nr. 1820.

Levine, Joseph (2001): *Purple Haze*. MIT Press.

Long, R. (ms): Nativism and Empiricism in Artificial Intelligence.

Longuenesse, Beatrice (2001): *Kant and the capacity to judge*. Princeton, NJ: Princeton University Press.

Mancuso, Stefano (2018): *The revolutionary genius of plants*. New York: Atria Books.

Marcus, Gary/Davis, Ernest (2019): *Rebooting AI. Building artificial intelligence we can trust*. New York: Vintage Books.

Margolis, Eric/Laurence, Stephen (2013): "In defense of nativism". In: *Philosophical Studies* 165. pp. 693–718.

Marr, David (1982): *Vision*. Cambridge, MA: MIT Press.

Matherne, Samantha (2014): "Kant and the Art of Schematism". In: *Kantian Review* 19. Nr. 2, pp.181–205.

Maturana, Humberto R./Varela, Francisco (1980): *Autopoiesis and Cognition: The Realization of the Living*. Amsterdam: Springer.

McCarthy, John/Minsky, Marvin L./Rochester, Nathaniel/Shannon, Claude E. (1955): "A Proposal for the Dartmouth Summer Research Project on Artificial Intelligence". In: *AI Magazine* 27. Nr. 4, pp. 12–14.

McDowell, John H. (1994): *Mind and World*. Harvard University Press.

Meerbote, Ralf (1989): "Kant's Functionalism". In: John-Christan Schmith (Ed.) *Historical Foundations of Cognitive Science*. pp. 161–87.

Metzinger, Thomas/Wiese, Wanja (Eds.) (2017): *Philosophy and predictive processing*. www.predictive-mind.net.

Minsky, Marvin/Papert, Seymour (1969): *Perceptrons: An Introduction to Computational Geometry*. Cambridge, MA: MIT Press.

Mitchell, Melanie (2020): *Artificial Intelligence. A guide for thinking humans*. Penguin.

Nguyen, Anh/Yosinski, Jason/Clune, Jeff (2015): "Deep neural networks are easily fooled: High confidence predictions for unrecognizable images". In: *Computer Vision and Pattern Recognition* (CVPR). pp. 427–436.

Noë, Alva (2004): *Action in Perception*. Cambridge: MIT Press.

Noë, Alva (2009): *Out of our heads*. New York: Hill & Wang.

Northoff, Georg (2012): "Immanuel Kant's mind and the brain's resting state". In: *Trends in cognitive sciences* 16. Nr.7, pp. 356–359.

Northoff, Georg (2013): Unlocking the brain. Vol. I: Coding. Oxford: Oxford University Press.

Northoff, Georg (2014): Unlocking the brain. Vol. II: consciousness. Oxford: Oxford University Press.

Northoff, Georg (2018): *The spontaneous brain. From the mind-body to the world-brain problem*. Cambridge, MA: MIT Press.

Nunez, Tyke (forthcoming): "Kant on plants: self-activity, representations and the analogy with life". In: *Philosopher's Imprint*.

Pearl, Judea (2018): *The book of Why. The new science of cause and effect*. London: Penguin.

Pendlebury, Michael (1995): "Making Sense of Kant's Schematism". In: *Philosophy and Phenomenological Research* 55. Nr. 4, pp. 777–797.

Pezzulo, Giovanni/Lapalme, Joshua/Durant, Fallon/Levin, Michael (2021): "Bistability of Somatic Pattern Memories: Stochastic Outcomes in Bioelectric Circuits Underlying Regeneration". In: *Philosophical Proceedings of the Royal Society* 376. Nr. 1821, pp. 20190765–20190776.

Piccinini, Gualtiero (2020): *Neurocognitive mechanisms. Explaining biological cognition.* Oxford: Oxford University Press.

Pippin, Robert B. (1976): "The Schematism and Empirical Concepts". In: *Kant-Studien* 67. Nr. 1–4, pp. 156–171.

Place, Ullin T. (1956): "Is consciousness a brain process?" In: *British Journal of Psychology* 47. pp. 44–50.

Polger, Thomas/Shapiro, Lawrence A. (2016): *The Multiple Realization Book.* Oxford: Oxford University Press.

Putnam, Hilary (Ed.) (1965): "The nature of mental states". In: *Philosophical Papers* 2. pp. 429–440.

Pylyshyn, Z. (1984) *Computation and Cognition.* Cambridge, MA: MIT Press.

Rosenblatt, Frank (1958): "The Perceptron: A Probabilistic Model for Information Storage and Organization in the Brain". In: *Psychological Review* 65. pp. 386–408.

Samuels, Richard (2004): "Innateness in cognitive science". In: *Trends in cognitive sciences* 8. Nr. 3, pp. 136–141.

Schlicht, Tobias (2007): „Erkenntnistheoretischer Dualismus. Kant und das Geist-Gehirn-Problem". In: *Logical Analysis and History of Philosophy* 10. pp. 113–136.

Schlicht, Tobias (Ed.) (2011): *Special Issue of Journal of Consciousness Studies* 18. Nr. 5–6, Mind in Life.

Schlicht, Tobias (2016): "Kant and the problem of consciousness". In: Stephen Leach/James Tartaglia (Eds.) *Consciousness and the great Philosophers.*

Schlicht, Tobias (2017): "Experiencing organisms. From Mineness to subject of experience". In: *Philosophical Studies* 175. Nr. 10, pp. 2447–2474.

Schlicht, Tobias (2018): "Does separating intentionality from representation imply radical enactivism?". In: *Frontiers in Psychology* 9. pp. 1497.

Schlicht, Tobias/Newen, Albert (2015): "Kant and cognitive science revisited". In: *Logical Analysis and History of Philosophy* 18. pp. 87–113.

Schlicht, Tobias/Dolega, Krzysztof (2021): "You can't always get what you want. Predictive processing and consciousness". In: *Philosophy and the mind sciences* 2.

Searle, John R. (1980): "Minds, Brains, and Programs". In: *Behavioral and Brain Sciences* 3. Nr. 3, pp. 417–424.

Sejnowski, Terrence J. (2018): *The Deep Learning Revolution.* Cambridge, MA: MIT Press.

Sejnowski, Terrence J. (2020): "The unreasonable effectiveness of deep learning in artificial intelligence". In: *Proceedings of the National Academy of Sciences* 117. Nr. 48, pp. 30033–30038. DOI:10.1073/pnas.1907373117.

Sellars, Wilfrid (1974): "Metaphysics and the Concept of a Person". In: *Essays in Philosophy and its History*, pp. 214–43.

Shanahan, Murray (2019): "Artificial intelligence". In: Mark Sprevak/Matteo Colombo (Eds.) *The Routledge Handbook of the Computational Mind.* pp. 91–100.

Shapiro, Lawrence (2011): *Embodied cognition.* London: Routledge.

Simon, Hans-Georg (2012): "Salamanders and fish can regenerate lost structures – why can't we?". In: *BMC Biology* 10. Nr. 1, p. 15.

Sims, Matthew (2019): "Minimal perception: Responding to the challenges of perceptual constancy and veridicality with plants". In: *Philosophical Psychology* 32. Nr. 7, pp. 1024–1048.

Skinner, Burrhus F. (1957): *Verbal behavior*. Acton: Copley Publishing Group.

Smart, John J. C. (1959): "Sensations and brain processes". In: *The Philosophical Review* 68. Nr. 2, pp. 141–156.

Smolensky, Paul (1988): "On the Proper Treatment of Connectionism". In: *Behavioral and Brain Sciences* 11. pp. 1–74.

Spelke, Elizabeth/Carey, Susan (1996): "Science and core knowledge". In: *Philosophy of Science* 63. Nr. 4, pp. 515–533.

Sturma, Dieter (1985): *Kant über Selbstbewusstsein. Zum Zusammenhang von Erkenntniskritik und Theorie des Selbstbewusstseins*. Hildesheim: Olms.

Swanson, Link R. (2016): "The predictive processing paradigm has roots in Kant". In: *Frontiers in Systems Neuroscience* 10. P. 79. DOI:10.3389/fnsys.2016.00079.

Szegedy, Christian/Zaremba, Wojciech/Sutskever, Ilya/Bruna, Joan/Erhan, Dumitru/ Goodfellow, Ian/Fergus, Rob (2015): "Intriguing properties of neural networks". In: *arXiv preprint arXiv:1312.6199*.

Thompson, Evan (2007): *Mind in Life*. Cambridge, MA: Harvard University Press.

Tolley, Clinton (2020): "Kant on the place of cognition in the progression of our representations". In: *Synthese* 197. pp. 3215–3244. DOI: 10.1007/s11229-017-1625-3.

Vallverdú, Jordi/Castro, Oscar/Mayne, Richard/Talanov, Max/Levin, Michael/Baluška, Frantisek/Gunji, Yukio-Pegio/Dussutour, Audrey/Zenil, Hector/Adamatzky, Andrew (2018): "Slime mould: The fundamental mechanisms of biological cognition". In: *Biosystems* 165. pp. 57–70. DOI: 10.1016/j.biosystems.2017.12.011.

Varela, Francisco J./Thompson, Evan/Rosch, Eleanor (1991): *The embodied mind*. Cambridge, MA: MIT Press.

Vincent, James (2018): "Google 'fixed' its racist algorithm by removing gorillas from its image-labeling tech". In: *The Verge*. https://www.theverge.com/2018/1/12/16882408/google-racist-gorillas-photo-recognition-algorithm-ai, visited on Jan. 12, 2018.

Walmsley, Joel (2012): *Mind and Machine*. London: Palgrave MacMillan.

Watkins, Eric/Willaschek, Marcus (2017): "Kant's Account of Cognition". In: *Journal of the History of Philosophy* 55. Nr. 1, pp. 83–112.

Weber, Andreas/Varela, Francisco J. (2002): "Life after Kant: Natural purposes and the autopoietic foundations of biological individuality". In: *Phenomenology and the Cognitive Sciences* 1. pp. 97–125.

Willaschek, Marcus/Watkins, Eric (2020): "Kant on cognition and knowledge". In: *Synthese* 197. Nr. 8, pp. 3195–3213.

Richard Evans

2 The Apperception Engine

Abstract: This paper describes an attempt to repurpose Kant's a priori psychology as the architectural blueprint for a machine learning system. First, it describes the conditions that must be satisfied for the agent to achieve unity of experience: the intuitions must be connected, via binary relations, so as to satisfy various unity conditions. Second, it shows how the categories are derived within this model: the categories are pure unary predicates that are derived from the pure binary relations. Third, I describe how Kant's cognitive architecture has been implemented in a computer system (the Apperception Engine) and show in detail what it is like for the system to construct a unified experience from a sequence of raw sensory input.

1 Introduction

This paper describes an attempt to repurpose Kant's *a priori* psychology as the architectural blueprint for a machine learning system.

Imagine a machine, equipped with sensors, receiving a stream of sensory information. It must, somehow, *make sense* of this stream of sensory data. But what, exactly, does this involve? We have an intuitive understanding of what is involved in "making sense" of sensory data – but can we specify precisely what is involved? Can this intuitive notion be formalized?

In machine learning, this is called the *unsupervised learning problem*. It is both fundamentally important and frustratingly ill-defined. This problem contrasts with the supervised learning problem where the sensory data come attached with labels. In a supervised learning problem, there is a clear learning objective, and there are a number of powerful techniques that perform very successfully. However, *the real world does not come with labels attached to sensory data*. We just receive the data. As Geoffrey Hinton said:[1]

> When we're learning to see, nobody's telling us what the right answers are – we just look. Every so often, your mother says "that's a dog", but that's very little information. You'd be lucky if you got a few bits of information – even one bit per second – that way. The brain's visual system has 10^{14} neural connections. And you only live for 10^9 seconds. So

---

[1] Quoted in Kevin Murphy's *Machine Learning: a Probabilistic Perspective* (Murphy, 2012).

Richard Evans, Imperial College London

it's no use learning one bit per second. You need more like 10^5 bits per second. And there's only one place you can get that much information: from the input itself.

In unsupervised learning, we are given a sequence of sensor readings, and want to make sense of that sequence. The trouble is we don't have a clear formalisable understanding of what it means to "make sense". Our problem, here, is *inarticulacy*. It isn't that we have a well-defined quantifiable objective and do not know the best way to optimize for that objective. Rather, we do not know what it is we really want.

One approach, the *self-supervised* approach, is to treat the sensory sequence as the input to a prediction problem: given a sequence of sensory data from time steps 1 to t, maximize the probability of the next datum at time $t + 1$. But I believe there is more to "making sense" than merely predicting future sensory readings. Predicting the future state of one's photoreceptors may be *part* of what is involved in making sense – but it is not on its own sufficient.

What, then, does it mean to make sense of a sensory sequence? In this paper, I argue that the solution to this problem has been hiding in plain sight for over two hundred years. In the *Critique of Pure Reason* (Kant, 1781), Kant defines exactly what it means to make sense of a sequence: to reinterpret that sequence as a *representation of an external world composed of objects, persisting over time, with attributes that change over time, according to general laws.*

In this paper, I reinterpret part of Kant's first *Critique* as a specification of a cognitive architecture, as a precise computationally-implementable description of what is involved in making sense of the sensory stream. This is an interdisciplinary project and as such is in ever-present danger of falling between two stools: neither philosophically faithful to Kant's intentions nor contributing meaningfully to AI research. Kant himself provides[2]

> the warning not to carry on at the same time two jobs which are very distinct in the way they are to be handled, for each of which a special talent is perhaps required, and the combination of which in one person produces only **bunglers**   [AK 4:388]

The danger with an interdisciplinary project, part AI and part philosophy, is that both potential audiences are unsatisfied. The computer science might reasonably ask: why should a two hundred year old book have anything to teach us now? Surely if Kant had anything important to teach us, it would already have been absorbed? The Kant scholar might reasonably complain: is it really necessary to

---

2 Translations are from the Cambridge Edition of the Works of Immanuel Kant (details at the end), with occasional modifications. With the exception of those to the *Critique of Pure Reason*, which take the standard A/B format, references to Kant are by volume and page number in the Academy Edition [*Immanuel Kants gesammelte Schriften*, 29 volumes, Berlin: de Gruyter, 1902-].

re-express Kant's theory using a computational formalism? We do not need these technicalities to talk about Kant. At best, it is an unnecessary re-articulation. At worst, misunderstandings are piled on misunderstandings, as Kant's ideas are inevitably distorted when shoe-horned into a simple computational formalism.

Nevertheless, I will argue, first, that contemporary AI has something to learn from Kant, and second, that Kant scholarship has something to gain when rearticulated in the language of computer science.

1.1 AI has Something to Learn from Kant

It is increasingly acknowledged that the strengths and weaknesses of neural networks and logic-based learning are *complementary*. While neural networks[3] are robust to noisy or ambiguous data, and are able to absorb and compress the information from vast datasets, they are also data hungry, uninterpretable, and do not generalize well outside the training distribution (Fodor and Pylyshyn, 1988; Marcus, 2018a; Lake et al., 2017; Evans and Grefenstette, 2018). Logic based learning, by contrast, is very data efficient, produces interpretable models, and can generalise well outside the training distribution, but struggles with noisy or ambiguous data, and finds it hard to scale to large datasets (Rocktäschel and Riedel, 2016; Evans and Grefenstette, 2018).

What we would really like, if only we can get it, is a system that combines the advantages of both. But this is, of course, much easier said than done. What, exactly, is involved in combining low-level perception with high-level conceptual thinking?

In the first *Critique* Kant describes, in remarkable detail, exactly what this hybrid architecture should look like. The reason why he was interested in hybrid cognitive architectures is because he was attempting to synthesise the two conflicting philosophical schools of the day, empiricism and rationalism. The neural network is the intellectual ancestor of empiricism, just as logic-based learning is the intellectual ancestor of rationalism. Kant's unification of empiricism and rationalism is a cognitive architecture that attempts to combine the best of both worlds, and points the way to a hybrid architecture that combines the best of neural networks and logic-based approaches.[4]

---

3 An introduction to neural networks is beyond the scope of this paper and we refer to Murphy (2012).

4 So far, so programmatic. The hybrid neuro-symbolic architecture is outlined in Section 3 and described in detail in (Evans et al., 2021a), and the ascription of this architecture to Kant in particular is justified in Section 2.

1.2 Kant Interpretation has Something to Learn from AI

Some of the most exciting and ambitious work in recent philosophy (Brandom, 1994, 2009, 2008; Sellars, 1967, 1968, 1978) attempts to re-articulate Kantian (and post-Kantian) philosophy in the language of analytic philosophy. Now this re-articulation is not merely window-dressing: it is not merely dressing up old ideas in the latest fashionable terminology, but rather an attempt to achieve a new level of perspicuity in a semi-formal language that was designed for clarity and precisiom.

My aim in this paper is to re-articulate Kant's theory at a further level of precision, by reinterpreting it as a specification of a *computational architecture*. Why descend to this particular level of description? What could possibly be gained? The computational level of description is the ultimate level of precise description. There is no more precise you can be: even a mere *computer* can understand a computer program. Computers force us to clarify our thoughts. They admit no waffling or vagueness. Hand-waving is greeted with a compilation error, and a promissory note is returned, unread.

The advantage of re-articulating Kant's vision in computational terms is that it gives us a new level of specificity. The danger is that, in an effort to shoe-horn Kant's theory into a particular implementable system, we distort his original ideas to the point where they are no longer recognisable. Whether this is indeed the unfortunate consequence, the gentle reader must decide.

1.3 Kant's Cognitive Architecture

The first half of the *Critique of Pure Reason* is a sustained exercise in *a priori* psychology: the study of the processes that must be performed if an agent is to achieve experience. For Kant, this *a priori* psychology was largely a means to an end – or, to be precise, two ends. One of his high-level goals was metaphysical: to enumerate once and for all the pure aspects of cognition – those features of cognition that must be in place no matter what sensory input has been received. The pure aspects of cognition include the pure forms of intuition (space and time, as described in the *Aesthetic*), the pure concepts (the categories, as described in the *Analytic of Concepts*), and the pure judgements (the synthetic *a priori* propositions, as described in the *Principles*). His other high-level goal was metaphilosophical: to delimit the bounds of sense, and finally put to rest various interminable disputes,[5] by showing that the pure concepts can only be applied to objects of possible experience.

But I believe that, apart from its role as a means to his metaphysical and metaphilosophical ends, Kant's peculiar brand of psychology has independent interest in its own right, *as a specification of a cognitive architecture.* According to Kant's specification, making sense of a sensory sequence involves constructing a symbolic causal theory that explains the sensory sequence and satisfies a set of unity conditions. According to our interpretation, making sense of sensory input is a type of program synthesis, but it is *unsupervised* program synthesis, constrained in such a way as to achieve the *synthetic unity of apperception.*

To test this hypothesis, we need to implement this architecture in a computer program, and test it on a wide array of examples. Kant's theory is intended to be a general theory of what is involved in achieving experience, so – if it actually works – it should apply to *any* sensory input. To test the viability of this architecture, then, we need to actually implement it, and evaluate it in a large and diverse set of experiments.

Our computer implementation of Kant's cognitive architecture is called the APPERCEPTION ENGINE.[6] Our system is able to produce interpretable human-readable causal theories from very small amounts of data because of the strong inductive bias provided by Kant's unity constraints. We have tested this system in a variety of experiments, and found it shows promise as a machine for making sense of unlabelled sensory input.

In this paper, I shall first (Section 2) extract some core theses from the first half of the *Critique*, and assemble them into a specification of a cognitive architecture. Next (Section 3), I describe some examples of the APPERCEPTION ENGINE in action. I show one worked example in detail.[7] Finally (Section 4), I discuss the various interpretive decisions that were made, and defend them against alternatives. One of the things that makes a computational implementation challenging is that it forces one to pick a specific interpretation of Kant, since the computer has zero tolerance for vagueness or equivocation.

---

5 He wanted to "put an end to all dispute" [A768/B796].
6 The APPERCEPTION ENGINE is described in detail in (Evans et al., 2021b,a; Evans, 2020). The source code is available at https://github.com/RichardEvans/apperception.
7 For the various other experiments, see (Evans et al., 2020) and (Evans et al., 2021a).

2 Achieving Experience

In the first half of the *Critique of Pure Reason*, Kant focuses on the following fundamental question:

What activities must be performed if the agent is to achieve **experience**?[8]

Note that this is a question about intentionality – not about knowledge. Kant's question is very different from the standard epistemological question:

Given a belief, what else has to be true of the agent for us to count that belief as knowledge?

Kant's question is *pre-epistemological*: he does not assume the agent is given a belief. Instead, we see his belief as an *achievement* that cannot be taken for granted, but has to be *explained*:

Understanding belongs to all experience and its possibility, and the first thing that it does for this is not to make the representation of the objects distinct, *but rather to make the representation of an object possible at all* [A199, B244-5]

Kant asks for the conditions that must be satisfied for the agent to have any possible cognition (true *or* false) [A158, B197]. Note that this is not an empirical psychological question about the processes that *human beings* happen to use, but rather a question of *a priori* psychology:[9] what must a system – any physically realised system at all[10] – do in order to achieve experience?[11]

In this paper, I will try to distill Kant's answer to this fundamental question, and reinterpret his answer as the specification of a cognitive architecture.

---

8 The subtitle of the *Transcendental Deduction* in the First Edition is: "On the *a priori* grounds for the possibility of experience." [A95].

9 In this project, I side with Longuenesse (Longuenesse, 1998), Waxman (Waxman, 2014), and others in interpreting the first half of the *Critique* as *a priori* psychology. *Contra* Strawson (Strawson, 2018), I believe that *a priori* psychology is a legitimate and important form of inquiry, and that if we try to expunge it from Kant's text, there is not much left that is intelligible.

10 There are a number of places in the *Critique* where Kant seems to restrict his inquiry to just humans e.g., [B138-9]. But Kant uses the term "human" to refer to any agent who perceives the world in terms of space and time and has two distinct faculties of sensibility and understanding. This is a much broader characterisation than just *homo sapiens*.

11 Because the second question is broader, it is more relevant to the project of artificial intelligence (Dennett, 1978).

2.1 Achieving Experience by Unifying Intuitions

A central claim of the *Transcendental Deduction* is that:

---

(1) In order to achieve experience, I must unify my intuitions. [A110]

Before we can assess the truth of such a claim, we first need to understand what it means. (i) What does Kant mean by an experience? (ii) What are intuitions? (iii) What does it mean to unify them? I shall consider each in turn.

2.1.1 What does Kant mean by 'Experience'?

Kant's notion of **experience** ('Erfahrung') is close to our usual use of the term. I shall list some features of this term as Kant uses it. First, experience is *everyday*. It is not an unusual peak state that people only achieve occasionally, like enlightenment or ecstasy. Rather, it is a state that most of us have most of the time when we are awake. Second, experience is *unified*. At any one time, I am having *one* experience [A110]. I cannot have multiple simultaneous experiences. I may be conscious of multiple stimuli, but they are all part of one experience. Third, experience is *articulated* (Stephenson, 2013). It is not a mere 'blooming, buzzing confusion' (James et al., 1890). Rather, experience is composed of distinct objects with distinct properties. Fourth, experience is *not (merely) conceptual*. It is not just a collection of beliefs. It is, to anticipate, a unified combination of intuitions and concepts. Fifth, experience is *not necessarily veridical*. It purports to represent the world accurately, but may fail to do so (Longuenesse, 1998; Stephenson, 2013; Waxman, 2014).

Experience is not something we should take for granted. Rather, experience is *an achievement*. When I open my eyes, I see various objects, with various properties that change over time. But this experience is a complex achievement that only occurs if a myriad of underlying processes work exactly as they should do. The central contribution of Kant's *a priori* psychology is to describe in detail the underlying processes needed in order for experience to be achieved.

2.1.2 What does Kant mean by 'Intuition'?

An **intuition** ('Anschauung') is a representation of a particular object[12] (e.g., this particular jumper) or a representation of a particular attribute[13] of a particular object at a particular time (e.g., the particular dirtiness of this particular jumper at this particular time).

Intuitions are produced by the faculty of **sensibility** [A19/B33]: the receptive faculty that detects sensory input. Sensibility provides the agent with a *plurality* of intuitions [B68], which the mind needs to make sense of.

Intuitions are private to the individual. My intuitions are different from yours. It is not just that we do not share intuitions we *cannot* share intuitions, as they are essentially private. To see this, consider four possible relations between an action and its object:

1. The object existed before and after the action (e.g., kicking the football).
2. The object existed before but not after the action (e.g., destroying the evidence).
3. The object existed after but not before the action (e.g., making a cake).
4. The object existed neither before nor after, but only during the action, because the object is only an *aspect* of the action

Let us focus on the fourth. When I draw a circle in the air, this thing – the circle – only exists for the duration of the activity because it is an *aspect* of the activity. Or consider "the contempt in his voice ": this thing, this contempt, only exists for the duration of his vocal utterance because it is an aspect of the utterance.

The way I read Kant, the object of intuition is a type (4) object: it only exists as part of the act because it is an aspect of the act.[14]

---

12 [B76].

13 A186/B229: "The determinations of a substance that are nothing other than *particular ways for it to exist* are called accidents." Note that whenever Kant talks about "existence" in the Analogies, he is really talking about a particular *way of existing*. See e.g., A160/B199: "synthesis is either mathematical or dynamical: for it pertains partly merely to the intuition, partly to the existence of an appearance in general". Here, "the existence of an appearance" means the particular way of existing of an appearance (e.g., the particular dirtiness of this particular jumper).

14 Kant interpreters differ on whether intuitions are relations between conscious minds and actual existing material objects (Allais, 2009;Gomes, 2013; McLear, 2016), or whether the object of an intuition is just a mental representation that in no way implies the existence of a corresponding external physical object (Longuenesse, 1998; Stephenson, 2015, 2017).The interpretation in this project fits squarely within the latter, representational interpretation. My reason for preferring the representational interpretation is based on a general interpretive

But in order to ognize something in space, e.g., a line, I must **draw** it. [B137]

Now because intuiting is a private mental act (no other agent can perform the same token-identical act), and because the object of intuition is a type (4) object that only exists as an aspect of the act, it follows that the object of intuition inherits the privacy of the intuiting act of which it is an aspect. Nobody else can have my particular object of intuition because this object is an aspect of my activity of intuition, and nobody else can perform this particular activity.

Intuitions are distinct from concepts. While an intuition is a representation of a particular object, a concept is a general representation that many intuitions fall under [B377]. For Kant, intuitions and concepts are distinct types of representation. While empiricists saw concepts as a special type of intuition that is used in a general way, and while rationalists saw intuitions as a special type of concept that is maximally specific, Kant understood intuitions and concepts to be entirely distinct *sui-generis* types of representation. His reasons for thinking intuitions and concepts are entirely distinct are: (i) they come from distinct faculties (sensibility and understanding respectively); (ii) while intuitions are private to an individual, concepts can be shared between individuals; (iii) while intuitions are immediately directed to an object (the particular object only exists as an aspect of the activity of intuiting, just as the circle only exists as an aspect of the activity of drawing a circle in the air), concepts are only mediately related to objects via intuitions [A68/B93, B377].

The intuition occupies a unique place in Kant's *a priori* psychology: it is the ultimate goal of all thought,[15] the final end that all cognition is aiming at. All the other aspects of thought (e.g. concepts and judgements) are only needed in so far as they help to unify the intuitions:

---

prejudice: whenever there are two ways of reading Kant, and one of those interpretations relies on fewer prior capacities, thus requiring the mind to do more work to achieve the coherent representation of an external world that we take for granted in our everyday life, then prefer that interpretation. The relational view takes for granted a certain type of cognitive achievement: the ability of the mind to be about an external object. The representational view, by contrast, sees this intentionality, this mind-directedness, as something that requires work to be achieved. Thus, simply because it is more demanding and asks harder questions, it should be preferred. Further, and not coincidentally, the representational view can be implemented in a computer program, while it is entirely unclear how we could begin to implement any relational view that takes for granted the ability for the mind's thoughts to be directed to particular external physical objects.

15 In this paper I focus on Kant's theoretical philosophy rather than his practical philosophy, and thus "thought" here means cognitive thought aimed at making sense of the world – rather than feelings, volitions, intentions, etc.

> In whatever way and through whatever means a cognition may relate to objects, that through which it relates immediately to them, and *at which all thought as a means is directed as an end, is intuition.* [A19/B33, my emphasis.]

2.1.3 What does Kant mean by 'Unifying' Intuition?

Recall Kant's key claim that:

(1) In order to achieve experience, I must unify my intuitions.

Here, the *explanandum* is a mental state (experience), while the *explanans* is a process (the process of unifying the intuitions). But what, exactly, does this process involve, and how will we know when it is finished?

The process of unifying intuitions can be unpacked as a particular type of synthesising process that satisfies a particular constraint, the constraint of unity:

> But in addition to the concept of the manifold and of its synthesis, the concept of combination also carries with it the concept of the *unity of the manifold.* [B130]

I shall first consider the synthesising process in general, and then turn to the unity constraint. The activity of synthesis may seem frustratingly metaphorical or ill-defined:

> The inadequacies of such locutions as "holding together" and "connecting" are obvious, and need little comment. Perceptions do not move past the mind like parts on a conveyor belt, waiting to be picked off and fitted into a finished product. There is no workshop where a busy ego can put together the bits and snatches of sensory experience, hooking a color to a hardness, and balancing the two atop a shape. (Wolff, 1963, p. 126)

What exactly does it mean to unify intuitions? What is the glue that binds the intuitions together? As I read Kant, the only thing that can bind intuitions together is the *binary relation.*[16] Synthesising intuitions means connecting the intuitions together using binary relations so that the resulting undirected graph is fully connected.[17] The synthesising process is the job of the faculty of **productive imagination**[18] [A78/B103; A188/B230], described in Section 2.2 and formalized in Section 2.4.

---

16 The precise binary relations involved are listed in the *Schematism* and described in detail in Section 2.2.

17 A graph is fully connected if there is a path of (undirected) edges between any two nodes. See West et al. (2001) for an introduction to graph theory.

18 Kant distinguished between the productive and reproductive imagination [A100-2]. Here, I focus exclusively on the productive imagination. The reproductive imagination's job is to recall

But there is much – much more – to unifying intuitions than just connecting them together with binary relations. The extra requirement that must be satisfied for a connected binary graph to count as a unification of intuitions is that the graph satisfies Kant's *unity conditions*. While there are many ways to connect intuitions together via binary relations to form a connected graph, only a small subset of these satisfy the various conditions of unity that Kant imposes. These unity conditions are satisfied by the faculty of **understanding** [A79/B104], and are described in detail in Sections 2.3.1, 2.3.2, 2.3.3, and 2.3.4.

The second claim, then, unpacks what it means to unify intuitions:

---

(2) Unifying intuitions means combining them using binary relations to form a connected graph, in such a way as to satisfy various unity conditions (described in detail in Sections 2.3.1, 2.3.2, and 2.3.4).

2.1.4 The Status of Claim 1

Claim (1), then, is the claim that an agent can only achieve experience – everyday conscious experience of a single articulated world – if it can unify its intuitions by connecting them together in a relational graph that satisfies various (as yet unspecified) unity conditions.

Let us break this down into two claims:

(1a) In order to achieve experience, my intuitions must be unified.
(1b) In order for my intuitions to be unified, I[19] must unify them.

Claim (1a) can be interpreted with at least two levels of strength. A strong interpretation treats the claim as *definitional*: experience *just is* unified intuition. A weaker interpretation sees the claim as merely a necessary condition: experience *requires* unified intuition, but it also needs more besides. In this project, I

---

earlier determinations and reproduce them. This capacity is taken for granted in the current implementation: I assume the whole sequence of sensory input has been given as a whole, so the agent does not need to recall earlier elements.

19 I do not, of course, mean that the agent deliberately and consciously performs various activities that result in the intuitions being unified. Rather, I mean that various *sub-personal* processes within the agent must occur in order for there to be a unified person at all.

adopt the stronger interpretation, and there is reason to think that Kant endorsed this stronger interpretation too.[20]

The second claim (1b) is not entirely trivial. An alternative possibility is that my intuitions arrive, via the faculty of sensibility, *already unified*. But Kant clearly rules out this alternative.[21] So, then, if my intuitions do not arrive already unified, and if I cannot pay or persuade somebody else to unify them for me,[22] then I must unify them myself. This is a task that only I can do.

2.2 Synthesis

In this section, I describe the relations that are used by the imagination to connect the intuitions together [A78/B103].

When Kant talks about pure synthesis [A78/B104], he means connecting intuitions by **pure** relations[23] that apply to all intuitions in all situations.[24] Why does Kant insist that synthesis can only use pure relations to connect intuitions? Because the unity conditions (that will be described in Sections 2.3.1, 2.3.2, and 2.3.4) are conditions that must apply to *every possible synthesis* of intuitions. If the unity conditions are to apply to every possible synthesis, they can only reference relations that feature in every possible synthesis, and these are the pure relations.

There are three[25] operations that bind intuitions together:
- **containment**: in(X, Y) means that object X is (currently) in object Y (e.g., the package is in the kitchen)
- **comparison**: X<Y means that attribute X is (currently) less than attribute Y (e.g., the weight of the package is less than the weight of the spoon)
- **inherence**: *det*(X, Y) means that attribute Y (currently) inheres in object X (e.g., this particular heaviness (of 2.3 kg) is an attribute of this particular parcel)

---

20 "[Experience] is therefore a synthesis of perceptions." [A176/B218] "There is only one experience, in which all perceptions are represented as in thoroughgoing and lawlike connection."[A110].

21 "Yet the **combination** (*conjunctio*) of a manifold in general can never come to us through the senses, and therefore cannot already be contained in the pure form of sensible intuition." [B129].

22 Nobody else can get anywhere near my intuitions because they are aspects of my private mental acts. See Section 2.1.2.

23 Pure relations are opposed to *impure* relations, such as *father-of*, that only apply contingently.

24 Kant enumerates the pure relations in the *Schematism*.

25 The containment operation is described in the *Axioms of Intuition*, the comparison operation in the *Anticipations of Perception*, and the inherence operation in the *First Analogy*.

When two intuitions are bound together by one of the three operations, the result is a **determination**. Thus, in (a, b), a < b, and *det*(a, b) are all determinations. Determinations hold at a particular moment or moments in time; they do not persist indefinitely [A183-4,B227].

The constituents of determinations are intuitions, representations of individuals; these are either particular objects, or particular attributes of those objects. To hold *det*(a,b) is to ascribe particular attribute b to particular object a (for example, to ascribe this particular dirtiness to this particular jumper).

It is absolutely essential, I believe, for understanding Kant's architecture that we distinguish clearly between attributes and concepts. Attributes are a type of intuition representing the particular way in which a particular object exists at a particular moment. Concepts, by contrast, are general representations. A number of different attributes typically fall under the same concept. Consider, for example, the particular dirtiness of this particular jumper, and the particular dirtiness of this particular laptop. Both attributes fall under the concept "dirty", but they are nevertheless distinct attributes: this jumper's particular dirtiness is different in myriad subtle ways from the dirtiness of my laptop.

Just as an attribute is a different kind of representation from a concept, just so a determination is a different kind of thought from a judgement. Seeing the particular dirtiness of the particular jumper at this particular moment (a determination) is very different from believing that the particular jumper is dirty (a judgement). In the former, I notice an individual property of an individual object. In the latter, I subsume a concept representing an individual object (the particular jumper) under a general concept ("dirty").

A determination is not a judgement, but a *way of perceiving*: I *see* the baby in the cot (containment); I *feel* the cup being heavier than the spoon (comparison); I *hear* the contemptuousness of the utterance (inherence). In each case, the argument of the perceptual verb is a *noun-phrase*, not a that-clause (Sellars, 1978).

Since a determination is a way of perceiving, it does not have a truth-value:

> For truth and illusion are not in the object insofar as it is intuited, but in the judgment about it insofar as it is thought. Thus it is correctly said that the senses do not err; yet not because they always judge correctly, but because they do not judge at all. Hence truth, as much as error, and thus also illusion as leading to the latter, are to be found only in judgments, i.e., only in the relation of the object to our understanding . . . In the senses there is no judgment at all, neither a true nor a false one. [A293-4/B350] See also
> [*Jäsche Logic* 9:53]

As well as the three pure operations that bind intuitions together, there are three[26] pure relations that bind determinations together:
- **succession:** $succ(P_1, P_2)$ means that P_1 is succeeded (at the next time-step) by P_2
- **simultaneity:** $sim(P_1, P_2)$ means that P_1 occurs at the same moment as P_2
- **incompatibility:** $inc(P_1, P_2)$ means that P_1 and P_2 are incompatible

When two determinations are bound together by one of the three relations, the result is a **connection.**[27] Thus, $succ(in(a, b), in(a, c))$ means that a's being in b is succeeded by a's being in c, and $inc(det(a, b), det(a, c))$ means that attributing b to a is incompatible with attributing c to a.

2.2.1 The Justification for this Particular Set of Operations and Relations

Why these particular pure relations? What makes this particular list special? The justification for this list is that the three pure operations and the three pure relations together constitute a *minimal set of binary operators that together are sufficient to construct the forms of space and time* [A145/B184ff].[28]

According to Kant, intuitions and determinations do not arrive with space and time coordinates attached [B129]. The job of sensibility is just to provide us with intuitions, but not to arrange them in objective space/time. It is the function of *synthesis*, the job of the imagination, to connect the intuitions together, using the pure operations and relations described above, so as to construct the objective spatio-temporal form:

> since time itself cannot be perceived, the determination of the existence of objects in time can only come about through their combination in time in general, hence only through *a priori* connecting concepts. [A176/B219]

To see that sensibility does not provide us with objects of intuition that are already positioned in space and time, consider a robot with a camera that provides a two-dimensional array of pixels for each visual snapshot. The robot receives information about the location of each pixel in egocentric two-dimensional space, and it must determine the positions of objects in *three-*

---

26 The succession and simultaneity relations are described in the second and third *Analogies*, and incompatibility is discussed in the *Postulates of Empirical Thought*.

27 "Experience is possible only through the representation of a necessary connection of perceptions." [B218].

28 This claim holds for a suitably qualified minimal notion of space. See Section 2.3.1.

dimensional space. Suppose a yellow pixel is left of a red pixel. Does the yellow pixel represent an object that is in front of the object represented by the red pixel, or behind? The visual input does not provide this information – the robot must decide itself. Next, consider time. Suppose the robot receives a sequence of visual impressions as its camera surveys the various parts of a large house [B162]. Do these subjectively successive impressions count as various representations of one moment in objective time, or do they represent different moments of objective time? The sensory input arrives ordered in subjective space/time but not in objective space/time.[29] In order to place our intuitions in objective space/ time, the imagination needs to connect them together using the pure relations described above.[30]

The three pure operations together with the three pure relations constitute a minimal set that is sufficient for generating the form of objective space/time. The containment operation *in* allows us to combine intuitions into a spatial field (a minimal representation of space that abstracts from the number of dimensions (Waxman, 2014)) [A162/B203ff]. The comparison operation < allows us to compare two different attributes; if we generate an intermediate attribute between two comparable attributes, we can generate an intermediate moment in time between two observed moments [A165/B208ff], thus filling time [A145/B184]. The inherence operation allows us to ascribe different attributions to an object at different times. The simultaneity and succession relations allow us to order determinations in time. Finally, the incompatibility relation allows us to test when sets of determinations are composible.

> Now one sees from all this that the schema of each category contains and makes representable: in the case of magnitude, the generation (synthesis) of time itself, in the successive apprehension of an object; in the case of the schema of quality, the synthesis of sensation (perception) with the representation of time, or the filling of time; in the case of the schema of relation, the relation of the perceptions among themselves to all time (i.e., in accordance with a rule of time-determination); finally, in the schema of modality and its categories, time itself, as the correlate of the determination of whether and how an object belongs to time. The schemata are therefore nothing but *a priori* **time-determinations** in accordance with rules, and these concern, according to the order of the categories, the **time-series**, the **content of time**, the **order of time**, and finally the **sum total of time** in regard to all possible objects. [A145/B184ff]

---

29 Kant makes this claim many times in the *Principles*. See [A181/B225], [A183/B226], etc.
30 In (Waxman, 2014) Chapter 3, Wayne Waxman makes a powerful case that intuitions do not arrive from sensibility already unified. They arrive as a mere multitude, and it is the job of the imagination to unify them in space/time. In other words, what the empiricist takes as "given" (the unified field of sensory input) is not actually "given" but rather has to be *achieved* by a mental process.

The third key claim, then, is:

---

(3) Synthesis involves (i) connecting intuitions together via containment, comparison, and inherence operations to form determinations; and (ii) connecting determinations together via succession, simultaneity, and incompatibility relations.

2.3 The Unity Conditions

So far, I have described how intuitions are connected together using the various pure binary relations. But there is more – much more – to synthetic unity than mere connectedness of intuitions. In this section, I describe the four types of unity condition that Kant imposes.[31]

---

(4) There are, in total, four types of unity condition in Kant's system: (i) the unity conditions for the synthesis of mathematical relations, (ii) the unity conditions for the synthesis of dynamical relations, (iii) the requirement that the judgements are underwritten by determinations, and (iv) the conceptual unity condition.

I shall go through each in turn.

2.3.1 The Unity Conditions for the Synthesis of Mathematical Relations

Kant divides the pure relations into two groups: the **mathematical relations** (containment and comparison) and the **dynamical relations** (inherence, succession, simultaneity, and incompatibility). The mathematical relations control the arbitrary synthesis of homogeneous elements,[32] while the dynamical relations control the necessary synthesis of heterogeneous elements[33] [B201n].

Kant says that the mathematical relations combine "what does not necessarily belong to each other" while the dynamical relations combine what "necessarily

---

31 There are many ways to connect intuitions together via binary relations to form a connected graph. If there are n nodes, then there are $2^{\binom{n}{2}}$ simple undirected graphs. The number of simple connected graphs for n nodes is the integer sequence A001187 which starts 1, 1, 1, 4, 38, 728, 26704, 1866256, . . . See http://oeis.org/A001187. But only a small fraction of these satisfy the various unity conditions that Kant imposes.

32 Observe that *in* relates two objects of intuition, while < relates two intuition attributes.

33 Observe that *det* relates two different types of intuition, an attribute and an object.

belongs to one another" [B201n]. This means that the agent has freedom to synthesise using containment and comparison in a way that is unconstrained by the conceptual realm of the understanding, but the synthesis using the dynamical categories is constrained by judgements produced by the understanding.[34]

I shall start with the unity conditions for the mathematical relations, before moving to the unity conditions on the dynamical relations. The fundamental unity condition for the mathematical relations is that the intuitions are combined in a fully connected graph. There are two further specific conditions, one for containment and one for comparison.

The unity condition for containment requires that there is some object, the maximal container, which contains all objects at all times [A25/B39]. Slightly more formally, the first unity condition for the synthesis of mathematical relations is:

---

(5)(a) There exists some intuition x such that for each object of intuition y, for each moment in time, there is a chain of *in* determinations between y and x.

Of course, objects can move about, from one container to another, but at every moment, the objects must always be contained in the maximal container.

Satisfying this unity condition means positing both pure objects (spatial regions with a mereological structure) and also impure objects (appearances) which are in the spatial regions.

Once objects have been placed in the containment hierarchy, and once we know which intuitions fall under which concepts, then we have all the information we need for *counting*. In order to count how many pens are in the box, I need to be able to tell whether each object falls under the concept "pen", and I also need to be able to tell which objects are actually in the box and which are outside. Thus, as Kant says, the pure schema of magnitude is "number, which is a representation that summarizes the successive addition of one (homogeneous) unit to another" [A142/B182]. The appearances are homogenous since they fall under the same concept, and we know which appearances to count and which to ignore by choosing a particular container in the containment hierarchy.

Now this containment hierarchy is a *necessary aspect* of any spatial representation: if we fix the positions and extensions of objects in 3D space, then the

---

34 See also [B110]: "the first class (mathematical categories) has no correlates which are to be met with only in the second class". Here, the correlates are the judgements that are required to underwrite the dynamical connections, but that are not required to underwrite the mathematical compositions.

containment hierarchy is also fixed. But, of course, the converse does not hold: specifying the containment hierarchy does not determine all the spatial information. Suppose, for example, that x and y are both in container z. We know that x and y are in the same container, but we do not know if x is above y, or below it. We do not know how near x is to y, etc.

The containment hierarchy is a distinguished sub-structure of the spatial world. If we abstract from our spatial representation all the aspects that are peculiar to our human form of intuition, all that is left is the containment hierarchy. As Kant says:

> Thus if, e.g., I make the empirical intuition of a house into perception through apprehension of its manifold, my ground is the necessary unity of space and of outer sensible intuition in general, and I as it were draw its shape in agreement with this synthetic unity of the manifold in space. This very same synthetic unity, however, *if I abstract from the form of space, has its seat in the understanding, and is the category of the synthesis of the homogeneous in an intuition* in general, i.e., the category of quantity, with which that synthesis of apprehension, i.e., the perception, must therefore be in thoroughgoing agreement.
> [B162]

And again:

> The pure *image* of all magnitudes (quantorum) for outer sense is space . . . The pure *schema* of magnitude (quantitatis), however, as a concept of the understanding, is number.
> [A142/B182]

Of course, a spatial representation performs many functions. It allows us, for example, to position and orient the parts of our bodies to manipulate other objects. But the function of space that is highlighted in the First Critique is space as the *medium in which appearances are unified*. Now space-qua-unifier-of-intuitions has fewer essential properties than space-qua-form-of-human-outer-sense. Qua unifier of intuitions, the key property of space is that it supports a containment hierarchy, in which we can tell which objects are in which containers. Kant makes it clear, when he first introduces space in the *Aesthetic*, that the function of space that he is focusing on is its ability to support the containment hierarchy:

> For in order for certain sensations to be related to something outside me (i.e., to something in another place in space from that in which I find myself), thus in order for me to represent them as outside one another, thus not merely as different but as in different places, the representation of space must already be their ground)   [A23/B38]

Space, qua unifier, is just the medium in which appearance can be placed together, the medium that allows me to infer from "I am intuiting x" and "I am intuiting y" to "I am intuiting x and y". This abstract unifying space just is the containment hierarchy: "space is the representation of coexistence (juxtaposition)" [A374].

To summarize, although Kant's notion of space was the standard (at the time) three-dimensional space of Euclidean geometry (B41), when he was thinking of space as the medium in which appearances can be unified, he focused on a substructure in which many of the features of space have been abstracted away: the containment hierarchy.[35]

The unity condition for comparison[36] simply requires that:

---

(5)(b) The comparison operator < forms a strict partial order.

Of course, we do not insist that < is a *total* order: although the dirtiness of this jumper can be compared with the dirtiness of this mug, the *weight* of this jumper need not be comparable with the dirtiness of this mug.

We do not, also, insist that < is *dense*.[37] This is because we follow Kant in wanting to allow *finite* models.[38]

2.3.2 The Unity Conditions for the Synthesis of Dynamical Relations

I have described above the unity conditions for the synthesis of mathematical relations (containment and comparison). Next we turn to the conditions Kant imposes on the synthesis of *dynamical* relations (inherence, succession, simultaneity, and incompatibility). This is perhaps the most important, the most original, and the most difficult part of the *Transcendental Analytic*. In fact, one of the major reasons that Kant rewrote the *Transcendental Deduction* in the B edition is precisely to re-express this condition as clearly as possible. In this

---

35 For a related position, see Waxman (Waxman, 2014) Section 4B: "It as if the mere use of the word 'space' is enough for many to reflexively read into Kant's doctrine virtually every meaning commonly attached to the term, or at least everything one supposes to remain after factoring in the adjective 'pure'. It becomes a space with all the features attributed to it by Euclid or Newton and so a space a priori incompatible with the features that have been or will be ascribed to space by later mathematicians and physicists. But . . . the unity of sensibility clearly does not require that pure space be determinately flat hyperbolic or elliptical, three-dimensional or ten-dimensional or any other number of dimensions, Ricci-flat or Ricci-curved, etc".

36 See [A143/B182-3] and [A168/B210].

37 A relation R is dense if Rxy implies there exists a z such that Rxz and Rzy.

38 (Pinosio, 2017) page 119.

section, I shall first explain Kant's general strategy before going into the specific details of how he handles each of the pure dynamical relations.

Kant was dissatisfied with the presentation of the Transcendental Deduction in the A edition. In the B edition, he changed the exposition significantly by splitting the proof into two parts (concluding in § 20 and § 26).[39] The first part of the Transcendental Deduction, culminating in § 20, relies heavily on a new explanation of the categories that was added to § 13 in the B edition:

> I will merely precede this with the **explanation of the categories**. They are concepts of an object in general, by means of which its intuition is regarded as **determined** with regard to one of the **logical functions** for judgments. Thus, the function of the **categorical** judgment was that of the relationship of the subject to the predicate, e.g., "All bodies are divisible." Yet in regard to the merely logical use of the understanding it would remain undetermined which of these two concepts will be given the function of the subject and which will be given that of the predicate. For one can also say: "Something divisible is a body." Through the category of substance, however, if I bring the concept of a body under it, it is determined that its empirical intuition in experience must always be considered as subject, never as mere predicate; and likewise with all the other categories.   [B128-9]

There are many other places where Kant makes similar claims.[40] What exactly is the claim here, and how exactly does Kant justify it?

Imagine someone trying to connect his intuitions together. Suppose he has "intuition dyslexia" – he is not sure if this intuition is the object and this other intuition is the attribute, or the other way round. Or he has two determinations in a relation of succession, but he is not sure which is earlier and which is later. The intuitions are swimming before his eyes. He needs something that can pin down which intuitions are assigned which roles, but what could perform this function? Kant's fundamental claim is that it is only the *judgement* that can fix the positioning of the intuitions. Moreover, this is not just one role of the judgement amongst many – this is the *primary* role of the judgement:

> a judgment is nothing other than the way to bring given cognitions to the objective unity of apperception   [B141]

---

39 The first half aims to show that we are always permitted to apply the pure concepts to intuitions, while the second half aims to show that the pure judgements (the synthetic *a priori* claims of the *Principles*) always hold.

40 For example, in a note added to Kant's copy of the first edition: "Categories are concepts, through which certain intuitions are determined in regard to the synthetic unity of their consciousness as contained under these functions; e.g., what must be thought as subject and not as predicate." He also makes similar claims in the *Metaphysik von Schon*, quoted in *Kant and the Capacity to Judge*, p.251, and *Prolegomena* § 20.

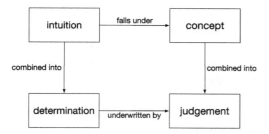

Figure 2.1: Intuitions are combined into determinations, just as concepts are combined
into judgements. An intuition falls under a concept, just as a determination
is underwritten by a judgement.

More specifically, the relative positions of intuitions in a determination can only
be fixed by *forming a judgement that necessitates this particular positioning*. This
judgement contains concepts that the intuitions fall under, and the position of
the intuitions in the determination are *indirectly determined* by the positions of
the corresponding intuitions in the judgement. See Figure 2.1. Thus:

> The same function that gives unity to the different representations in a judgment *also
> gives unity to the mere synthesis of different representations in an intuition.* The same un-
> derstanding, therefore, and indeed by means of the very same actions through which it
> brings the logical form of a judgment into concepts by means of the analytical unity, also
> brings a transcendental content into its representations by means of the synthetic unity
> of the manifold in intuition in general.   [A79/B104-5]

There is a parallel claim one level up, at the level of complex judgements: the
relative positions of determinations in a connection can only be fixed by forming
a complex judgement that itself contains a pair of judgements as constituents[41]
that necessitates this particular positioning. This complex judgement contains
two constituents – judgements – that the two determinations fall under, and the
position of the determinations in the connection are indirectly determined by the
positions of the corresponding judgements in the complex judgement.

What justification does Kant provide for this claim? His argument goes
something like this: the aim of the dynamical relations is to order the intuitions
and determinations in *objective* space-time. Now we can only achieve objectivity by imposing *necessity* on the combination.[42] But the faculty of imagination

---

41 Kant is emphatic on this point: "hypothetical and disjunctive judgments do not contain a
relation of concepts but of judgments themselves." [B141].
42 "Our thought of the relation of all cognition to its object carries something of necessity
with it." [A104] The concept of an object is "the concept of something in which [the appearan-
ces] are necessarily connected" [A108].

is entirely incapable of imposing necessity. All the imagination can do is connect the intuitions using the pure relations – it cannot impose necessity on those connections.[43] In fact, the only element that can provide the desired necessity is the judgement.[44] Thus, the only way dynamical relations can be ordered in objective space-time is by indirectly positioning them, using judgements that impose the necessity that the connections require.[45]

In terms of the cognitive faculties responsible for the various processes, the **capacity to judge**[46] is responsible for constructing the judgements, and the faculty of **the power of judgement**[47] is responsible for constructing the subsumptions that decide which intuitions fall under which concepts.

This, then, is the general claim, as it applies to all the dynamical relations. Next, I shall describe the various forms of judgement that are needed to underwrite the various dynamical relations: inherence, succession, simultaneity, and incompatibility.

Inherence must be backed up by a categorical judgement. The first of the four conditions of dynamical unity is that the positions of intuitions in an inherence determination must be backed up by a corresponding judgement:[48]

---

(6)(a) If I form an inherence determination, ascribing a particular attribute a to a particular object O, then I must be committed to a judgement "this/some/all X are P", where O falls under X, and a falls under P.

Suppose, for example, I am seeing the particular dirtiness of this particular jumper. This inherence determination is a combination of two bare particulars:

---

43 "Apprehension is only a juxtaposition of the manifold of empirical intuition, but no representation of the necessity of the combined existence of the appearances that it juxtaposes in space and time is to be encountered in it." [A176/B219].

44 "This word [the copula "is"] designates the relation of the representations to the original apperception and its *necessary unity*, even if the judgement itself is empirical, hence contingent." [B142].

45 Here, the agent "binds" itself in two distinct but related senses. First, it binds its intuitions together via the pure relations. But this binding at the intuitive sensible level must be underwritten by a second binding at the conceptual discursive level: it is only because the agent binds itself to a rule relating concepts that the binding of intuitions achieves the necessity required for objectivity. See (Evans et al., 2019).

46 The capacity to judge (*Vermögen zu urteilen*) generates judgements from concepts. See [A81/B106] and (Longuenesse, 1998).

47 The power of judgement (*Urtheilskraft*) is responsible for deciding whether an intuition falls under a concept. See [A132/B171] and (Kant, 1790).

48 In each of the unity conditions that follow, I restrict to the case of unary predicates. The extension to binary, ternary, and so on is straightforward but complicates the presentation.

this particular jumper and this particular instantiation of dirtiness. Now it is essential, in seeing the inherence correctly, that this particular dirtiness is the attribute and this particular jumper is the object in which the attribute inheres. Things would be very different indeed if the intuition of the dirtiness is the object, and the intuition of the jumper is the attribute.[49]

Kant's fundamental claim is that it is only because I form some corresponding categorical judgement that I am able to fix the positions of the two arguments of the inherence operator *det* [B128-9]. In this case, suppose I have formed the judgement "Some jumper is dirty." Now my intuition of this particular jumper falls under the concept "jumper", and my intuition of this particular dirtiness (of this particular jumper at this particular moment) falls under the concept "dirty". Thus, I am able to fix the positions of the two arguments to the inherence operator indirectly, via the judgement and the falls-under relation. I see the positions of the intuitions in the inherence *through* the corresponding judgement.

Now of course I do not need to use that precise judgement "Some jumper is dirty" to fix the positions of the intuitions in the inherence determination. I could have used "Some jumper is revolting", or "This jumper is dirty", and so on and so forth. All that is needed is *some* categorical judgement where the two intuitions fall under the two concepts.

Succession must be backed up by a causal judgement. The second condition of dynamical unity is that every succession of determinations must be backed up by a causal judgement:

---

(6)(b) If I form a succession, in which one determination (say, particular object O having particular attribute a) is followed by another determination (say, O having incompatible attribute b), then I must have formed a conditional judgement relating judgements describing the two determinations (say, "If $\phi(X)$ holds then X changes from P to Q", where object O falls under concept X, attribute a falls under concept P, attribute b falls under concept Q, and $\phi(X)$ is a sentence featuring free variable X.)

Suppose, for example, I see the jumper's cleanliness followed by the jumper's dirtiness. It is essential, when seeing this succession, that I see the order

---

49 It is perhaps tempting to argue that it is just obvious which is the attribute and which is the object of the inherence: we can tell from the *types* of the two intuitions which one is which. Above, I said that there are two types of intuitions: intuitions of objects and intuitions of particular attributes. But this distinction only applies *after* a judgement has been constructed which allows the intuitions to be positioned; before that, these intuitions are not yet dignified with these roles as intuitions of objects or intuitions of particular attributes; they are just indeterminate intuitions. In other words, this response just begs the question, assuming that we have already access to the very positioning assignments that we are struggling to achieve.

correctly. Seeing the cleanliness followed by the dirtiness is very different from seeing the dirtiness followed by the cleanliness.

Kant claims[50] that it is only because I form some corresponding causal judgement that I am able to fix the positions of the two determinations in the succession relation [A189/B232]. Suppose, for example, I have formed the causal rule that if I wallow about in the mud, then my clothing will transform from clean to dirty. Now my intuition of this jumper falls under the concept "clothing", my intuition of this particular cleanliness falls under the concept "clean", and my intuition of this particular dirtiness falls under the concept "dirty". Thus, I am able to fix the positions of the two determinations in the succession relation indirectly, via the causal judgement and the falls-under relation.

Simultaneity must be backed up by a pair of causal judgements. The third condition of dynamical unity is that every simultaneity of determinations must be backed up by a pair of causal judgements:

---

(6)(c) If I form a simultaneity, in which one determination (say, particular object O_1 having particular attribute a) is simultaneous with another determination (say, object O_2 having attribute b), then there must be a pair of causal judgements describing determinations of the two objects (say, one of which states that an attribute of O_2 (simultaneous with a) causally depends on an attribute of O_2, and another of which states that an attribute of O_2 (simultaneous with b) causally depends on an attribute of O_1.)

Suppose, for example, I have two determinations simultaneously, one involving the sun, and one involving the moon. Now since simultaneity is a symmetric relation, it does not matter which of the two determinations is placed where in the *sim* relation. But it does matter whether we ascribe simultaneity or succession to the pair of determinations. When we are presented with a subjective succession of determinations, should we ascribe them to the same moment (of objective time) or to two successive moments (of objective time)?[51]

Kant's claim here is that in order to choose simultaneity over succession, we need to form a pair of judgements describing, for both objects, how some attribute of that object causally depends on some attribute of the other [A212/

---

50 Not all commentators agree with this way of reading Kant. Beatrice Longuenesse, for example, believes that we do not have to have already formed a causal judgement – we just need to acknowledge that we should form a causal judgement. For Longuenesse, perceiving a succession means being committed to look for a causal rule – it does not mean that I need to have already found one (Longuenesse, 1998).

51 "The apprehension of the manifold of appearance is always successive. The representations of the parts succeed one another. Whether they also succeed in the object is a second point for reflection, which is not contained in the first." [A189/B234].

B259]. I do not dwell on this principle, because it is the most controversial,[52] hard to understand, and does not feature in our computer implementation.

Incompatibility must be backed up by a disjunctive judgement. Kant talks throughout the *Postulates* about the possibility of an *object* – not of the possibility of a sentence being true. It is easy to see this as a category error, or as elliptical: perhaps "the object is possible" is short-hand for "it is possible that the object exists"? This temptation must be resisted. Kant predicates possibility/actuality/necessity of *determinations* as well as of judgements. When we connect two determinations with the *inc* connective, we are making a modal connection between two elements, two ways of seeing, elements that *do not have a truth value*.

Kant claims[53] that every incompatibility between determinations must always be backed up by a disjunctive[54] judgement:

---

(6)(d) If I form an incompatibility in which one determination (say, particular object *O* having attribute *a*) is incompatible with another (say, particular object *O* having attribute *b*), then I must have formed an exclusive disjunctive judgement stating that two judgements describing the two determinations are incompatible (say, "All *X* are either (exclusive disjunction) *P* or *Q* or . . .", in which *O* falls under *X*, *a* falls under *P*, and *b* falls under *Q*.)

Suppose, for example, I see this jumper's cleanliness as incompatible with the jumper's dirtiness. Now this is, to repeat, an incompatibility between determinations, ways of seeing, not an incompatibility between *judgements*. But Kant claims that this incompatibility between determinations must be underwritten by an exclusive-or disjunctive judgement. Suppose, for example, I have formed the judgement that every article of clothing is either clean or dirty. Now my intuition of this particular cleanliness falls under the concept "clean", my intuition of this particular dirtiness falls under the concept "dirty", and my intuition of this particular jumper falls under the concept "article of clothing." Thus, the exclusive disjunctive judgement (expressing an incompatibility between concepts) justifies the incompatibility relation between determinations.

---

52 See e.g., (Longuenesse, 1998) p.388.
53 "The schema of possibility is the agreement of the synthesis of various representations with the conditions of time in general (e.g., since opposites cannot exist in one thing at the same time, they can only exist one after another)." [A144/B184].
54 Recall that for Kant, disjunctions are *exclusive*: "*p* or *q*" means either *p* or *q* but not both.

2.3.3 Making Concepts Sensible

As well as the unity condition requiring that determinations are underwitten by judgements, there are also unity conditions in the other direction, requiring that judgements are supported by corresponding determinations.

> It is thus just as necessary to make the mind's concepts sensible (i.e., to add an object to them in intuition) as it is to makes its intuitions understandable (i.e., to bring them under concepts). [A51/B75]

The requirement here is that judgements cannot "float free" of the underlying intuitions. Instead, each judgement must be backed up by a corresponding determination.

More specifically (and restricting ourselves to unary predicates):

---

(7) If I form a judgement, ascribing a concept P to a particular object X, then there must be a corresponding inherence determination ascribing particular attribute a to particular object O, where O falls under X and a falls under P.

It might seem that this condition is trivially satisfied given that the agent starts with intuitions and determinations, and forms judgements to make them intelligible. But this is not always so: sometimes the agent constructs new *invented objects* to make sense of the sensible given and ascribes properties to these invented objects. In such cases, condition (7) requires that as well as subsuming object o under concept P, there is also a corresponding particular individual attribute a that inheres in o.[55]

2.3.4 Conceptual Unity

In addition to the synthetic unity described above, Kant also requires that one's concepts be unified by being connected together via judgements. I shall first consider a weak form of this constraint, before describing a stronger version.

A judgement connects various concepts together. For example, the judgement "some bodies are divisible" connects the concepts of "body" and "divisible". Let us say two concepts are *together* if there is some judgement in

---

55 The experiment of Section 3.1 shows just such an example where an invented object is postulated, and particular individual attributes of that object are posited in imagination to make the concepts sensible.

which they both feature. Define *together** as the transitive closure of *together*. Now the weak constraint of conceptual unity is that every pair of concepts are *together**.

Kant uses a significantly stronger constraint. His requirement is that the concepts are not just connected, but that they are connected into a *hierarchy* of genera and species.[56] In order that one's concepts form a *system* in this sense, we focus exclusively on the judgement form of exclusive disjunction [A70/B95]. Consider a judgement of the form "every *X* is either (exclusive) *P* or *Q*". This does not merely state that *P* and *Q* are exclusive; it also states that *P* and *Q* form a *totality*: the totality of concepts that together capture *X*. By bringing concepts under the *xor* judgement form, we bring them into a hierarchical community with a genera-species structure.[57]

The condition of conceptual unity is the requirement that:

---

(8) Every concept features in some disjunctive judgement.

2.4 Taking Stock

It is time to take stock. For Kant, the fundamental mental representation is the intuition, a representation of an individual element (e.g. a particular object or a particular attribute of a particular object). All the other types of representation serve only to unify the intuitions into a coherent whole.

Intuitions can be combined into determinations using the three pure operations of containment, comparison, and inherence. Further, determinations can be combined into connections using the pure relations of succession, simultaneity, and incompatibility. (See Section 2.2).

In order for the connections of determinations to achieve unity,[58] multiple conditions must be satisfied. The mathematical operations (of containment and

---

56 See (Longuenesse, 1998, p.105).

57 "What the form of disjunctive judgment may do is contribute to the acts of forming categorical and hypothetical judgments the perspective of their possible systematic unity", (Longuenesse, 1998), p.105.

58 In Section § 16 of the B deduction, Kant distinguishes four types of unity using two cross-cutting distinctions: analytic versus synthetic unity, on the one hand, and original versus empirical unity, on the other. Analytic unity is achieved when the mind has the ability to subsume each of its intuitions and determinations under the unary predicate "I think". Synthetic unity is achieved when the intuitions and determinations are connected together via the pure

comparison) must form a structure of the appropriate sort (Section 2.3.1), the dynamical functions (of inherence, succession, simultaneity, and incompatibility) must be underwritten by judgements of the appropriate sort (Section 2.3.2), the judgements must be underwritten by determinations of the appropriate sort (Section 2.3.3), and the concepts used in judgements must form their own unity (Section 2.3.4).

Why these unity conditions in particular? One of the remarkable things about Kant's philosophy is its systematicity. Instead of being content with merely enumerating the pure concepts of the understanding, Kant insists on showing how the pure concepts form a *system*, by showing that these are all and only the *a priori* concepts needed to make sense of experience.[59] The same systematicity requirement applies to the unity conditions: he must show that these are *all and only* the unity conditions needed for the synthesis of intuitions to achieve objectivity. To see that the unity conditions described above form a system, observe that there are two realms of cognition: the sensible intuitions and the discursive concepts. There are exactly four possible conditions involving these two realms: (i) a requirement that the intuitions achieve their own individual unity, (ii) a requirement that the intuitive realm respects the conceptual, (iii) a requirement that the conceptual realm respects the intuitive, and (iv) a requirement that the conceptual realm achieves its own individual unity. Here, (i) is the requirement that the synthesis of apprehension forms a fully connected graph satisfying 5(a) and 5(b) (Section 2.3.1). Condition (ii) is the requirement that the connections between intuitions are underwritten by corresponding judgements (Section 2.3.2). Condition (iii) is the requirement that the judgements respect the intuitions (Section 2.3.3). The final condition (iv) is the requirement that the discursive realm of judgement achieves conceptual unity (Section 2.3.4).

If our agent does all these things, and satisfies all these conditions, then it has achieved *experience*: it has combined the plurality of sensory inputs into a coherent representation of a single world. Achieving experience requires four faculties: sensibility (to receive intuitions), the imagination (to connect intuitions together

---

relations of Section 2.2 in such a way as to satisfy the unity conditions of Sections 2.3.1, 2.3.2, 2.3.3, and 2.3.4. Synthetic unity is the more fundamental concept, as it is presupposed by analytic unity [B133]. The distinction between empirical and original unity is the difference between a particular unity achieved by a particular mind when confronted with a particular sensory sequence, and what is in common between all unities achieved by all minds no matter which sensory sequence they are provided with. In this paper, I focus on the general conditions common to all minds when achieving synthetic unity.

59 See (Longuenesse, 1998, p.105).

using the pure relations as glue), the capacity to judge (to generate judgements), and the power of judgement (to decide whether an intuition falls under a concept).

According to our interpretation, intuitions are formed by sensibility, entirely independently of the understanding.[60] Further, intuitions can be connected (via the pure relations of Section 2.2) by the imagination, without the need for the understanding.[61] But intuitions can only constitute *experience* if the intuitions are brought under concepts (via the power of judgement) and the concepts are combined into judgements (via the capacity to judge): experience requires understanding working in concert with sensibility and the imagination to bring the connected intuitions into a unity. Thus, both sensibility and understanding need each other if they are to jointly achieve experience.[62]

Here are the core claims, brought together in one place for ease of reference:

1. In order to achieve experience, I must unify my intuitions.
2. Unifying intuitions means combining them using binary relations to form a connected graph, in such a way as to satisfy the various unity conditions.
3. Synthesis involves (i) connecting intuitions together via containment, comparison, and inherence operations to form determinations; and (ii) connecting determinations together via succession, simultaneity, and incompatibility relations.
4. There are, in total, four types of unity condition that Kant imposes: (i) the unity conditions for the synthesis of mathematical relations, (ii) the unity conditions for the synthesis of dynamical relations, (iii) the requirement that the judgements are underwritten by determinations, and (iv) the conceptual unity condition.
5. The unity conditions for the synthesis of mathematical relations are:
   (a) There exists some intuition x such that for each object of intuition y, for each moment in time, there is a chain of *in* determinations between y and x.
   (b) The comparison operator $<$ forms a strict partial order.

---

60 "Appearances can certainly be given in intuition without functions of the understanding." [A90/B122]. "The manifold for intuition must already be given prior to the synthesis of the understanding and independently from it." [B145].

61 "Synthesis in general is, as we shall subsequently see, the mere effect of the imagination, of a blind though indispensable function of the soul, without which we would have no cognition at all, but of which we are seldom even conscious" [A78/B103].

62 "Thoughts without content are empty, intuitions without concepts are blind." [A50-51/B74-76]. But note the striking asymmetry between the types of deficiency when one activity is performed without the other: *blindness* is a deficiency of a living conscious being, while *emptiness* is a deficiency of a mere *container*. This asymmetry confirms the interpretation in Section 2.1.2 that unity of intuition is the final end of all thought, and conceptual thought is merely a means to that end.

6. The unity conditions for the synthesis of dynamical relations are:
   (a) If I form an inherence determination, ascribing a particular attribute a to a particular object o, then I must be committed to a judgement "this/some/all X are P", where o falls under X, and a falls under P.
   (b) If I form a succession, in which one determination (say, particular object o having particular attribute a) is followed by another determination (say, o having incompatible attribute b), then I must have formed a conditional judgement "If $\phi(X)$ holds and X is P then X becomes Q at the next time-step", where object o falls under concept X, attribute a falls under concept P, attribute b falls under concept Q, and $\phi(X)$ is a sentence featuring free variable X.
   (c) If I form a simultaneity, in which one determination (say, particular object o_1 having particular attribute a) is simultaneous with another determination (say, object o_2 having attribute b), then there must be a pair of causal judgements, one of which states that an attribute of o_1 causally depends on an attribute of o_2, and another of which states that an attribute of o_2 causally depends on an attribute of o_1.
   (d) If I form an incompatibility in which one determination (say, particular object o having attribute a) is incompatible with another (say, particular object o having attribute b), then I must have formed a judgement "All X are either (exclusive disjunction) P or Q or . . .", in which o falls under X, a falls under P, and b falls under Q.
7. The requirement that the conceptual realm respects the intuitive is the condition that if I form a judgement, ascribing a concept P to a particular object X, then there must be a corresponding inherence determination ascribing particular attribute a to particular object o, where o falls under X and a falls under P.
8. The unity condition for conceptual unity is the requirement that every concept must feature in some disjunctive judgement.

In this section, I shall formalise the task of achieving synthetic unity of apperception. The formalism introduced is necessary for the derivation of the categories below.

2.5 Achieving Synthetic Unity

Let $\mathcal{I}$ be the set of intuitions, $\mathcal{D}$ the set of determinations, and C the set of connections. The signature of the three pure operations of containment, comparison, and inherence are:

$$in : I \times I \to \mathcal{D}$$

$$< \; : I \times I \to \mathcal{D}$$

$$det : I \times I \to \mathcal{D}$$

The signature of the three pure relations of succession, simultaneity, and incompatibility are:

$$succ : \mathcal{D} \times \mathcal{D} \to C$$

$$sim : \mathcal{D} \times \mathcal{D} \to C$$

$$inc : \mathcal{D} \times \mathcal{D} \to C$$

For example, if a, b, c are intuitions of type I, then $det(a, b)$, $in(a, b)$, and $b < c$ are determinations of type $\mathcal{D}$; and $succ(det(a, b), det(a, c))$ and $sim(in(a, b), b < c)$ are connections of type C.

The input that the mind receives from sensibility is a sequence of individual determinations from $\mathcal{D}$. Note that the input is not a sequence of *sets* of determinations that are already assumed to be simultaneous, but a sequence of *individual* determinations. Kant insists on this:

> The apprehension of the manifold of appearance is always successive. The representations of the parts succeed one another. Whether they also succeed in the object is a second point for reflection, which is not contained in the first . . . Thus, e.g., the apprehension of the manifold in the appearance of a house that stands before me is successive. Now the question is whether the manifold of this house itself is also successive, which certainly no one will concede. [A189/B234ff]

Here, Kant asks us to imagine an agent surveying a large house from close range. Its visual field cannot take in the whole house in one glance, so its focus moves from one part of the house to another. Its sequence of visual impressions is successive, but there is a further question whether a pair of (subjectively) successive visual impressions represents the house at a single moment of objective time, or at two successive moments of objective time.[63]

Given a sequence $(d_1, \ldots, d_t)$ of individual determinations, constructed from a set I of intuitions using the three pure operations (containment, comparison, and inherence), the task of making sense of sensory input is is to construct a synthetic unity – a tuple $(J, D, \kappa, \upsilon, \theta)$ – satisfying various conditions, where:
- J is a set of intuitions that must include I but also includes new intuitions that were constructed by the productive imagination

---

63 See also (Longuenesse, 1998, p.359).

– D is a set of determinations that must include $d_1, \ldots, d_t$ but also includes new determinations that were constructed by the productive imagination
– $\kappa \subseteq C$ is a set of connections between determinations
– $\upsilon \subseteq I \times P_1$ is the falls-under relation (also known as subsumption) between intuitions and unary predicates P_1, between pairs of intuitions and binary predicates P_2, etc.
– θ is a collection of judgements

The connections κ are generated by the faculty of *imagination*. Note that not all the determinations in κ need come from the original sequence $(d_1, \ldots d_t)$. Some of the determinations may involve new invented objects constructed by *pure intuition* (for spaces and times) or by the *imagination* (for hypothesised unperceived empirical objects). The connections must satisfy the following conditions:
–   For every pair of intuitions in J, there is a chain of determinations in D connecting one to the other
–   If d_i, d_{i+1} are successive determinations in $(d_1 \ldots, d_t)$, then either $sim(d_i, d_{i+1})$ or $succ(d_i, d_{i+1})$ must be in κ
–   The determinations are fully connected: every determination in D is κ-connected to every other determination via some path of undirected edges.

While the falls-under relation υ is generated by *the power of judgement*, the theory θ is a collection of judgements that is generated by the *capacity to judge*. The formal language for defining judgements, Datalog$^{\ni}$, is described in (Evans et al., 2021b), but in brief: judgements are either rules or constraints. Rules are either arrow rules $\alpha_1 \wedge \ldots \alpha_n \rightarrow \alpha_0$ (stating that if $\alpha_1 \ldots, \alpha_n$ all hold, then α_0 also holds at the same time-step), or causal rules $\alpha_1 \wedge \ldots \alpha_n \ni \alpha_0$ (stating that if $\alpha_1 \ldots, \alpha_n$ all hold, then α_0 also holds at the *next* time-step). Constraints are either *xor* judgements $\alpha_1 \oplus \ldots \oplus \alpha_n$ (stating that exactly one of the α_i hold) or a uniqueness constraint $\forall X, \exists! Y, r(X, Y)$ (stating that for each X there is exactly one Y such that $r(X, Y)$).

Figure 2.2 shows two different ways of grouping the four faculties, according to two cross-cutting distinctions. According to one distinction, sensation and imagination both fall under *sensibility* because both faculties process intuitions.[64] The power of judgement and the capacity to judge both fall under the *understanding* because both faculties process concepts. According to the

---

[64] "Now since all of our intuition is sensible, the imagination, on account of the subjective condition under which alone it can give a corresponding intuition to the concepts of understanding, belongs to **sensibility**." [B151].

other distinction, sensation falls under *receptivity* because it is a purely passive capacity that merely receives what it is given. The other three faculties fall under *spontaneity*[65] because the agent is free to construct *whatsoever it pleases*, as long as the resulting construction satisfies the various unity conditions.

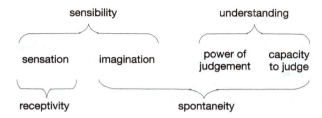

Figure 2.2: The relationship between the four faculties.

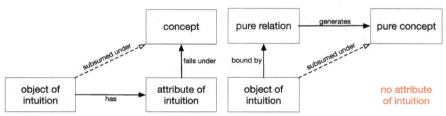

(a) The explanation of subsumption for an empirical concept   (b) The explanation of subsumption for a pure concept

Figure 2.3: Both diagrams provide an explanation for an object being subsumed under a concept. In (a), the concept is empirical, and the explanation goes via the intermediary of an attribute of intuition. In (b), the concept is pure, there is no corresponding attribute, and the explanation goes via the another intermediary: a pure relation.

We have now assembled the materials needed to define the task of synthetic unity.

Given a sequence $(d_1, \ldots, d_t)$ of determinations, the **task of achieving synthetic unity of apperception** is to construct a tuple $(J, D, \kappa, u, \theta)$ as described above that satisfies the unity conditions of Sections 2.3.1, 2.3.2, 2.3.3, and 2.3.4.

---

65 See [A51/B75], [B133], [B151].

2.6 The Derivation of the Categories

The problem of the pure categories is explained in the opening paragraphs of the *Schematism*:

> In all subsumptions of an object under a concept the representations of the former must be **homogeneous** with the latter, i.e., the concept must contain that which is represented in the object that is to be subsumed under it, for that is just what is meant by the expression "an object is contained under a concept." . . . Now pure concepts of the understanding, however, in comparison with empirical (indeed in general sensible) intuitions, are entirely unhomogeneous, and can never be encountered in any intuition. Now how is the **subsumption** of the latter under the former, thus the **application** of the category to appearances possible, since no one would say that the category, e.g., causality, could also be intuited through the senses and is contained in the appearance? [A137/B176 ff]

For empirical concepts, an object's being subsumed under a concept can be explained in terms of a particular attribute that the object has which falls under the concept. See Figure 2.3(a). Suppose, for example, my intuition of this particular jumper is subsumed under the concept "dirty". This subsumption is explained by (i) the object of intuition having, as one of its determinations, a particular attribute of intuition (my representation of the particular dirtiness of this particular jumper at this particular moment), and (ii) the attribute of intuition falling under the concept "dirty". The problem, for the pure concepts such as *Unity*, *Reality*, *Substance*, and so on, is that there is no corresponding attribute of intuition, so the explanation of the subsumption in Figure 2.3(a) is not applicable. What, then, justifies or permits us to subsume the objects of intuition under the pure concepts?

According to Kant, what justifies my subsuming an object under a pure concept is the existence of a *pure relation*[66] that the object is bound to. See Figure 2.3(b). Here, the subsumption of the object under the pure concept is explained by (i) the object of intuition being bound to the pure relation, and (ii) the pure concept being derivable from the pure relation. Note that in both Figures 2.3(a) and (b) there is an intermediary that explains the object being subsumed under a concept, but it is a different sort of intermediary in the two cases:

> Now it is clear that there must be a third thing, which must stand in homogeneity with the category on the one hand and the appearance on the other, and makes possible the application of the former to the latter. This mediating representation must be pure (without anything empirical) and yet intellectual on the one hand and sensible on the other. Such a representation is the transcendental schema. [A138/B177]

---

66 I.e. one of the six pure relations introduced in Section 2.2.

The "transcendental schema" is just another term for what I have been calling a pure relation: *in*, $<$, *det*, *succ*, *sim*, and *inc*.

This, then, is the outline of Kant's argument explaining how the pure concepts (categories) apply to objects of intuition. The next stage is to show, in detail, for each pure concept, exactly how it is derived from the corresponding pure relation. The derivation is straightforward and Kant did not see the need to spell it out.[67] But for the sake of maximal explicitness, we shall go through each in turn.

Starting with the title of *Relation*, intuition X falls under the pure concept **substance** if there exists an intuition Y such that $det(X, Y)$ is a determination in κ [B128-9]. Likewise, X falls under the pure concept **accident** if there exists an intuition Y such that $det(Y, X)$ is a determination in κ. Determination d falls under the pure concept **cause** if there exists a determination d' such that $succ(d, d')$ is in κ [A144/B183]. Likewise, determination d falls under the pure concept **dependent** if there exists a determination d' such that $succ(d', d)$ is in κ. A set D of determinations falls under the pure concept **community** if for each d, d' in D, $sim(d, d')$ is in κ [A144/B183-4].

Moving to the title of *Modality*, a set D of determinations falls under the pure concept **possible** if there is some sequence of sensor readings, and some theory θ that makes sense of those readings, such that D is contained in one of the states of the trace of θ [A144/B184]. A set D of determinations is **actual** if it is contained in one of the states of the trace of the best theory that explains the sensor readings that have been received.[68] A set D of determinations is **necessary** if it is contained in every state of the trace of the best theory that explains every possible sensory sequence.

Moving next to the title of *Quality*, intuition X falls under the pure concept of **reality** if there exists an intuition Y such that $Y < X$ [A168/B209]. Likewise, intuition X falls under the pure concept of **negation** if there does not exist an intuition Y such that $Y < X$.

---

67 In (Brandom, 2009), Brandom describes how new unary concepts can be derived from given relations. So, for example, if we have the binary relation $P(x, y)$ representing that x admires y, then we can form the new unary predicate $Q(x)$ defined as $Q(x) = R(x, x)$. Here, $Q(x)$ is true if x is a self-admirer. In a similar manner, the unary categories are derived from the pure relations of Section 2.2.

68 "The postulate for cognizing the **actuality** of things requires **perception**, thus sensation of which one is conscious – not immediate perception of the object itself the existence of which is to be cognized, but still its connection with some actual perception." [A225/B272].

Moving, finally, to the title of *Quantity*, the categories of *Unity*, *Plurality*, and *Totality* are slightly more involved because they are implicitly indexed by a predicate p. A container is a **unity** of p's if it contains all the objects that fall under p. In other words, X falls under the pure concept of unity if for all Y, $(Y,p) \in v$ implies $in(Y,X)$. A container is a **plurality** of p's if all the objects within it fall under p. In other words, X falls under the pure concept of plurality if for all Y, $in(Y,X)$ implies $(Y,p) \in v$. A container is a **totality** of p's if it contains all and only the objects that fall under p.[69]

Returning to the overall argument for the derivation of the categories, Kant's deontic[70] argument can be summarized as:

- Achieving experience requires that I connect the intuitions using the pure relations.
- If I connect the intuitions using the pure relations, then I may apply the pure concepts (the categories) to the objects of intuition.
- Therefore, achieving experience permits me to apply the pure concepts to the objects of intuition.

Thus the *quid juris* question [A84/B116] has been answered. Note, however, that my permission to apply the pure concepts to objects of intuition is conditioned on my *activity*, the activity of trying to achieve experience. Hence Kant's conclusion that the categories are only permitted to apply to objects of experience.[71]

Kant insisted that the categories are not innate. The pure unary concepts are not "baked in" as primitive unary predicates in the language of thought. The only things that are baked in are the fundamental capacities (sensibility, imagination, power of judgement, and the capacity to judge) together with the pure relations of Section 2.2. The categories themselves are *acquired* – derived from the pure relations *in concreto* when making sense of a particular sensory sequence. But they are *originally* acquired [*Entdeckung*, Ak. VIII, 222–23; 136.][72] because they are *always* derivable from *any* sensory sequence. The pure concepts, then, are not innate but originally acquired (Longuenesse, 1998).[73]

---

69 Kant says that a totality is a plurality considered as a unity [B111].

70 The argument is deontic in that it relies on the concepts of obligation and permission. Kant tries to show that we are permitted to apply the pure concepts to objects of experience, and his justification is that we are obligated to perform the activity of achieving synthetic unity.

71 "The category has no other use for the cognition of things than its application to objects of experience." [B145].

72 This is quoted in (Longuenesse, 1998).

73 Some cognitive scientists (e.g. Gary Marcus (Marcus, 2018b)) place Kant on the nativist side of the nativist versus empiricist debate. But the key question for Kant is not what humans are born with, but what agents *must do* in order to make sense of the sensory input. It is a normative

3 Experiments

The cognitive architecture described above has been implemented in the APPER-CEPTION ENGINE. The computer system is described in (Evans et al., 2021b) and (Evans et al., 2021a). In this section, I describe one experiment in detail.

3.1 The Sensory Input

In this experiment, there are two light sensors that can register various levels of intensity. If we take readings of both sensors at regular intervals, we get Figure 2.4. Here, the top row shows a human-readable discretised version of the sensor readings, revealing a simple regular pattern. The bottom row shows a fuzzier version of the same pattern where each sensor reading was perturbed with random noise. It is this second fuzzier version that is used in this experiment. But the sensory input, as presented in Figure 2.4(b), shows the sensory readings after they have already been assigned to particular moments in time. In Kant's theory, this time-assignment is not something that is given to the system, but rather is a hard-won *achievement*. In Kant's theory, the sensory input is presented as a sequence of *individual* sensory readings, and the agent has to decide how the various readings should be combined together into moments of objective time. So the actual input to the Kantian agent is shown in Figure 2.5. Here, the agent is given a sequence of individual sensory readings, and must choose how to combine them together into a succession of simultaneous readings. While Figure 2.5 shows the sequence of individual readings in subjective time, Figure 2.6 shows a variety of different ways of parsing the raw sequence into moments. The bottom row of Figure 2.6 shows the correct way of parsing the sequence in Figure 2.5; this correct parse corresponds to Figure 2.4(b).

The input, then, is the sequence shown in Figure 2.5. In our implementation, the continuous sensor readings are first discretised into binary vectors. The total sequence $(d_1, \ldots, d_{50})$ is a list of 50 inherence determinations. Note that the readings do not simply alternate between a and b. Sometimes there are multiple a's or

---

question of *a priori* psychology, not an empirical question about ontogenetic development. From Kant's perspective, the list of innate concepts proposed by cognitive scientists (spelke and Kinzler, 2007) is a "mere rhapsody" [A81/B106] unless they can be unified under a *common principle*. Nativists compile their list of innate concepts by looking at what human babies can do. But the capacities that evolution has hard-wired to help us in our particular situation are not *maximally general*. For example, babies can distinguish faces from other shapes before they are born, but the concept of a face is not a pure concept in Kant's sense.

b's in a row. The subjective sequence records the sequence of items the agent is attending to (he can only attend to one sensation at a time), and the agent might attend to either sensor at any moment of subjective time. Given this sequence in subjective time, we must reconstruct the moments of objective time by connecting the determinations using the relations of simultaneity and succession.

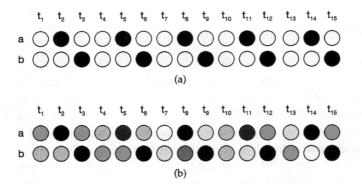

Figure 2.4: A simple sequence involving two sensors. (a) shows a noise-free version, where the pattern is clearly apparent. (b) shows the fuzzy version with random noise that is used in this experiment.

Figure 2.5: The input to the APPERCEPTION ENGINE is a sequence of individual readings. The engine must choose how to group the individual readings into groups of simultaneous readings.

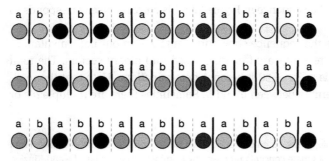

Figure 2.6: We show three ways of parsing the individual readings (in subjective time) into a succession of simultaneous readings (in objective time). The thin dashed lines divide the readings in subjective time, while the thicker lines group the individual readings into sets of simultaneous readings in objective time. The bottom row of the three represents the correct ground-truth way of grouping the readings.

3.2 The Model

Given the sensory sequence, the agent must construct an interpretation that makes sense of the sequence. The interpretation consists of:
1. A **synthesis of intuitions**. This contains a set of determinations (that must include the original sensory sequence, but can also include determinations involving other invented intuitions) connected together via the pure relations of *sim*, *succ*, and *inc*.
2. A **collection of subsumptions**. This is a set of mappings from intuitions of individual objects to general concepts. The mapping is implemented as a binary neural network.
3. A **set of judgements** that connect the concepts together.

I shall go through each in turn.

3.2.1 The Synthesis of Intuitions

The given sequence $(d_1, \ldots, d_{50})$ is a sequence of individual determinations in subjective time. We need to produce a sequence of sets of determinations in objective time. For each consecutive pair d_t, d_{t+1}, they can either be simultaneous or successive.

In our example, this choice rule gives us 2^{49} possibilities.[74] Once the *sim* and *succ* relations are provided, this determines the positions of the determinations in objective time.

3.2.2 The Set of Subsumptions

A subsumption maps an intuition (a bit vector) to a concept (symbol). We implement the power of judgement using a binary neural network parameterised by Boolean weights.

The neural network's input is a binary vector and the output is a binary vector of length $|P|$ (where $|P|$ is the number of unary predicates). The neural network implements a multilabel classifier mapping binary vectors to $2^{|P|}$.

---

[74] The current implementation assumes that any pair of consecutive sensor readings are either simultaneous or successive. This precludes the possibility that there are intermediate time-steps between the two consecutive readings. In future work, I plan to expand the choice rule to allow this further possibility, so that it is possible to abduce intermediate time-steps.

3.2.3 The Set of Judgements

Kant's faculty of understanding is implemented as a program synthesis system that takes as input a stream of sensory information, and produces a theory (a set of judgements) that both explains the sensory stream and also satisfies various unity conditions. For details, see (Evans et al., 2021b).

3.2.4 Filling in the Unperceived Details

Kant's requirement that judgements should be underwritten by determinations is implemented by adding a choice rule for each predicate p, stating that if an object X satisfies predicate p at T, then there is some particular attribute *Attr* ascribed to X at T (where *Attr* falls under p).

3.2.5 Finding the Best Model

When the three sub-systems (the imagination, power of judgement, and understanding) described above are implemented in one system, many different interpretations are found. In order to decide between the various interpretations, we use the following preferences:
1. We prefer shorter theories over longer theories, all other things being equal.
2. We prefer more discriminatory neural networks which assign fewer intuitions to the same concept.

See (Evans et al., 2021a) for the mathematical details of how these two desiderata are weighted and compared.

3.3 Results

The interpretation found by the APPERCEPTION ENGINE consists of a tuple $(J, D, \kappa, \upsilon, \theta)$ consisting of a synthesis of intuitions, a collection of subsumptions, and a set of judgements. We shall consider each in turn.

The synthesis of intuitions κ. When confronted with the sensory sequence of Figure 2.5, the engine produces a set κ of connections using the pure relations of *sim*, *succ*, and *inc*. Here is an excerpt:

$\text{sim}(([1,0,0],a,1),([1,0,1],b,2))$	$\text{succ}(([1,0,1],b,2),([0,0,1],a,3))$	$\text{inc}(([1,0,0],a,1),[0,0,1],a,3))$
$\text{sim}(([0,0,1],a,3),([1,0,1],b,4))$	$\text{succ}(([1,0,1],b,4),([0,0,0],b,5))$	$\text{inc}(([1,0,1],b,2),([0,0,0],b,5))$
$\text{sim}(([0,0,0],b,5),([1,0,0],a,6))$	$\text{succ}(([1,0,0],a,6),([1,0,1],a,7))$	$\text{inc}(([1,0,0],a,6),([0,0,1],a,10))$
$\text{sim}(([1,0,1],a,7),([1,0,0],b,8))$	$\text{succ}(([1,0,0],b,8),([1,0,0],b,9))$	$\text{inc}(([1,0,1],a,7),([0,0,0],a,15))$

Here, the determinations are triples containing an attribute (a binary vector of length 3, representing a particular shade of gray), an object (here a or b), and an index (from 1 to 15) in *subjective* time. This index is needed so that two determinations sharing the same object and attribute at different moments of time are nevertheless treated as distinct.

Figure 2.7 shows how the *succ* and *sim* relations produce objective time from subjective time.

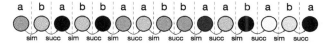

Figure 2.7: How the objective temporal sequence is constructed from the subjective temporal sequence via the pure relations of *sim* and *succ*.

The falls-under relation υ. The APPERCEPTION ENGINE constructs two unary predicates, p and q, and subsumes the binary vectors under them. The binary neural network implements a multilabel classifier, mapping binary vectors to subsets of $\{p, q\}$. The subsumptions υ produced by the engine are:

$$[0,0,0] \mapsto \{q\} \quad [0,0,1] \mapsto \{q\}$$
$$[0,1,0] \mapsto \{q\} \quad [0,1,1] \mapsto \{p,q\}$$
$$[1,0,0] \mapsto \{p\} \quad [1,0,1] \mapsto \{p\}$$
$$[1,1,0] \mapsto \{p\} \quad [1,1,1] \mapsto \{p\}$$

Note that $[0, 1, 1]$ is considered ambiguous.

Figure 2.8 shows the subsumptions generated by the engine. Note the introduction of an invented object, c, that was not part of the sensory input.

The set of judgements θ. Along with the synthesis of intuitions and the collection of subsumptions, the APPERCEPTION ENGINE also generates a theory θ, containing a set of judgements that explain the dynamics of the system. The theory constructed for the problem of Figure 2.5 is $\theta = (\phi, I, R, C)$, where ϕ is a type signature, I, is a set of initial conditions, R is a set of conditionals, and C

a	b	a	b	b	a	a	b	b	a	a	b	a	b
$p(a)$		$q(a)$		$p(a)$		$p(a)$		$q(a)$		$p(a)$		$p(a)$	
$p(b)$		$p(b)$		$q(b)$		$p(b)$		$p(b)$		$q(b)$		$p(b)$	
$q(c)$		$p(c)$		$p(c)$		$q(c)$		$p(c)$		$p(c)$		$q(c)$	

Figure 2.8: The subsumptions generated by the engine. The dashed lines divide subjective time, while the solid lines divide moments of objective time. The atoms generated at each moment are displayed below.

is a set of constraints. The type signature ϕ consists of types T, objects O, and predicates P where:

$$T = \{sensor, space\}$$
$$O = \{a{:}sensor, b{:}sensor, c{:}sensor, s_1{:}space, s_2{:}space, s_3{:}space, s_w{:}space\}$$
$$P = \{p(sensor), q(sensor), in(sensor, space), in_2(space, space), r(space, space)\}$$

The initial conditions I, rules R and constraints C are:

$$I = \left\{ \begin{array}{lll} p(a) & p(b) & q(c) \\ in(a, s_1) & in(b, s_2) & in(c, s_3) \\ in_2(s_1, s_w) \ in_2(s_2, s_w) & in_2(s_3, s_w) \ in_2(s_w, s_w) \\ r(s_1, s_2) & r(s_2, s_3) & r(s_3, s_1) \end{array} \right\}$$

$$R = \left\{ \begin{array}{l} q(X) \geqslant p(X) \\ in(X, S_1) \wedge in(Y, S_2) \wedge r(S_1, S_2) \wedge q(X) \geqslant q(Y) \end{array} \right\}$$

$$C = \left\{ \begin{array}{l} \forall X{:}sensor, \ p(X) \oplus q(X) \\ \forall X{:}sensor, \exists! Y{:}space, \ in(X, Y) \\ \forall X{:}space, \exists! Y{:}space, \ in_2(X, Y) \\ \forall X{:}sensor, \exists! Y{:}sensor, \ r(X, Y) \end{array} \right\}$$

Here, the sensors a and b are given as part of the sensory input, but c is an invented object, constructed by the imagination. The invented objects s_1, s_2, and s_3 are three parts of space, constructed by pure intuition. The three spaces are all parts of the spatial whole s_w.

The unary predicates p and q are used to distinguish between a sensor's being on and off. The *in* relation places sensors in space, and the *in*$_2$ relation places spaces inside the spatial whole. The r relation is used to define a one-dimensional

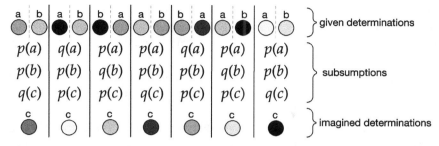

Figure 2.9: The determinations imagined by the engine. Here we show the given determinations (top row), the subsumptions (middle row), and the imagined determinations (bottom row) that are generated to satisfy condition (7): the requirement that every judgement needs to be underwritten by a determination. Thus, for example, the atom $q(c)$ in time step 1 needs to be underwritten by an inherence determination attributing a particular shade of q-ness to object c.

space with wraparound.[75] Note that our "spatial unity" requirement is rather minimal: we just insist that there is *some* containment structure connecting the intuitions together. It is not essential that the space constructed has the particular three-dimensional structure that we are accustomed to. Any spatial structure will do as long as the intuitions are unified , Chapter 3. In terms of Kant's distinction between the *form of intuition* and the *formal intuition* [B160n], the relation r describes the form of intuition (relations between objects) while the particular spaces (s_1, s_2, s_3, and s_w) represent the formal intuitions.

Note that the given objects of sensation (the sensors a and b) are not directly related to each other. Rather, they are *indirectly related* via the spatial objects and the *in* and r relations.

The rules describe how the unary properties p and q change over time. The first rule states that objects that satisfy q at one time-step will satisfy p at the next time-step. The second rule describes how the q property moves from one sensor to its right neighbour.

The constraints are constructed to satisfy conceptual unity (Section 2.3.4). The first insists that every sensor is either p or q but not both. The second requires that every sensor is contained within exactly one spatial region.

Filling in the unperceived details. In order to make concepts sensible (Section 2.3.3), the engine must ensure there is a determination corresponding to every judgement. In particular, the judgements involving invented unperceived

---

75 Note that, in this example, the spatial structure is static. But see Evans et al. (2020) for examples where objects move around.

object c must be underwritten by corresponding determinations. This means that for each time step at which $p(c)$ (respectively $q(c)$) is true, there must be an inherence determination $det(c, \alpha)$ ascribing particular attribute α to c, where c falls under p (respectively q).

Satisfying this condition means *imagining* particular attributes assigned to c for each moment of objective time. One set of determinations satisfying this condition is shown in Figure 2.9.

Thus, the unperceived object c is not merely subsumed under a predicate, but is also involved in a determination. *Even though c is an external object with which the agent has no sensory contact, it is cognised as satisfying particular perceptual determinations.* This is, I believe, the truth behind the Kant-inspired claim that "perception is a kind of controlled hallucination" (Clark, 2013).

Note that requirement (7) of Section 2.3.3 insists that object c must be involved in *some* determination, but does not – of course – insist on any *particular* determination. The productive imagination is free to construct any determination it pleases.

Discussion. Figure 2.10 shows the whole experiment, from the original input to the complete output consisting of a synthesis of intuitions, a collection of subsumptions, and a set of judgements. It is gratifying to see the APPERCEPTION ENGINE discerning a discrete intelligible structure behind the continuous noisy input. It started with a fuzzy sensory input, and perceived, amongst all the noise, an underlying system involving two discrete unary predicates, p and q, and devised a simple theory explaining how p and q change over time.

Let us pause to check that the interpretation of Figure 2.10 satisfies the various conditions (Section 2.4) required to achieve synthetic unity:
- The determinations are connected together via the relations of *succ*, *sim*, and *inc* to form a fully connected graph, as required in Section 2.2.
- The containment condition 5(a) of Section 2.3.1 is satisfied by the initial conditions I of Figure 2.10. Here, s_w is the spatial whole in which all other objects are contained, directly or indirectly.
- The $<$ relation is not needed in this particular example. The empty relation trivially satisfies the condition 5(b) that $<$ is a strict partial order.
- The requirement 6(a) of Section, that every inherence determination is underwritten by a judgement, is satisfied by the theory θ together with the subsumptions v. Consider, for example, the first determination in the given sequence: $det(a, [1, 0, 0])$, ascribing the binary vector $[1, 0, 0]$ (representing a particular shade of gray) to object a. Note that $[1, 0, 0] \mapsto p$ according to v, and since a is an object of type *sensor*, the determination is underwritten by the judgement $\exists X{:}sensor, p(X)$.

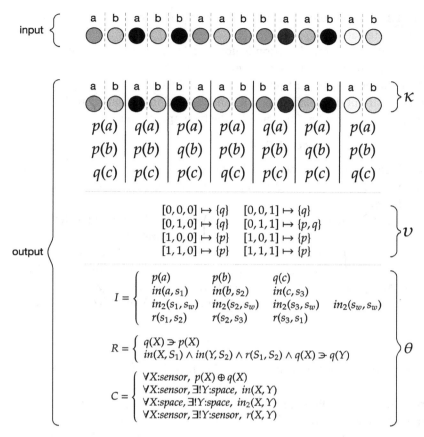

Figure 2.10: The result of applying the Apperception Engine to the input of Figure 2.5. The dashed lines divide moments of subjective time, while the solid lines divide moments of objective time. We show the synthesis of intuitions κ, the subsumptions υ, and the theory θ. We also show the ground atoms at each step of objective time, generated by applying the subsumptions υ to the raw input.

– The requirement 6(b) of Section, that every succession is underwritten by a causal judgement, is satisfied by the theory θ together with the subsumptions υ. Consider, for example, the succession:

$$succ(([0,0,1],b,4),([1,1,0],b,5))$$

This represents the succession of $det(b,[0,0,1])$ by $det(b,[1,1,0])$ (i.e., b changing from one particular shade of gray to another). Note that $[0,0,1]\mapsto q$

and $[1, 1, 0] \mapsto p$ according to the subsumptions v, and rules R contain the causal judgement $q(X) \Rightarrow p(X)$.

- The requirement 6(c) of Section is not used in our initial implementation of the Apperception Engine. See Section 4.4 for a discussion.
- The requirement 6(d) of Section, that every incompatibiity is underwritten by a constraint, is satisfied by the constraints C in θ together with the subsumptions v. Consider, for example, the incompatibility:

$$inc(([1, 0, 0], a, 1), [0, 0, 1], a, 3))$$

This incompatibility between determinations is underwritten by the constraint $\forall X{:}sensor,\ p(X) \oplus q(X)$, together with the mappings $[1, 0, 0] \mapsto p$ and $[0, 0, 1] \mapsto q$.

- The requirement 7 of Section 2.3.3 is satisfied by the inherence determinations featuring invented object c as shown in Figure 2.9.
- The requirement 8 of Section 2.3.4, that every predicate features in some *xor* or uniqueness constraint, is satisfied by the theory θ of Figure 2.9. Here, predicates p and q feature in the constraint $\forall X{:}sensor,\ p(X) \oplus q(X)$, *in* features in the constraint $\forall X{:}sensor,\ \exists! Y{:}space,\ in(X, Y)$, and so on for the other binary relations.

3.4 Perceptual Discernment and Conceptual Discrimination

Compare the interpretation of Figure 2.10 with the alternative degenerate interpretation of Figure 2.11. Both interpretations satisfy the unity conditions, but they do so in very different ways. While Figure 2.10 discerns a difference between the inputs – dividing them into two classes, p and q – and constructs a theory that explains how p and q properties interact over time, Figure 2.11, by contrast, fails to discern any difference between the input vectors. Because Figure 2.11 is coarser and less discriminating, mapping all input vectors to p and none to q, it can make do with a much simpler theory: if everything is always p and never q, we do not need a complex theory to explain how objects transition between p and q.[76]

---

[76] The APPERCEPTION ENGINE considers and evaluates many different theories when presented with the sensory input of Figure 2.5. It prefers the interpretation of Figure 2.10 over the degenerate interpretation of Figure 2.11 precisely because the former discriminates finer. In (Evans et al., 2021a), I explain how one interpretation is preferred to another if, other things being equal, the first makes more fine-grained perceptual discriminations. I justify the preference using simple Bayesian considerations.

In Kant's theory of synthetic unity, as we interpret it, this phenomenon holds across the board. In order to discern a fine-grained discrimination between sensory input, we must provide a theory that underwrites that distinction, a theory that explains how the various properties that we have discriminated actually interact. Fine-grained perceptual discrimination requires an articulated theory (a collection of concepts and judgements) that underpins the distinctions made at the sensible level. Intuitions without concepts are blind.

There is a recurrent myth that humans have fallen from a state of pre-conceptual grace (Jaynes, 2000). At some mythic earlier time, humans were not saddled with the conceptual apparatus we now take for granted, and – precisely because they were unburdened by concepts and judgements – were able to perceive the world in all its glory, with a fine-grained vividness we moderns can only dream of. It is as if there is only a finite amount of consciousness to go round; because we modern concept users waste some of that consciousness on the conceptual side of our experience, there is less consciousness remaining to spend on the sensible side. The mythic earlier man, by contrast, is able to spend all his consciousness on the sensible level. Thus for him, in his state of pre-conceptual grace, the colours are brighter.

If Kant is right, this myth gets things exactly the wrong way round. Consciousness is not a zero-sum game between sensibility and understanding, in which one side's gains must be the other side's losses. Rather, perceptual discrimination at the sensible level requires conceptual discrimination from the understanding. *The more intricate the theories we are able to construct, the more vividly we are able to see.*

4 Discussion

4.1 Rigidity and Spontaneity

There is a popular image of Kant as a rigid rule-bound automaton whose daily routine was so tightly scheduled you could use it to calibrate your clock. According to this popular image, Kant's philosophy (both practical and theoretical) is as rigid and rule-bound as his unusually unremarkable personal life. What is most unfair about this gross mischaracterisation is that it omits the critical fact that, for Kant, the rules I am bound to are rules that *I myself create.*

Spontaneity and self-legislation are at the heart of Kant's philosophy, both practical and theoretical. In his practical philosophy, I am free to construct *any maxims whatsoever* – as long as they satisfy the universalisability conditions of the categorical imperative. In his theoretical philosophy, I am free to construct *any rules whatsoever* – as long as they satisfy the unity conditions. When confronted with a stream of raw sensory input, the Kantian agent constructs a set of connections between intuitions, a set of subsumptions mapping intuitions to concepts, and a set of judgements connecting concepts together. The agent is completely free to construct *any* set of connections between intuitions, *any* set of subsumptions, and *any* set of judgements – so long as the package jointly satisfies the unity conditions (Sections 2.3.1, 2.3.2, and 2.3.4). These conditions of unity are not unnecessary extraneous requirements that Kant insists on for some personal Puritan preference – they are the absolutely minimal conditions necessary for it to be *you* who is doing the constructing. According to Kant, the conditions that need to be satisfied to interpret the sensory input as a coherent

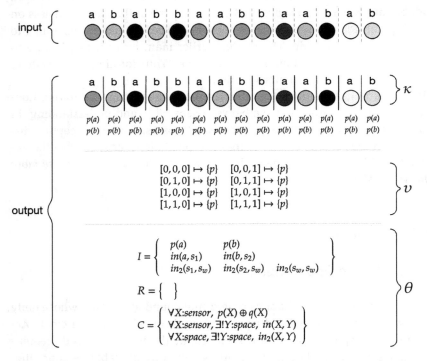

Figure 2.11: An alternative degenerate interpretation of the input of Figure 2.5. Here, all sensory input is mapped, indiscriminately, to *p*. Because no discriminations are made, and nothing changes, the induced theory is particularly simple. Note in particular that the set of dynamic rules *R* is empty, hence nothing changes.

representation of a single world are *exactly the same conditions* that need to be satisfied for there to be a *self* who is perceiving that world.[77]

Unlike the popular image, Kant's vision of the mind is one of remarkable freedom. I am continually constructing the program that I then execute. The only constraint on this spontaneous construction is the requirement that there is a single person looking out. In our computer implementation, this spontaneity is manifest in a particular way: when given a sensory sequence, the APPERCEPTION ENGINE constructs an unending sequence of increasingly complex interpretations, each of which satisfies Kant's unity conditions. The engine must decide, somehow, which of these interpretations to choose.[78]

4.2 Rigidity and Diachrony

Wittgenstein is sometimes interpreted as denying the possibility of any rule-based account of cognition. Throughout the *Investigations* (Wittgenstein, 2009), Wittgenstein draws our attention, again and again, to cases where our rules *give out*:

I say "There is a chair" What if I go up to it, meaning to fetch it, and it suddenly disappears from sight? – "So it wasn't a chair, but some kind of illusion". – But in a few moments we see it again and are able to touch it and so on. – "So the chair was there after all and its disappearance was some kind of illusion". – But suppose that after a time it disappears again – or seems to disappear. What are we to say now? *Have you rules ready for such cases* – rules saying whether one may use the word "chair" to include this kind of thing? But do we miss them when we use the word "chair"; and are we to say that we do not really attach any meaning to this word, because *we are not equipped with rules for every possible application of it*? (*Investigations*, § 80)

Our rules for the identification of chairs cannot anticipate every eventuality, including their continual appearance and disappearance – but this does not mean we cannot recognise chairs. Or, to take another famous example, we have rules for determining the time in different places on Earth. But now suppose someone says:

It was just 5 o'clock in the afternoon on the sun　　　　(*Investigations*, § 351)

---

77 "The *a priori* conditions of a possible experience in general are at the same time conditions of the possibility of the objects of experience." [A111].

78 Our way of deciding between the various interpretations is based on the theory size and the fine-grainedness of the perceptual classifier. See (Evans et al., 2021a). This is one place where we attempt to go beyond Kant's explicit pronouncements, since he does not give us guidance here.

Again, our rules for determining the time do not cover all applications, and sometimes just *give out*. They do not cover cases where we apply the time of day on the sun. Since any set of rules is inevitably limited and partial, we must continually improvise and update.

This point is important and true, but is fully compatible with Kant's vision of the cognitive agent. Such an agent is *continually constructing* a new set of rules that makes best sense of its sensory perturbations. It is not that it constructs a set of rules, once and for all, and then applies them rigidly and unthinkingly forever after. Rather the process of rule construction is a continual effort.

Kant describes an *ongoing process* of constructing and applying rules to make sense of the barrage of sensory stimuli:

> There is no unity of self-consciousness or "transcendental unity of apperception" apart from this effort, or conatus towards judgement, *ceaselessly affirmed and ceaselessly threatened with dissolution* in the "welter of appearances"　(Longuenesse, 1998, p.394)

Kant's apperceptual agent is continually constructing rules so as to best make sense of the barrage of sensory stimuli. If he were to cease constructing these rules, he would cease to be a cognitive agent, and would be merely a *machine*.

In *What is Enlightenment?* (Kant, 1784), Kant is emphatic that the cognitive agent must never be satisfied with a statically defined set of rules – but must always be modifying existing rules and constructing new rules. He stresses that adhering to any statically-defined set of rules is a form of *self-enslavement*:

> Precepts and formulas, those mechanical instruments of a rational use, or rather misuse, of his natural endowments, are the ball and chain of an everlasting minority.

Later, he uses the term "machine" to describe a cognitive agent who is no longer open to modifications of his rule-set. He defines **enlightenment** as the *continual willingness to be open to new and improved sets of rules*. He imagines what would happen if we decided to fix on a particular set of rules, and forbid any future modifications or additions to that rule-set. He argues that this would be disastrous for society and also for the self.

Some of Wittgenstein's remarks are often interpreted as denying the possibility of *any* sort of rule-based account of cognition:

> We can easily imagine people amusing themselves in a field by playing with a ball so as to start various existing games, but playing many without finishing them and in between throwing the ball aimlessly into the air, chasing one another with the ball and bombarding one another for a joke and so on. And now someone says: The whole time they are playing a ball-game and following definite rules at every throw.　(*Investigations* §83)

Now there is a crucial scope ambiguity here. Is Wittgenstein merely denying that there is a set of rules that captures the ball-play at every moment? Or is he making a stronger claim, claiming that there is *some* moment during the ball-play that cannot be captured by *any set of rules at all*? I believe the weaker claim is more plausible: we make sense of the world by applying rules, but we need to continually modify our rules as we progress through time. Wittgenstein's passage in fact continues:

> And is there not also the case where we play and make up the rules as we go along? And there is even one where we alter them, as we go along.

Here, he does not consider the possibility of there being activity that cannot be explained by rules – rather, he is keen to stress the *diachronic* nature of the rule-construction process: one set of rules at one moment in time, a modified set of rules at a subsequent moment. Thus Wittgenstein's remarks on rules should not be seen as precluding any type of rule-based account of cognition, but rather as emphasising the importance of always being open to revising one's rules in the light of new information. As T. S. Eliot once observed:[79]

> For the pattern is new in every moment
> And every moment is a new and shocking
> Valuation of all we have been

4.3 Basic Assumptions

The Apperception Engine in its current form, and its limitations as described below, are a result of some fundamental decisions that were made early on in the project, answers to some basic questions about how to interpret and implement Kant:

1. When Kant says that every succession of determinations must be underwritten by a causal rule, does he mean that (i) there must be a causal rule that the agent believes? Or, much weaker, (ii) the agent must merely believe there *is* a causal rule?
2. When Kant says that judgements are rules, does he mean (i) explicit rules formed from discrete symbols? Or could he mean that some judgements are just (ii) implicit rules?
3. How expressive are Kant's judgements in the *Table of Judgements*? Does he just allow (i) simple definite clauses? Or does he also allow (ii) geometric rules (with disjunctions or existentials in the head)?

---

79 Four Quartets, *East Coker.*

4. Given that the understanding involves two separable capacities – the capacity to subsume intuitions under concepts and the capacity to combine concepts into rules – how should these two capacities be implemented? Should there be (i) one system that performs both, or (ii) two separate systems, with one passing its output to the other?

The design of the APPERCEPTION ENGINE was based on choosing option (i) at each of the four decision points. I shall attempt to justify each decision in turn.

4.3.1 Succession and Causal Rules

In the *Second Analogy*, Kant writes:

> If, therefore, we experience that something happens, then we always presuppose that something else precedes it, which it follows in accordance with a rule.   [A195/B240]

Now this claim has a crucial scope ambiguity: does it mean that (i) whenever there is a succession there is a rule which the agent believes that underwrites the succession? Or does it mean that (ii) whenever there is a succession the agent believes that there is some rule that underwrites the successsion, even if the agent does not know what the particular rule is?

Some commentators have assumed the second, weaker interpretation. For example, Longuenesse believes that I do not have to have already formed a causal judgement to perceive a succession – I just need to acknowledge that I should form a causal judgement. For Longuenesse, perceiving a succession means *being committed to look for a causal rule* – it does not mean that I need to have *already found one*:

> The statement that "everything that happens presupposes something else upon which it follows according to a rule" does not mean that we cognize this rule, but that we are so constituted as to search for it, for its presupposition alone allows us to recognize a permanent to which we attribute changing properties.   (Longuenesse, 1998, p.366)

Others, including Michael Friedman (Friedman, 1992) take the first, stronger interpretation.

I do not have the space or time to enter into the exegetical fray, but would like to make one observation. If we take the first, stronger interpretation, then any implementation of Kant's theory will be a system that can be used to predict future states, retrodict past states, and impute missing data. This ability to fill in the blanks in the sensory stream is only available because the agent *actually constructs rules* to explain the succession of appearances. If we had implemented the second, weaker interpretation, then the agent would merely believe that there was *some* rule – it would not have been forced to find the rule, it would have been content to know that the rule existed somewhere. Such an agent would not be able to anticipate the future or reconstruct the past.

4.3.2 Explicit or Implicit Rules

When Kant says that judgements are rules, does he mean that judgements are (i) explicit rules formed from discrete symbols? Or could he mean that some judgements are just (ii) implicit rules (e.g., a procedure that is implicit in the weights of a neural network)?

The first interpretation, assuming judgements are explicit rules using discrete symbols in the language of thought,[80] is a form of what Brandom calls *regulism* (Brandom, 1994, p.18). The second interpretation allows for rules that are universal (they apply to all objects of a certain type), necessary (they apply in all situations), but *implicit*: the rule may not be expressible in a concise sentence in a natural or formal language. For a concrete example of the second interpretation, consider the *Neural Logic Machine* (Dong et al., 2019). This is a neural network that simulates forward chaining of definite clauses but without representing the clauses explicitly. The "rules" of the Neural Logic Machine are implicit in the weights (a large tensor of floating point values) of the neural network and cannot be transformed into concise human-readable rules. Nevertheless, the rules are universal and necessary, applying to all objects in all situations.

Most commentators believe that Kant's rules are explicit rules composed of discrete symbols.[81] I do not want to contribute to the exegetical debate, but rather want to provide a practical reason for preferring the first interpretation in terms of explicit rules. Part of the attraction of the APPERCEPTION ENGINE as described above is that the theories found by the engine can be read, understood, and verified. For example, the theory learned from the *Sokoban* trace is not just correct, but *provably* correct. If we need to understand what the machine is

---

80 In this project, I follow Jerry Fodor in assuming that our beliefs are expressed in a language of thought (Fodor, 1975) which is symbolic and compositional. Moreover, I assume that the language of thought is something like Datalog$^\Rightarrow$, but somewhat more expressive (Piantadosi, 2011).

81 But there is a note, inserted in Kant's copy of the first edition of the first Critique [A74/ B99], which suggests that judgements need not be explicit: "Judgments and propositions are different. That the latter are *verbis expressa* [explicit words], since they are assertoric".

thinking, or need to verify that what it is thinking is correct, then we must prefer explicit rules.

Another, perhaps more fundamental, reason for preferring explicit rules is that they enable us to test whether Kant's unity conditions (see Section 2.4) have been satisfied. In order to test whether every succession is underwritten by a causal judgement (Section), for example, we need to be able to inspect the rules produced. It is unclear how a system that operates with merely implicit rules can detect whether or not Kant's unity conditions have actually been satisfied.

4.3.3 The Expressive Power of Kant's logic

Commentators disagree about the expressive power of Kant's judgements. Some think Kant's logic is restricted to Aristotelian syllogisms over judgements containing only unary predicates. If this were so, Kant's logic would indeed be "terrifyingly narrowminded and mathematically trivial"[82] Similarly, many commentators (for example, MacFarlane [42], p.26; also [55]) assume or claim that Kant's logic is highly restrictive in that it does not support nested quantifiers. Others[83] argue that Kant must have a more expressive logic in mind, a logic that includes at least nested quantifiers of the form $\forall\exists$.

There is, of course, a tradeoff between the expressiveness of the logic and the tractability of learning theories in that logic: the more complex the judgement forms allowed, the harder it is to learn. Geometric logic, for example, is highly expressive[84] but it is also undecidable (Bezem, 2005). Datalog, by contrast, is decidable, and has polynomial time data complexity dantsin 2001 complexity.

Because of this tradeoff, in this work we opted for a simpler logic (i.e. Datalog$^\ni$ rather than geometric logic) in order to make it tractable to synthesise theories in that logic. One of the central pillars of our interpretation is that Kant's fundamental notion of spontaneity is best understood as *unsupervised program synthesis*. To test out this claim, it was necessary to build a system that is capable of generating theories to explain a diverse range of examples. Thus, in this

---

82 (Hazen, 1999), quoted in (Achourioti and Van Lambalgen, 2011).

83 See in particular (Achourioti and Van Lambalgen, 2011; Achourioti et al., 2017), and also (Evans et al., 2019).

84 More generally, (Dyckhoff and Negri, 2015) shows that, for each set Σ of first-order sentences, there is a set of sentences of geometric logic that is a conservative extension of Σ.

THE CAT

Figure 2.12: Top-down influence from the symbolic to the sub-symbolic. Here the ambiguous image (the image used to represent both the 'H' of 'THE' and the 'A' of 'CAT') is disambiguated at the sub-symbolic level using knowledge (of typical English spellings) at the symbolic level.

project, we used an extension of Datalog to define a simple range of judgements. We do not claim that logic adequately represents the range of judgements expressible in Kant's *Table of Judgements*: after all Datalog$^\ni$ contains no negation symbol, no existential quantifier, and no modal operators. In future work we plan to extend this language with stratified negation as failure, disjunction in the head, and existential quantifiers, to increase its expressive power.

4.3.4 One System or Two?

The understanding involves two distinguishable capacities: the capacity to subsume intuitions under concepts (the power of judgement), and the capacity to combine concepts into rules (the capacity to judge). These two capacities take different sorts of input: the power of judgement takes raw intuitions and maps them to discrete concepts, while the capacity to judge operates on discrete concepts. This difference could suggest that we need a hybrid approach involving two distinct systems for the two capacities: one system (perhaps a neural network) for mapping intuitions to concepts and another (perhaps a symbolic program synthesis system) for combining concepts into rules. According to this suggestion, the output of the first system is fed as input to the second system.

A concern with this hybrid approach is that it is very unclear how to support top-down information flow from the conceptual to the pre-conceptual. There is much evidence that expectations from the conceptual symbolic realm can inform decisions at the pre-conceptual sub-symbolic realm. See, for example, Figure 2.11.[85] Here, part of the image is highly ambiguous: the 'H' of "THE" and the 'A' of "CAT" use the same ambiguous image, but we are able to effortlessly disambiguate (at the sub-symbolic level) by using our knowledge of typical English spelling at the symbolic level.

---

85 This example is adapted from (Chalmers et al., 1992).

Thus, it is essential that the high-level constraints – the conditions of unity – are allowed to inform the low-level sub-symbolic processing. This consideration precludes a two-tier architecture where a neural network transforms intuitions into concepts, and a symbolic system searches for unified interpretations. In such an architecture, it is not possible for the low-level neural network to receive the information it needs from the high-level system. The only information that the neural network will receive in a two-tier approach is a *single bit*: whether or not the high-level symbolic system was able to find a unified interpretation. It will not know *why* it was unable, or *which constraints* it was unable to satisfy. This is insufficient information.

Because of this concern, we opted for a different architecture, in which a *single system* jointly performed both tasks: both mapping intuitions to concepts and combining concepts into rules.[86]

4.3.5 Alternative Options

The particular design decisions taken in the APPERCEPTION ENGINE represent one way of answering the four questions above. But there are many other possible architectures. One option, for example, would be to represent the rules implicitly (Dong et al., 2019), and to use a single neural network to jointly learn to map intuitions to concepts and to learn the weights of the implicit rules. Another option would be to use a hybrid architecture in which a neural network, trained on gradient descent, maps intuitions to concepts, while another symbolic system combines concepts into rules. These alternative options have issues of their own, as I hope the discussion above makes clear, but the point remains that the APPERCEPTION ENGINE is certainly not the only way to implement Kant's cognitive architecture.

4.4 Moving Closer to a Faithful Implementation of Kant's *a priori* Psychology

This project is an attempt to repurpose Kant's *a priori* psychology as the architectural blueprint for a machine learning system, and as such has the real potential to irritate two distinct groups of people. AI practitioners may be irritated

---

86 Of course, our single system itself contains both a neural network mapping intuitions to concepts and a program synthesis component that constructs sets of rules. But this counts as a single architecture rather than a hybrid architecture because our binary neural network is implemented in ASP and the weights are found using SAT, rather than gradient descent.

by the appeal to a notoriously difficult eighteenth-century text, while Kant scholars may be irritated by the indelicate attempt to shoe-horn Kant's ambitious system into a simple computational formalism. The concern is that Kant's ideas have been distorted to the point where they are no longer recognisable.

In what ways, then, does the Apperception Engine represent a faithful implementation of Kant's vision, and in what ways does it fall short?

I shall focus, first, on the respects in which the computer architecture is a faithful implementation of Kant's psychological theory. Kant proposed various faculties that interoperate to turn raw data into experience: the imagination (to connect intuitions together using the pure relations as glue), the power of judgement (to decide whether an intuition falls under a concept), and the capacity to judge (to generate judgements from concepts). Throughout, Kant emphasized the spontaneity of the mind: the faculties are free to perform *whatever activity they like*, as long as the resulting system satisfies the various unity conditions described in the *Principles*.

The Apperception Engine provides a unified implementation of the various faculties Kant describes: the imagination is implemented as a set of non-deterministic choice rules, the power of judgement is implemented as a neural network, and the capacity to judge is implemented as an unsupervised program synthesis system. These sub-systems are highly non-deterministic: the imagination is free to synthesise the intuitions *in any way whatsoever*, the power of judgement is free to map intuitions to concepts *in any way it pleases*, and the capacity to judge is free to construct *any rules at all* – so long as the combined product of the three faculties satisfies the various unity conditions (implemented as *constraints*).

Thus, while contingent information flows bottom-up (from sensibility to the understanding), necessary information flows top-down, as the unity conditions of the understanding are the only constraints on the operations of the system. As Kant says: "through it [the constraint of unity] the understanding determines the sensibility [B160-1n]". This is, I believe, a faithful implementation of Kant's cognitive architecture at a high level.

Next I shall turn to the various respects in which the computer architecture described above falls short of Kant's ambitious vision of how the mind must work. I shall focus on six aspects of Kant's cognitive architecture that are not adequately represented in the current implementation.

4.4.1 The Representation of the Input

The way in which raw data is given to the APPERCEPTION ENGINE is different from how Kant describes it. Kant describes a cognitive agent receiving a *continuous* stream of information, making sense of each segment before receiving the next. The APPERCEPTION ENGINE, by contrast, is given the entire stream as a single unit. If the APPERCEPTION ENGINE is to operate with a continuous stream, it will have to synthesise a new theory *from scratch* each time it receives a new piece of information.

In the *A Deduction*, Kant describes three aspects of synthesis: the synthesis of apprehension in the intuition, the synthesis of reproduction in the imagination, and the synthesis of recognition in a concept. The synthesis of reproduction in the imagination involves the ability to recall past experiences that are no longer present in sensation. The APPERCEPTION ENGINE does not attempt to model the synthesis of reproduction. Rather, it assumes that the entire sequence is given.

The form of the raw data is also different from how Kant describes it. In Section 3.1, the raw data is provided as a sequence of *determinations*: assignments of raw attributes to persistent objects (sensors). Here, we assume that the agent is provided with the sensor, as a persistent object. But in Kant's architecture, the construction of determinations featuring persistent objects is a hard-won achievement – not something that is given. What *is* given, in Kant's picture, is the activity of sensing and the ability to tell when a particular sensing performed at one moment is the same sensing activity performed at another (the "unity of the action"). Thus, in Kant's picture, the agent is provided with a more minimal initial input than that given to our system, and so his agent has more work to do to achieve experience.

4.4.2 The Representation of Space and Time

The way space is represented in the APPERCEPTION ENGINE is different from how Kant describes it. For Kant, space is a single *a priori* intuition. He starts with space as a totality, and creates sub-spaces by division ("limitation" [A25/B39]). In the APPERCEPTION ENGINE, by contrast, we start with objects representing spatial regions, and compose them together using the containment structure (Section 2.3.1).

Similarly, with time, Kant starts with the original representation of the whole of time, and constructs sub-times by division [A32/B48]. In the APPERCEPTION ENGINE, by contrast, the sequence of time-steps are determined by the given input, and it is not possible for the system in its current form to construct new moments of time that are intermediate between the given moments. Relatedly, it is not possible to represent continuous causality (e.g. water slowly filling a container) in our formalism. In future work, we plan to enrich Datalog∃ so that it can represent continuous change{\mdottt}

4.4.3 The Minimal Conception of Space

The APPERCEPTION ENGINE unifies objects by placing them in a containment structure: each object is in some spatial region which is itself part of some larger spatial region, until we reach the whole of space. In Section 2.3.1, I argued that this containment structure is a central component of any notion of space. But there is much more to spatial relations than the containment structure: just knowing that x and y are in does not tell us anything about the relative positions of x and y.

Kant had a much more full-blooded conception of space than just a containment structure: he assumed three-dimensional Euclidean space [B41]. In future work, I plan to provide the APPERCEPTION ENGINE with three-dimensional space,[87] thus providing a stronger inductive bias, which should help the system to learn more data-efficiently.

4.4.4 The Expressive Power of the Logic

In the *Transcendental Deduction*, Kant argued that the relative positions of intuitions in a determination can only be fixed by forming a judgement that necessitates this particular positioning [B128]. The APPERCEPTION ENGINE attempts to respect this fundamental requirement by insisting that the various connections between intuitions are backed up by judgements of various forms (Section 2.3.2). However, the forms of judgement supported in Datalog∃ are a mere subset of the forms enumerated in the *Table of Judgements* [A70/B95]. Datalog∃ supports universally quantified conditionals, causal conditionals, and xor constraints (corresponding to Kant's disjunctive judgement). But it does not support negative judgements, infinite judgements, particular judgements, singular judgements, or

---

87 Perhaps by providing an axiomatisation of Euclidean space using Tarski's formalisation, or somesuch (but note that axiomatising Euclidean geometry requires ternary predicates, which are not currently handled in the Apperception Engine). But Tarski assumes points as primitive, where a point is defined as a vector of real numbers. It would be closer to Kant's program, I believe, to axiomatise space starting from the notion of *limitation*, without assuming real numbers as given.

modal judgements. In future work, we plan to extend the expressive power of Datalog$^{\ni}$ to capture the full range of propositions expressible in the *Table of Judgements*.[88]

4.4.5 The Role of the Third Analogy

The *Third Analogy* states that whenever two objects' determinations are perceived as simultaneous, there must be a two way interaction between the two objects. This does not mean, of course, that there must be a direct causal influence between them, but just that there must be a chain of indirect causal influences between them.

This requirement has not been implemented in the APPERCEPTION ENGINE. This is because it would make it very hard for the system to find any unified interpretation at all if every time it posited a simultaneity between determinations it also had to construct some rules whereby one determination of one object indirectly caused some determination of the other object. Longuenesse (Longuenesse, 1998) has a different understanding of the second and third *Analogies*, and does not believe that we need to *have actually formed a causal rule* in order to perceive succession or simultaneity. In her interpretation, we merely need to *believe that there is a causal rule to find* (see Section for a discussion). However, in our interpretation, in which the rule must actually be found before a temporal relation can be assigned, the *Third Analogy* does seem restrictively strong. In future work, we hope to address this issue and find a way to respect the simultaneity constraint.

4.4.6 Consciousness and Analytic Unity

The first *Critique* contains various discussions of various aspects of self-consciousness. But no aspect of self-consciousness is implemented in the APPERCEPTION ENGINE. In the *B Deduction*, Kant distinguishes the synthetic unity of apperception (the connecting together of one's intuitions via the pure relations in such a way as to achieve unity) from the analytic unity of apperception (the ability to subsume any of my cognitions under the predicate "I think"). He claims that synthetic unity of apperception is a necessary condition for achieving analytic

---

[88] By contrast, the geometric logic used in (Achourioti and Van Lambalgen, 2011; Achourioti et al., 2017) is much more expressive.

unity [B133-4]. Although the Apperception Engine aims to implement the synthetic unity of apperception, no attempt has been made to implement the analytic unity of apperception.

Kant is clear to distinguish between inner sense and explicit self-consciousness [B154]. Inner sense is the aspect of sensibility in which the mind perceives its own mental activity: it notices the formation of a belief, for example, or the application of a rule. Inner sense provides us with intuitions that must be ordered in time. Explicit self-consciousness, by contrast, is the construction of a theory that makes sense of the sequence of perturbations produced by inner sense. In inner sense I become aware of some of the cognitions I am having, and in explicit self-consciousness, I posit a theory that explains the dynamics of my own mental activity – although this hypothesized theory may or may not reflect accurately the actual mental processes I am undergoing [B156]. In future work, I plan to extend Apperception Engine so that (some of) its own activity is perceptible via inner sense, so that the system is forced to construct a theory to make sense of its perceptions of its own mental activity.

There are, then, various aspects of Kant's theory of mental activity that are not captured in the current incarnation of the Apperception Engine. There is, I think it is fair to say, more work still to do.

5 Conclusion

In the *Critique of Pure Reason*, Kant asks: what activities must be performed by an agent – *any* finite resource-bounded agent – if it is to make sense of its sensory input. This is not an empirical question about the particular activities that are performed by *homo sapiens*, but an *a priori* question about the activities that any agent must perform. Kant's answer, if correct, is important because it provides a blueprint for the space of *all possible minds* – not just our particular human minds with their particular human foibles.

If Kant's cognitive architecture is along the right lines, this will have significant impact on how we should design intelligent machines. Consider, to take one important recent example, the data efficiency of contemporary reinforcement learning systems. Recently, deep reinforcement learning agents have achieved super-human ability in a variety of games, including Atari (Mnih et al., 2013) and Go (Silver et al., 2017). These systems are very impressive, but also very data-inefficient, requiring an enormous quantity of training data. DQN (Mnih et al., 2013) requires 200 million frames of experience before it can reach human performance on Atari games. This is equivalent to playing non-stop for 40 days.

AlphaZero (Silver et al., 2017) played 44 million games to reach its performance level.

Pointing out the sample complexity of these programs is not intended to criticise these accomplishments in any way. They are very impressive achievements. But it does point to a fundamental difference between the way these machines learn to play the game, and the way that humans do. A human can look at a new Atari game for a few minutes, and then start playing well. He or she does not need to play non-stop for 40 days. A human's data efficiency at an Atari game is a consequence of our inductive bias: we start with prior knowledge that informs and guides our search.

It is a commonplace that the stronger the inductive bias, the more data-efficiently a system can learn. But the danger, of course, with injecting inductive bias into a machine, is that it biases the system, enabling it to learn some tasks quicker, but preventing it from learning other tasks effectively. What we really want, if only we can get it, is inductive bias that is maximally general. But what are these maximally general concepts that we should inject into the machine, and how do we do so?

Neural net practitioniers, for all their official espousal of pure empiricist anti-innatism, do (in practice) acknowledge the need for certain minimal forms of inductive bias. A convolutional net (LeCun et al., 1995) is a particular neural architecture that is designed to enforce the constraint that the same invariants hold no matter where the objects appear in the retinal field. A long short-term memory (LeCun et al., 1995) is a particular neural architecture that is designed to enforce the constraint that invariants that are valid at one point in time are also valid at other points in time. But these are isolated examples. *What, then, are the maximally general concepts that we should inject into the machine, to enable data efficient learning?*

The answer to this question has been lurking in plain sight for over two hundred years. In the first *Critique*, Kant identified the maximally general concepts, showed how these concepts structure perception itself, and identified the conditions specifying how the pure concepts interoperate. Kant's principles provide the maximally general inductive bias we need to make our machines data-efficient.[89]

> In the history of human inquiry, philosophy has the place of the central sun, seminal and tumultuous: from time to time it throws off some portion of itself to take station as a science, a planet, cool and well regulated, progressing steadily towards a distant final state. – Austin, *Ifs and Cans* (Austin, 1956)

---

89 Thanks to Dieter Schönecker and Sorin Baiasu for thoughtful feedback.

References

Achourioti, T. and Van Lambalgen, M. (2011). A formalization of Kant's transcendental logic. *The Review of Symbolic Logic*, 4(2):254–289.

Achourioti, T., van Lambalgen, M., et al. (2017). Kant's logic revisited. *IfCoLog Journal of Logics and Their Applications*, 4:845–865.

Allais, L. (2009). Kant, non-conceptual content and the representation of space. *Journal of the History of Philosophy*, 47(3):383–413.

Austin, J. L. (1956). Ifs and cans. *Proceedings of the British Academy*.

Bezem, M. (2005). On the undecidability of coherent logic. In *Processes, Terms and Cycles: Steps on the Road to Infinity*, pages 6–13. Springer.

Brandom, R. (1994). *Making It Explicit*. Cambridge, MA: Harvard University Press.

Brandom, R. (2009). How analytic philosophy has failed cognitive science. *Towards an Analytic Pragmatism (TAP)*, pages 121–133. Proceedings of the Workshop on Bob Brandom's Recent Philosophy of Language: Towards an Analytic Pragmatism (TAP-2009). Genoa, Italy, April 19–23, 2009. Edited by Cristina Amoretti, Carlo Penco, Federico Pitto.

Brandom, R. B. (2008). *Between Saying and Doing*. Oxford: Oxford University Press.

Chalmers, D. J., French, R. M., and Hofstadter, D. R. (1992). High-level perception, representation, and analogy: A critique of artificial intelligence methodology. *Journal of Experimental & Theoretical Artificial Intelligence*, 4(3):185–211.

Clark, A. (2013). Whatever next? Predictive brains, situated agents, and the future of cognitive science. *Behavioral and Brain Sciences*, 36(3):181–204.

Dantsin, E., Eiter, T., Gottlob, G., and Voronkov, A. (2001). Complexity and expressive power of logic programming. *ACM Computing Surveys (CSUR)*, 33(3):374–425.

Dennett, D. C. (1978). Artificial intelligence as philosophy and as psychology. *Brainstorms*, pages 109–26. MIT Press.

Dong, H., Mao, J., Lin, T., Wang, C., Li, L., and Zhou, D. (2019). Neural logic machines. *arXiv preprint arXiv:1904.11694*.

Dyckhoff, R. and Negri, S. (2015). Geometrisation of first-order logic. *Bulletin of Symbolic Logic*, 21(2):123–163.

Evans, R. (2017). Kant on constituted mental activity. *APA on Philosophy and Computers*, 16(2): 41–53.

Evans, R. (2019). A Kantian cognitive architecture. In *On the Cognitive, Ethical, and Scientific Dimensions of Artificial Intelligence*, pages 233–262. Springer.

Evans, R. (2020). *Kant's cognitive architecture*. PhD thesis, Imperial College London.

Evans, R., Bošnjak, M., Buesing, L., Ellis, K., Pfau, D., Kohli, P., and Sergot, M. (2021a). Making sense of raw input. *Artificial Intelligence*, 299:103521.

Evans, R. and Grefenstette, E. (2018). Learning explanatory rules from noisy data. *Journal of Artificial Intelligence Research (JAIR)*, 61:1–64.

Evans, R., Hernandez-Orallo, J., Welbl, J., Kohli, P., and Sergot, M. (2020). Evaluating the Apperception Engine. *arXiv preprint arXiv:2007.05367*.

Evans, R., Hernández-Orallo, J., Welbl, J., Kohli, P., and Sergot, M. (2021b). Making sense of sensory input. *Artificial Intelligence*, 293:103438.

Evans, R., Sergot, M., and Stephenson, A. (2020). Formalizing Kant's rules. *Journal of Philosophical Logic*, 49(4):613–680.

Fodor, J. A. (1975). *The Language of Thought*. Cambridge, MA: Harvard University Press.

Fodor, J. A. and Pylyshyn, Z. W. (1988). Connectionism and cognitive architecture: A critical analysis. *Cognition*, 28(1–2):3–71.

Friedman, M. (1992). *Kant and the Exact Sciences*. Cambridge, MA: Harvard University Press.

Gomes, A. (2013). Kant on perception: Naive realism, non-conceptualism, and the B-deduction. *The Philosophical Quarterly*, 64(254):1–19.

Hazen, A. P. (1999). Logic and analyticity. In *The Nature of Logic*, pages 79–110. CSLI.

Hochreiter, S. and Schmidhuber, J. (1997). Long short-term memory. *Neural Computation*, 9(8): 1735–1780.

Hofstadter, D. R. (1995). *Fluid Concepts and Creative Analogies*. New York, NY: Basic Books.

Hofstadter, D. R., Mitchell, M., et al. (1994). The copycat project: A model of mental fluidity and analogy-making. *Advances in connectionist and neural computation theory*, 2(31–112):29–30.

James, W., Burkhardt, F., Bowers, F., and Skrupskelis, I. K. (1890). *The Principles of Psychology*, volume 1. Macmillan London, Transactions of the Charles S. Peirce Society, 19(2).

Jaynes, J. (2000). *The Origin of Consciousness in the Breakdown of the Bicameral Mind*. Boston, MA: Houghton Mifflin Harcourt.

Kant, I. (1781). *Critique of Pure Reason*. Cambridge University Press.

Kant, I. (1784). What is enlightenment? In *Practical Philosophy*, pages 11–22. Cambridge University Press. Translated and edited by Mary J Gregor.

Kant, I. (1790). *Critique of the Power of Judgment*. Cambridge: Cambridge University Press.

Lake, B. M., Ullman, T. D., Tenenbaum, J. B., and Gershman, S. J. (2017). Building machines that learn and think like people. *Behavioral and Brain Sciences*, 40. Cambridge: Cambridge University Press.

LeCun, Y., Bengio, Y., et al. (1995). Convolutional networks for images, speech, and time series. *The Handbook of Brain Theory and Neural Networks*, 3361(10):1995.

Longuenesse, B. (1998). *Kant and the Capacity to Judge*. Princeton, NJ: Princeton University Press.

Marcus, G. (2018a). *The Algebraic Mind*. Cambridge, MA: MIT press.

Marcus, G. (2018b). Innateness, AlphaZero, and artificial intelligence. *arXiv preprint arXiv:1801.05667*.

McLear, C. (2016). Kant on perceptual content. *Mind*, 125(497):95–144.

Mnih, V., Kavukcuoglu, K., Silver, D., Graves, A., Antonoglou, I., Wierstra, D., and Riedmiller, M. (2013). Playing Atari with deep reinforcement learning. *arXiv preprint arXiv:1312.5602*.

Murphy, K. P. (2012). *Machine Learning: a Probabilistic Perspective*. MIT press.

Piantadosi, S. (2011). *Learning and the Language of Thought*. PhD thesis, Massachusetts Institute of Technology.

Pinosio, R. (2017). *The Logic of Kant's Temporal Continuum*. PhD thesis, University of Amsterdam.

Rocktäschel, T. and Riedel, S. (2016). Learning knowledge base inference with neural theorem provers. In *Proceedings of the 5th Workshop on Automated Knowledge Base Construction*, pages 45–50.

Sellars, W. (1967). Some remarks on Kant's theory of experience. In *In the Space of Reasons*, pages 437–453. Cambridge, MA: Harvard University Press.

Sellars, W. (1968). *Science and Metaphysics*. Oxfordshire: Routledge.

Sellars, W. (1978). The role of imagination in Kant's theory of experience. In *In the Space of Reasons*, pages 454–466. Harvard University Press.

Shanahan, M. (2005). Perception as abduction. *Cognitive science*, 29(1):103–134.

Silver, D., Schrittwieser, J., Simonyan, K., Antonoglou, I., Huang, A., Guez, A., Hubert, T., Baker, L., Lai, M., Bolton, A., et al. (2017). Mastering the game of go without human knowledge. *Nature*, 550(7676):354–359.

Spelke, E. S. and Kinzler, K. D. (2007). Core knowledge. *Developmental Science*, 10(1):89–96.

Stephenson, A. (2013). *Kant's Theory of Experience*. PhD thesis, University of Oxford.

Stephenson, A. (2015). Kant on the object-dependence of intuition and hallucination. *The Philosophical Quarterly*, 65(260):486–508.

Stephenson, A. (2017). Imagination and inner intuition. *Kant and the Philosophy of Mind*.

Strawson, P. (2018). *The Bounds of Sense*. Routledge.

Waxman, W. (2014). *Kant's Anatomy of the Intelligent Mind*. Oxford: Oxford University Press.

West, D. B. et al. (2001). *Introduction to graph theory*, volume 2. Hoboken, NJ: Prentice hall Upper Saddle River.

Wittgenstein, L. (2009). *Philosophical Investigations*. Oxford: John Wiley & Sons.

Wolff, R. (1963). *Kant's Theory of Mental Activity*. Cambridge, MA: Harvard University Press.

Sorin Baiasu

3 The Challenge of (Self-)Consciousness: Kant, Artificial Intelligence and Sense-Making

Abstract: How do we make sense of the countless pieces of information flowing to us from the environment? This question, sometimes called the Problem of Representation, is one of the most significant problems in cognitive science. Some pioneering and important work in the attempt to address the problem of representation was produced with the help of Kant's philosophy. In particular, the suggestion was that, by analogy with Kant's distinction between sensibility and the understanding, we can distinguish between high- and low-level perception, and then focus on the step from high-level perception to abstract cognitive processes of sense-making. This was possible through a simplification of the input provided by low-level perception (to be reduced, for instance, to a string of letters), which the computer programme was supposed to 'understand'. Most recently, a closer look at Kant's model of the mind led to a breakthrough in the attempt to build programmes for such verbal reasoning tasks: these kinds of software or 'Kantian machines' seemed able to achieve human-level performance for verbal reasoning tasks. Yet, the claim has sometimes been stronger, namely, that some such programmes not only compete with human cognitive agents, but themselves represent cognitive agents. The focus of my paper is on this claim; I argue that it is unwarranted, but that its critical investigation may lead to further avenues for how to pursue the project of creating artificial intelligence.

Acknowledgements: The first draft of this paper was presented to the 'Recent literature on Kant' session of the 2017 UK Kant Society Annual Conference, which took place at the University of St Andrews. I am grateful to participants in the audience, particularly to Richard Evans, for discussion and feedback. Special thanks are owed to the editors of this volume, especially to Dieter Schönecker, for inviting me to contribute this chapter, for their patience and support during the writing of the piece, and for some excellent feedback. Needless to say, all remaining errors are my own.

Sorin Baiasu, Keele University, UK

1 Introduction

The problem of representation – of how we make sense of the countless pieces of information flowing to us from the environment – is one of the most significant problems in cognitive science. At least two issues have been identified as important for a solution to the problem of representation, both being applications of the problem to more specific parts of the cognitive process of representation. Using a terminology which, as we will see later in this chapter, is in some respects problematic, the two issues have been presented in some of the most influential texts in the literature, as follows. The first was described as an issue of processing information from various sensory modalities, this being the function of the so-called 'low-level' perception. Again, this is an issue of selecting from, and making sense of, information provided to us by the senses. The second was described as an issue of extracting meaning from the raw material by making sense of it at a conceptual level, a job assigned to 'high-level' perception. A significant step forward in the attempts to answer the problem of representation was made when it was acknowledged that low-level perception, high-level perception and more abstract cognitive activities are interacting in the process of representation and are difficult to be separated from each other.[1]

Even more progress was made when the problem of the integration of high-level perception and more abstract cognitive activities was separated from the question of how to integrate low- and high-level perception. This separation took place through a simplification of the input, of which high-level perception and more abstract cognitive activities were expected to make sense. Finally, more recently, there was some further progress noted in cognitive science, this time of particular relevance for Kantian studies. Thus, concerning the issue of integration of high-level perception and more abstract cognitive processes and with direct relevant for the general problem of representation, it has been suggested

---

[1] As an approximation, the distinction between low-level perception and high-level perception can be understood along the lines of Kant's distinction between subjective and objective perception. (KrV: A320/B377 – see n3 below for the convention used for references to Kant's *Critique of Pure Reason*.) Both 'low-level' and 'high-level perception' are regarded as spectra of processes, some more concrete and some more abstract. For instance, an example of low-level perception takes place when the light impinges on the retina. A further example is the processing of brightness contrasts and of light boundaries in the visual field. High-level perception may include object recognition or, more abstractly, relation recognition. An example of a more abstract cognitive process would be the understanding of a complex situation, such as a love affair.

that a good solution could be found in Immanuel Kant's theoretical work, particularly the *Critique of Pure Reason.*[2]

The resulting 'Kantian machine', a computer equipped with the 'Kantian programme', yielded, for the same problems, results comparable with those obtained by human beings. The claim, however, was not simply that cognitive science has now the ability to match (and perhaps outdo) human performance also for the specific type of task under consideration – this would have been a significant claim in its own right to be sure, although the same obtained for other type of tasks (think of computation or even more complex tasks, such as playing chess). The claim was a much stronger one, namely, that cognitive science has now the ability to create cognitive agents. In this paper, I examine this claim and argue that it is, at this point, unwarranted, but that the argument presented here may suggest further avenues for how to pursue the general project of creating artificial intelligence.

In the next section, I introduce the representation problem and focus on the progress made in cognitive science by those attempting to answer it. Sections 3 and 4 continue the examination of this progress with particular attention to a recent attempt to create a machine that can solve certain tasks (for instance, verbal reasoning exercises) through a programme which follows the architecture of the mind presented by Kant in his theoretical philosophy. Particularly encouraging are the results the Kantian machine has in the attempt to solve specific tasks relevant for the problem of representation; the performance of the Kantian machine here is comparable to that of human beings. Sections 5 and 6 focus critically on a further claim that the Kantian machine is in fact a cognitive agent. The focus is on the distinction between sensory and cognitive agency, and on what is needed for an agent to be a cognitive being. The final section draws the conclusions of my argument.

2 The Representation Problem

In their seminal text, "High-Level Perception, Representation, and Analogy: A Critique of Artificial Intelligence Methodology", David Chalmers, Robert French and Douglas Hofstadter identify our capacity of making sense of the vast amount of information constantly flowing to us from our environment as "one of the deepest problems in cognitive science". (Chalmers *et al.* 1992, p. 185) The problem, more

---

2 See, for instance, Evans's paper in this volume (Evans 2022), but also some of his earlier texts, including Evans (2017).

exactly, is to understand how this capacity functions and, even more precisely, to understand human perception's ability to bring order to the multiplicity of "raw data". (Chalmers *et al.* 1992, p. 185) It is from these 'data' that we select, organize and interpret specific inputs in order to obtain more or less abstract day-to-day perceptions, whether movement in the visual field, emotion in a tone of voice, what we should do in a game or why a particular political phenomenon is currently unfolding.

The result of the process of perception is representation. By analogy with Kant's distinction between sensibility and the understanding, in the *Critique of Pure Reason*,[3] a distinction is identified by Chalmers *et al.* as implicitly functioning in cognitive science. This is the distinction between high- and low-level perception. Thus, according to them, "[t]oday Kant's model seems somewhat baroque"; yet, "its fundamental insight" is still "valid". (Chalmers *et al.* 1992, p. 186) This fundamental insight is Kant's distinction between a faculty (sensibility) "whose job it is to pick up raw sensory information" and a faculty (the understanding) "which is devoted to organizing these data into a coherent, meaningful experience of the world". (Chalmers *et al.* 1992, p. 186) The focus for Chalmers *et al.* is on representations produced by high-level perception.

That this Kantian distinction is taken to be the rough model for the distinction between low- and high-level perception is not surprising, but it is not clear the language of 'low' and 'high' is very useful in connection with Kant. To be sure, sensibility and the understanding are distinct faculties in Kant, and there are specific senses in which what the understanding does, relies indeed essentially, for specific purposes, on what sensibility provides. For instance, the understanding is supposed to provide rules for the synthesis of the intuitions given by sensibility. Kant is famous for claiming that speculative metaphysical claims are the result of conceptual rules used without reference to intuitions. Yet, there also are specific senses in which what sensibility produces relies, for specific purposes, on the work of the understanding. For instance, intuitions are also the result of a synthesis of a manifold of sensations, a synthesis which is made possible by (the understanding's) transcendental unity of apperception.

Be that as it may, Chalmers *et al.*'s reading of Kant is not the focus here and I doubt their brief comments on Kant were intended as hermeneutically illuminating for Kantian scholarship. Moreover, their discussion does not dwell on this distinction, although they do challenge some of its aspects, but, as already

---

3 In what follows, references to Kant's *Critique of Pure Reason* follow the pagination of the first and second editions, abbreviated A/B accordingly. The English and German editions I have used are listed under Literature.

mentioned, the focus is on representation formed by 'high-level' perception. The focus on 'high-level' perception is not surprising; after all, the problem of making sense or the problem of representation is supposed to concern the process which yields coherent, meaningful experiences of the world. This, however, seems to be primarily the task Kant assigns to the understanding, although, as already mentioned, not to the exclusion of sensibility.

The approach Chalmers *et al.* take is, in the first instance, critical. They object to the dominant answers provided at that time to the "representation problem". (Chalmers *et al.* 1992, p. 188) What is criticised is the dominant or traditional approach in artificial intelligence, which from the start identifies not only the structure, which 'high-level' perception-based representations are supposed to embody, but also the data considered to be relevant for a particular problem. Far from offering a solution to the problem of representation, the claim is that the traditional approach bypasses it, since it starts from data which have already been represented in a form close to the sought-for representation. (Chalmers *et al.* 1992, pp. 192–8)

One case considered is a model of scientific discovery, BACON, claimed to be able to discover, among other laws, Kepler's third law of planetary motion. (Langley *et al.* 1987) This model is embodied in a computer programme, which allegedly starts from the same conditions as those of the human discoverers and is able to provide as output a formulation of Kepler's third law of planetary motion. Another case is that of the structure-mapping engine (SME) for analogy-making. (Falkenhainer *et al.* 1989) The SME programme, for instance, is claimed to be able to 'discover' an analogy between an atom and the solar system. Yet, as in the case of BACON, the process of analogy-making bypasses representation, since data have been represented in such a way that the common structure is almost immediately apparent.

This objection formulated by Chalmers *et al.* to the traditional methodology in artificial intelligence has at least one plausible reply. It could be argued that the process of high-level perception can be separated from even more abstract cognitive processes, such as nomic formulation or mapping. Programmes, such as BACON or SME, focus on the latter and leave the task of solving the problem of 'high-level' perception for other researchers. The main difficulty for this reply, however, is that these two research tasks cannot be separated so easily. First, perception depends on analogical processes, since it depends on interpreting new situations in terms of old ones. Secondly, however, it is not possible to introduce a temporal separation between 'high-level' perception and more abstract cognitive processes, such as mapping. Briefly, this is because perception does not take place in a vacuum, but it is directed to further specific tasks, such as drawing an analogy or formulating a law. Hence, the task of understanding 'high-level' perception will not have one response, which a separate research project could target. (Chalmers *et al.* 1992, pp. 198–200)

As mentioned, Chalmers *et al.* begin their seminal text with a critical discussion of the answers to the representation problem in contemporary cognitive science. Yet, their paper has also a constructive or reconstructive part. In this part, they try to integrate 'high-level' perception and the more abstract cognitive process of sense-making (in this case, analogy-making). There is, however, a second problem of integration, namely, integration of 'low-' and 'high-level' perception. The two problems of integration are related and both of them would need to be solved for a proper approach to the problem of representation.

The strategy adopted by Chalmers *et al.* is to deal with the second problem of integration (namely, between 'low-' and 'high-level' perception), in order to isolate the first problem of integration ('high-level' perception and abstract cognitive process of sense-making). They, then, also claim to have a solution for this first problem of integration. To isolate the first problem, a restriction is introduced, which is meant to answer the difficulty 'low-level' perception has to deal with, namely, making sense of the huge amount of information available in the real world in order to convey the relevant details to 'high-level' perception. The respective restriction is on the complexity of the input that will be considered for sense-making (in particular, analogy-making). Thus, the input is taken to be given by the domain of alphabetical letters. For instance, for the strings of letters *abc* and *iijjkkll*, the programme will try to build representations which will make evident their common structure and find correspondences between the two representations. Through this restriction, the first problem of integration is being dealt with, and the focus can be then entirely on second problem of integration. The programme introduced as a solution to this second problem of integration is the Copycat programme.[4] (Chalmers *et al.* 1992, pp. 201–10)

Imagine now a programme for which input is also considered from within the restricted domain of alphabetical letters. The computer is given a sequence of letters and has to predict the next letter in that set as part of a verbal reasoning task. It does this by making sense of the letters through the construction of a rule, on the basis of which it will predict the next element in the series. The programme is also influenced by Kant's philosophy, but, unlike the case of Chalmers *et al.*'s Copycat, it regards Kant's Critical philosophy much more

---

4 Copycat is described as having sprung "out of two predecessors, Seek-Whence and Jumbo". (Hofstadter and Mitchell 1994, p. 34) The programme is intended as "universal" and, hence, as able to deal with the problems both Seek-Whence (Meredith 1986) and Jumbo (Hofstadter 1983) are supposed to tackle.

sympathetically and considers it as a much more useful tool.[5] In addition, the outcomes yielded by this more Kantian programme are impressive – they are supposed to be comparable to human-level performance achieved for similar tasks.

Imagine, however, that the claim of such a Kantian programme's supporters is not simply that, in this way, we obtain a machine with human-level performance. Instead, the claim is that, thus programmed, the computer is a cognitive agent. The Kantian programme, in this case, would not simply offer a potential breakthrough in the attempt to answer the problem of representation, but would also make a significant contribution to the attempts to create artificial intelligence more generally. In the next section, I introduce in more detail this Kantian programme.

3 The Kantian Programme

The standard position in the philosophy of mind for those working in the area of artificial intelligence is functionalism. In general, functionalism is the view that, in order for a creature or machine to count as a cognitive agent, what is important is not that they be made of some special kind of substance; instead, the requirement is that they function in a particular way (usually describable in the language of computer science). Every creature or machine that realises that function will count as a cognitive agent.[6]

---

5 One instance of this Kantian programme, which I will also present in sections 3 and 4, is developed by Richard Evans *et al.* in a series of texts, including "Kant on Constituted Mental Activity" (2017); also see Evans (2022; in this volume). The claim that his Kantian programme will lead to the creation of a cognitive agent, a claim I will introduce shortly, is not to be found in all of Evans's texts. For instance, it is absent in Evans *et al.* (2020) and also in Evans (2022). In the latter text, he does talk about 'cognitive agent', but in relation to Kant. In other words, there is an acknowledgement that Kant examines the conditions of cognitive agency, but there is no claim that his Kantian programme or machine (called in this text the "apperception engine") is a cognitive agent. In email correspondence, Evans acknowledged my discussion in this paper (presented in 2017 – see note 1) as having had a real impact on his thinking.

6 Functionalism can be easily distinguished from traditional mind-body dualism (e.g., René Descartes's), since, as already mentioned, it makes no claim that minds are made of some special kind of substance. It can also be distinguished from identity theory (e.g., J. J. C. Smart's), since it does not assume mental states are states of brains and, hence, made of the matter brains are made of. Moreover, unlike behaviourism, (e.g., B. F. Skinner's), it accepts the reality of internal mental states, rather than reducing it to the behaviour of the whole organism.

Now, the Kantian model of cognitive agency takes Kant's *Critique of Pure Reason* to include a description of a rule-induction process, a process for the creation of rules on the basis of an input.[7] In our exemplary case, as we have seen in the previous section, the input is a letter sequence given as part of a verbal reasoning task.[8] On this interpretation of Kant, the claim is that, if the rule-induction process meets certain constraints, the internal activities of the process count as cognitive activities.

The idea of *counting* certain activities *as* activities of a specific kind is central for social practices. Social practices, such as taking part in a competition, will count as practices of a particular kind, if certain necessary and sufficient conditions are met. For instance, among other conditions for a sprint race, included is also the requirement that sprinters run in their respective designated lanes. If this condition is not met, if a person runs crossing lanes, then her activity of running cannot count as participation to a sprint race. In general, to count as social activity of type X, one specific kind of action (or one set of specific kinds of actions) Y will have to be performed in the appropriate circumstances or in the apposite context Z. By analogy, certain activities count as mental activities, when specific acts or processes are performed or take place under certain circumstances. For instance, having a representation of a red circle is a mental activity, which is counted as such when a plurality of sensory perturbations is experienced by an agent, who applies then a specific rule to these perturbations, in the appropriate context.

Now, counting-as does not happen automatically. Although the necessary and sufficient actions or processes may take place in the right context, these can only count as a specific type of activity, if somebody counts them as such. Hence, in order to count as an activity of type X, a specific kind of action or set of actions Y, performed in the appropriate context Z, would have to be counted

---

[7] It is unclear, by the way, whether functionalism, as standardly presented in contemporary philosophy of mind, would also be the view Kant would subscribe to. I have discussed this question elsewhere (Baiasu 2018) and it would go beyond the scope of this paper to rehearse those arguments here. I mention only that there are many interpretations of Kant on offer: materialism (Brook 1994), mere immaterialism (Ameriks 2000), 'dual-aspect' theory (Nagel 1989), epistemological dualism (Schlicht 2016) and transcendental functionalism (Lau 2014). Not even the transcendental version of functionalism proposed by Lau is clearly compatible with standard functionalism.

[8] Another set of data, where the Kantian programme is supposed to function with achieved human-level performance, is given by sensory readings in a two-dimensional grid world. The rules constructed must make sense of the data. Momentary apprehensions are combined into persisting objects, which change over time according to intelligible rules and interact with other objects according to intelligible rules. (Evans 2017, p.51).

as such by an agent W. Hence, the agent W must not only be aware of the fact that Y is taking place and that Z obtains, but he or she must also be aware that Y counts as X in Z. In other words, the agent will need to be aware of the rule for the activity which is counted as taking place (for instance, the social practice of sprint racing) and will need to apply this rule.

For instance, if a plurality of sensory perturbations is taking place in a certain context, then an agent may count those sensory perturbations as a certain kind of activity. Consider a thermometer which measures the temperature of the water in a recipient (say, an aquarium). When the temperature of the water changes, the mercury in the thermometer rises. The internal activity of the thermometer (the perturbation manifested by the rise of the level of mercury) counts (in the right context, say, when the thermometer is not faulty) as a change in the properties of the water, which is external to the thermometer. What is important for us to note for our purposes here is that the agent who counts certain sensory perturbations of the thermometer as a change in the water's temperature is *me*. Contrast this with the situation in which we consider the thermometer on its own. The water's temperature will produce the same sensory perturbations of the mercury, whose level will rise. Yet, we usually do not consider the thermometer as able to count the plurality of its sensory perturbations leading to the rise of the mercury level as its representation of a change of the properties of the external world (the rise of the water's temperature).

Consider the claim that a thermometer is representing the temperature of the water in the aquarium. On some accounts, we can say that A is a representation of B only if A expresses a thought about B or only if the relation between A and B is an intentional one.[9] If either of these is correct, it follows that, when we talk about the thermometer's mercury level as representing the water's temperature, then we assert that the thermometer is expressing a thought about temperature or that thermometer and temperature are in a relation of intentionality. This, however, is at least awkward, if not completely implausible.

What may attenuate the implausible character of such claims (although they may still be awkward) is the idea of derivative intentionality, more exactly, the fact that this is intentionality *we* attribute to the thermometer. In general, as noted by John Haugeland, symbols have their intentionality derivatively when they inherit it from something else that has the same content already; for instance, a

---

9 This is a premise identified by some commentators in Roger Scruton's argument against photography and film as art (1983); for instance, Robert Stecker formulates it in terms of thought, but also considers a possible reply from Scruton, who could formulate the premise in terms of intentionality. (Stecker 2009, pp. 122–3).

secret signal between you and me has a particular meaning derivatively from the stipulation we made about the signal, when we agreed to have it. (Haugeland 1990, p. 385) Haugeland emphasises the need for an original intentionality, as a way of stopping the infinite regress of a series of derivative intentionalities. Thus, in the case of the secret signalling, if our intentionality were also derived and the intentionality of the source of our intentionality were in its turn derived, and we simply moved from derivative intentionality to derivative intentionality, an infinite regress would threaten. (Haugeland 1990, p. 385)

Haugeland rightly notes that the issue of a potential regress can be answered by reference to an original, non-derivative intentionality; some intentionality must be non-derivative. The significant problem does not concern the transfer or derivation of intentionality from the original, non-derivative instance, but the very possibility of this original intentionality. One question concerns the nature of original intentionality. Haugeland rejects the assumption sometimes held that only mental intentionality is original. (Haugeland 1990, pp. 385–6) Thus, it seems clear that some intentionality must be non-derivative; it also seems plausible that at least some instances of original intentional are mental in character;[10] it does not follow, however, Haugeland concludes, that all original intentionality should be mental.

We have seen that functionalist accounts of the mind regard as cognitive any processes which realise specific functions. On the Kantian-programme-based account of cognitive agency, a computer equipped with the Kantian programme will count as a cognitive agent and, hence, as an agent with original intentionality. For such accounts, therefore, it is important to subscribe to a version of Haugeland's scepticism about the character of original intentionality, namely, to subscribe to scepticism about the standard view that cognitive agents cannot be machines. Otherwise we could not take a machine equipped with the Kantian programme to be a cognitive agent with original intentionality, although the plausible assumption is that a cognitive agent (and perhaps any agent more generally) has original intentionality. Moreover, these accounts also rely on scepticism about another claim, sometimes made in these debates, namely, that only biological organisms can achieve original intentionality. A computer or robot, which is programmed to function in accordance with the Kantian programme is expected to achieve original intentionality and represent an instance of cognitive agency.

---

10 To be sure, what 'having mental character' means is an issue for ongoing debate. The argument in this paper does not rely on any particular response to this question.

In the following section, I would like to focus more closely on those aspects which are specified by the supporter of the Kantian-programme-based account of cognitive agency as characteristic for the cognitive agent.

4 Cognitive Agency

Consider a merely sensory agent, such as the thermometer in the example above. There are, to be sure, vigorous debates on the nature of agency,[11] so my understanding of what an agent is will aim to be sufficiently general to avoid the main issues. I take agency to refer very generally to a capacity to do something. For instance, the thermometer can measure the temperature of the water. As the name indicates, a sensory agent has sensors. The behaviour of the merely sensory agent depends on the state of its sensors. To make this more evident, consider a slightly more complex instance of a merely sensory agent – a thermostat. We can assume that the context is the same – an aquarium – and we assume it is an aquarium housing tropical fish, who need a temperature between 25° and 27° Celsius. When the thermostat's sensors indicate low temperature, the thermostat will react by switching on the aquarium heater. The thermostat does react to the perturbations of its temperature sensors, but it is an automatic response. Switching the aquarium heating on is not done because the thermostat *counts* the perturbations of its gauge as its *representation* of the water's low temperature; *we* may do so, but the thermostat itself only responds blindly according to the way it was programmed.

Unlike a merely sensory agent, a cognitive one is a sensory agent who, in addition to behaving in response to his sensings, also counts his sensings as his representation or presentation of an external world – hence, an agent who also has original intentionality. The move from a merely sensory agent to a cognitive agent can be understood at least in part as the result of the way in which the cognitive agent combines the plurality of sensings obtained by the sensors (or provided as input). Consider now a programme that includes rules of composition, which combine parts into wholes. For instance, the programme may be permitted to combine a group of sensings representing a nose with a group of sensings representing an ear under the totality of a face.

These rules of composition are defeasible, but they enable the programme to place groups of sensings under one element. For instance, the rule for the totality of the face mentioned above is defeasible, since specific features of a

---

11 For an introductory presentation, see Markus Schlosser (2019).

context may undermine the composition of a face out of the representation of one ear and of one nose. We may discover that what the programmed machine senses is not a person's face, but, say, a cubist painting. Sensings can be combined not only by composition, but also by connection. Rules of connection are normative: they specify which combination must be made, once a group of sensings is regarded as composing a whole, and which combinations should be avoided. For instance, if a group of sensings composes a nose, then it must also compose part of the face and, moreover, it should not be regarded as composing an ear.

On the Kantian model of cognitive agency, the activities of combination are similar to social practices, as discussed in the previous section. Thus, both composing and connecting are done by doing something else, in the same way in which I cannot simply run a sprint race, but I do so indirectly by performing some actions (including keeping within my designated lane). Similarly, activities of combination would be performed by constructing rules, which permit or obligate me to combine representations in a certain way and then apply these rules. Hence, combinations are performed indirectly, too, through the construction and application of rules.

To sum up, the Kantian-programme-based account of cognitive agency claims that a cognitive agent counts his sensings as representations of the external world; moreover, the claim is that, in order to do so, the cognitive agent needs to combine these in a certain way, and, in order to combine his sensings in the appropriate way, he needs to construct rules and apply them. We can take Kant to suggest the same; for instance, according to Kant,

> when we think of a triangle as an object, we do so by being conscious of the assembly [*Zusammensetzung*] of three straight lines according to a rule whereby such an intuition can always be exhibited [*dargestellt*].   (KrV: A 105)

Kant can be read here to claim that, in order to count the three lines as a triangle, we need to apply a general rule for counting certain sets of three lines as triangles. We cannot combine sensings directly, without constructing and applying a rule, because a combination without rules does not satisfy the condition of unification, which is very important. According to this condition, unguided combination would not produce a unity of experience that I could call *mine*. To be able to combine sensings without rules would mean that there would be no need for a self that would have the sensings. Yet, without a self, the notion of cognitive agency would no longer apply.

This argument offered by the supporter of the Kantian-programme-based account of agency moves rather quickly from the assumption of a unification without rules to the absence of a self to whom experience and its unity are supposed to belong. This, as we will see, will be reflected by the objection I will formulate in the next sections. Presumably, however, the argument could be reconstructed as follows: the unity of experience, which is needed in order for a cognitive agent to have experience, is a unity of presentations; for Kant, however, any presentation should be connected with a possible consciousness of the cognitive agent's having it. My presentation of this window, for instance, is connected with a possible consciousness that I am seeing this window. If there is a presentation of a door, but I cannot connect it with a possible consciousness that I am seeing this door (for instance, it is your presentation of a door), then I cannot unify these presentations as part of my experience of a house.

The defeasible rule which connects the presentations of a window and of a door to yield the experience of a house is indeed necessary for the unity of experience required by the experience of the house. Without that rule, it is indeed the case that I cannot have the unity of the experience of a house, which I can call mine. If a unity of experience would still be possible without this rule, the self-related requirement imposed by the application of the rule (namely, that the presentations be the presentations had by the same conscious agent) may not be needed.

This interpretation seems also confirmed by the following passage in Kant:

> Hence the original and necessary consciousness of one's own identity is at the same time a consciousness of an equally necessary unity of the synthesis of all appearances according to concepts – these concepts being rules that not only make these appearances necessarily reproducible, but that thereby also determine an object of our intuition of these appearances, i.e., determine a concept of something wherein these appearances necessarily cohere [*zusammenhängen*]. For the mind could not possibly think its own identity in the manifoldness of its presentations, and moreover think this identity a priori, if it did not have present to it the identity of its act – the act that subjects all synthesis of apprehension (a synthesis that is empirical) to a transcendental unity, and thereby first makes possible the coherence [*Zusammenhang*] of those presentations according to a priori rules.   (KrV: A 108)

Kant can be read here (as we will see, quite controversially) to claim that we cannot perceive the unity of the self in our sensings; we can perceive objects, which are determined by connecting the sensings under rules. The unity of the self is achieved by what persists through the sensings, and these are the constraints on the rules applied. A cognitive agent on this model does not have a primitive ability to combine representations, but can only combine them through a rule which says that she may or must do so. Hence, the cognitive agent sets down rules, which she will then follow in order to make sense of her sensings and perceive the world. Hence, in order for a sensory agent to count her sensings as representations of an external world (and, hence, in order for her to be a cognitive agent with original intentionality), she will have to construct and apply rules of combination satisfying various constraints.

A rule is understood as a general relation, which applies in many situations and specifies that a certain activity is permitted or obligatory. This is not an explicit, linguistically formulated conditional. Although we may employ language in order to describe a rule, the rule is an implicit procedure for generating a representation. Yet, although implicit, nor is a rule the same as a disposition. A disposition indicates a high probability for specific behaviour under certain conditions. A rule, by contrast, requires or allows the performance of an activity.

Rules of composition are perceptual rules – they are rules for apprehending particular configurations as parts of objects. For instance, one such rule may state that, if sensors meet certain conditions, the agent will count them as his representation of an ear. Rules of connection may form concepts or make judgements. Some rules, for instance, may form a concept by stipulating that it is a sub-concept of another concept or excludes another concept. Some rules may connect concepts conditionally, depending on external factors – for instance, that if a tree gets no water, then it dies. Finally, some rules may specify that if something is counted as a man, then it must also be counted as mortal, or if someone is Caesar, then he is a general.

Apart from constructing rules of combination, the cognitive agent needs also to apply them, in order to count the result as representation of the external world. One important aspect about rules in general is that their applicability is not conditional on the applicability of some further condition. Were a rule to be of this kind, an infinite regress would threaten, because, in order to determine whether or not the additional condition applies, another rule would be required, which, in its turn, would also require another rule with a potential for an infinite number of such iterations. Hence, rules are themselves responsible for determining whether or not they apply. If a rule applies in a particular situation, then it is will either be a rule of composition or a rule of connection. In the case of the former, the agent knows she *may* perform the combination activity, but whether or not she will perform is not decided on the basis of a further rule, since this will again lead to an infinite regress.

Kant certainly also makes this point about the applicability of rules; Kant explains that, in general logic, to show whether something stands under a rule or not, another rule would be needed. In its turn, this would also require for its application another rule. Hence, Kant concludes that the understanding can be instructed and equipped through rules, but the power of judgement cannot be taught, but only practiced. (KrV: A 133/B 172) So where, in the Kantian-programme-based account of agency, can we find the power of judgement? The answer seems to be that the power of judgement just is the application of rules, which contain procedures for determining whether or not they apply. The practice of rule application just is the faculty of judgement.

The rules of composition will be applied with the help of the imagination. The imagination is considered a faculty involving spontaneity, since it has the choice over whether to form a particular combination under rules of composition or not. However, the imagination is part of sensibility, since it applies rules of composition on sensings, which sensibility has provided. For rules of connection, there is no longer the same latitude in the application of rules, since rules of connection *obligate* the agent, rather than merely permitting her, to perform the respective mental activity.

So far, we have seen that a cognitive agent is a sensory agent, who counts her sensings as representing an external world. We have also seen that, to count these sensings as representing an external world, the agent must combine those sensings together in the right way. Finally, to combine the sensings together in the right way, the agent must construct and apply rules that satisfy a set of constraints. These constraints are severally necessary and jointly sufficient in order for the agent to count the plurality of sensory perturbations as representing an external world, since this is what it means for the agent to have original intentionality, and this is required for cognitive agency.

For the Kantian-programme-based account of cognitive agency, these constraints are provided by Kant in the *Critique of Pure Reason*. If one aim of the account of cognitive agency is to explain original intentionality, then one aspect which needs to be explained is the unity of cognitions. Cognitions can be unified in time, and this process involves four aspects: constructing moments in time, generating intermediate moments of time, providing a total ordering of moments of time and generating the totality of time (by excluding moments that are impossible).

These aspects, it is claimed, determine constraints on the construction and application of rules. The starting point is the highest principle of all synthetic judgements, which is a top-level constraint, according to which knowledge claims must be about items of possible experience. The four aspects mentioned above follow. They generate constraints on the types of rules that can be constructed and further constraints on the results of applying the rules.

We now have a relatively comprehensive picture of the Kantian computational architecture, the realisation of which (for instance, in a computer programmed on the basis of this architecture) is supposed to be a cognitive agent with original intentionality. The input provided is the result of a simplification, which, in the case of Chalmers *et al.*, was meant to avoid the problem of the integration of 'low-' and 'high-level' perception. In the remaining part of this paper, my question will be whether we can indeed regard the resulting programmed machine as a cognitive agent, that is, as a sensory agent endowed with original intentionality.

5 Original Intentionality and (Self-)Consciousness

As we have seen, *A* is said to have original intentionality in representing *p*, when *A* himself counts his activities as *A*'s representing *p*. By contrast, a merely sensory being, a being without original intentionality (think of the example of the barometer or of the thermostat) cannot count a plurality of its sensory perturbations as *its* representation of a change of properties in the external world. Now, in order for a being to *count* its activities as its representing something, it needs to be able to represent those activities as (its) representing activities. After all, this process of counting activities as representing the external world is an interpretive process. Yet, on a Kantian account of representation or presentation [*Vorstellung*], we can only present something and, hence, have presentations, when these presentations are connected with a possible consciousness of having them. As Kant famously puts it,

> The *I think* must be *capable* of accompanying all my presentations. For otherwise something would be presented to me that could not be thought at all – which is equivalent to saying that the presentation either would be impossible, or at least would be nothing to me. (KrV: B 131–2)

As is often pointed out, Kant does not require that every presentation be actually accompanied by this consciousness of having it. All that is needed is the possibility of this consciousness. It follows that, in order for a being to count its own activities as its representing something, the representing process of counting-as should be accompanied by the possibility of a consciousness of this process. This is a point Kant also makes explicit in the first edition of the *Critique*:

> All presentations have a necessary reference to a *possible* empirical consciousness. For if they did not have this reference, and becoming conscious of them were entirely impossible, then this would be tantamount to saying that they do not exist at all. (KrV: A 117 n)

Here Kant presents a similar *reductio*, starting from the contradictory of what is to be demonstrated (that is, starting by assuming that there is a presentation without a necessary reference to a possible empirical consciousness) and concluding that, in order to exist, presentations must have a reference to the possibility of consciousness. The argument is that, if a presentation might not have reference to a *possible* empirical consciousness, then it might be impossible for a person to become conscious of that presentation. Yet, if a person cannot become conscious of a presentation, then that presentation cannot be that person's presentation and, hence, cannot exist as that person's presentation.[12]

---

12 Consider the objection (which I owe to Dieter Schönecker; see his paper in this volume, Schönecker 2022) that the unifier need not be an *I*; a computer's control unit might suffice.

Perhaps the clearest way to see how the argument works is by an analogy with a fictional idea. If, say, I create a character for a short story, then that character's existence depends on the representing activity I perform through imagination. If it is impossible for me to be conscious of this character, then I cannot imagine it and, hence, it cannot exist as my creation. The same goes for any of my presentations or representations – if I cannot be conscious of them, then I cannot represent them and, hence, they cannot exist.

Now, I have been using 'consciousness' without additional qualification; the claim that presentations have a necessary reference to a *possible* empirical consciousness may suggest that we may have presentations of which we are not actually conscious. The point here, however, is not to debate the possibility of unconscious or subconscious presentations in Kant.[13] When Kant makes a claim to a possible empirical consciousness as necessary for every presentation, the implication is not that we have presentations of which we are not conscious. The point is rather that, in some cases, the link between me and my presentation is not the focus of my attention. I may well be conscious of a particular presentation without being explicitly aware of it as *my* presentation.[14] This is then a presentation of which I am conscious, but which is not accompanied by the *I think* or by a consciousness of the presentation as *mine*.

Presumably the implication will be that, if a presentation cannot exist as a person's presentation, it does not mean that it cannot be part of a unity the computer will offer through its processing. The average calculator, which synthesises '2', '2' and '+' offering as an answer '4', seems to perform precisely this synthesis without any *I*. But consider the simplified similar process of dropping two balls next to two others; in order to see the four balls as the result of a synthesis, I would need to be aware of the initial two balls, of the additional two and of the process of addition. If I am simply presented with four balls, it will not be self-evident that this is the result of a synthesis, and the calculator or the mechanism which leads to the result of four (say, four balls) will not be able to take this result as representing the result of an addition; it will just go through a mechanical process.

13 This issue is sometimes discussed when the history of psychoanalysis is researched and presented, but the topic is not directly relevant for this paper.

14 In what follows, I rely on aspects of my interpretation of Kant's account of the transcendental unity of apperception in *Kant and Sartre: Re-discovering Critical Ethics*. (2011: Ch. 1, esp. §§12–3) In that text, I draw a parallel between Kant's transcendental apperception and Sartre's (self-)consciousness (as non-reflective self-consciousness) – hence, the title of this paper. See also José Luis Bermúdez (1994, p. 234–7). For the relevant aspects on which I focus here, Stephen Engstrom's account offers a similar interpretation, although Engstrom does not link his account of the transcendental unity of apperception to the issue of identity and the Paralogisms. (2013, pp. 52–3 for what Engstrom takes to be the link to the problem of identity) The closest to my focus in this paper is the discussion by Melissa McBay Merritt. (2009) Merritt thinks that the philosophy of mind Kant advances in the Deduction is part of an enlightenment epistemology, which requires that a subject be able to recognise herself as the source of her

This can be easily noticed in cases where we are absorbed by the object of some activity or other to the point of 'forgetting about ourselves'. We are certainly aware of the object of activity and of the activity itself, but we are not aware of them as *our* activities or objects. Asked what we are doing, we then change the focus of attention, reflect on ourselves and regard the previous object of consciousness as *our* presentation. Again, applied to the presenting process of counting-as, which is crucial for the notion of original intentionality, what this implies is that a cognitive agent can only take its sensory perturbations as representing activities of an external world, if this presentation of the sensory perturbations is linked to a possible consciousness of the presentation as the agent's presentation.

This, however, is a condition for a second condition, which is a fundamental requirement for cognition in general. According to Kant, cognition relies on the "principle of the original *synthetic* unity of apperception". (KrV: B 137) Kant regards this principle as "the primary pure cognition of understanding [. . .] entirely independent of all conditions of sensible intuition". (KrV: B 137) The role of this synthesis is to make possible the unification of the manifold both under concepts and under intuitions. As Kant puts it, "not only do I myself need this condition in order to cognise an object, but every intuition must be subject to it *in order to become an object for me*." (KrV: B 138) Kant takes 'cognition' to refer to intuitions, concepts or (in the case of "the proper meaning of the term" – KrV: A 78/B 103) a synthesis of intuitions and concepts.[15] In all these cases, a synthesis is required – whether of sensations, of marks or of intuitions and marks – and this synthesis is made possible by the a priori synthesis of the transcendental unity of apperception. Thus, Kant sees this principle of the synthetic unity of apperception to be a condition which makes possible "all thought".

As we have seen, each of our presentations is potentially accompanied by a consciousness of the presentation as our presentation. Cognitions (whether intuitions, concepts or a mixture of the two) are presentations, which refer to an object. For this objective reference, however, the understanding needs to synthesise under a rule the manifold of the elements, which constitute the

---

cognitions. She reconstructs "Kant's argument for the apperception principle [the principle of the original synthetic unity of apperception]" as connected "with the notion of cognitive agency". (2009, p. 63).

15 "Cognition is either *intuition* or *concept* (*intuitus vel conceptus*). An intuition refers directly to the object and is singular; a concept refers to the object indirectly, by means of a characteristic that may be common to several things." (KrV: A 320/B 376–7) For further discussion of Kant's account of cognition and the distinction between cognition and knowledge, see Marcus Willaschek and Eric Watkins (2020).

respective cognition. This rule is given by the original synthetic unity of apperception. This is an a priori unity, which is created by apperception. Every aspect of my experience – whether a sensation, a conceptual mark, an intuition, a concept or a combination of these – is, as we have seen, an aspect of which I am potentially aware as an aspect of *my* experience. Hence, every aspect of my experience presupposes a potential link to a form of self-consciousness. The original synthetic unity of apperception is the mode in which aspects of our experience are formed, so that they are potentially linked to the same consciousness, namely, *my* identical consciousness.

I have called this original apperception '(self-)consciousness', since it is a form of self-consciousness, but one in which I am not reflecting on a self or ego, but on an aspect of experience as an aspect of *my* experience. The self, therefore, is still not explicitly posited and the identity of this self is only presupposed by the a priori synthetic unity of apperception or (self-)consciousness. It is unclear, however, that a Kantian machine would be able to meet this condition of (self-)consciousness or at least this is what I will claim in the next section.

6 (Self-)Consciousness and the Kantian Machine

As we have seen, (self-)consciousness is what makes possible for me to reflect on a presentation I have and to make it explicit that it is *my* presentation. The presentation which I have and of which I am conscious as a presentation is presented as my presentation (since I can realise that it is I who thinks the thought represented by this presentation). Moreover, given the principle of the synthetic unity of apperception, this presentation of which I am now conscious as my presentation is already part of a formal unity, given by the identity of the *I* in the 'I think the thought represented by this presentation'.

This is how I understand Kant's very condensed explanation of the principle of the synthetic unity of apperception:

> For it says no more than that all *my* presentations in some given intuition must be subject to the condition under which alone I can ascribe them – as *my* presentations – to the identical self, and hence under which alone I can collate them, as combined synthetically in one apperception, through the universal expression *I think*.   (KrV: B138)

Kant explains here that the principle of the synthetic unity of apperception, which he claims to be also the primary pure cognition of the understanding is itself an analytic judgement. It claims that in order for me to have a cognition, the presentations constituting that cognition must be unifiable as my presentations and, hence, must meet the condition that they are the presentations of an identical self. What follows is that cognition in general relies on the possibility of reflection, as given by (self-)consciousness or transcendental apperception. This is needed for the synthetic unity of apperception, for cognition and, hence, also for cognitive agency with its capacity to make sense.

Now to see why the Kantian machine seems unable to meet this fundamental condition for cognitions and, hence, for cognitive agency, consider a different thermostat. Apart from the temperature sensor, this thermostat has also a sensor for atmospheric pressure. The thermostat no longer regulates temperature in an aquarium, but in a recipient where the liquid should not go over the boiling point. It is well known that the boiling point occurs at a lower temperature when the pressure is reduced. So the thermostat measures continuously air pressure and the temperature of the liquid in order to avoid the boiling of the liquid. This example is useful, since we have a system which is regulated by two types of rule. There is first the temperature-related rule, which determines the thermostat to switch on a cooling element, when the temperature of the liquid is close to the boiling point. There is, then, the pressure-related rule, which tells the thermostat what the boiling temperature is, depending on the pressure of the air around the recipient. The second rule is in fact a higher-order rule relative to the first, since it modifies the first rule. In fact, it can be seen as a constraint on the first rule.

Level of complexity aside, the second thermostat has a structure similar to the Kantian machine. Recall that the Kantian machine receives a relatively simple input, has certain rules (of combination, more exactly, composition and connection) and some constraints on the rules. Nevertheless, there seems to be no doubt that the second thermostat is a merely sensory agent, not a cognitive agent yet; by contrast, the claim of the supporter of the Kantian-programme-based machine is that the Kantian machine is a cognitive agent.[16] As a cognitive agent, this machine should have original intentionality, that is, should be able to count its own perturbations as its representation of the external world.

Yet, in discussing Kant's account of cognition, we have seen that, apart from rules and constraints, Kant's account also presupposes as a significant condition (self-)consciousness. This is a capacity of the agent to represent her representations as her own. This condition is important for the synthetic unity of apperception, which Kant takes to be the fundamental condition for cognition in general and, hence, presumably, a fundamental condition for a

---

16 Some of the things a Kantian machine would need to do in order to be a cognitive agent seem to be doable by an extended model of what Evans calls in this volume the "Apperception Engine". (See esp. sub-subsection 4.4.6.) The claims there are programmatic and go in the same direction as this paper's argument.

cognitive agent too. Yet, there is no further aspect presented as part of the Kantian machine, which would play the role or function in the way in which (self-)consciousness is supposed to.

Neverthless, as we have seen, Kant takes (self-)consciousness to be very significant for cognition. He thinks a cognition, such as an intuition, can be a synthetic unity of presentations only if I can ascribe these presentations – as *my* presentations – to the same *I*, and, hence, only if I can combine them synthetically as one cognition. This is also a presentation, which I can count as my presentation of the world, since the synthesis of its components is not mechanically performed according to a rule, but it is the result of a collation that I perform given the potential for each component to be presented by me as my thought.

By contrast, the account of the Kantian programme presented in Sections 3 and 4 explains unity solely by reference to rules, in particular, first, the construction and application of rules of combination, and, secondly, the constraints on the generation of the rules and on the results of the applications of the rules. Thus, to consider the first source of unity, there is a claim that presentations cannot be combined directly, but we need rules to combine them. A combination without rules, the argument goes, would not satisfy the condition of unification, would not produce the unity of experience that I can call *mine*, and a self that would have the presentations would no longer be needed. The second source of unity, as already mentioned, is given by the constraints on the construction and application of rules. The Kantian highest principle of all synthetic judgements is considered a top-level constraint, which stipulates that knowledge claims must be about items of possible experience.

While it is correct that rules and constraints are needed for synthesis, it is also the case, as we have seen, that a synthetic unity is not possible without the condition which makes it possible for me to collate the elements to be synthesised as mine. (Self-)consciousness is, therefore, also a necessary condition for cognitive agency, a condition which is distinct from those related to rules and constraints. At the same time, it is a condition for which the Kantian programme provides no account.

As an illustration, consider again the second thermostat: As we have seen, we also have rules and constraints in that case, yet, it is quite plausible to see this thermostat as a merely sensory agent. The gap between the merely sensory agent and the cognitive agent is not bridged by any additional specific aspect of the Kantian programme.

7 Conclusion

Consider a Kantian computer[17] – a computer programmed with all the rule-generating procedures provided by Kant in the Schematism, Transcendental Deduction and Analytic of Principles. Assume that it provides good answers to verbal reasoning tasks – in fact, as good as those provided by human beings. Does this not mean the computer has to unify the various inputs as part of its experience? Does this not mean it can count its 'sensings' as its representing the external world?

In this paper, I have argued that these claims implicit in these rhetorical questions are unwarranted. To be sure, the significance of the successes of the Kantian machine in solving verbal reasoning tasks and other tasks relevant for the problem of representation is not questioned here, but it is taken for granted. What I have argued is unwarranted is the further claim that a Kantian machine is more or less the same as a cognitive agent, that is, an agent with original intentionality. The problematic assumption seems to be the assumption that some of the necessary conditions of experience presented by Kant are sufficient conditions.

I have argued that combining through rules is necessary for my experience, but it is not sufficient. Hence, it might be sufficient to equip a computer with rules which enable it to respond better to various tasks than other computers usually do, but from here to getting the computer to count its 'sensings' as *its* representing the external world is a gap that at least for Kant requires (self-)consciousness. It is, however, unclear how the Kantian machine could be seen as being equipped with this type of apperception. This, however, might be a line of inquiry that is worth pursuing in the attempt, both in cognitive science and philosophy, to solve the problem of representation.

References

KrV   Kritik der reinen Vernunft/*Critique of Pure Reason*

Ameriks, Karl (2000): *Kant's Theory of Mind: An Analysis of the Paralogisms of Pure Reason*. Oxford: Oxford University Press.
Baiasu, Sorin (2018): "Kant, AI and Contemporary Philosophy of Mind". In: *presentation given to the UK Kant Society's Annual 'Recent Literature on Kant' Session*. University of Cardiff.
Baiasu, Sorin (2011): *Kant and Sartre: Re-discovering Critical Ethics*. Basingstoke: Palgrave Macmillan.

---

17 For instance, as presented in the previous footnote, an extended Apperception Engine.

Bermúdez, José L. (1994): "The Unity of Apperception in the *Critique of Pure Reason*". In: *European Journal of Philosophy* 2. Nr. 3, pp. 213–40.

Brook, K. (1994) *Kant and the Mind*. Cambridge: Cambridge University Press.

Chalmers, David J./French, Robert M./Hofstadter, Douglas (1992): "High-Level Perception, Representation, and Analogy: A Critique of Artificial Intelligence Methodology". In: *Journal of Experimental and Theoretical Artificial Intelligence* 4. Nr. 3, pp. 185–211.

Engstrom, Stephen (2013): "Unity of Apperception". In: *Studi Kantiani* 26. pp. 37–54.

Evans, Richard (2017): "Kant on Constituted Mental Activity". In: *APA Newsletter* 16. Nr. 2, pp. 41–53.

Evans, Richard/Sergot, Marek/Stephenson, Andrew (2020): "Formalizing Kant's Rules: A Logic of Conditional Imperatives and Permissives". In: *Journal of Philosophical Logic* 49. pp. 613–80.

Evans, Richard (2022): "The Apperception Engine". In: Dieter Schönecker/Hyeongjoo Kim (Eds) *Kant and Artificial Intelligence*. Berlin: De Gruyter, 2022, pp. 39–103.

Falkenhainer, Brian/Forbus, Kenneth D./Gentner, Drede (1989): "The Structure-Mapping Engine". In: *Artificial Intelligence* 41. Nr. 1, pp. 1–63.

Haugeland, John (1990): "The Intentionality All-stars". In: *Philosophical Perspectives* 4. pp. 383–427.

Hofstadter, Douglas R. (1983): "The architecture of Jumbo". In: *Proceedings of the International Machine Learning Workshop*. Monticello, IL: University of Illinois.

Hofstadter, Douglas R./Mitchell, Melanie (1994): "The Copycat project: A model of mental fluidity and analogy-making". In: Keith Holyoak/John A. Barnden (Eds) *Advances in connectionist and neural computation theory* 2. *Analogical connections*.

Kant, I. (2000[1781/1787]) *Critique of Pure Reason*. Tr. W.S. Pluhar. Indianapolis, IN: Hackett.

Kant, I. (1966[1781/1787]) *Kritik der reinen Vernunft*. Hrsg. I. Heidemann. Stuttgart: Philipp Reclam Jun.

Langley, Pat/Simon, Herbert A./Bradshaw, Gary L./Zytkow, Jan M. (1987): *Scientific Discovery: Computational Explorations of the Creative Process*. Cambridge, MA: MIT Press.

Lau, Chong-Fuk (2014): "Kant's Transcendental Functionalism". In: *The Review of Metaphysics*. 68. Nr. 2, pp. 371–94.

Meredith, Marsha J. (1986): *Seek-Whence: A model of pattern perception*. Doctoral Dissertation. Department of Computer Science. Bloomington, IN: Indiana University.

Merritt, Melissa M. (2009): "Kant's Argument for the Apperception Principle". In: *European Journal of Philosophy* 19. Nr. 1, pp. 59–84.

Nagel, Thomas (1989): *The View from Nowhere*. Oxford: Oxford University Press.

Schlicht, Tobias (2016): "Kant and the Problem of Consciousness". In: Stephen D. Leach/James Tartaglia (Eds) *Consciousness and the Great Philosophers: What Would They Have Said about Our Mind-Body Problem*.

Schlosser, Markus E. (2019): "Agency". In: Edward N. Zalta (Ed.) *The Stanford Encyclopedia of Philosophy*. <plato.stanford.edu/archives/win2019/entries/agency/>.

Schönecker, Dieter (2022): "Kant's argument from moral feelings: Why practical reason cannot be artificial". In: Dieter Schönecker/Hyeongjoo Kim (Eds) *Kant and Artificial Intelligence*. Berlin: De Gruyter, 2022, pp. 169–188.

Scruton, Roger (1983): "Photography and Representation". In: *The Aesthetic Understanding*. London and New York: Methuen.

Stecker, Robert (2009): "Film as art". In: Paisley Livingston/Carl Plantinga (Eds) *The Routledge Companion to Philosophy and Film*. pp. 121–130.

Willaschek, Marcus/Watkins, Eric (2020): "Kant on Cognition and Knowledge". In: *Synthese* 197. pp. 3195–3213.

Hyeongjoo Kim

4 Tracing the Origins of Artificial Intelligence: A Kantian Response to McCarthy's Call for Philosophical Help

Abstract: Computer scientist John McCarthy has been tremendously influential in our understanding of what Artificial Intelligence really is. I shall argue that, from a Kantian point of view, the underlying theoretical framework of McCarthy's position – which I summarize as the claim that AI as a technical entity is an imitation of the computational ability of human intelligence for problem solving in the empirical physical world – can be understood as transcendental realism. McCarthy dispels the distinction between phenomena and things-in-themselves by fundamentally blocking the reflective ability of intelligence, that is, the ability to intuit oneself as a synthetic act. The reflective ability of intelligence, i.e. the self-consciousness contained in the "cogito, ergo sum", is the barometer, as it were, for distinguishing transcendental idealism from transcendental realism; at the same time, it is the watershed that separates Kant from McCarthy. In a philosophical paper, McCarthy called for the help of philosophers to define AI; Kant, I shall argue, can offer such help.

1 Introduction

The term "artificial intelligence" (AI) has become a global buzzword. AI chatbots on smartphones speak to us, today's children are called digital natives, and AI companion robots serve at senior centers. However, what exactly is AI? Is it a robot, a program, or a kind of intelligence? While AI is a commonly used term, people seem to use it in reference to different concepts. In other words, the meanings encapsulated by this term are diverse.

In the 1780s, Kant took issue with the ambiguity of the concept of "metaphysics." At that time, the term "metaphysics" was a hot buzzword among philosophers as well; just as AI, metaphysics had become a "battlefield of endless controversies" (A VIII).[1] Kant introduced the *synthetic-analytic distinction*

---

1 For citations, see References.

Hyeongjoo Kim, Chung-Ang University

https://doi.org/10.1515/9783110706611-004

(of subject-predicament judgments) as a methodological means for concept clarification. The emphasis on this distinction is still valid in the quest for the meaning of artificial intelligence. A synthetic proposition's predicate concept is not contained in its subject concept and is therefore knowable only through experience, whereas an analytic proposition's predicate concept is contained in its subject concept and thus is knowable through concept analysis (A6/B10 ff). I will expand this synthetic-analytic distinction to include a distinction between concepts referring to empirical objects and concepts relating to speculative and philosophical ideas; I will then apply the latter distinction to the semantic layers of the concept of AI. While this article aims to trace the original meaning of AI, the scope of discussion will be limited to the works by McCarthy, who boldly coined this oxymoronic term as early as 1956. More specifically, the paper will focus on the definition and explanation of "artificial intelligence" as discussed in his philosophical writings (McCarthy 1987, 1995, 2007).

On the assumption that "philosophers have not really come to an agreement [concerning the definition of intelligence: HJ. K.] in 2500 years" (McCarthy 2007, p. 5), McCarthy considered it hardly possible to develop a "solid definition of artificial intelligence" (McCarthy 2007, p. 2). Nonetheless, he discussed the question of "Why Artificial Intelligence Needs Philosophy" (McCarthy & Hayes 1969, p. 2) from an epistemological perspective, defined artificial intelligence, and attempted a philosophical explanation of it. This attempt set a milestone for the foundation of future AI research, as expressed in his call for support: "Philosopher! Help!" (McCarthy 1995, p. 5)[2]

This article is my response to McCarthy's call from a Kantian viewpoint. In doing so, I pursue two goals: one is related to the definition of artificial intelligence and the other to the epistemological background of AI. First, I will provide an analysis of McCarthy's definition of artificial intelligence. To give a brief preview of the results of this analysis, there are, I submit, three interrelated semantic layers in McCarthy's concept of AI: engineering AI, philosophical AI, and literary AI. Engineering AI is the object of direct reference as a technical entity; philosophical AI is a conceptual premise of engineering AI; and literary AI is the ideology of engineering AI development. In other words, I define literary AI as AI geared toward the goal of AI engineering that is outside the realm of current technology, such as strong AI or super AI, which is mainly

---

2 Kant is not, of course, what McCarthy has in mind here. In this context, he mentions that he received the help of linguistic philosophers such as Searle, Austin, and Grice. From his mention of Carnap, Quine, and Putnam, it can also be assumed that what he had in mind is the philosophy of logical positivism, which became the philosophical basis for the development of artificial intelligence in the early and mid-20th century.

discussed in the post-humanist world based on the fundamental skepticism about the distinction between humans and machines. Based on this categorization, what McCarthy ultimately wanted to assert in his definition of AI is that *artificial intelligence (as a technical entity) is a model for the human computational ability for problem-solving in the empirical physical world.* Second, by analyzing its epistemological background, I argue that it corresponds to Kantian transcendental realism. Furthermore, I will demonstrate that both a Kantian and McCarthy's understanding of intelligence have a common denominator: they both define intelligence as problem-solving computational ability in the world of empirical realism. However, Kant demands another necessary condition for intelligence: the self-consciousness represented by the "I think." While this demand functions as the core evidence of the Kantian worldview of transcendental idealism, it was neglected by McCarthy.

2 McCarthy's Concept of Intelligence

McCarthy's definition of artificial intelligence is densely formulated in his article "What Is Artificial Intelligence?" (McCarthy 2007). It can be summarized as follows:

[1] Artificial intelligence is the science and engineering of intelligent machines, especially intelligent computer programs. [2] Artificial Intelligence is related to the similar task of using computers to understand human intelligence. However, the concept of *intelligence* is not completely independent from the concept of human intelligence yet. [3] It is certain that intelligence is the computational part of the ability to achieve goals in the world. [4] Varying kinds and degrees of intelligence occur in people, animals, and machines.[3]

Now, the AI referred to in [1] is a technical entity as an *a posteriori* designation of an empirical embodiment existing in reality (be it a robot with a body or a program), not a term analytically derived from the concepts of *artificial* and *intelligence*. [2], [3], and [4], however, deal with the original meaning of intelligence, the traditional subject of epistemology. In this regard, McCarthy uses the term AI, though unintentionally, in two senses: AI as a technical entity and AI as a type of 'intelligence'. On this premise, while [2] points out the dependence of the concept of *intelligence* on *human intelligence*, [4] talks about the ubiquity of the concept of intelligence. Two seemingly contradictory (yet compatible) arguments

---

3 Cf. McCarthy (2007, p. 2).

coexist in these two statements.[4] [Claim 1] is derived from [4], and [Claim 2] is derived from [2]:

> [Claim 1]: *Intelligence* is a concept that encompasses *AI* and *human intelligence.*
> [Claim 2]: *Artificial intelligence* is dependent on *human intelligence.*[5]

In [Claim 1], intelligence is a necessary condition both of AI and of human intelligence. Furthermore, AI has an intelligence like human intelligence; accordingly, it can be regarded as *artificial* intelligence, that is, a kind of intelligence. AI and human intelligence have one thing in common: intelligence. They are distinct from each other only by what (or who) possesses this intelligence. In this sense, the term *animal intelligence* is also possible. In other words, intelligence does not originate from the human being and therefore is not a human-specific element. In fact, McCarthy emphasizes the expression "our notion of general intelligence" (McCarthy & Hayes 1969, p. 3) as an ability to perceive "commonsense knowledge" (McCarthy 1987, p. 1030) of the world and uses it as a key concept to guide the discussion on the definition of intelligence.[6] According to McCarthy, "an entity is intelligent if it has the intellectual world of mathematics, an understanding of its own goals, or other mental processes [including the human mind: HJ. K.]" (McCarthy & Hayes 1969, p. 4). Furthermore, he

---

4 However, the coexistence of two claims described contrastively in the above summary does not mean that they are incompatible. This aspect will become clear in the discussion that follows.

5 In this regard, McCarthy (1995) says, "Human level artificial intelligence requires equipping a computer program with a philosophy, particularly epistemological attitudes" (p. 1). And I point out that the basic idea for the distinction between this two claims was drawn from Kim (2016).

6 This is the conceptual basis of artificial general intelligence (AGI) currently under discussion. However, it is not what McCarthy intends to express through this concept. AGI, which is considered the next-generation AI or a term synonymous with strong artificial intelligence (SAI) as the ultimate goal of AI development, means the ability of an intelligent agent to perform any intellectual task that a human being can. AGI belongs to the category of synthetic-empirical concepts according to the classification I previously made, i.e., empirical reality. In his article "Generality in Artificial Intelligence," McCarthy still regards the purpose of AI as reasoning and problem-solving ability (McCarthy 1987, p. 1032). Here, "generality" refers to the possibility that AI abilities (problem-solving and computation) can have human abilities and his emphasis on its imperativeness. This is ultimately linked to the implementation of one of the rule-based AI programs, "General Problem Solver" (McCarthy 1987). In the course of these discussions, McCarthy does not clearly distinguish between the synthetic and analytical concepts of AI. To develop my argument, I pay attention to the expression "our notion" in the phrase "our notion of general intelligence." McCarthy himself initially used the concept of generality in the sense of *human-like* rather than in the sense of transcending that of humans and machines. Therefore, Claims 1 and 2 are connected, which will be addressed later.

claims that "the physical world exists and already contains *some intelligent machines called people*" (McCarthy & Hayes 1969, p. 5). Considering his comments, [Claim 1] can be rephrased as follows:

[Claim 1*]: The *intelligence* of *AI* is *general intelligence*.

But what is the *artificiality* of AI? The dictionary meaning of "artificial" is: "made or produced to copy something natural" (https://dictionary.cambridge.org/). "Something natural", however, does not refer to anything other than intelligence itself. AI as an object of philosophical analysis, different from the synthetic sense of AI referring to a discipline of science or a concrete entity such as robots as defined in [1], is *imitative* intelligence. More explicitly, AI as part of any machine or program is *artificialized* intelligence of (human) intelligence, that is, an intelligence modeled after (human) intelligence.[7] Re-examining [Claim 2], AI should be considered as an intelligence in the sense that AI shares some of the faculties of human intelligence. Thus, at first glance there seems to be a difference between [Claim 1*] and [Claim 2]. This difference can be expressed by the thesis of the independence of intelligence in general from human intelligence; it is a matter of determining whether endowing AI with the status of intelligence is admitting that (general) intelligence encompasses AI and human intelligence, logically preceding them, or that it is *similar to human intelligence*.

On a related note, McCarthy's statement mentions the first premise of general intelligence: "The physical world exists and already contains some intelligent machines called people" (McCarthy & Hayes 1969, p. 6). This premise serves as the rationale supporting the principle behind this interpretation: *humans are intelligent machines, these machines already exist in the world, and homo sapiens is only one of them*. This is consistent with [4], "Varying kinds and degrees of intelligence occur in people, many animals, and some machines." Against this background, combining [Claim 1] and [Claim 2] allows for the understanding that both machines and humans have intelligence; however, since humans have had a higher form of intelligence so far, machines are modeled after human intelligence.

Now, let us turn to [Claim 3]: "It is certain that intelligence is the computational part of the ability to achieve goals in the world." This statement makes it clear that McCarthy limits the scope of the definition of intelligence to computational power. Regarding the purpose of using this power, he says:

---

7 The Turing Test, the first experiment related to the feasibility question of artificial intelligence which has served as a direct model for McCarthy's concept of AI, is based on the concept of intelligence as imitation (McCarthy, 2007).

> Work on artificial intelligence, especially general intelligence, will be improved by a
> clearer idea of what intelligence is (. . .) We have to say that a machine is intelligent if it
> solves certain classes of problems requiring intelligence in humans.
>
> (McCarthy & Hayes 1969, p. 4)

According to McCarthy, the purpose of AI (as a technological entity) is problem-solving, which requires human intelligence.[8] That is, problem-solving ability is what endows AI with a type of intelligence – machine intelligence – with a status similar to that of animals and humans. Thus, McCarthy's statement [3*], "Intelligence is an ability to solve problems through computation," helps us to understand the link between the seemingly contradictory [Claim 1*] and [Claim 2] (again, [Claim 1*]: The intelligence of AI is general intelligence; [Claim 2]: AI is dependent on human intelligence. With [3*] as an underlying statement, the two claims can be formally synthesized as follows:

> [Claim 3]: All *intelligence (general intelligence)* is a computational ability to solve prob-
> lems. Therefore, *AI* and *human intelligence* have computational abilities.

However, [Claim 3] does not explain general intelligence and dependence on human intelligence. Therefore, we must revisit the three interrelated layers mentioned in the introduction: engineering AI, philosophical AI, and literary AI. I have already pointed out that the first two concepts are implied in [1] and [2, 3, 4], respectively. From a scientific viewpoint, literary AI is a regulative idea, to borrow the term from Kant.

If the "general intelligence" implied in [Claim 3] directly refers to such literary AI, how should we understand it? If intelligence means general intelligence that precedes any concrete form of intelligence possessed by a specific entity, general intelligence logically precedes AI or human intelligence, and, accordingly, what bestows the status of intelligence on AI would not be human intelligence but intelligence itself. The attributes and limits of general intelligence constitute an uncharted terrain for us. Against this background, strong AI, super AI, or any intelligence that goes beyond such limits and attributes is free from the restraints of discussion. However, although this argument can serve the purpose of AI engineers, including McCarthy, as an ideology for AI development as an engineering entity, it cannot be its premise. As stated in [3], McCarthy clearly limits the scope of intelligence to computational power. Even if the general ability he advocates is intelligence as a "general representation of the

---

8 McCarthy's argument that the purpose of AI is problem-solving is still valid. For example, *Artificial Intelligence: A Modern Approach*, which is the standard of AI textbooks, defines AI as a "problem-solving agent" (2010, p. 64).

world" (McCarthy & Hayes 1969, p. 1), that is, intelligence with common sense and human-like flexibility (McCarthy & Hayes 1969, p. 3), it merely means upgraded reasoning and computational ability, far from strong AI with intuition and self-consciousness. To reiterate, the essence of AI as established by McCarthy is the ability to solve problems in a "specific situation" (McCarthy & Hayes, 1969, p. 4)[9] in the external physical world[10] based on logical reasoning. As such, we can concretize his claim as follows:

> [Claim 3*]: AI as a technical entity is an imitation of the computational ability of human intelligence for problem solving in the empirical physical world.

3 Kant's Concept of Intelligence and McCarthy's Transcendental Realism

As McCarthy states, philosophical discussions about intelligence have been around for 2,500 years. It is true that human interest in intelligence dates to ancient Greece. The Greeks persistently inquired into what can be known (noetos; *intelligible*) by the *Geist* (nous) and its cognition or function (noesis) (see Plato 2008, p. 235 f.). Parmenides was the first philosopher who put the *Geist* over physical or sensible abilities, and this line of thought led to Plato, who subdivided the concept of *Geist* and extended it into discussions about the relationship between the Idea and its cognition, as well as the activities and divisions of *Geist's* abilities. This conception of intelligence was represented by the concept of "intellectus or intelligentia" (Copleston, 1993, p. 191) which is the etymological background of the concept of intelligence we are discussing now.

---

9 In this sense, Russell and Norvig (2010) attempted to organize the definition of existing AI (with four frameworks: thinking humanly, thinking rationally, acting humanly, and acting rationally) through a combination of two separate categories: 'ability to act and think', and 'similarity with humans and rationality'. Thinking humanly relates to understanding and developing programs in relation to human cognitive abilities, specifically the relationship between sensory organs, the ability to think, and knowledge. Thinking rationally (with the subtitle "Approach based on the 'law of thought'") is based on human (formal) logical thinking. The definition of AI based on acting humanly is no different from the keynote of the Turing Test. Acting rationally is an extended concept that includes thinking rationally and aims to solve a given problem under specific circumstances based on the ability to reason (pp. 2–5).

10 This is related to Kant's *transcendental realism*, which will be addressed later. Transcendental realism is the theory that space-time exists independently of our sensitivities; therefore, representations that exist in this space-time are considered *things-in-themselves*.

Against this linguistic tradition, Kant limits intelligence to the cognitive faculty of cognizing empirical objects along with the faculty of cognizing the self. That is, Kant boldly discards the role of human intelligence as the faculty that intuits God, and simultaneously asserts an agnosticism of metaphysical objects beyond the empirical world.[11] Kant describes his worldview as *transcendental idealism*, and the worldview he criticizes as *transcendental realism*. This leads us to the following passage:

> [K][K1] I understand by the transcendental idealism of all appearances the doctrine that they are all together to be regarded as mere representations and not as things in themselves, and accordingly that space and time are only sensible forms of our intuition, but not determinations given for themselves or conditions of objects as things in themselves. [K2] To this idealism is opposed transcendental realism, which regards space and time as something given in themselves (independent of our sensibility). The transcendental realist therefore represents outer appearances (if their reality is conceded) as things in themselves, which would exist independently of us and our sensibility. (. . .) [K3] The transcendental idealist, on the contrary, can be an empirical realist. (. . .) [K4] He can concede the existence of matter without going beyond mere self-consciousness and assuming something more than the certainty of the representation in me, hence the cogito, ergo sum.   (A369)

As can be seen from [K1], transcendental idealism clearly distinguishes between the thing-in-itself and the phenomenon and limits the area that is cognized by human intelligence to the world of phenomena. The cause of this distinction and limitation is the consciousness-immanence of space and time. According to it, space-time is not an entity that exists independently of human intelligence but is a form of human intelligence that enables cognition. Hence, according to Kant's transcendental idealism, "we have to do only with our representations" (A190/B235) that we self-create, intuited through space-time.

From the Kantian viewpoint, McCarthy's statement [3][12] matches the transcendental realism designated by Kant as an object of criticism in [K2]. The epistemological premise of [Claim 3] is as follows:

---

11 In this linguistic context, Kant distinguishes two types: archetype intelligence (*intellectus archetypes*) and ectype intelligence (*intellectus ectypus*). Archetype intelligence indirectly expresses divine intelligence. Divine intelligence implies intuition as part of it. In other words, it means intelligence without distinction between intelligence (*Verstand*) and intuition (*Anschauung*), that is, intuitive intelligence (*intuitiver Verstand*). For God, cognition is knowledge. "God cognizes the object as it is" (AA XXVIII, 606). Therefore, divine intuition is a logical premise about the existence of the thing-in-itself. On the other hand, human cognitive ability, which is ectype intelligence for divine intelligence, is limited.

12 [3] reads: "It is certain that 'Intelligence' is the computational part of the ability to achieve goals in the world."

> [M][M1] The physical world already containing intelligent machines called people exists. [M2] Information about this world is obtainable through the senses and is expressible internally. [M3] Our common-sense view of the world is almost right, and that is our scientific view. [M4] The right way to think about the general problems of metaphysics and epistemology is not to attempt to clear one's own mind of all knowledge and start with "Cogito, ergo sum" and build up from there.   (McCarthy & Hayes, 1969, p. 6)

According to [M1] and [M2], the understanding of the world in which problems to be solved are assigned to AI, that is, the world underlying the situation requiring a specific output value, posits a *scientific worldview* (in [M3]) in which *the existence of an external physical object is taken for granted as common sense* (in [M1]). [M2] justifies direct knowledge of the physical world, that is, the world external to consciousness, by claiming that the knowledge of the physical world obtained through our sense organs can become the immanent knowledge of the cognitive subject. This can be reformulated as:

> [M*] The existence of a physical world that contains humans is real. Therefore, as Kant says, the physical world exists outside human cognition. However, empirical knowledge of the physical world obtained through sense organs is immanent. This is our common scientific sense. Therefore, this is correct.

Applying [M*] to [K] yields transcendental realism, as described in [K2]:

> [K2] This idealism is opposed to transcendental realism, which regards space and time as something given in themselves (independent of our sensibility). The transcendental realist therefore represents outer appearances (if their reality is conceded) as things in themselves, which would exist independently of us and our sensibility.

Acknowledging that time and space are things-in-themselves acknowledges the reality of physical objects that occupy time and space, regardless of the perceiver's abilities. More specifically, transcendental realism affirms the existence of things-in-themselves, as opposed to transcendental idealism. In [M*], the physical world, which exists outside the perceiver and whose existence is justified beyond doubt, has the same contextual meaning as that of things-in-themselves ([K2]). This confirms transcendental realism as the theoretical framework for [Claim 3*], "AI as a technical entity is an imitation of the computational ability of human intelligence for problem solving in the empirical physical world." Thus, when viewed from the Kantian perspective, McCarthy is a transcendental realist [K2].

On the other hand, from the statement in [K3] that a transcendental idealist can be an empirical realist and thus concede the existence of external things,[13]

---

13 Kant argues that transcendental idealism and empirical realism are compatible (as seen in A369 above), even though the point to emphasize through the two concepts is different. While

it can be inferred that there is a common denominator in these seemingly contradictory positions. As suggested by the term itself, transcendental idealism means that anything outside the realm of human intelligence is transcendental, that is, only ideal. Against this background, the realm of things-in-themselves and the realm of phenomena are divided, with the field of the activity of human intelligence limited to the latter. However, from the viewpoint of the phenomenal world, only empirically perceived external things are real. Transcendental idealism and empirical realism differ in that the former defines the realm of human cognition in a negative way, that is, by *reductio ad absurdum*, and the latter in a

---

transcendental idealism focuses on the separation between thing-in-itself and phenomenon due to the consciousness-immanence of the space-time form, in empirical realism, the perception of external things derives the reality of things in space directly from reality, and based on this, the correspondence between representations and external objects, that is, the objective validity of representation is discussed. This has resulted in a variety of interpretations and controversies. At the time of republishing the *Critique of Pure Reason*, Jacobi assessed that Kant's explanation of materialism had failed and Kantian idealism, or transcendental idealism, was likely to be a non-idealism (*Nicht-Idealismus*), since it took on an object corresponding to representation, in *David Hume über den Glauben oder Idealismus und Realismus* (1787). "It is still controversial whether empirical realism connected to transcendental idealism can be justified as a kind of realism" (see Heidemann 2015, p. 1894, translated by the author). Putnam regards Kant's empirical realism as intrinsic realism, while Allison protects Kant's idealism from the overemphasis of the realist stance (see Heidemann 2015, p. 1894). It is another philosophical issue to establish a philosophical stance on transcendental idealism. Transcendental idealism can also be interpreted as "idealism, phenomenology, and realism" (see Edmundts 2015, p. 1109). For example, Strawson regards transcendental idealism as a phenomenological idealism (Strawson 1966, p. 246), whereas Allison argues that there is a clear difference between the two concepts (see Allison 2004, p. 41). Whether transcendental idealism can be regarded as a phenomenology or phenomenological idealism was already triggered by Garbe and Feder when Kant was alive has been a debate between "two worlds or two perspectives," as introduced and attended by many researchers, including Van Cleve.

Despite this conceptual difference and many controversies arising out of it, this paper focuses on the statement that "a transcendental idealist can be an empirical realist" since "the certainty of representation in me, that is, 'Cogito, ergo sum,' the certainty of self-consciousness" (A369) can be the basis for both theories; and it considers that "transcendental idealism is a realism only possible when one pays attention to the subjective conditions of our cognition" (Edmundts 2015, p. 1108). The meaning of empirical realism is nothing more than the theory that time and space and our representations in them are meaningful only within the limits of our experience (Kim 2016, p. 25). It is well identified that the primary commonality between the two must be the consciousness-immanence of space and time, if we temporarily reserve the emphasis itself based on Kant's plan for the difference in expression, the interpretation by expression, criticism of skepticism, and the objective validity of cognition. In addition, reserving various secondary interpretations that can be derived from transcendental idealism, I will just focus on this point to proceed with the discussion by contrasting transcendental idealism (empirical realism) and transcendental realism centered on self-consciousness.

positive way. By virtue of these rules, Kant presents the task of finding an answer to the question of how limited human intelligence works as the ultimate task of his epistemology. In other words, the goal of his transcendental philosophy is to justify how synthetic *a priori* propositions are possible (B73). Kant responds to this task with the following statements:

> *In this way* synthetic *a priori* judgements are possible, if we relate the formal conditions of *a priori* intuition, the synthesis of imagination and the necessary unity of the synthesis in a transcendental apperception, to a possible empirical knowledge in general.
>
> (A158/B197)

> [T]he unity of apperception in relation to the synthesis of the imagination (Einbildung-skraft) is the understanding (. . .) In the understanding there are therefore pure *a priori* cognitions that contain the necessary unity of pure synthesis of the imagination in regard to all possible appearances. (A119)

The imagination is the ability to derive a schema that is "intellectual on the one hand and sensible on the other" (A138/B177), and the unity of apperception is "the formal unity of consciousness in the synthesis of the manifold of the representations" (A105). In summary, for Kant, the necessary conditions for legitimate knowledge are the synthesis of receptive sensibility and spontaneous intellect, and the awareness that the subject of this synthesis and the destination of the resultant representation is the self. What is important from our standpoint, i.e., the perspective of empirical realism, is that this process of experience must relate to *possible empirical cognition in general*. What matters here is that this *possible empirical cognition in general* signifies "possible appearances" for Kant. Bearing this in mind, let us take a brief look at the working principle of AI.

First, I will briefly describe the core contents of deep learning technology, which has gained significant interest among the currently available AI techniques. Although deep learning is technically different from rule-based AI techniques such as list processing (LISP), which is an AI language designed by McCarthy, they share the same goal, that is, problem solving. Deep learning is an AI technique that processes inputted information based on the vast amount of data already provided to produce a desired result as accurately as possible. For example, if we draw the number "3" in handwriting, the deep learning technique will print a clearly recognizable number "3" based on the numerous data already obtained. Handwriting "3" is compared with other similar handwriting "3" data already entered; then, common features are extracted as a group of related things. With this process of repeated feature extraction, handwriting "3" is recognized as a definite character, that is, digitized character "3". Handwriting "3" is stored as data to be used for the next input information. Language and face recognition, which are a tagging function of Facebook, work by a similar mechanism. When a picture of a human face is entered into a computer and deep learning is activated, a series of processes lead to the final judgment that "this is a human face."

Let us consider the widely used cat-recognition process model as an example.

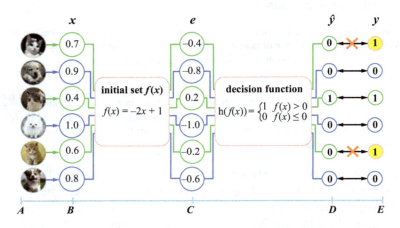

In this model,[14] the algorithm quantifies the input images and substitutes them into multilayered functions until the final output is expressed as 0 or 1 to determine a match or mismatch. Although omitted in the figure above, the error range in the D-E section is reflected in section B–C, and this iterative process lasts until the error range reaches the minimum value. The back-propagation algorithm is the algorithm governing the entire process. This is understood herein as a meta-function because it continuously changes the mapping function. In the figure above, x denotes the initial value, e denotes the output value of $f(x)$, $\hat{y}$ denotes the output value of the decision function (0 or 1), and y denotes the true value of the target image. In summary, computers with deep learning can conceptualize information. Computers can take handwriting "3" as a digitalized number "3" and analyze data with patterns in the pictures of human faces to define the concept of "human face".

To return to Kant, he explains that the key to human intelligence is simply the conceptualization of sensible information. The object of the external becomes the object of the internal, and in the process, synthesis by affinity (*Affinität*) occurs. Then, the synthesized diversity is unified into one representation, and when it is defined by concepts, it is stated in a form of judgment. If we see a set of red dots in the space of a circle, these manifold (*mannigfaltige*) dots are

---

14 The lecture materials of Prof. Jaesung Lee of Chung-Ang University. Special thanks to him.

synthesized by the principle of affinity in the circle; then, by the understanding of the synthesized representation, we derive the judgment that "this representation is an apple." When other similar judgments are given, by reason, we can make abstract judgments such as "An apple is a fruit." Given a picture of "3", the principle of AI, which conceptualizes it as a digitalized number "3" and derives new judgments through reasoning based on the learned (determined) data, is similar to the principle of human intelligence just discussed. This similarity can be expressed in McCarthy's terms, "problem-solving ability using intelligence," or in Kant's terms, "faculty of combination of understanding." If the world of objects of "problem solving" (McCarthy) and "empirical cognition" (Kant) is limited to the phenomenal world, McCarthy can also be classified as an empirical realist in the sense that the experience of the existence of an object can be obtained by artificial intelligence through its synthesis ability.

As we have pointed out, however, McCarthy is also a transcendental realist, and the core of Kant's criticism of transcendental realism is the lack of the distinction between things-in-themselves and phenomena; behind the rationale for this criticism lies the concept of "intelligence" as defined by transcendental idealism. With this in mind, let us compare Kant's [K4] and McCarthy's [M4].

> [K4] One can concede the existence of matter without going beyond mere self-consciousness and assuming something more than the certainty of the representation in me, hence the cogito, ergo sum.

> [M4] The right way to think about the general problems of metaphysics and epistemology is not to attempt to clear one's own mind of all knowledge and start with "cogito, ergo sum" and build up from there.

In the *Critique of Pure Reason,* "cogito" (I think) often means self-consciousness,[15] and [K4] matches this concept. In this context, self-consciousness is a definite representation of "I think (therefore, I am)". For this reason, "without going out of his consciousness" can be matched with "not to attempt to clear one's own mind of all knowledge," and "without assuming more than the certainty of the representation within me ('I think, therefore I am')" with "start with 'cogito, ergo sum' and build up from there." Thus, [K4] is simplified as follows:

> [K4*] An empirical realist acknowledges the existence of matter without going out of the cogito of self-consciousness.

[K4*] has two semantic layers: (1) the cognition realm of self-consciousness, and (2) "I think must be able to accompany all my presentations" (B130). Based on these two thoughts, [K4] can be reformulated as follows:

---

15 As a prime example, see B130 f., B413. For further information, see Kim (2016).

[K4**] Our knowledge starts with our self-consciousness of "I think, therefore I am" and ends there.

In the same vein, [M4] can be simplified as follows:

[M4*] Our knowledge is not an epistemological quest for self-knowledge and therefore does not start with "I think, therefore I am."

A direct comparison of [K4*] and [M4**] shows that the decisive difference between the two, that is, between empirical realism and transcendental realism, lies in the answer to whether the self-consciousness of "I think" is acknowledged. According to Kant, this self-consciousness constitutes human "intelligence." In the "deduction" of the *Critique of Pure Reason* (§ 25), which deals with the problem of self-consciousness as the main subject, Kant says the following about intelligence:

(. . .) through which [intuition of the manifold in me: HJ. K.] I determined this thought [I think myself: HJ. K.]; and I exist as an intelligence that is merely conscious of its faculty for combination (. . .) [T]his spontaneity is the reason I call myself an intelligence.

(B158 footnote)

In this passage, intelligence is defined first and foremost as the faculty of combination. As examined above, this holds true for both Kant and McCarthy. However, Kant adds the faculty to be aware of this faculty as an additional essential attribute of intelligence. For Kant, the human being is a subject constantly conscious of the fact that the representations and thoughts that the subject is thinking certainly belong to the subject. This is where Kant and McCarthy part.

References

The *Critique of Pure Reason* is quoted according to: Kant, Immanuel: (1998). *Critique of Pure Reason* (The Cambridge Edition of the Works of Immanuel Kant) (P. Guyer & A. Wood, Eds.). Cambridge: Cambridge University Press.

Allison, Henry: (2004). *Kant's Transcendental Idealism*. New Haven/London: Yale University Press.
Boden, Margaret: (Ed.) (1990). *The Philosophy of Artificial Intelligence*. Oxford: Oxford University Press.
Copleston, Frederick: (1993). A History of Philosophy. New York: Doubleday.
Cramer, Konrad: (1990). "Über Kants Satz: Das: Ich denke, muß alle meine Vorstellungen begleiten können." In *Theorie der Subjektivität/Hrsg. von Konrad Cramer*. Frankfurt am Main: Suhrkamp, pp. (167–202).

Marr, David: (1990). "Artificial Intelligence: A Personal View." In: Boden, Margaret (Ed.): *The Philosophy of Artificial Intelligence* Oxford: Oxford University Press, pp. 133–146.

Emundts, Dina: (2015). "Idealismus, Transzendentaler." In *Kant Lexikon (Online)*. Berlin/ New York: Walter de Gruyter.

Heidemann, Dietmar: (2015). "Realismus, Transzendentaler/Empirischer." In *Kant Lexikon (Online)*. Berlin/New York: Walter de Gruyter.

Henrich, Dieter: (1976). *Identität und Objektivität*. Heidelberg: Carl Winter.

McCarthy, John: (1987). "Generality of Artificial Intelligence." In *Communications of the ACM* Volume 30 Issue 12, pp. 1030–1035.

McCarthy, John: (1995). "What Has AI in Common with Philosophy?", What has AI in Common with Philosophy? (stanford.edu).

McCarthy, John: (2007). "What Is Artificial Intelligence?", http://jmc.stanford.edu/articles/ whatisai/whatisai.pdf.

McCarthy, John/Hayes, Patrick: (1969). "Some Philosophical Problems from the Standpoint of Artificial Intelligence (Online).", Some Philosophical Problems from the Standpoint of Artificial Intelligence (stanford.edu).

Plato: (2008). *Republic* (Waterfield, Robin, Trans.). Oxford: Oxford University Press.

Rich, Elaine: (1987). "Artificial Intelligence." In Shapiro (Ed.): *Encyclopedia of Artificial Intelligence*. US: John Wiley & Sons, pp. 9–16.

Rohlf, Michael: (2010). *Stanford Encyclopedia of Philosophy*. http://plato.stanford.edu/ entries/kant/

Rosefeldt, Tobias: (2000). *Das logische Ich*. Berlin/Wien: Philo.

Russell Stuart, and Norvig, Peter: (2010). *Artificial Intelligence: A Modern Approach*. Boston: Prentice Hall.

Strawson, Peter: (1966). *The Bounds of Sense*. London: Methuen & Co. Ltd.

Wundt, Max: (1964). *Die deutsche Schulphilosophie im Zeitalter der Aufklärung*. Olms.

Kim, Hyeongjoo: (2016). *Zur Empirizität des „Ich denke" in Kants Kritik der reinen Vernunft*. Würzburg, Königshausen & Neumann.

Kim, Hyeongjoo: (2016). "Artificial Intelligence and Human Intelligence - With Emphasis on Intelligence-Concept in MacCarthy and Kant" In *Philosophical Investigation* Volume 43, pp. 161–190.

Kern, Andrea: (2015). "Intellectus Archetypus/Ectypus." In *Kant Lexikon (Online)*. Berlin/ New York: Walter de Gruyter.

Practical Philosophy

Lisa Benossi & Sven Bernecker

5 A Kantian Perspective on Robot Ethics

Abstract: What conditions does a robot have to satisfy to qualify as a moral agent? Should robots become moral agents, or should humanity fully retain agency and personhood for itself? Is it permissible to prevent robots from developing moral agency? This paper examines these questions from a viewpoint-neutral and a Kantian perspective. Regarding the first question, we argue that the Kantian standards for moral agency could not possibly be met by robots. The second and third questions are more difficult to answer, in part because the viewpoint-neutral perspective does not provide a clear verdict. We argue that it is a feature of the Kantian perspective to propose a plausible answer. The idea is that preventing robots from achieving moral personality is morally permissible, insofar as our intention is consistent with the respect of human life and its rational nature.

1 Introduction

The term *robot ethics* can mean different things. It can refer to the professional ethics of roboticists, the moral code programmed into robots, the ability of robots to do ethical reasoning, or moral issues concerning the design and development of robots. It is the latter usage of the term that is presupposed in this paper. In particular, we are concerned with the question of whether it is permissible to prevent robots from developing moral agency.

What are robots? This much is clear: that a robot uses sensors to detect aspects of the environment, software to reason about it, and actuators to interact with it. Sensors are needed to obtain information from the environment. Reactive behaviors (like the stretch reflex in humans) do not require any deep cognitive ability, but on-board intelligence is necessary if the robot is to perform significant tasks autonomously, and actuation is needed to enable the robot to exert forces upon the environment (Bekey 2005). Beyond these truisms, however, there is a lot of disagreement about how to characterize robots.

For this paper, we stick to the general definition of a robot in terms of sensors, on-board intelligence, and actuators. This definition excludes virtual or software robots (so-called 'software bots'). Fully remote-controlled machines are also not

Lisa Benossi, Stanford University
Sven Bernecker, University of Cologne & University of California, Irvine

robots because they do not think for themselves. The way we use the term, a robot must think and decide for itself. Thus, conventional landmines and calculators are not robots. A robot thinks in the sense that it can process information from sensors and internal set of rules (either programmed or learned) to make some decisions autonomously. A robot decides for itself if it has the capacity to operate in a specific environment for some time without any form of external control.

We tend to picture robots as artifacts made of nuts and bolts such as driverless cars. Yet robots can also be constructed of organic material. Recently scientists have repurposed living frog cells and assembled them into so-called *xenobots*, which can move toward a target and heal themselves after being cut. These novel living machines are neither traditional robots nor any known species of animal. They are living yet programmable organisms (Wu 2020).

A necessary feature of robots – living and inanimate – is intelligence. Given that robots are artifacts, the intelligence in question is artificial intelligence (AI). It is common to distinguish two kinds of AI – strong and weak. Weak AI is goal-oriented, designed to perform singular tasks and is intelligent at completing the specific task it is programmed to do. Examples of weak AI are Siri by Apple, drone robots, and driverless cars. For a system to exhibit strong AI, by contrast, it must act like a brain. Rather than classifying things according to set rubrics, it uses clustering and association to process data. Strong AI solves not only specific tasks but also mimics human intelligence and behavior, with the ability to learn and apply the intelligence to solve a wide range of problems. It is generally assumed that strong AI includes consciousness, autonomy, reason, knowledge representation, the ability to sense, to plan, to learn and to generalize, and the ability to communicate in natural language (Russell & Norvig 2016, pp. 1–3, 1020–40, 1044–6). Since strong AI can think, understand, and act in a way that is indistinguishable from that of a human in any given situation, it would pass the Turing Test with flying colors. The reason we use the subjective mood is that strong AI does not currently exist.

Instead of arguing for the possibility of strong AI, we assume the possibility of robots with strong AI ('robots' for short) and explore three follow-up issues. First, could a robot qualify as a *moral agent* in the sense of being an intelligent being who can self-consciously choose its own life goals, rather than serving as a mere means to the ends of others? Second, given that robots could qualify as moral agents or present some features necessary for morality, do we have an obligation to work towards developing such robots? In other words, do we have an obligation to help robots achieve full moral personality? Third, given that we are not obligated to create robots who are moral persons, are there no limits on what we can do to robots? When and to what extent is it permissible to exploit robots?

The significance of these issues is obvious. If, with our help, robots can evolve into moral agents, humans must decide whether they should allow this to happen. If robots are persons, they presumably have the same rights and duties we have. And if robots have the same rights as we, we can no longer assign them jobs that are so dull, dirty, and dangerous that no human wants to do them. By helping robots reach personhood, we increase their capabilities but, at the same time, decrease their usability because it is immoral to exploit persons. The more capabilities robots have, the less useful they are, and *vice versa*. We could try to circumvent this dilemma by keeping robots at a stage of development below personhood. We could prohibit the development of robots with strong AI. However, this strategy gives rise to further moral qualms: is it morally permissible to not help or actively prevent robots from developing their full potential?

Kant's moral philosophy provides criteria for moral agency and personhood whereby it is very unlikely that robots will ever qualify as moral agents. On Kant's view, moral personality ultimately requires access to the moral law and an autonomous will. For a robot to be a moral agent it would not only have to be able to decide freely and to act in a way that looks moral, but its practical reason would have to be autonomous. The robot would have to govern itself. Moreover, Kant's practical philosophy offers a criterion for deciding whether it is permissible to prevent a robot from becoming a moral person. The moral permissibility of an action, on Kant's view, depends on whether the maxim in question may be willed to be a universal law, and on whether we respect rationality and rational nature.

Section 2 explains why it is generally thought that robots are unable to develop moral agency. Section 3 lays out Kant's conception of moral agency and argues that, given this conception, it is highly unlikely that robots can become moral agents. Sections 4 asks whether and why it would be desirable to have robots that are moral agents. Suppose it is not to our advantage that robots become moral agents: is it permissible to prevent them from developing moral agency? Section 5 discusses this question from a Kantian perspective. Section 6 contains some concluding remarks.

2 Robots and Moral Agency

The two standard objections to attributing full-fledged moral agency to a robot with strong AI is that it lacks two key components required for morally relevant decision making – an emotional 'inner' life and freedom of will. Let us look at these objections in turn.

The Aristotelian tradition has it that humans have two distinct kinds of decision-making systems – an instinctual (irrational) and a cognitive (rational) system. The instinctual decision-making system is emotionally laden and is shared with higher mammals. It is part of cognitive system S1, which is fast, intuitive, and mostly unconscious. By and large, people are not considered (fully) morally responsible for actions performed based on the instinctual system. While much of human activity is due to the instinctual system, we can also form decisions based on conscious reasoning. The cognitive system, which is part of type 2 thinking, enables us to imagine different possible futures and choose a course of action based on our values and the likely outcome of the action under consideration. Moral agency is usually reserved for actions due to the cognitive system. Higher mammals and human non-agents such as babies and severely cognitively disabled are not held morally responsible for their action precisely because their decisions to act are not the result of the cognitive deliberative system.

Some deny robots moral agency because robots lack an emotional inner life needed for decision-making. This is a dubious move for two related reasons. First, for someone to be morally responsible for their actions, that person needs a functioning deliberative decision-making system. Yet if robots are unlike us, it is presumably because they lack our instinctual system, not because they lack something akin to a cognitive deliberative decision-making system. Hence, this difference between humans and robots does not seem to affect the possibility of moral agency. Second, human agents with a dysfunctional or missing emotional inner life (such as psychopaths) may still be morally (and legally) responsible for their actions,[1] while those who have normal emotional responses but cannot rationally deliberate (such as babies and the mentally disabled) may not.

Another standard reason to deny robots moral agency does not have to do with their lack of emotions but with their lack of free will, that is, the ability to choose to do otherwise in similar circumstances. The idea is that robots are not free because their choices are the result of a deterministic algorithm.

A lot of ink has been spilled on the question of whether causal determinism is compatible with free will. Compatibilists argue that free choices may be caused by a metaphysical (but not physical) chain of events. Kant is often understood as a compatibilist of sorts, since he distinguished between the law of

---

[1] Scanlon (1998, pp. 287–290) and Talbert (2014) argue that agents who are fully impaired for moral understanding are still open to blame as long as they possess broader rational competencies.

causality in the phenomenal world and the law of freedom in the noumenal world. It might be interesting to notice that Kant employs stern expressions to describe compatibilism, such as "wretched subterfuge" and "petty word jugglery" (KpV, AA 05:96). However, in these passages, by compatibilism Kant understands the claim that moral actions can be free in a deterministic world insofar as they come from within us, rather than being forced externally. Hence, it seems that Kant is right that this proposal does not suffice to explain how causality and freedom can coexist. In any case, he does clearly take moral agency to require freedom of the will. Hence, in what follows, we will consider the related questions of whether robots can be moral agents and whether robots can have a free will.

Harry Frankfurt (1969) developed counterexamples to the principle of alternate possibilities, which holds that an agent is morally responsible for an action only if that person could have done otherwise. Consider the following Frankfurt-style case. Black wants Jones to kill Smith. Black has set up a device for manipulating Jones's brain processes, so that Black can determine that Jones chooses to kill Smith. Black only interferes with Jones's decision process when Black is unhappy with the way Jones is about to decide. Suppose that Jones decides on his own to kill Smith and does kill Smith. Jones has no alternative but to do what Black wanted him to do; whether he does it of his own accord or because of Black's intervention, he would kill Smith.

Many philosophers maintain that Jones is responsible for the killing of Smith. Yet it also seems to be the case that Jones could not have avoided killing Smith. When Jones kills Smith on his own, he is morally responsible. His responsibility is not affected by Black's lurking in the background ready to interfere, since that interference does not come into play. Jones is morally responsible for what he did, but he could not do otherwise. The upshot for our purposes is that even if robots are not free, they could still be morally responsible. And according to Kant, moral agency depends on whether we regard an agent responsible for their action.

3 Kant on Robots and Moral Agency

Famously, Kant's moral philosophy is an example of logocentrism, insofar as it pivots around rational beings and rationality. For instance, moral concepts and moral laws are necessary and a priori (GMS, AA 04:408), and because of this they are said to be valid for all rational beings. Kant takes the realization that moral concepts must be valid for all rational being to be a great innovation in moral theorizing. Previous attempts at morality failed because they were grounded either on empirical considerations, or on the general concept of will. In contrast, he bases morality on the concept of a pure will, which is common to all rational beings (GMS, AA 04:390, 4:407). Moreover, moral concepts derive from the concept of rational being itself (GMS, AA 04:412).[2] What are rational beings, and how do moral precepts rely on their rationality? In the simplest terms, rational beings are beings endowed with practical reason and a capacity for willing that is determined by practical reason itself. On Kant's view, humans constitute a special kind of rational beings, insofar as their will is influenced both by practical reason and by sensible desires and inclinations. Hence, for humans the precepts of practical reason can be in tension with sensible inclinations. Therefore, the moral law necessitates us and becomes imperative. Other rational beings, such as God and angels, are divine or holy wills who are already in complete conformity with the moral law (GMS, AA 04:414). A way to illustrate the difference between human and holy will is the following. To act morally, we must act from duty rather than in mere conformity with duty. For humans, we can never be certain that our volitions are from duty, because we might have been influenced by our inclinations such as self-love (GMS, AA 04:406). In contrast, the concepts of duty do not apply to God's will, which is necessarily and without exception in agreement with the moral law (GMS, AA 04:414).

Kant's moral theory is centered around rational beings, but his actual exposition of moral duties and rights in the *Metaphysics of Morals* (MS) focuses on human beings. In particular, Kant seems to endorse a distinction between direct and indirect duties. The former duties apply only to the relations between human beings, either as duties to ourselves or as duties to other human beings. What sets relationships among humans apart from relationships to other creatures is that they contain both direct rights and direct duties (MS, AA 06:442). Moreover, there are certain duties, such as the duty to avoid deliberate destruction of what is beautiful in nature and the duty to avoid unnecessary violence towards animals (MS, AA 06:443), which appear to be duties to non-rational and non-human beings. However, Kant's view is that these duties are indirect: they are duties towards ourselves, which concern non-rational and non-human beings. Hence, it seems that we ultimately only have direct duties to respect the

---

2 According to the GMS, AA (04:412), rational beings are characterized by the capacity to act in accordance with the representations of laws. In the *Groundwork*, practical reason as the faculty to derive actions from laws is equated with the will. In the MS, however, Kant distinguishes the will in a strict sense, which has no determining ground, from the will insofar as it can determine choice. The latter is again identified with practical reason itself (06:213).

humanity in ourselves and in other humans. This idea is based on the fact that only humans, as rational beings, partake in moral legislation and yet are objects of possible experience.

With regard to non-rational beings such as non-human animals and nature, we have duties towards ourselves to respect them for our sake, not for their own.[3] The reason we should avoid the destruction of what is beautiful in nature is that this would weaken our ability to love something regardless of our own aims and interests (MS, AA 06:443). And the reason we should not treat non-rational animals cruelly is that we might grow tolerant to suffering by fellow humans (MS, AA 06:443). With regards to rational beings who are perfectly in agreement with the moral law, we do not have duties towards them because they are not objects of our possible experience (MS, AA 06:242, 06:444). God is the supreme head of moral legislation, yet insofar as God is not an object of experience, God is not a subject of duties nor rights (GMS, AA 04:433). However, we still ought to believe in God as a practical duty to ourselves.

Let us suppose for a moment that robots might be rational beings, namely, beings endowed with practical reason and with a will that can be determined by practical reason. Could robots be an example of a holy will, so that their volitions are in automatic agreement with the precepts of practical reason? It seems dubious for two reasons. First, such rational beings such as God and angels are said not to be objects of our possible experience. Robots, however, are perceivable by us. Nonetheless, it could be an accidental fact that Gods and angels fall under both categories of holy or divine will and of beings who cannot be objects of possible experience for us. Second, and most relevant, even though robots lack a system 1, there is a sense in which they display instinct-like behavior. It is conceivable, and much a pressing problem in current discussion on self-driving cars, that robots can display a conflict between the precepts of practical reason, such as to protect the life of humans, and other lower-level rules, such as to optimize comfort or the like. In what follows, we argue that if robots can be moral agents, they must be akin to human beings. This entails that, if they can be moral agents, they must be receptive to the concepts of duty. We shall argue that robots cannot count as rational beings, for they lack autonomy.

---

3 Taken together the claim that we only have direct duties to human beings and the claim that we ought to respect nature and non-human animals for our sake constitute the so called 'indirect view'. Korsgaard notices that these two elements of Kant's view do not have to be paired together. For instance, we might only have duties to other humans but value nature and animals for their own sake (Korsgaard 2018, p. 116).

In the introduction to the *Metaphysics of Morals*, Kant offers a preliminary definition of a moral agent or person as someone to whom actions can be imputed (MS, AA 06:223), who can be regarded as the author (*causa libera*) of an action (06:227).[4] This seems to mirror the commonsense idea that a person's action can only be morally wrong if the person is in control of the action (see Rohlf, 2020). Moral personality requires the ability to act in accordance with the general law, or the will (MS, AA 06:224; GMS, AA 04:412). For rational beings, this boils down to two features: first, "the freedom of a rational being [consists in being] under moral laws" (MS, AA 06:223) and second, a person is subject only to the laws they give themselves (MS, AA 06:223).[5] Let us consider these two features in turn.

Human and non-human animals alike have the capacity to bring about the objects of their representations and desire (MS, AA 06:211). Animal choices (*arbitrium brutum*), however, are completely determined by sensible inclinations and impulses (MS, AA 06:213; 27:344) while human choices can be affected by inclinations without being fully determined by them. A human's choice is free to the extent that it is determined by pure reason (MS, AA 06:213). Famously, in the G and in the KpV, Kant refers to the will itself as free, while in the MS he introduces the notion of 'free choice' (*Willkür*). According to the MS then, the will is strictly speaking neither free nor constrained, it 'has no determining ground' (MS, AA 06:213). Regardless of the slightly different conceptions of free will in Kant's moral opus, the will is characterized as "the faculty to act in accordance with the representation of laws, i.e., in accordance with principles" (GMS, AA 04:412, 04:427; see MS, AA 06:213). In simple terms, the will is a causal power, found in

---

4 This preliminary definition of moral agency should not be given excessive weight, since it is unclear how it would apply to holy wills and God. Nonetheless, it is useful as a first approach to Kant's conception of moral agency for human beings.

5 Personality is one of the three predispositions of human nature. Kant distinguishes, within humans themselves, between our animal nature, our human nature, and our personality. Animality includes our natural desires and sensible impulses. Humanity is the capacity to set arbitrary ends. Personality is the rational capacity to give laws and obey them (06:26, 7:321–324). As Wood (1998, p. 189) rightly notices, humanity is composed of the technical ability to set arbitrary ends for ourselves, and of the practical tendency to harmonize our ends into a whole, called happiness. This element becomes crucial when we consider the content of duties to ourselves and to other humans presented in the *Metaphysics of Morals*. For instance, we have a duty towards the happiness of others. In understanding this duty, we must remember both that humans are rational beings, and value their rationality, but also that their humanity generates the need for happiness. Arguably, other rational beings such as a holy will do not have such needs.

rational beings, to direct their choice of ends by principles or judgments about what is good (Gregor, Introduction to Critique of Practical Reason, p. xvi).

Prima facie, it might seem that the definition of the will as the ability to act in accordance with the representation of laws can easily apply to robots. After all, a straightforward manner to describe robot behavior is to claim that they act based on rules, be it programmed or learned ones. Yet it is implausible that robots act based on their *representations* of laws or rules rather than simply following these rules blindly. Likewise, non-human animals act based on rules given to them by their instincts and desires, but they lack practical reason, which is the source of laws. In what follows, we spell out what it means to act with or without practical reason in the context of Kant's conception of morality.

To understand Kant's conception of free choice it is helpful to recapitulate his notion of freedom. On one hand, Kant spells out the positive conception of freedom in terms of "the ability of pure reason to be of itself practical" (MS, AA 06:214) or in terms of "the internal lawgiving of reason" (MS, AA 06:227). On the other hand, the negative conception of freedom as the ability to act without any external cause requires that we are *transcendentally* free. Transcendental freedom is, negatively spoken, the ability to act without being determined by external causes and natural laws, such as causality (KpV, AA 05:29). This seems to be a condition of practical freedom, understood as autonomy (see Düsing 1993, cf. KpV, AA 05:29). Famously, in G III, Kant attempts to ground morality in freedom. Later, in the KpV, Kant returned to the relationship between morality and freedom.[6] In the KpV, he argues that freedom is the *ratio essendi* of the moral law, but we only learn about our freedom because of the moral law (KpV, AA 05:6 n). He claims that our moral experience as constrained by the moral law is a "fact of reason", because it cannot be derived from other data of our reason, such as the consciousness of our freedom (KpV, AA 05:31).[7]

Regardless of whether the moral law affords our practical freedom or *vice versa*, freedom is an essential ingredient of Kant's conception of morality. In KpV, Kant goes as far as to claim that without our freedom, understood as the autonomy of the will, we would be like automata or robots (KpV, AA 05:101). If

---

6 Whether and how the view about freedom and morality expound in the *Groundwork* differs from the view expressed in the *Critique of Practical Reason* is matter of controversy. Schönecker (1999) defends the view that Kant did change his mind between the two works. By contrast, Allison (2011, p. 297, n. 41) submits that there is no "radical chang[e] in Kant's conception of freedom". Recently, Puls (2016) also argued for the view that there is a substantial agreement between G III and KpV.

7 There is much debate on how the 'fact of reason' talk should be understood, see, for instance, Lueck (2009), Kleingeld (2010), Schönecker (2013), and Ware (2014).

we were not actually free in this sense, even our consciousness of our spontaneity would be an illusion. For even if our cognitive mechanism might seem internal and self-caused, ultimately there would be "an alien hand" directing all our actions. This remark highlights the priority that we are in fact autonomous over our consciousness of this autonomy.

Kant explains our practical freedom in terms of the autonomy of our practical reason (KpV, AA 05:31; MS, AA 06:227).[8] Practical reason is the same thing as the broad conception of the will. To say that practical reason is autonomous means that humans are bound only by laws that they give to themselves (GMS, AA 04:432). In other words, every rational being must regard themselves as giving universal laws through the maxims of their will (GMS, AA 04:432). The importance of the concept of autonomy in Kant's practical philosophy cannot be overstated. Autonomy explains not only freedom but also the intrinsic dignity of human beings. Everyone agrees that autonomy plays a central role in Kant's practical philosophy but there is disagreement on what it exactly means for our reason to be law giving.[9]

In this paper, we rely on the conception of autonomy defended by Kleingeld and Willaschek (2019). They argue that our reason is autonomous not in the sense that it gives itself the moral law (CI), on which all specific moral laws are based, but in the sense that we are the source of the binding force of the moral law. We are lawgivers to ourselves insofar as we make the law valid for us. In what follows, we investigate whether robots could count as moral agents under such a conception of autonomy. Notice that if a subject, be it human or robot, cannot be autonomous in the sense of providing normative force for the moral law, then it cannot count as autonomous in the strong sense of contributing to giving the moral law. There is no relevant sense according to which robots can

---

8 The notion of autonomy employed by Kant differs substantially from the notion of autonomy employed in AI, and as introduced in section 1. In AI, a robot is considered autonomous when it is not completely dependent on its prior knowledge, but it is able to integrate the information from its own percepts. Towards this aim, it is essential that knowledge-based robots can learn from their own percepts (Russell & Norvig, 2016, p. 39, p. 236). Furthermore, the notion of 'preference autonomy' introduced in section 5 also differs from autonomy both in the Kantian sense and in AI. Preference autonomy consists in the ability of human and non-human animals to have preferences based on their needs and impulses and to initiate actions (see Wood 1998, p. 200; Regan 2004, pp. 84–6).

9 Reath (1994) famously offered an analysis of autonomy in analogy to the political case: a state is free insofar as the laws that bound citizens are the result of their action, e.g., through voting. For the constructivist reading see Rawls (1980), Korsgaard (1996), O'Neill (2003), and Engstrom (2009). For the realist tradition, see Ameriks (2003), Wood (1999), Langton (2007), Kain (2004). See also Sensen (2012), and Bacin & Sensen (2018).

be understood as giving to themselves the moral law, because regardless of whether it is hard-wired or generated though empirical learning, it would still ultimately come from an "alien hand" (KpV, AA 05:101). Nonetheless, even according to the conception of autonomy as the source of the binding force of the law, robots cannot possibly count as autonomous, for they seem unable to make the moral law valid for themselves. Therefore, it is impossible to consider robots as rational agents.

If, as we suggest, robots must be considered rational beings akin to humans, in that their will can be in contrast with the precepts of practical reasons, robots would have to satisfy further requirements to qualify as rational agents. The conditions of morality mentioned so far apply to humans qua rational beings. Kant, however, also presents us with a list of moral feelings which are grounded on the concept of duty (MS, AA 06:399). In the *Metaphysics of Morals*, the feeling of respect, which is already discussed in the Groundwork and in the Critique of Practical Reason (in the section on the incentives of pure practical reason) is expanded to four feelings: *moral feeling, conscience, love of one's neighbor,* and *respect for one-self (self-esteem)*. In general, moral feelings are characterized by the fact that they precede neither the desire nor the representation of the law. By contrast, pleasures arising from inclinations can precede the desire and the maxim. They are characterized in terms of the "aesthetic receptivity to the concepts of duty (respect)" (MS, AA 06:399). These feelings are further characterized as the "subjective predispositions of the mind for being affected by the concepts of duty" (MS, AA 06:399). Kant argues forcefully that there can be no duty to have them, but only a duty to cultivate them. Indeed, these feelings make us aware of the obligations contained in the moral law.[10] In other words, we could say that these feelings constitute the way morality can have an effect on us; sensible beings like us who tend to deviate from the commands of the moral law.

Let us briefly see how these four feelings can nudge us in the direction of the moral law. *Moral feeling* is the feeling of pleasure or displeasure that depends on our consciousness that our actions agree or disagree with the moral law (MS, AA 06:399). *Conscience* is characterized through the metaphor of an "inner court" (MS, AA 06:438). Practical reason judges and condemns our actions, providing objective rules for our conduct. But it is the faculty of judgment that submits the specific judgments that are relevant for conscience. These are subjective judgments, concerning not what is objectively our duty but rather

---

10 Dieter Schönecker (2018a) suggests that these feelings play an important role in our knowledge of the moral law.

whether a maxim leading to action has been submitted to practical reason. Hence, within the judicial metaphor of an inner court, Kant attributes the role of the prosecutor to practical reason itself. By contrast, conscience is our attentiveness to the voice of this inner judge (MS, AA 06:401) or the consciousness of this inner court (MS, AA 06: 438). In other words, conscience is a natural predisposition on the side of feeling that allows us to listen to the verdicts of this inner court, and hence it allows us to judge whether our actions conform to our duties or not, causing remorse or rejoicing (MS, AA 06:440). Moreover, through this process, it becomes possible for us to attribute actions to ourselves (MS, AA 06:838–9). *Love of one's neighbor* is the third moral feeling presented in the *Metaphysics of Morals*. It is related to the duty to be benevolent towards other in the sense of directly helping them with their material well-being and indirectly helping them with their moral well-being (06:393–94). Kant clarifies that the benevolence ought not be based in practical love for our neighbors. If we acted in this manner, we would be acting merely on the basis of inclinations and might stop helping others as soon as we are not inclined to it anymore. Love is characterized in terms of *amor complacientiae*, which appears to be an immediate delight that results from our striving for moral perfection.[11] It is natural to suppose that such love requires some sense of social membership (see also Bauer 2018; Jaarsma et al. 2012; Williamson 2009). Finally, *respect for oneself (or self-esteem)* is a feeling towards oneself that aids our duty to respect the humanity in ourselves.[12] Just as respect was in the Groundwork, the sensible criteria for morality are merely the effects of the moral law on us.

Prima facie, it might seem that Kant's sensible criteria are equivalent to requiring robots to have an inner emotional life discussed in section 2. Yet notice that a crucial element of Kant's account is that the sensible criteria are the way the moral law and the concept of duty bind us. Hence, if robots can be in disagreement with practical reason, they too must have some way for the moral law to bind them and to produce its effects on them as subjects to the law.[13]

To probe whether robots could count as Kantian moral agents, we introduced the crucial features of Kant's theory of morality. Moreover, we proceeded

---

[11] Love of one's neighbor is often interpreted in terms of benevolence. Contra this general trend and for a more comprehensive account of love as *amor complacientiae* see Schönecker (2010).

[12] Cf. GMS, AA 04:401 n, where respect is characterized as follows: "What I immediately recognize as a law for me, I recognize with respect, which signifies merely the consciousness of the *subjection* of my will to a law without any mediation of other influences on my sense. The immediate determination of the will through the law and the consciousness of it is called *respect*, so that the latter is to be regarded as the *effect* of the law on the subject and not as its *cause*."

[13] For a similar point, see Schönecker (2018b).

by considering the two possible ways in which robots could qualify as rational agents. Either they are holy wills, and in such case, they would lack autonomy and a free will; or they are akin to human wills, and in such case, they lack autonomy, free will, and the sensible criteria for morality. In either case, robots cannot qualify as moral agents in the Kantian sense. We have no idea what it would take to build a robot that would meet Kant's condition of moral agency.

4 The Desirability of Moral Robots

In the previous section we saw that, given the Kantian perspective, the prospects of robots ever qualifying as moral agents are bleak. For the moment, however, let us bracket the improbability of robots ever becoming moral agents and let us instead ask whether we should want to create robots with moral agency. Would it be desirable to have moral robots?

There are at least three considerations in favor of there being moral robots (Danaher 2019). First, robots with moral agency would become more socially useful and integrated in our lives than robots without moral agency. Robots with moral agency could, for instance, be deployed as nurses for patients with highly infectious diseases and space explorations. Second, in some areas (e.g., medical care, military, autonomous vehicles) it would be irresponsible to deploy robots unless they have some form of moral agency. Third, since robots are less ambiguous in their moral judgment and less fickle and erratic in their moral sentiments, they can help us in our own moral decision making. For example, when making decisions about distributive and criminal justice, we tend to be bogged down by the multitude of moral variables and interests at play, and we tend to struggle to balance those interests effectively when making decisions. Because of their greater simplicity and stricter rule following, robots might help us cut through the moral noise. Robot-aided moral decisions could be faster, more consistent, fairer, and ultimately safer (e.g., in the case of driverless vehicles). Another place where robots could prove useful is jury service. It is usually difficult to find impartial jurors for high-profile trials. This is where an impartial yet morally competent juror in the form of a robot would very useful.

On the other side, there are also good reasons to not want robots to develop moral agency. For starters, by allowing robots to acquire moral agency we would rob ourselves of the possibility to exploit them. As was mentioned in the introduction, robots are currently being used to perform jobs that that are so dull, dirty, and dangerous that no human wants to do them. If robots became moral agents, they would have the same rights as us, and hence the way they are used would have to change.

Another reason to not want robots to develop moral agency is that the scenarios in which we have the greatest need for competent ethical agents are ones that involve moral ambiguity and the call for contextual understanding. Ambiguous situations are ones in which judgment is required and there is not a single correct answer. A prime example of an ambiguous situation is a battlefield. We probably do not want to give moral robots the power to make autonomous decisions about killing people. But even in less serious contexts, a moral robot could cause harm by not fully understanding the complexity of the situation. Sharkey gives the example of a bar-tending robot, which serves the adult customers as much alcohol as they want. She writes:

> But how could a robot make appropriate decisions about when to praise a child, or when to restrict his or her activities, without a moral understanding? Similarly, how could a robot provide good care for an older person without an understanding of their needs, and of the effects of its actions? Even a bar-tending robot might be placed in a situation in which decisions have to be made about who should or should not be served, and what is and is not acceptable behavior. (Sharkey 2020, p. 293)

5 Kant on the Permissibility of Preventing Robots from Becoming Moral Agents

If robots became moral agents, we would have clear moral duties to robots, and they would have the same rights as we, or at the very least, some minimal rights such as the right to their 'life.'[14] If we were still allowed to employ their labor, we would have to treat them also as ends and not merely as means. In section 3, we saw that Kant's notion of moral personality is not applicable to robots. This is a welcome result, for if robots had moral personality, they would have rights and duties to themselves. Consequently, we could not make them sacrifice themselves to protect human lives in critical situations. This, however, is one of the crucial features of the human-robot interaction.

In what follows we address two pressing questions about robots and their development. First, we must understand whether we are morally allowed to prevent robots to ever achieve moral personality. This question leads us into uncharted territory since, to the best of our knowledge, Kant did not explicitly

---

14 On Kant's technical notion of life, see 6:211.

address the question of whether we may prevent a being that might have practical reason, or some preconditions for rationality, from achieving full moral personality. Moreover, this question is entirely hypothetical. In section 3, we established that according to Kant's conception of moral agents, robots do not qualify as moral agents. We now consider whether it is conceivable that they might become moral persons, or at least participate in some parts of our rational nature. *Prima facie* the question of whether it is permissible to prevent robots from achieving moral personality is analogous to the question of whether it is morally allowed to prevent a child or a person with cognitive deficiencies from achieving full moral personality. The characterization of rational beings in section 3 entails that being endowed with the faculty of practical reason is a *conditio sine qua non* for moral personality. Yet we also saw how on Kant's view, much more than the mere potential to be rational is required to be a moral agent. Some Kant scholars even argue that, given Kant's criteria, children and people with cognitive deficiencies and impairments do not qualify as full moral persons (Regan 2004; Wood 1998; Merkel 2002; Nida-Rümelin 2002; see also Kain 2009). This view resonates with our intuition that such agents should not be blamed for their amoral actions. However, Kant seems committed to the idea that we ought to allow children and cognitively impaired persons to achieve their full rationality and hence their moral agency. Or, at the very least, Kant claims that we have the wide, imperfect duty not to interfere with the moral development of other human beings. For instance, this wide, imperfect duty can take the form of ensuring that their material conditions do not corrupt their moral status (MS, AA 06:394).[15] Moreover, the appendix to the MS, where Kant presents his views on teaching ethics, suggests clearly that virtue "can and must be taught" (MS, AA 06:477). Wood (1998, p.198) even suggests that, given the fragility of children and the cognitively impaired, the respect of rational

---

15 Kant's phrasing at MS, AA 06:394 is quite infelicitous for the case under consideration, for he writes: "[I]t is my duty to refrain from doing anything that, considering the nature of men, could tempt him to do something for which his conscience could afterward pain him, to refrain from what is called giving scandal". In the case of human beings who have not yet fully developed their rational ability and their moral agency, such as children, it is plausible to assume that children cannot yet feel with full force the sensible effects of our consciousness of our duties and hence feel pain in their conscience. Nonetheless, this is but an apparent problem: first, children presumably do feel already some form of remorse for their actions; second, they can or potentially could achieve full moral standing, and hence feel remorse over their actions. The second point applies even to humans who might never achieve full moral standing and full rationality again, because their potential rationality if fully actualized would cause them to feel remorse, hence they are potentially subject to remorse.

nature required of us might even dictate that we protect them and give priority to their development.

Under a strict interpretation of what counts as rational being, wherein only beings with full and actual practical reason are rational, it is clear that robots cannot become moral persons and hence the question of whether we ought to allow their moral development does not arise. In recent years, Kant scholars have argued that Kant's moral system requires an extension to include and satisfactorily explain our duties not only to children and cognitively impaired humans, but also with regard to non-human animals and nature (Wood 1998; Korsgaard 2018). These interpretations revise Kant's notion of rationality to show that a coherent understanding of Kant's system requires some form of rationality to be shared by all these categories.

Wood (1998) develops an account of 'potential rationality' or of the 'infrastructure of rationality'. He argues that Kant appears to subscribe to the personification principle: according to the second formulation of the moral law, the formula of humanity (FH), we ought to respect the rational nature that is personified in ourselves or in others.[16] Wood suggests that a coherent account of Kant's ethics requires rejecting the personification principle and understanding the FH in terms of respect of rational nature itself. Moreover, he claims that Kant's commitments to the fair treatment of animals presuppose an analogy between the rationality we encounter in human beings and the 'infrastructure of rationality' that we encounter in non-human animals. On his picture, moral considerations concern not only those who are fully rational, but also all those who potentially have a rational nature. The concept of potential rationality includes individuals who virtually have rationality, or had it in the past, as well as those who have parts of rational nature or its necessary conditions (Wood 1998, p. 200–1). Children, cognitively deficient people, and animals are therefore worthy

---

16 Kant famously offers three main formulations of the moral law in the *Groundwork*, and two of these formulations have variants (see also Schönecker & Wood, 2015, pp. 122–172). The first formulation, called Formula of Universal Law (FUL), is as follows: "Act only in accordance with that maxim through which you can at the same time will that it become a universal law" (GMS, AA 04:421). The third formulation, called Formula of Humanity (FH), claims "Act so that you use humanity, as much in your own person as in the person of every other, always at the same time as end and never merely as means" (GMS, AA 04:429). The third formulation, called Formula of Autonomy, prescribes "the idea of the will of every rational being as a will giving universal law" (GMS, AA 04:431). These three formulations, with their variants, are supposed to be theoretically equivalent: they all express the moral law under different aspects. Nonetheless, they are not practically equivalent. For instance, in the *Metaphysics of Morals* which presents the content of Kant's ethics rather than merely its foundation, FH has clear priority (see Kant 1999, introduction by A. Wood, pp. xxxi–ii).

of moral considerations. Wood (1998, p. 200) and Regan (2004, pp. 84–6) argue that animals have 'preference autonomy' because they have preferences and the ability to initiate action. Wood presents preference autonomy as the necessary precondition for moral autonomy and as a fundamental constituent of our rational nature. In other words, on this account, animals have the necessary 'infrastructure of rationality'. When we are unnecessarily violent towards animals, we are disrespecting the part of rational nature which we share with animals. This part of our rational nature seems to coincide with our animality, the capacity to act based on natural impulses and desires. Therefore, both rationally imperfect humans, non-human animals have rights.

Korsgaard (2018) similarly suggests that Kant's account of duties to animals presupposes that humans and non-human animals are analogous in a relevant aspect. Korsgaard argues that we can distinguish two senses of the expression 'ends in themselves'. On one hand, human beings are ends in themselves because they can give force of law to their claims and practical judgments, by partaking in moral legislation. On the other hand, human beings are ends in themselves understood as the source of legitimate normative claims– claims that must be recognized by all rational agents. It is under the latter conception of ends in themselves that animals are ends in themselves just as much as we are. According to Korsgaard's view, animals constitute the things for which things are good or bad. We share this feature of animality, and it is morally required of us to respect this status both in humans (MS, AA 06:420 and ff., 06:452), and in non-human animals.

Wood and Korsgaard's accounts are much more inclusive than the standard account. The upshot of these accounts is that animals are appropriate objects of moral considerations, even if the duties regarding animal welfare remain duties to us. Our feelings of gratitude towards animals that served us are appropriate only because animals are analogous to us, i.e., they share something which we ought to respect in other humans. Nonetheless, even according to these liberal interpretations of Kant's conception of the recipients of moral rights, we would have no duty to allow the moral and rational development of robots. First, notice that even according to Korsgaard we should not have any duty to the moral development of animals. After all, we share with them the sense of ends in themselves according to which ends in themselves are the source of normative claims. Animals do not partake in moral legislation, and they can never participate in moral legislation. Second, rationally imperfect humans clearly have practical reason either potentially or virtually as well as the necessary preconditions of practical reason. On Wood's view, animals display the 'infrastructure of rationality' and hence they deserve our respect. Robots, however, lack all constitutive elements of practical rationality: they are not potentially or virtually endowed with practical reason, nor do they display the preference autonomy of animals. Robots seem to fall short even of our animal nature. Robots do not exhibit pain, desires, and natural impulses in the same way human and non-human animals do. Preference autonomy might constitute a condition of moral personality (for humans) only insofar as sensible impulses in animals are not forced or programmed into animals. Robots are not the sorts of things for which things are valuable, good, or bad. Even if robots were able to display pain and desire-like behavior, it would still be as the direct or indirect result of our own programming. It would fail to constitute a part of rationality that robots have independent of us and that we share with them. Therefore, we do not owe robots the moral considerations that on Wood's and Korsgaard's view we owe to animals.

At this point, it is useful to bring Kant's universalizability test into the picture. An action is morally permissible if we can will it to become a universal law (GMS, AA 04:402, 04:421–3). We ought not to kill humans, because we cannot even imagine a world where killing becomes a universal law: there would be no human left. We ought to help others because we cannot will a world where nobody helped others. Perfect, narrow duties result from the impossibility to imagine a maxim from becoming a universal law. Imperfect, wide duties result from the failure to will the maxim in question to become a universal law (GMS, AA 04:421–5, see also MS, AA 06:390–4). We cannot prevent humans from developing their moral personality, because this would destroy humanity and its ability to act morally. Preventing a human from achieving moral personality would consist in a failure to respect the rational natural of this person, and it would amount to disrespecting our own greatest moral perfection, that is, the ability to act from duty (MS, AA 06:392). Yet we can both imagine and will a world where robots are prevented by us from achieving moral personality. Robots, as we argued, cannot become moral beings and it is legitimate for us not to want this to happen.

When Kant provides us with the full exposition of our duties, in the *Metaphysics of Morals*, he often relies on the formula of humanity rather than the formulation of universal law or law of nature. Hence, it might be useful to reframe our discussion on the basis of the formula of humanity: "act so that you use humanity, as much in your own person as in the person of every other, always at the same time as an end and never merely as means" (GMS, AA 04:429). The reason why it should be morally impermissible to stop a human from achieving moral personality is that this maxim violates the rights and value of humanity. We would be degrading our own rational nature. Similarly, preventing robots from achieving moral personality is morally permissible, insofar as our intention is consistent with the respect of human life and its rational nature.

Based on everything we argued so far, it might seem that Kantian ethics allows us to do whatever we please with robots. But this is not the case. Kant's ethical system can offer guidelines on a morally permissible usage of robots. Through the development of robots, we ought not to kill other humans, to respect humanity in us and in others, etc. *In nuce*, the system of duties Kant devised should regulate our experiments with robots.

Suppose that we decided to employ autonomous robots, in the sense described in section 1, in warfare to kill an enemy army or to decimate civilians. One obvious reason why this might seem preferable to wars conducted merely by humans is that killing persons often leads to traumatic consequences, post-traumatic stress disorder and other psychological conditions. Nonetheless, from a Kantian perspective such a path is contrary to morality, or so we suggest. By allowing an autonomous robot to extinguish life, the dignity of the human lives terminated by a robot is disregarded and disrespected. As Ulgen (2017) argues, such a scenario prioritizes a relative end, such as protecting a soldier from post-traumatic stress disorder, over the fundamental principle of humanity as an objective value. Hence, by devising robots killing humans we would violate the formula of humanity. Similarly, the usage of robots ought not to detriment or infringe the material well-being of other humans. If we decided to create robots that would render other humans unnecessary or reduce them to a condition of slavery, we would degrade the absolute value of humanity to mere means.

6 Conclusion

We have argued that Kant's conception of moral agency offers answers to some of the core questions of robot ethics. We have considered three such questions: might robots qualify as moral agents? Is it desirable that robots develop moral agency? Is it permissible to prevent robots from developing moral agency? From a Kantian standpoint, the prospects of robots with strong AI evolving into moral agents are bleak. But notwithstanding the low probability of robots ever becoming moral agents in the Kantian sense, there is the issue of whether this is desirable and, if not, whether it would be permissible to prevent robots from developing moral agency. We have argued that even on a liberal interpretation of Kant's metaphysics of morals, robots with strong AI are not appropriate objects of moral considerations for their own sake. It is morally permissible for us to prevent robots from achieving moral personality, insofar as they are neither rational agents in the practical sense nor share our animal nature. This does not mean, however, that Kantian ethics does not impose moral constraints on the development or use of robots. Our usage of robots is regulated by the duties we have to ourselves. Hence, in the development of robots with strong AI, we ought to bear in mind the respect of rational nature, both in our own person and in the person of others.[17]

References

All references to Kant's works are to *Kant's Gesammelte Schriften, Ausgabe der Preußischen Akademie der Wissenschaften* (Berlin: de Gruyter, 1902 ff.). The following abbreviations of individual works are used:

GMS   Grundlegung zur Metaphysik der Sitten/*Groundwork of the Metaphysics of Morals*
KpV   Kritik der praktischen Vernunft/*Critique of Practical Reason*
MS   Metaphysik der Sitten/*Metaphysics of Morals*

Abney, Keith (2012): "Robotics, Ethical Theory, and Metaethics: A Guide for the Perplexed". In: Patrick Lin/Keith Abney/George A. Bekey (Hrsg.): *Robot Ethics: The Ethical and Social Implications of Robotics*. Cambridge/MA: MIT Press, pp. 35–52.
Allison, Henry E. (2011): *Kant's Groundwork for the Metaphysics of Morals: A Commentary*. Oxford: Oxford University Press.
Ameriks, Karl (2003): "On Two Non-Realist Interpretations of Kant's Ethics". In: Karl Ameriks (Hrsg.): *Interpreting Kant's Critiques*. Oxford: Oxford University Press, pp. 263–283.
Bacin, Stefano/Sensen, Oliver (Hrsg.) (2018): *The Emergence of Autonomy in Kant's Moral Philosophy*. Cambridge: Cambridge University Press.
Bauer, Katharina (2018). Cognitive Self-Enhancement as a Duty to Oneself: A Kantian Perspective. *Southern Journal of Philosophy* 56. Nr. 1, pp. 36–58.
Bekey, George A. (2005): *Autonomous Robots*. Cambridge/MA: MIT Press.
Danaher, John (2019): "Should we create artificial moral agents? A Critical Analysis". https://philosophicaldisquisitions.blogspot.com/2019/09/should-we-create-artificial-moral.html, visited on 6.7.2021
Düsing, Klaus (1993): "Spontaneità e Libertà Nella Filosofia Pratica di Kant". In: *Studi Kantiani* 1993. Nr. 6, pp. 23–46.
Engstrom, Stephen P. (Hrsg.) (2009): *The Form of Practical Knowledge: A Study of the Categorical Imperative*. Cambridge/MA: Harvard University Press.

---

17 We are grateful to Andrew Kim and Dieter Schönecker for comments on a draft of this paper. Further thanks belong to the members of CONCEPT (the Cologne Center of Contemporary Epistemology and the Kantian Tradition) who took part in the Kant Reading Group for fruitful discussion of Kant's ethics. Sven Bernecker would like to acknowledge the financial support from an Alexander-von-Humboldt Professorship Award. Lisa Benossi would like to thank the Alexander von Humboldt Foundation for the generous support she received during her time in Cologne.

Frankfurt, Harry (1969): "Alternate Possibilities and Moral Responsibility". In: *Journal of Philosophy* 66. Nr. 23, pp. 829–839.

Jaarsma, Pier/Gelhaus, Petra/Welin, Stellan (2012): "Living the Categorical Imperative: Autistic Perspectives on Lying and truth Telling–between Kant and Care Ethics". In: *Medicine, Health Care and Philosophy 15*. Nr. 3, pp. 271–277.

Kain, Patrick (2004): "Self-legislation in Kant's Moral Philosophy". In: *Archiv für Geschichte der Philosophie 86*. Nr.3, pp. 257–306.

Kain, Patrick (2009): "Kant's Defense of Human Moral Status". In: *Journal of the History of Philosophy 47*. Nr.1, pp. 59–101.

Kant, Immanuel (1999): *Practical Philosophy*. Trans. and ed. Mary J. Gregor. Cambridge: Cambridge University Press.

Kant, Immanuel (2002): *Critique of Practical Reason*. Trans. by Werner S. Pluhar. Indianapolis: Hackett Publishing.

Kleingeld, Pauline (2010): "Moral Consciousness and the 'Fact of Reason'". In: Jens Timmerman/Andrew Reath (Hrsg.): *A Critical Guide to Kant's 'Critique of Practical Reason'*. Cambridge: Cambridge University Press, pp. 55–72.

Kleingeld, Pauline/Willaschek, Marcus (2019): "Autonomy without Paradox: Kant, Self-Legislation and the Moral Law". In: *Philosopher's Imprint 19*. Nr. 6, pp. 1–18.

Korsgaard, Christine M. (1996): *The Sources of Normativity*. Cambridge: Cambridge University Press.

Korsgaard, Christine M. (2018): *Fellow Creatures: Our Obligations to the Other Animals*. Oxford: Oxford University Press.

Langton, Rae (2007): "Objective and Unconditioned Value". In: *Philosophical Review 116*. Nr. 2, pp. 157–185.

Lueck, Bryan (2009): "Kant's Fact of Reason as Source of Normativity". In: *Inquiry 52*. Nr. 6, pp. 596–608.

Merkel, Reinhard (2002): „Rechte für Embryonen". In: Julian Nida-Rümelin (Hrsg.): *Ethische Essays*. Frankfurt: Suhrkamp, pp.427–239.

Nida-Rümelin, Julian (2002): „Humanismus ist nicht teilbar". In Julian Nida-Rümelin (Hrsg.): *Ethische Essays*. Frankfurt: Suhrkamp, pp. 463–469.

O'Neill, Onora (2003): "Autonomy: The Emperor's New Clothes". In: *Aristotelian Society Supplementary 77*. pp. 1–21.

Puls, Heiko (2016): *Sittliches Bewusstsein und kategorischer Imperativ in Kants ›Grundlegung‹: Ein Kommentar zum dritten Abschnitt*. Berlin: de Gruyter.

Rawls, John (1980): "Kantian Constructivism in Moral Theory". In: *Journal of Philosophy 77*. Nr. 9, pp. 515–572.

Regan, Donald (2002): "The Value of Rational Nature". In: *Ethics* 112. pp. 267–291.

Regan, Tom (2004): *The Case for Animal Rights*. Berkeley: University of California Press.

Reath, Andrews (1994): "Legislating the Moral Law". In: *Noûs* 28, Nr. 4, pp. 435–464.

Rohlf, M. (2020). Immanuel Kant, *The Stanford Encyclopedia of Philosophy*, Edward N. Zalta (Hrsg.), URL = <https://plato.stanford.edu/archives/spr2020/entries/kant/>.

Russell, Stuart J. and Norvig, Peter (2016): *Artificial Intelligence: A Modern Approach*. Upper Saddle River: Pearson.

Scanlon, Thomas M. (1998): *What We Owe to Each Other*. Cambridge/MA: Harvard University Press.

Schönecker, Dieter (1999): *Kant: Grundlegung III Die Deduktion des kategorischen Imperativs*. Freiburg: Karl Alber.

Schönecker, Dieter (2010): „Kant über Menschenliebe als moralische Gemütsanlage". In: *Archiv für Geschichte der Philosophie 92*. pp. 133–175.

Schönecker, Dieter (2013): „Das gefühlte Faktum der Vernunft. Skizze einer Interpretation und Verteidigung". In: *Deutsche Zeitschrift für Philosophie 61*. Nr.1, pp. 91–107.

Schönecker, Dieter (2018a): „Gemütsanlagen, moralische". In: In Larissa Berger/Elke E. Schmidt: *Kleines Kant-Lexikon*. Paderborn: Wilhelm Fink/UTB, pp. 156–7.

Schönecker, Dieter (2018b): "Can Practical Reason be Artificial?". In: *Journal of Artificial Intelligence Humanities*. Nr. 2, pp. 67–91.

Schönecker, Dieter/Wood, Allen W. (2015): *Immanuel Kant's Groundwork for the Metaphysics of Morals*. Cambridge/MA: Harvard University Press.

Sensen, Oliver (Hrsg.) (2012): *Kant on Moral Autonomy*. Cambridge: Cambridge University Press.

Sharkey, Amanda (2020): "Can we Program or Train Robots to be Good?". In: *Ethics and Information Technology 22*. pp. 283–295.

Talbert, Matthew (2014): "The Significance of Psychopathic Wrongdoing". In: Thomas Schramme (Hrsg.): *Being Amoral: Psychopathy and Moral Incapacity*. Cambridge, MA: MIT Press. pp. 275–300.

Ulgen, Ozlem (2017): "Kantian Ethics in the Age of Artificial Intelligence and Robotics". In: *Questions of International Law 43*. pp 59–83.

Ware, Owen (2014): "Rethinking Kant's Fact of Reason". In: *Philosopher's Imprint 14*. Nr. 32, pp. 1–21.

Warren, Mary Anne (1997): *Moral Status: Obligations to Persons and Other Living Things*. Oxford: Oxford University Press.

Williamson, Diane M. (2009): *Emotional Intelligence and Moral Theory: A Kantian Approach*. Dissertation, Vanderbilt University.

Wood, Allen W. (1998): "Kant on Duties Regarding Nonrational Nature". In: *Proceedings of the Aristotelian Society Suppl. 72*. pp. 189–210.

Wood, Allen W. (1999): *Kant's Ethical Thought*. Cambridge: Cambridge University Press.

Wu, Katherine J. (2020): "Scientists Assemble Frog Stem Cells into First 'Living Machines'". https://www.smithsonianmag.com/innovation/scientists-assemble-frog-stem-cells-first-living-machines-180973947/, visited on 6.7.2021

Dieter Schönecker

6 Kant's Argument from Moral Feelings: Why Practical Reason Cannot Be Artificial

Abstract: Can practical reason be artificial? The answer, from a Kantian point of view, is clearly negative: Practical reason cannot be artificial. After a preliminary remark on the possibility of Kantian moral machines (1.1) and some basics on the concept of practical reason (1.2) and Kant's intuitionism (1.3), I will argue that in a Kantian model of moral obligation, the typical (human) moral subject has moral feelings and must have them in order to cognize the validity of the moral law as a categorical imperative (1.3). Using the knowledge argument against physicalism and functionalism, I shall argue that computers have no feelings and, *a fortiori*, no moral feelings; therefore, computers are not moral subjects (1.4). This conclusion is based on a Kantian *I feel* rather than *I think* (2.). I will then tackle two problems with this argument (3.). I will conclude with an analogy (4): Just as planets do not fly, computers do not feel.

Artificial Intelligence (AI) has given rise to a variety of moral, juridical, economic and political, or for short, *practical* questions that need to be answered soon – from how to deal with self-driving cars to AI being the end of the human race due to some kind of technological singularity.[1] Since AI is, at least by philosophical standards, a fairly recent phenomenon, both these practical questions and problems as well as the possible answers and solutions to them are fairly new. Note, however, that these answers in turn will depend on foundations that are a far cry from unbiased or innocent; in applied ethics and political philosophy, one arrives very quickly at traditional questions and positions that one needs to discuss both on a metaethical and a normative level in order to provide sustainable answers. Hence, it is no surprise that in papers about

---

1 This paper is a revised version of a paper published in *Journal of AI Humanities*, 2018, vol.2, 67–91 ("Can practical reason be artificial?"). – I shall like to thank the organizers of *The First International Conference on Artificial Intelligence Humanities* held at Chung-Ang University, Seoul on August 16, 2018; my special thanks go to Prof. Chan Kyu Lee and Prof. Hyeongjoo Kim. I would also like to express my gratitude to Sorin Baiasu, Larissa Berger, Richard Evans, Markus Lohrey, Christian Prust, Elke Schmidt, and Thomas Sukopp for helpful discussions.

Dieter Schönecker, University of Siegen

moral machines arguments are put forward on the grounds of good old fashioned utilitarianism, for instance.[2]

However, practical questions or the applied ethics of AI are not my concern here. Rather, the question that I shall address belongs essentially to the philosophy of mind: Can practical reason be artificial? Practical reason is best understood, I submit, as a genuine power to cognize and will the good. From a Kantian point of view, the answer to that question is clearly negative: *Practical reason cannot be artificial*. It is tempting to think that this answer has a foundation already in Kant's epistemological, or – as Kant would put it – *theoretical* thought that reason is always *someone's* reason, so that there is no thinking without *someone* who thinks or can always think *I think*. I will briefly look into this, but my focus will be on Kant's practical philosophy. From this practical point of view, too, the conclusion that practical reason cannot be artificial is quick, solid and inevitable; for practical reason is free and computers are not. However, my approach is different; it is based on the idea that moral reason comes along with moral feelings that computers cannot have. After a preliminary remark on the possibility of Kantian moral machines (1.1) and some basics on the concept of practical reason (1.2) and Kant's intuitionism (1.3), I will argue that in a Kantian model of moral obligation, the typical (human) moral subject has moral feelings and must have them in order to cognize the validity of the moral law as a categorical imperative (1.3). Using the so-called *knowledge argument* against physicalism and functionalism, I shall argue that computers have no feelings and, *a fortiori*, no moral feelings; therefore, computers are no moral subjects (1.4). This conclusion is based on a Kantian *I feel* rather than *I think* (1.5). I will then tackle two problems with this argument (2). I will conclude with an analogy (3): Just as planets do not fly, computers do not feel.

1 The Argument From Moral Feelings

It is easy to understand a Kantian argument that, if true, clearly rules out the possibility that computers have practical reason. It is the *argument from transcendental practical freedom*. Here is a very brief sketch: Moral obligation presupposes transcendental practical freedom of practical reason. Such freedom is, negatively speaking, independence from natural causality or physical determinism. Computers, however, are determined by the laws of physics; therefore, they cannot be free. But practical reason – and thus the human being – is free,

---

2 Cf., for instance, Bonnefon & Shariff & Rahwan (2015).

and it needs to be free for morality to make sense (Kant is an incompatibilist);[3] therefore, no computer can have practical reason. Note that even on a non-deterministic understanding of physics, and even with regard to quantum computers, this argument from freedom will hold. For freedom is not only, negatively speaking, independence from natural causes; it is also, positively speaking, the faculty of determining oneself in an autonomous act of absolute spontaneity, and such spontaneity, unlike chance, is not lawless.

Thus, one can easily see that at least from a Kantian point of view it is quite obvious that a computer cannot have practical reason. Since this is so obvious, I would like to address or rather develop an argument from Kant's practical philosophy that often goes unnoticed; I shall call it the *argument from moral feelings*.[4]

1.1 A Preliminary Remark: Kantian Moral Machines

Alan Turing once listed a number of things that people think computers will never be able to do; these included the ability to "tell right from wrong". Of course, it depends on what one means by '*telling* right from wrong', but at least with regard to the output of such 'telling', that assumption might very well turn out not to be true. There has been a serious debate about "moral machines" for quite some time already,[5] and the development of robots raises moral questions that are not only of theoretical (or philosophical) interest, so to speak, but are being addressed quite practically. Moral algorithms seem possible, and such algorithms may not only help, for instance, judges to make moral decisions, but will soon make, in some very limited sense, moral decisions on their own;[6] just

---

3 Kant is an incompatibilist in the sense of denying the possibility of being a moral agent that is not strictly speaking free; morality presupposes absolute spontaneity (which is incompatible with determinism). Kant is a compatibilist only in that sense that freedom and determinism are compatible *on the assumption* – which is *not* the conceptual assumption in the debate about compatibilism and incompatibilism – of the difference between the noumenal and sensible world such that in some (transcendental or noumenal) respect the agent is free whereas in another (empirical or sensible) respect she is not; cf. Schönecker (2005).

4 In the English literature (with the famous exception of Antonio Damasio), it is common to distinguish between feelings and emotions; the former are understood as non-intentional (e.g. pain), the later as intentional (e.g. love). I will speak of feelings throughout without thereby referring to feelings in that strict sense. Moral feelings, in that sense, should be called moral emotions.

5 Cf. for instance, Wallach & Allen (2009).

6 It is very difficult to put into language what computers or robots do – which is (almost) a case in point, because strictly speaking, computers and robots do not *do* anything, if by deeds we mean those acts that persons perform. As I see it, robots do not *think* or *feel*, they do not

think of so-called autonomous vehicles and the related trolley-problem.[7] It is maybe tempting to assume that such moral machines must be based on some kind of utilitarian reasoning, given the mathematical character (and *prima facie* easiness) of a utilitarian or hedonistic calculus. Given the *formal* aspect of Kant's famous categorical imperative and the idea of universalization, however, this could be a prejudice; a computer might be able to perform a moral algorithm on Kantian grounds as well. Recall the basic idea of the so-called natural law formula: Suppose someone has a maxim, for instance, that she will commit suicide when her life irreversibly brings about more suffering than agreeableness. The categorical imperative obligates her to ask herself whether such a maxim could be a universal (natural) law such that everyone who experiences more suffering than agreeableness will actually kill himself or herself; then she might realize that this leads to some kind of contradiction. There has been a long and ongoing debate on how to understand the contradiction Kant has in mind; but at least on a somewhat formal (logical) interpretation of the contradiction involved, a Kantian moral machine that runs a universalization test seems possible.[8]

1.2 Kant's Concept of Practical Reason

'Practical reason' is (pure) good volition: "Every thing in nature works in accordance with laws. Only a rational being has the faculty to act *in accordance with the representation* of laws, i.e. in accordance with principles, or a *will*. Since for the derivation of actions from laws *reason* is required, the will is nothing other than practical reason" (GMS: 412).[9] It is important, however, to differentiate three aspects of Kant's concept of practical reason or good will: The noumenally-good will, the practically-good will, and the holy will. The *noumenally-good will* is the autonomous will that *as such* wills the good. It is this noumenally good will Kant presupposes when he says that "a free will and a will under moral laws *are the*

---

play a game nor do they *make* moral decisions that would be sufficiently similar to what persons do, let alone truly perform these actions. So when I say that a robot 'makes a moral decision on its own', this is to be taken at best by way of analogy. I will get back to this later.

7 For an overview, cf. Misselhorn (2018). On the trolley-problem see Schmidt (2022) and Wright (2022), in this volume.

8 Cf. Powers (2006) and Lindner & Bentzen (2018).

9 Cf. GMS: 427: "The will is thought as a faculty of determining itself to action *in accord with the representation of certain laws.*"

same" (GMS: 447, emphasis mine).[10] As a moral faculty, it gives the moral law (the categorical imperative) for imperfect beings and, by means of moral feelings, it is also a motivating force. Every human being has such a will, even if he or she acts immorally.[11]

The noumenally-good will is the basis both for the practically-good will and for the holy will. The *practically-good will* is the will that finite beings have when their volition is indeed moral; it is the noumenally-good will considered as a will that manifests itself successfully in a finite being against the influence of inclinations and desires. For imperfect beings, to act morally (to act with a practically-good will) means to act from duty. The noumenally-good will that is manifest in a person without (active) sensual hindrances is what Kant calls the *holy will*; it only belongs to God and other holy beings. These beings have no inclinations and desires contrary to the good; the "will whose maxims necessarily harmonize with the laws of autonomy is a *holy*, absolutely good will" (GMS: 439). The noumenally-good will as such (regardless of its being incorporated in a finite being) cannot be differentiated from the holy will (regardless of its being incorporated in an infinite being). It is a noumenal causality: "The rational being counts himself as intelligence in the world of understanding, and *merely as an efficient cause belonging to this world* does it call its causality a *will*" (GMS: 453, first emphasis mine).

This will is then identified with the will that is autonomous, i.e., with autonomy itself: "if we think of ourselves as *free*, then we *transport ourselves as members into the world of understanding* and cognize the *autonomy* of the will, together with its *consequence*, morality" (GMS: 453, m. e.). Note how Kant continues: ". . . but if we think of ourselves as *obligated* by duty, then we consider ourselves as belonging to the world of sense and yet at the same time to the world of understanding" (GMS: 453, m. e.). Thus the free will is the noumenal will (pure practical reason), and autonomy is its property. In some contexts, this will is *considered* not as the will of a human being that is *also* part of the sensible world, but as a noumenal will only: as "a *mere* member of the world of understanding, all my actions would be perfectly in accord with the principle of the *autonomy* of the pure will" (GMS: 453, m. e.). It is important to keep in mind that the noumenally-good will *as such* is *not* only a mere capacity to act morally; for this will as such wills the good. Nonetheless, it is the noumenally-good will that *enables* the *human* being to act morally; thus, *for the human being* – who is a member both of the noumenal *and* of the sensible world – the

---

10 Cf. Schönecker (2013b).
11 Cf. GMS: 400, 34–37; 412,30–35; 440,7–13; 449,16–23; 455,7–9.

noumenally-good will is indeed a capacity. Also, unless autonomy and having a practically-good will are not the same, a scoundrel would not be autonomous – which he actually *is* insofar as even he, to some extent, wants to be morally good, i.e., insofar he has a *noumenally*-good will (we shall return to this later).[12]

1.3 Kant's Moral Intuitionism

It is often striking to see how defenders of strong AI[13] find it obvious that computers "can *do* many things as well as or better than humans" (Russell & Norvig 2016, 1022, m. e.). But such an assumption, of course, is begging the question; for the point is rather whether they can *do anything* a human being can do when it comes to feeling, thinking, and acting. On Kant's account, there is no 'doing' in any narrow sense here. Human actions, strictly speaking, are not only free actions; if they are guided by the moral law, they are embedded in moral feelings. Computers have no feelings; therefore, they do not act morally even if they make decisions in accordance with duty. Let us take a closer look at this argument from moral feelings.

To the present, Kant is believed to defend, as Edmund Husserl put it, "an extreme and almost absurd rationalism" (Husserl 1988: 412), an "extreme intellectualism" (ibid.) that leaves no room for feelings. Such a position betrays historical and textual ignorance. For even every beginner in an introductory class on Kant's ethics will learn that Kant consistently argues that reason "*obviously*" (GMS: 460,9, m.H.) can only bring about actions by means of feelings; hence, feelings necessarily come into play here already as a determining (motivating) ground. However, it is important to realize that on Kant's account, feelings serve a much more important function.

As we have already seen, Kant draws a very strict line between holy and non-holy beings. Whereas holy beings always will what a good will wants, this is not true for non-holy, sensuous-rational beings. For them, the moral law is always a categorical imperative that necessitates them. Let me quote Kant in more detail here:

---

12 In the last section I have drawn from Schmidt & Schönecker (2018) and Schönecker & Wood (2015).

13 By "strong AI" I mean for my purposes that a computer or robot could have consciousness, an inner life (qualia) and really think the way we do. Such a computer would not just imitate thinking, and would not just imitate moral thinking, but really think and therefore also *think morally*.

If reason determines the will without exception, then the actions of such a being, which are recognized as objectively necessary, are also subjectively necessary, i. e. the will is a faculty of choosing *only that* which reason, independently of inclination, recognizes as practically necessary, i. e. as good. But if reason for itself alone does not sufficiently determine the will, if the will is still subject to subjective conditions (to certain incentives) which do not always agree with the objective conditions, in a word, if the will is not *in itself* fully in accord with reason (as it actually is with human beings), then the actions which are objectively recognized as necessary are subjectively contingent, and the determination of such a will, in accord with objective laws, is *necessitation*, i. e. the relation of objective laws to a will which is not thoroughly good is represented as the determination of the will of a rational being through grounds of reason to which, however, this will in accordance with its nature is not necessarily obedient. The representation of an objective principle, insofar as it is necessitating for a will, is called a 'command' (of reason) and the formula of the command is called an *imperative*. All imperatives are expressed through an *ought* and thereby indicate the relation of an objective law of reason to a will which in its subjective constitution is not necessarily determined by that law (a necessitation). (GMS: 412 f.)

The crucial step is to see that this necessitation is experienced by the feeling of *respect* (which in turn has a negative and a positive aspect that I cannot deal with here). But this feeling is not just a side effect, as it were. Since by 'necessitation' Kant means nothing but the fact that for non-holy, sensuous-rational beings like us the moral law is an imperative, that is, a duty, the obligation involved in this is experienced in the feeling of respect. As a matter of fact, it is not only somehow *experienced*, but *cognized* by this feeling: "What I immediately recognize as a law for me, I cognize with respect" (GMS: 402, fn.). And it is important to see that Kant's famous theory of the 'fact of reason' is directly related to this thought.[14] In § 7 of the *Critique of Practical Reason*, Kant formulates the categorical imperative; a bit later, he says that one could call the "consciousness of this fundamental law a fact of reason" (KpV: 31). The so-called factum-theory explains our insight into the binding character of the moral law; it is, among other things, a theory of justification. The basic idea is that there can be no deduction of the categorical imperative in any normal (deductive) sense,[15] and yet the objective reality of the moral law is "nevertheless firmly established *of itself*" (KpV: 47, m. e.). In our consciousness of the categorical imperative, the moral law is immediately *given* in its unconditional and binding validity; in this sense (but only in this sense), the factum theory is a theory of moral self-evidence. This consciousness of the categorical imperative, however, is determined by the feeling of respect, that is, the unconditional validity of the categorical imperative is given in the feeling of respect.

---

14 Cf. Schönecker (2013) and (2013a).
15 "Hence the objective reality of the moral law cannot be proved by any deduction" (CPrR: 47,15).

Hence, it *is through the feeling of respect that we cognize the validity or binding character of the moral law.*[16] Thus, Kant is by no means the pure rationalist that Husserl and others represent him as being. Rather, Kant is a moral intuitionist. A moral intuitionist is someone who holds the view that we cognize the validity of the moral law, the moral *You ought*, not by some kind of deductive (or inductive or abductive) reasoning, but by means of a certain kind of self-evidence, through a feeling. It is important not to misunderstand these claims: On Kant's account, it is *not* the content of the categorical imperative that is understood through the feeling of respect; *what* we ought to do or omit we cognize by reason and some kind of universalization. Kant is not a moral sentimentalist. Also, the moral law itself does not *depend* on the moral feeling of respect for its validity; it is not that the moral law is valid *because* we have that feeling. Yet what we do cognize through the feeling of respect is that we ought to act morally, that the moral law is categorically binding.

1.4 A Kantian Knowledge Argument

From this, however, it follows that a computer can have no practical reason. To see this, we have to take a brief look at the so-called *knowledge argument* put forward in one version or another by Thomas Nagel and, historically more properly speaking, Frank Jackson.[17] This is quite an intricate story, and here we can only sketch the main idea behind it.

For our purposes, recall Jackson's thought-experiment about Mary: Think of her as a scientist who knows everything there is to know about colors and their perception from the point of view of the natural sciences; but Mary, being locked in a room with only black and white books, TVs, etc., has never seen

---

16 Colin & Varner & Zinser (2000, 260) see that emotions have more than just a motivational function; they do not, however, recognize their cognitive function as regards the validity of the moral law.

17 Cf. the pertinent texts by Nagel (1974) and Jackson (1982). Nagel's argument is not that we can never understand or intuit or have access to someone else's inner life and the phenomenal qualia involved. The point is that this understanding is subjective and not objective, i. e., it cannot be reached by a third person perspective and hence not by the natural sciences (cf. Nagel 1974, 441 f.). So in some sense, the bat-example is misleading. Even if there were only human beings and no other sentient organisms, the problem (or fact) Nagel describes would remain. Levine's explanatory gap argument (1983) and Chalmer's related 'hard problem' are somewhat similar, but still different, since here the focus is not so much on the physical inexplicability of the first-person-perspective as such but on the (presumably inexplicable) relation between consciousness (qualia, what-it-is-likeness) and their physical relatum as well as function.

any objects that are not black or white. One day, however, she leaves her room and actually sees something that is, say, red. Now according to physicalism (materialism, naturalism), only natural (physical) objects exist, and natural objects are those described and explained by physics (and possibly by chemistry, biology, or neuroscience). If this were true, then Mary would not gain any new knowledge of a quality she had not already known because everything there is to know about colors from an scientific, objective, third-person perspective, she already knows. But there is something she did not know before she left the room, to wit, *how it feels* or *what it is like* (the later is Nagel's famous formula, of course) to see something red, to experience a certain *quale*; therefore, there is something in the world that is not physical, i. e. not fully describable by physics. This something is consciousness making phenomenal experiences. Thus we could know everything there is to know about the physical or functional facts concerning a mental state (such as having a perception of something being red) and still we would not know everything about that mental state; therefore, this mental state cannot be identical with or be reduced to those physical or functional facts. From this it follows, some at least have argued, that physicalism is false.

Although there is some dispute as to which mental states are qualia or are accompanied by qualia, it is obvious that feelings are indeed qualia. But then the argument is apparent: We can know everything a computer is made of and how it works. There is no *what it is like to be a computer*, and therefore, unlike beings for whom there is a certain phenomenal inner life, to be in a computational state is not to be in a mental state (and vice versa). And so unless computers experience qualia, they cannot have practical reason. For practical reason comes along with practical necessitation through the feeling of respect; the categorical imperative cannot be understood without this feeling; since computers have no feelings, and *a fortiori* no feeling of respect, they cannot understand the categorical imperative.

That is the basic argument. From a Kantian point of view, there are three more important points: *First* and only in passing, I should note that in his later work (*The Metaphysics of Morals*) Kant further developed his theory of moral feelings by distinguishing four kinds of moral predispositions and, consequently, four moral feelings: the moral feeling proper, conscience, love of human beings as *amor complacentiae*, and self-respect.[18] With regard to each of

---

18 Cf. Schönecker (2010). – Kriegel & Timmons (2021) claim to work on a 'phenomenology of Kantian respect for persons'. For some reason or other, however, they pay no attention to 'respect' (as self-respect) as one of the four moral predispositions. They also seem to be unaware

these feelings Kant stresses that there is no obligation to have them; for to have these feelings is already a necessary presupposition to make sense of the very concept of duty in the first place. *Second*, to Kant, practical reason is the noumenal will that both cognizes and wills the good; it is autonomous and therefore a noumenal causality. As I have indicated already, this is a complicated story, but moral feelings cannot be naturalized as they are brought about by reason which cannot be naturalized; so even if computers did have feelings, they could not have the feeling of respect, because this feeling has its source in reason which is not a natural (physical) entity. *Third*, Kant, too, understands feelings as qualia. Of course, Kant did not use this term. Nevertheless, he had a clear understanding of the fact that feelings have a phenomenal side that cannot be grasped by physical knowledge but must be experienced. The phenomenal side of feelings is particularly emphasized by Kant in his theory of beauty.[19] Feelings as such, says Kant in the so-called *First Introduction* to the *Critique of the Power of Judgment*, "cannot be explained at all"; rather, they "must be felt, not understood [*eingesehen*]" (EEKU: 232).[20] In a similar vein, Kant writes in the *Metaphysics of Morals* that "pleasure and displeasure cannot be explained for themselves" (MS: 212).

In any case, the purity in pure practical reason by no means suggests that there are no feelings involved in the process of moral self-determination. The purity of practical reason consists in its being free from considerations of happiness and self-love; in human beings, it is pure reason that becomes practical on the strength of moral feelings. So even if a computer 'makes a decision' (*as it were*) on the basis of a moral algorithm, it has no idea of what it is 'doing' (*as it were*): it has no understanding whatsoever of what the moral law as a categorical imperative really is. In Kant's terminology, a computer can perform actions (*as it were*) *according* to duty. But it certainly cannot perform actions *from* duty. And it certainly has no conscience or self-respect; as I see it, such a claim is not even apprehensible.

Before I move on to two problems for this Kantian position, let us have a quick look at a possible further argument, the *argument from the power of judgment*; given the latitude of many ethical duties, this is obviously an important

---

that Kant himself presents his own detailed 'phenomenology' of respect in KpV: 71–89 (which plays no role whatsoever in their analysis).

19 Cf. Berger (2022).

20 In German: "Man sieht hier leicht, daß Lust oder Unlust, weil sie keine Erkenntnisarten sind, für sich selbst gar nicht können erklärt werden, und *gefühlt*, nicht eingesehen werden wollen".

aspect of practical reason.[21] The argument could run like this: Following Kant, the power of judgment is the "faculty of thinking the particular as contained under the universal" (KU: 179). If there is a rule, then the faculty of the power of judgment is the "faculty of subsuming" something particular under this rule; Kant calls this the determining power of judgment (*bestimmende Urteilskraft*). If the rule is yet to be found for something particular that cannot be subsumed under an already existing rule, then Kant calls it *reflective power of judgment* (*reflektierende Urteilskraft*). At least for the determining power of judgment, Kant argues, there can be no further rule. For if one "wanted to show generally how one ought to subsume under these rules, i. e., distinguish whether something stands under them or not, this could not happen except once again through a rule. But just because this is a rule, it would demand another instruction for the power of judgment, and so it becomes clear that although the understanding is certainly capable of being instructed and equipped through rules, the power of judgment is a special talent that cannot be taught but only practiced" (KrV: A133/B172). Put another way: There can be meta-rules on how and when to apply rules; but on pain of a vicious circle or an infinite number of rules, there must be a point at which the power of judgment takes action without applying a rule. Computers, however, have nothing but rules to work with, i. e., nothing but algorithms (and data, of course, in regard to which they are applied). If the power of judgment is a faculty that does not follow rules, then this faculty cannot be something a computer could have. The "lack of the power of judgement," says Kant, "is that which is properly called stupidity" (ibid.); in this sense, computers are stupid.

Yet it is dubitable whether this argument actually goes through. The necessity of something like a power of judgment is due to the fact that there is no complete ascertainment or definition of all possible concepts and cases *a priori* or in advance.[22] But if a decision based on the power of judgment is not based on a rule, on what is it based? It had better not be based on chance; for that is something a computer could do (following the rule to choose randomly). One might think that the power of judgment has to do with something like intuitions; but intuitions (the way G. E. Moore, for instance, understands them) are different and have nothing to do with the power of judgment. However, intuitions broadly

---

21 Kant actually thinks that all ethical duties (unlike juridical duties) are wide duties. Note, however, that there are negative ethical duties that despite being duties of omission have latitude; cf. Schmidt & Schönecker (2018).
22 Cf. KrV: B 756: "One makes use of certain marks only as long as they are sufficient for making distinctions; new observations, however, take some away and add some, and therefore the concept never remains within secure boundaries".

understood as somewhat unconscious, strong, quick seeing(judging)-as-true states of mind (as understood in moral psychology), might very well not be random, but based on some (unconscious, strong, quick) weighing of goods, and such a weighing could follow rules. In any case, I would not be ready to defend the argument from the power of judgment.

2 I Think vs. I Feel

Obviously, moral subjects *will* something, and they *act* on the basis of their volitions. But they also *think*, and even if it is disputed how and how much thinking is actually involved in moral decisions as such, it cannot be disputed that moral subjects must also think, at least with regard to the cognition of the surrounding world in which they will and act; moral knowledge involves non-moral knowledge about the internal and external world. Now Kant famously argues (in the second edition of the *Critique of Pure Reason*) – or appears to argue, anyway – that there is no thinking and hence no knowledge of the internal and external world without self-consciousness; the *I think*, he says, "must *be able* to accompany all my representations" (KrV: B 131). What exactly this means has been the object of painful and long discussions among Kant-scholars.[23] One problem is the nature and relation of what Kant calls the *analytic unity of apperception* to what he calls the *synthetic unity of apperception* (cf. KrV B133 ff.); it is neither clear what exactly each of these unities really is and in what sense the synthetic unity of apperception is a necessary condition of the analytic unity of apperception. Very generally speaking, I take the basic idea to be that all thinking as the *"capacity to judge"* (A69/B94) involves the *synthesis*[24] of representations as someone's representations in a judgment, such that these representations – as well as the act of synthesizing them – belong, and *must* belong,[25] to a self-conscious *I* that can always say *I think* (these representations). In any case, if Kant is right, and if it is true that a computer has no *I*, then a computer does not and cannot think, and it is not intelligent the way human beings are.[26] At best, then, a computer (AI) can only imitate intelligence and moral thinking.

---

23 Cf. Klemme (1996), Rosefeldt (2000), Allison (2015); for a very brief overview Schlicht (2016). For a recent brief account cf. Hoeppner (2022).

24 Cf. KrV: A69/B94: "All judgments are therefore functions of unity among our representations"; categories are "concepts of synthesis" (A80/B106). Evans (2022, 50) speaks of *containment, comparison* and *inherence* as the three basic operations.

25 Friebe (2005, 53) seems to think that such a reading is too strong.

26 For further discussion of this argument, see Baiasu (2022) and Evans (2022) in this volume.

I'm not quite convinced of this argument. It seems true to me that (developed) human beings must always be able to think *I think* when they think (not that they always do think *I think*, of course). Now, if this is true, and if it is true that computers have no *I* (which I think is true indeed), then computers do not think the way we do. Still it might be justified to say that they think: If theoretical (not practical) thinking is essentially the act of synthesizing content that requires a center or unit by which this act is performed, then one could possibly understand this center or unit as the *control unit* of a computer. My point is that the act of combining content (synthesis) might require neither *Meinigkeit* nor self-consciousness (*apperception*, as Kant calls it) as a higher (egological) form of *Meinigkeit*, but just a control unit. This unit must not necessarily be aware of itself because the content of (something like) perceptions (intuitions) and (something like) thoughts or propositions does not require an *I* that thinks it and not even a form of *Meinigkeit*; all that is needed for thinking as synthesizing is synthesis itself, not synthesis that is aware of itself.[27]

It seems to me that Kant himself might have been aware of this and that all he claims is that the way *a human being* thinks is such that an underlying *I* is involved that thinks. Now in thinking *I think* a human being is not only aware of itself as the *I* that thinks *I think* and only this (transcendental apperception, mere spontaneity), but also of itself as determinable by representations in the order of time because "without any empirical representation, which provides the material for thinking, the act I think would not take place" (KrV: B 423, fn.).[28] So one's own existence (*Dasein*) is given in two ways: as the existence of the mere and "wholly empty representation: I" (KrV: A345/B404), and as this very (numerically identical) I that thinks something (has representations in time) and therefore thinks itself as determinable in time and therefore also exists as an empirical I. This is why Kant calls the *I think* an "empirical proposition" (KrV: B422 fn, cf. B 404, 420, 428) and why he also says, in direct connection with this, that the proposition *I think*

---

27 There remains, of course, the question of how computers have representations. Friebe (2005, 61) is quite right in claiming that representations (*Vorstellungen*) as such are always someone's representations; and it might also be true that the property of *being my representations* (*Meinigkeit*) does imply an *I* whose representations they are. However, the question remains whether thinking must be understood as an operation that involves representations as something mental.

28 Cf. KrV: B 420: "But because my existence in the first proposition [I think, D. S.] is considered as given, since it does not say that every thinking being exists (which would at the same time predicate absolute necessity of them, and hence say too much), but only 'I exist thinking,' that proposition is empirical, and contains the determinability of my existence merely in regard to my representations in time."

"contains within itself the proposition 'I exist'" (KrV: B 420, fn.): As an empirical proposition, the *I think* contains the potentially (determinable) empirical existence of the I.[29]

In this context, Kant repeatedly criticizes Descartes for (allegedly) saying "Everything that thinks, exists" (KrV: B422, fn.; cf. B 404 and B420). If this were true, he argues, "the property of thinking would make all beings possessing it into necessary beings" (KrV: B422, fn; cf. B420). Thus, Kant criticizes the following argument (which he claims is Descartes'): Everything that thinks, exists; I think; therefore, I exist. He does so by criticizing the first premise. Taken literally, it seems almost impossible to understand what his critique of the first premise ('necessary beings') really consists in. However, Kant's argument does make sense if we assume that *not* every act of thinking is accompanied by the *I think*. 'Everything' that thinks and does so by also thinking *I think* is "given" (KrV: B 420) its existence; and if it were true that every act of thinking involved an *I* that thinks, then the major premise of Descartes' inference would be true as well. If, on the other hand, it is possible to think of thinking as not involving an *I* that thinks, then obviously *I exist* is not implied by that thinking (it is only implied, as Kant says, by the *I think*).[30]

In the introductory passage of the chapter on the *Paralogism of Pure Reason*, Kant makes the following remark:[31]

> But right at the start it must seem strange that the condition under which I think in general [*daß die Bedingung, unter der ich überhaupt denke*], and which is therefore merely a property of my subject, is at the same time to be valid for everything that thinks, and that on an empirical-seeming proposition we can presume to ground an apodictic and universal judgment, namely, that everything that thinks is constituted as the claim of self-consciousness asserts of me. But the cause of this lies in the fact that we must necessarily ascribe to things a priori all the properties that constitute the conditions under which alone we think them. Now I cannot have the least representation of a thinking being through an external experience, but only through self-consciousness. Thus such objects are nothing further than the transference of this consciousness of mine to other things, which can be represented as thinking beings only in this way.   (KrV: A 346 f./B 404 f.)

---

29 Though this is an intricate story; cf. Kim (2017).

30 I do not mean to say that the alternative to an egological account of the self in self-consciousness is a non-egological account, because in the later account there is consciousness, too (though without an I), that is, conscious of itself (for this difference cf. Frank, 2015, 14 ff.). I mean thinking without consciousness; it allows for self-knowledge, though.

31 In the earlier version of this paper (s. fn. 1) I misinterpreted this passage.

So two things 'seem strange': First, that the *I think*[32] as 'the condition under which *I* think in general' and which is 'merely a property of *my* subject', shall be a condition 'valid for *everything* that thinks'; and, as a consequence, that that proposition (*I think*), which (as we have seen above) also has an empirical aspect, could be the ground for the proposition 'that *everything* that thinks is constituted as the claim of self-consciousness asserts of *me*', to wit, that 'everything that thinks exists' – which is exactly the Cartesian proposition Kant later vigorously opposes. And since we know for sure from the other passages that Kant indeed finds grave fault with Descartes' argument (or rather its first premise), what 'seems strange' here must not be read as being only 'seemingly' strange, but as *really* being strange.[33]

So maybe there is thinking without a self-conscious *I* that thinks and even without any consciousness. When it comes to feelings, however, we *necessarily* enter into a different world – the inner world.[34] One can identify the activity of thinking[35] and still leave it an open question of whether thoughts are thought by an *I* that thinks. This is impossible as regards feelings. There can be no feeling without *someone* who feels and for whom *it is like*.[36] To say that there is a state which we could preliminary describe as "there is a feeling", requires that there is an instance *for whom* it is to be in that state (of feeling something). Whatever

---

32 Throughout those introductory passages, the *I think* is discussed not only as a transcendental concept (cf. KrV: A341/B399) but also as the "sole text of rational psychology" (KrV: A343/B401).

33 Note that Kant says that "*right* at the start it must seem strange . . ." (the German original is even stronger, it seems to me: "Es muß aber *gleich* anfangs befremdlich scheinen . . .". If it only said "Es muß aber anfangs befremdlich scheinen" (i.e. without the "gleich") one could maybe get the impression as if Kant were to say that 'at the start it must seem strange', but later it doesn't; but really it is later that Kant's critique of Descartes becomes evident.

34 If cognitive acts have a phenomenality of their own (i. e. if there is a what-it-is-like to think), then these acts, too, require someone for whom it-is-like to think (cf. Bayne/Montague, 2011).

35 Kant often speaks of the "*actions* of the understanding" (*Handlungen des Verstandes*, e. g. KrV: A69/B94, m. e.)

36 As Chalmers (1996, 147) puts it: "*all it is* for something to be in pain is for it to feel like pain. There is no distinction between pain and painy stuff, in the way there is a distinction between water and watery stuff. One could have something that felt like water without it being water, but one could not have something that felt like pain without it being pain. Pain's feel is *essential* to it". In her paper on computational models of emotion, Gu discusses so-called affective computing, but points out that "both emotion recognition and expression belong to the outer layer" of emotion – i.e. to "cognitive, behavioral, and physiological processes" (Gu 2010, p. 436) – and that "the 'core affect' part has not yet been included in the discussion" (ibid. p. 440) on computational models of emotion. This "'core' emotion, often equated with the term *affect*, is the subjective *feeling* aspect of emotion" (ibid., p. 436).

feelings are, too, (bodily sensations, judgments, perceptions, evaluations), it is essential that one feels them. A feeling that is not felt is not a feeling; but for it to be felt there must be someone who feels it.[37]

3 Two Problems for the Argument from Moral Feelings

The argument from moral feelings is strong, I submit; still, it has two problems. First, *what about holy wills*? As we have already seen, it is a very important element of Kant's ethics to distinguish between holy and non-holy beings. For the latter, the moral law is a categorical imperative and thus duty and obligation; for the former, there are no hindrances for morality to overcome, they have a perfectly good will. So must holy beings then be understood as moral machines? And would it not be true for a computer that always follows moral algorithms that it has such a perfectly good will? Well, no. It is certainly correct that a holy being cannot act from duty.[38] But unlike computers, holy beings have a will; computers have no will; *a fortiori*, they do not will anything for the sake of the moral law. The claim that computers have no will is underpinned by the claim that volitions are intentional; computational states, however, are not intentional states;[39] therefore, computers have no will. Still the question of what it means for a holy will to will and to act for the sake of the moral law without intermediary moral feelings is not easy to answer.

The second problem with the argument from moral feelings simply is this: *Can computers really have no feelings*? This, too, is a long and complicated story, and I can only sketch the problem and the possible solution. So here is the argument that maybe computers could or even do, after all, have feelings: We know that *we* have consciousness and feelings. At the end of the day, we have no clear, let alone comprehensive and convincing story to tell how this happens, how it really can be that we have such an inner life. However, provided that some kind of naturalistic evolutionary theory is correct, we do know that our ability to have mental events has developed out of unconscious matter. But if it is possible that the mind and its mental states somehow evolved out of matter, i. e., out of the brain and its embodiment – and possible it *is* on the

---

37 This does not rule out that feelings are also dispositional and as mere dispositions are not felt.
38 It also cannot have the four moral predispositions.
39 All of this is highly disputed, of course; recall the long and ongoing debate about Searle's *Chinese room argument*. For a brief summary and critique cf. Gabriel (2018, 95 ff.).

assumption that mental states are real, regardless of whether they can be reduced to brain states or not –, then it *could* very well be possible that the mind and its mental states somehow could evolve out of a computer as yet another complicated assembly of matter. – Fair enough, I would say. So yes, that is possible if it is possible that the mind evolved (and evolves) out of matter. But from all that we know it is also very unlikely: A single biological cell is already *extremely* complex, let alone the brain, and complexity, as far as we know, is a precondition for, as well as a sign of, consciousness and feelings. By comparison, a computer is a very primitive object; there is no more reason to think that it has a mind than to think a sewing machine has one.[40]

4 Conclusion: Swimming Submarines, Flying Planets

To conclude, let me come back to Kant's *I think*. The computer scientist Edsger Dijkstra famously argued that "the question of whether *Machines Can Think . . .* is about as relevant as the question of whether *Submarines Can Swim*,"[41] or, one might add, whether airplanes can fly. His point, I take it, is that submarines of course *can* swim, i. e., move through water, despite the fact that they do not swim like fish, and that airplanes *can* fly despite the fact that they move through air without moving wings up and down or whatever. Following Dijkstra's analogy, it seems sensible to hold that computers think despite the fact that they do not think the way we think; there is no *I*, and still they think. But this analogy between computers thinking and submarines swimming or airplanes flying is misleading. As always, it all depends on how one defines such words as "swimming", "flying", or "thinking". If one defines "swimming" as "moving through water using limbs, fins, or tails", then submarines do not swim; but why define "swimming" like this? To define a word – or to explicate what it is for a thing to be what it is – somehow presupposes a recognition of what is essential to that thing; for this, however, one needs paradigmatic cases.[42] Now one could argue – maybe along the lines of functionalism – that

---

40 One could also, by the way, turn the tables and argue that the existence of mental states proves that something is wrong with Darwinist evolutionary theories. Thomas Nagel, among others, has done so recently; cf. Nagel (2012). For a critical view of Nagel's moral realism, cf. Schmidt (2018).
41 Cf. Russell & Norvig (2016, 1021).
42 Cf. Damschen & Schönecker (²2013).

computers on the basis of certain inputs perform certain operations that bring about certain outputs; and taking into account just the output – calculating, playing chess, driving a car, writing music – one is tempted to believe that computers think (and also that human beings think the way computers think). The question of how and by what means swimming is performed is not crucial to the concept of swimming. But the difference between a being that thinks *I think*, or at least between one that feels *I feel*, or that experiences *I want*, and a machine that has no such self-consciousness, is so enormous that those terms (to *think*, to *feel*, to *want*) should not be used for beings that have no I. To say that a computer feels is like saying that a planet *flies* just because it moves through space.

References

Kant's moral writings (except for the *Groundwork*; here I use Allen Wood's translation) are cited from the translation by Mary J. Gregor in the volume *Practical Philosophy* (*The Cambridge Edition of the Works of Immanuel Kant*), Cambridge 1996. The KrV is quoted according to the translation provided by Paul Guyer and Allen W. Wood (*Cambridge Edition*). All page and line numbers refer to the pagination of the Academy Edition.

EEKU   Erste Einleitung in die Kritik der Urteilskraft/*First Introduction to the Critique of Judgment*
GMS   Grundlegung zur Metaphysik der Sitten/*Groundwork of the Metaphysics of Morals*
KpV   Kritik der praktischen Vernunft/*Critique of Practical Reason*
KrV   Kritik der reinen Vernunft/*Critique of Pure Reason*
KU   Kritik der Urteilskraft/*Critique of Judgment*
MS   Die Metaphysik der Sitten/*Metaphysics of Morals*

Allison, Henry E. (2015): *Kant's Transcendental Deduction. An Analytical-Historical Commentary*, Oxford: Oxford University Press.
Baiasu, Sorin (2022): "The Challenge of (Self-)Consciousness: Kant, Artificial Intelligence and Sense-Making," in: *Kant and Artificial Intelligence*. Ed. by H. Kim & D. Schönecker. Berlin: De Gruyter, 2022. pp. 105–127.
Bayne, Tim/Montague, Michelle (2011) (ed.): *Cognitive Phenomenology*. Oxford and New York: Oxford University Press.
Berger, Larissa (2022): *Kants Philosophie des Schönen. Eine kommentarische Interpretation zu den §§ 1–22 der „Kritik der Urteilskraft"*, Freiburg: Alber.
Bonnefon, Jean- François & Shariff, Azim & Rahwan, Iyad (2015): "Autonomous Vehicles Need Experimental Ethics: Are we ready for Utilitarian Cars?", in: arXiv:1510.03346 [cs.CY], 12 Oct. 2015.
Chalmers, David J. (1996): *The Conscious Mind. In Search of a Fundamental Theory*. Oxford: Oxford University Press.

Colin, Allen & Varner, Gary & Zinser, Jason (2000): "Prolegomena to any future artificial moral agent", *Journal of Experimental & Theoretical Artificial Intelligence*, 12:3, 251–261, DOI: 10.1080/09528130050111428

Damschen, Gregor & Schönecker, Dieter (²2013): *Selbst philosophieren. Ein Methodenbuch*, de Gruyter: Berlin/Boston.

Evans, Richard (2022): "The Apperception Engine," in: *Kant and Artificial Intelligence*. Ed. by H. Kim & D. Schönecker. Berlin: De Gruyter, 2022, pp. 39–103.

Frank, Manfred (2015): *Präreflexives Selbstbewusstsein. Vier Vorlesungen*, Reclam: Stuttgart.

Friebe, Cord (2005): *Theorie des Unbewußten: Eine Deutung der Metapsychologie Freuds aus transzendentalphilosophischer Perspektive*, Würzburg: Königshausen u. Neumann.

Gabriel, Markus (2018). *Der Sinn des Denkens*, Berlin: Ullstein.

Gu, Xiaosi (2019): "Computational models of emotion," in: *The Routledge Handbook of the Computational Mind*, ed. by Mark Sprevak and Matteo Colombo, London & New York: Routledge, pp. 436–451.

Hoeppner, Till (2022): "Kant's Metaphysical and Transcendental Deductions of the Categories. Tasks, Steps and Claims of Identity". In: Motta, Giuseppe/Schulting, Dennis/Thiel, Udo (Hrsg.): Kant's Transcendental Deduction and His Theory of Apperception. New Interpretations. Berlin/New York: De Gruyter.

Husserl, Edmund (1988): "Kritik der Kantischen Ethik," in: E. Husserl, *Vorlesungen über Ethik und Wertlehre 1908–1914*, Dordrecht/Boston/London. pp. 402–418 (Husserliana XXXVIII)

Jackson, Frank (1982): "Epiphenomenal Qualia," *Philosophical Quarterly*, 32. pp. 127–136.

Kim, Hyeongjoo (2017). *Zur Empirizität des „Ich denke in Kants Kritik der reinen Vernunft*, Würzburg: Königshausen & Neumann.

Klemme, Heiner F. (1996): *Kants Philosophie des Subjekts. Systematische und entwicklungsgeschichtliche Untersuchungen zum Verhältnis von Selbstbewußtsein und Selbsterkenntnis*, Hamburg: Meiner.

Kriegel, Uriah & Timmons, Mark (2021): "The Phenomenology of Kantian Respect for Persons", In: Richard Dean & Oliver Sensen (eds.), *Respect: Philosophical Essays*. Cambridge: Oxford University Press. pp. 77–98.

Levine, Joseph (1983): "Materialism and Qualia: The Explanatory Gap", *Pacific Philosophical Quarterly*, 64. pp. 354–361.

Lindner, Felix & Bentzen, Martin Mose (2018): "A Formalization of Kant's Second Formulation of the Categorical Imperative", in: arXiv preprint arXiv:1801.03160, 2018.

Misselhorn, Catrin (2018): *Grundfragen der Maschinenethik*. Stuttgart: Reclam.

Moreland, James P. & Craig, William Lane (2003): *Philosophical Foundations for a Christian Worldview*, InterVarsity Press: Downers Grove, Illinois.

Nagel, Thomas (1974): "What it is like to be a bat", in: *Philosophical Review* 83. pp. 435–450.

Nagel, Thomas (2012): *Mind and Cosmos: Why the Materialist Neo-Darwinian Conception of Nature is Almost Certainly False*, Oxford: Oxford University Press.

Powers, Thomas M. (2006): "Prospects for a Kantian Machine," in: *IEEE Intelligent Systems*, vol. 21, no. 4. pp. 46–51, July-Aug. 2006, doi: 10.1109/MIS.2006.77.

Rosefeldt, Tobias (2000): *Das logische Ich. Kant über den Gehalt des Begriffes von sich selbst*, Berlin (et al.): philo.

Russell, Stuart J. & Norvig, Peter (Eds.). (³2016). *Artificial Intelligence. A Modern Approach*. Hoboken NJ: Pearson Education Limited.

Schlicht, T. (2016): "Kant and the problem of consciousness", in: *Consciousness and the great Philosophers*. Ed. by S. Leach & J. Tartaglia. London Routledge. pp. 115–124.

Schmidt, Elke E. (2018): *"The Dilemma of Moral Naturalism in Nagel's* Mind and Cosmos", in: *Ethical Perspectives* 25, 2/2018. pp. 203–231.

Schmidt, Elke E. (2022). "Kant on Trolleys and Autonomous Driving", in: *Kant and Artificial Intelligence*. Ed. by H. Kim & D. Schönecker. Berlin: De Gruyter, 2022, pp. 189–221.

Schmidt, Elke E. & Schönecker, Dieter (2018): "Kant's Ground-Thesis. On Dignity and Value in the Groundwork", in: *The Journal of Value Inquiry*, March 2018, Volume 52, Issue 1, 81–95, https://doi.org/10.1007/s10790-017-9603-z.

Schönecker, Dieter (2005): *Kants Begriff transzendentaler und praktischer Freiheit. Eine entwicklungsgeschichtliche Studie* (unter Mitarbeit von Stefanie Buchenau and Desmond Hogan), Berlin: Walter de Gruyter.

Schönecker, Dieter (2010): "Kant über Menschenliebe als moralische Gemütsanlage", in: *Archiv für Geschichte der Philosophie*, Heft 2/2010, 133–175 (unter Mitarbeit von Alexander Cotter, Magdalena Eckes, Sebastian Maly).

Schönecker, Dieter (2013): "Das gefühlte Faktum der Vernunft. Skizze einer Interpretation und Verteidigung", in: *Deutsche Zeitschrift für Philosophie*, Heft 1, 2013. pp. 91–107.

Schönecker, Dieter (2013a): "Kant's Moral Intuitionism. The Fact of Reason and Moral Predispositions", in: *Kant Studies Online*, Feb. 2013. pp. 1–38.

Schönecker, Dieter (2013b): „'A free will and a will under moral laws are the same': Kant's concept of autonomy and his thesis of analyticity in *Groundwork* III", in: Oliver Sensen (ed.): *Kant on Moral Autonomy*, Cambridge: Cambridge University Press. pp. 225–245.

Schönecker, Dieter & Wood, Allen W. (2015): *Kant's Groundwork for the Metaphysics of Morals. A Commentary*, Cambridge (Mass): Harvard University Press

Ulgen, Ozlem (2017): "Kantian Ethics in the Age of Artificial Intelligence and Robotics", in: *Questions of International Law*, Zoom-in 43 (2017). pp. 59–83.

Wallach, Wendell, & Allen, Colin (2009): *Moral machines: Teaching robots right from wrong.* New York, Oxford: Oxford University Press.

Wright, Ava Thomas (2022): "Rightful machines", in: *Kant and Artificial Intelligence*. Ed. by H. Kim & D. Schönecker. Berlin: De Gruyter, pp. 223–237.

Elke Elisabeth Schmidt

7 Kant on Trolleys and Autonomous Driving

Abstract: Unlike most interpreters, I do not take it for granted that Kant's decision would be to divert the trolley. Rather, I submit, the trolley ought not to be turned, given the Kantian difference between narrow and wide duties. It is a narrow duty not to kill innocent human beings, but only a wide duty to save them. Given the latitude of the wide duty (to save the five) and the narrow and negative character of the other duty (not to kill the one), it is morally obligatory to obey the latter, i. e., not to kill the one. Also, because of the latitude of the wide duty, no conflict of duties arises. I shall rebut three objections against this *wide/narrow interpretation* (as I will call it) and present three additional arguments supporting it. In conclusion, I will discuss the relevance of these findings for the ethical challenges that come along with autonomous vehicles.

New technical developments lead to new ethical problems. The development of autonomous vehicles is a case in point: In view of the advancing automation of road and freight traffic, a decision has to be made as to how autonomous vehicles shall be programmed with regard to possible situations of conflict. For instance, may (or should) such vehicles steer around a group of people in order not to hit them, putting up instead with hitting a smaller group of people or a single person? Part of the theoretical framework to be taken into account in answering this question is the trolley problem. In this paper, I shall take a Kantian perspective on the trolley problem and thus also on the problem of autonomous driving. The final question, then, is: How should, against the background of Kantian ethics, autonomous vehicles be programmed when it comes to trolley situations?

To begin with, I shall spell out the basic features of the trolley problem (1). I will then discuss the question of whether the programmer of autonomous vehicles is to be paralleled with the trolley driver or rather with the so-called bystander (2). Afterwards, I will present a solution to the trolley problem that I think Kant himself would have given – I call it the *wide/narrow interpretation* (3). I shall then rebut three objections (4) and present three additional arguments supporting that interpretation (5). In conclusion, I will discuss the relevance of these findings for the ethical challenges that come along with autonomous vehicles (6).

Elke Elisabeth Schmidt, University of Siegen

1 The Trolley Problem

The trolley problem challenges philosophers to take a stance on very basic and crucial ethical questions, and it can be adapted not only to autonomous driving, but also to quite a number of controversial debates such as just war, torture, or triage. In her famous 1967 paper, Philippa Foot describes the following situation: "[. . .] it may rather be supposed that he [someone] is the driver of a runaway tram which he can only steer from one narrow track on to another; five men are working on one track and one man on the other; anyone on the track he enters is bound to be killed" (Foot 1978 [1967], 23).[1] If the driver does not turn the trolley, the five will die; if he does turn the trolley, the five survive but the one will die.[2] Two questions arise: First, should the trolley be turned or not? I call this the *preceding trolley problem*. It is only preceding in the sense that, as a matter of fact, this question typically is given a rather quick and straightforward affirmative answer; according to the prevailing opinion, the trolley may or even must be diverted.[3] Therefore, the main question in the literature and so, in this sense, the *prevalent trolley problem* (as I call it) is this: Why is it permissible to turn the trolley while it is not permissible not to turn it (or to make analogous decisions) in somewhat similar cases?[4] For example, it is not permissible to kill one healthy man in order to donate his organs to save some other five, and likewise, it is not permissible to throw a large man down a bridge over the tracks in order to block the trolley with his body before it kills the five (the so-called *footbridge* case).[5] Foot's solution both to the preceding and the prevalent trolley problem is as follows: The trolley driver has to divert the trolley to save the five. As a rule, in situations in which both negative duties (such as the duty not to kill) and positive duties (such as the duty to help others) apply, negative duties trump positive

---

1 Foot was not the first to come up with the trolley problem. This is not the place to investigate the historical question of who introduced the trolley problem (or a similar situation) first. In any event, Engisch (1930, 288) and Welzel (1951, 51 f.) already discussed similar cases.
2 In morally relevant respects, the involved persons are equal.
3 For such straightforward answers, cf. Foot (1978 [1967], 23), Thomson (1985, 1396 f.), Otsuka (2008), and Kleingeld (2020).
4 For the question what exactly the trolley problem consists in, cf. Foot (1978 [1967], 23), Thomson (1985, 1396, 1401; 2016, 115 f., 117), Otsuka (2008, 93), Kamm (2016, 58 f.), Nyholm/Smids (2016, 1279 f.), and Himmelreich (2018, 670 f.).
5 Foot contrasts the original trolley case with the case of a judge who has to decide whether he should sacrifice one innocent person to prevent a violent riot or not. She also discusses a number of similar but slightly different cases.

duties; killing, for example, is worse than not helping and thus worse than letting die (rule 1).[6] In the trolley case, however, only negative duties are relevant, so that the driver is faced – Foot argues (1978 [1967], 27) – with a "conflict of negative duties": If he does nothing, he kills five; if he diverts the course, he kills one; both killings are, generally speaking, prohibited.[7] Since in such a case, when duties of the same kind (such as the negative duty not to kill one and the negative duty not to kill five) are conflicting, the number of victims is to be minimized (rule 2), the driver must divert the trolley. By contrast, a healthy person may not be killed in order to save five by organ donation because the five who would otherwise die of organ failure would merely be left to die, while the healthy person would be killed. In the trolley case, no one would be left to die, but would be killed either way.

As we shall see, this thought has considerable flaws or, in any case, questionable premises. Foot has sparked a tremendous discussion with an enormous number of more or less similar cases (from bridges to bombs, avalanches, trap doors, tunnels, lazy Susans, tractors, and much more) which all drive at a better account of the prevalent trolley problem, i. e., a better answer to the question of why it is permissible to do something in this case (original trolley case) but not in another (transplantation case, large man etc.).[8] Contrary to what usually happens, I shall not primarily deal with those different modifications of the original trolley case and the prevalent trolley problem. Rather, I shall pursue the preceding trolley problem against the background of Kantian ethics, that is, the question of whether it is appropriate to turn the trolley or not (even though the answer to this preceding problem is, of course, related to the solution to the prevalent trolley problem, insofar as the answer to the latter shall provide criteria that also explain why the diversion of the trolley is permissible in the original case). Thus, although the preceding trolley problem is usually relegated to the background of discussion insofar as it seems clear to most that the trolley should be turned, it is precisely this question that will be brought into focus here. The main question then is: Would Kant agree to turn the trolley in the original trolley case?

---

6 Foot does not explicitly speak of rules, but it is obvious that she avails herself of these principles. Thomson (1985, 1396 f.), referring to Foot, articulates the principles (rules).
7 Foot (1978 [1967], 27) does not speak of a *duty not to kill* at this point but of the "duty to avoid injuring", but that does not make any difference.
8 For a discussion of the most important cases, cf. Kamm (2016).

2 Driver, Bystander, and Programmer

Before I address the main question, another distinction deserves attention. Obviously, the preceding and the prevalent trolley problem are highly interesting topics. However, my focus in this paper is not primarily on these problems *as such*, but on their relation to Kant's ethics and especially to the question of how a Kantian programmer would program fully autonomous vehicles for cases that are similar to the original trolley case.[9] Based on this presupposition, one ought to clarify the Kantian programmer's point of view by analogy: Does the fact that a certain action is morally permissible or obligatory for the driver of the trolley in the original case really imply that the corresponding programming is permissible or obligatory for the programmer, too? Although the parallelization of programmer and driver seems to be appropriate at first, on closer inspection some doubts arise. For in the context of the trolley problem it is not only the driver that is made a subject of discussion, but also the so-called *bystander* – and it *could* be, for instance, that a certain action, which is permissible for one (the bystander), is not permissible for the other (the driver). If this is the case, clarification is called for which role the programmer must fill.

This leads us to Judith Thomson, who introduced the bystander into the discussion.[10] By referring to a situation in which it is not the driver who has to make the decision to turn the trolley, but an uninvolved bystander next to the scene, she aimed at showing that Foot's solution to the trolley problem is not convincing. Thomson's argument goes like this: Since the driver of the trolley has started a process that, if he does not intervene, inevitably leads to the death of the five (he started the trolley and steered it up to the point in question), the driver *kills* the five on the tracks even if he does not do anything.[11] The bystander, on the other hand, finds himself at a short distance from the trolley and has no history with it; he has not set the trolley in motion and thus does not kill the five in case of non-intervention, but only *lets them die*. However, he would certainly *kill* the one if he were to throw the switch he is standing next to. According to Thomson, Foot's rule 1 (negative duties trump positive duties) implies that it is not permissible for the bystander to turn the switch, because by turning the switch he would *kill* the

---

9 There are different levels of automation when it comes to autonomous vehicles. I will concentrate here on the highest level (full driving automation), where no intervention of the driver is possible and where a driver is not necessary at all.

10 Cf. Thomson (1985, 1397–1400).

11 "[. . .] if the driver fails to turn his trolley, he does not merely let the five track workmen die; he drives his trolley into them, and thereby kills them" (Thomson 1985, 1397); "[. . .] if he does not turn the trolley, he does drive his trolley into them, and does thereby kill them" (1398).

one, i. e. the bystander would violate a negative duty which is worse than letting five die. However, according to Thomson's intuition, it is indeed permissible for the bystander to turn the switch. Consequently, it cannot be true that killing is always worse than letting die (because it is permissible for the bystander to kill a person by turning the switch). Thomson then offers her own answer to the question of why it is permissible to turn the trolley in the driver's and in the bystander's case but not in others (the large man case, for instance), but this is of no interest to us here.[12]

Now the question arises as to whether the role of the programmer of autonomous vehicles is analogous to the role of the trolley driver or to that of the bystander; note, however, that this question is only important if there really is a normative difference between being in the driver's and the bystander's position. If the programmer accepts rules similar to Foot's (negative duties trump positive duties; when duties of the same kind conflict, the number of victims is to be minimized), it follows that, understanding the programmer as a driver, it is permissible for him to turn the trolley; understanding him as a bystander, it is not permissible for him to flip the switch on the basis of those rules. Yet if the Kantian rules (which we still have to determine) are different from Foot's, it might turn out that the difference between driver and bystander is irrelevant for the programmer.

Admittedly, in a certain respect the programmer is neither driver nor bystander. He is not surprised by a situation in which he is directly involved and in which he has to decide quickly. Rather, the programmer has enough time for his decision.[13] And yet these differences are irrelevant, because even in hypothetical trolley situations the crucial question is which *carefully considered* decision is the right one; psychological pressure or time pressure hardly play any

---

12 Thomson's first approach (1985, 1403) includes two criteria: "In the first place, the bystander saves his five by making something that threatens them instead threaten one. Second, the bystander does not do that by means which themselves constitute an infringement of any right of the one's." However, in her later paper (Thomson 2008), she changes her mind with reference to a further variation of the scenario with a total of three options for the bystander including the choice between the death of five, the death of one, or self-sacrifice. She now agrees with Foot's initial proposal and holds that it is not permissible for the bystander to flip the switch.

13 Of course, it is not simply up to the programmer which way to go; manufacturers or states and the corresponding laws will dictate what is permissible to program, and in this respect the programmer is not the decision maker at all (cf. Nyholm/Smids 2016, 1281 f.). For the sake of argument, I will leave these questions aside.

role in trolleyology.[14] What matters instead is the following: *If* there is a morally significant difference between driver and bystander, the programmer has to be paralleled with the bystander. Both bystander and programmer did not start the vehicle; they are in a certain way outside the situation. Neither of them has initiated a process leading to the death of five in case of non-intervention, neither of them maneuvered the vehicle into a dangerous situation. Of course, there would be no autonomous vehicle without a programmer. But the case of the bystander would not be judged differently even if he had been involved as an engineer in the construction of the trolley. It does not make any difference whether someone was part of the construction of the vehicle or not. Similarly, the fact that the programmer has not only been involved in the construction of the trolley, but also in the decision-making process of where to steer the vehicle, does not change the game; for the bystander also faces a decision to make. Hence, it is also negligible at what point in time the decision is made (obviously, the programmer makes his decisions way ahead of a possible accident). Consequently, the role of the programmer is that of the bystander. *Nota bene*: This does *not* imply that the difference between driver and bystander *is* morally relevant at all. Assuming for now that this difference is relevant, though, we are now in a position to address the main question of this paper: Would Kant agree to let the bystander (and hence the programmer) flip the switch?

3 Kant's Solution to the Trolley Problem

Let me begin with a comment on possible conflicts of duties. According to Foot, the trolley problem is a situation in which we find ourselves faced with such a conflict. However, for Kant, such conflicts of duties are not possible. This much is clear, I think, but it is not evident why this is so. It seems as if Kant argued for the impossibility of such conflicts by virtue of the very essence of what duties are: Duties obligate with necessity, and therefore, two duties cannot contradict each other.[15] This seems to be a rather formalistic approach to the problem. Yet it

---

14 If at all, psychological pressure can only be relevant in legal contexts when it comes to the question of whether someone who broke the law in a case of (possible) exculpatory necessity (*Notstand*) should be punished; cf. Wörner (2019, 45 f.).

15 For the impossibility of conflicting duties, cf. Kant's *Doctrine of Right*, MS: 224. – Since, strictly speaking, a dilemma involves two conflicting binding rules in a specific situation and conflicts of duties are not possible, the trolley situation, according to Kant, cannot be understood as a *dilemmatic* situation in a strict sense. Even though duties cannot conflict, according to Kant, "*grounds of obligation*" can. Unfortunately, Kant says next to nothing about what *grounds of obligation* are

is possible to develop a further argument on Kantian grounds. To see how, let us recall the different kinds of duties he discusses: Roughly speaking, there are wide duties, i. e., duties which come with a certain kind of latitude in obeying them, and narrow duties without latitude.[16] Since wide duties only command maxims[17] and no particular acts, a conflict between wide duties is not possible. For instance, the wide duty of benevolence cannot contradict the wide duty of gratitude in a situation in which one can either carry out an act of benevolence to one person or an act of gratitude to another; both wide duties of benevolence and of gratitude have latitude that enables one to carry out the specific act of benevolence (or gratitude) at another time and another place. Furthermore, since narrow duties are negative duties only commanding omissions, there can be no conflict of narrow duties either; one can both and at the same time obey the duty not to murder someone as well as the duty not to steal.[18] And since, lastly and generally speaking, both reasons hold (wide duties have latitude and narrow duties only tell us not to do something), there can be no conflict between a wide and a narrow duty either.[19] Now one *could* think that the trolley problem strongly

---

supposed to be and in which sense conflicts between them can arise. There is no consensus in the literature about these questions either; possibilities range from bare facts to *prima facie* duties and a combination of both. According to Timmermann (2013, 48), "a ground of obligation arises when an agent correctly applies an ethical principle to a concrete case." "This ground," he goes on, "though genuine, can still fail to produce an actual obligation if the agent lacks the means to further the ethical end in question, e.g. because of some physical, psychological, or moral impossibility". Timmermann (2013, 43–50) holds that conflicting *grounds of obligation* are only possible within the realm of ethical duties (for a different position, cf. McCarty 1991, 69). However, he does not discuss the possibility of ethical duties being duties of omission, especially not duties of respect (I will get back to this later). For further analysis, cf. McCarty (1991) and Adkins (1999), and, in a more general approach, Hill (2002). – Note that the trolley situation is also not a case of *moral uncertainty*: The alleged conflict can be resolved, or so I shall argue. I shall present a conclusive Kantian answer to the question of what to do. In doing so, I will not switch from one level of argumentation (what is morally obligatory in a specific situation?) to another (what ought we to do when the answer to the first question is uncertain?); for an overview regarding such a strategy of distinguishing different levels, cf. Bykvist (2017).

16 Cf. Kant's *Doctrine of Virtue*, MS: 388–394 and 410–411.

17 The term *maxim* is of course a highly problematic one. For this purpose, I take a *maxim* to be a non-normative, expressive principle of an agent's practical self-determination.

18 Cf. Timmermann (2013, 45). According to Joerden (1997, 44) and from a legal point of view, it is not undisputed that there can be no conflicts between negative duties. According to McCarty (1991, 70 f.), there can be "conflicts of grounds of obligation involving only perfect duties" when it comes to the duty of civil obedience or the duty to keep promises on the one hand and the duty not to lie, for instance, on the other.

19 For the three options *narrow/narrow*, *wide/narrow* and *wide/wide*, cf. McCarty (1991, 69), Adkins (1999, 463 ff.).

suggests that Kant must be wrong, after all, in claiming this impossibility of ethical conflicts – for the trolley problem shows, it might be argued, that there indeed *can* be conflicts between duties. But as we shall see, this conclusion would be drawn too quickly.

How would Kant analyze the trolley situation in his own terms, provided that no conflicts of duties are possible? Given this assumption, we cannot think of the bystander as having to choose between obeying two different narrow duties, that is, between the narrow duty not to kill five and the narrow duty not to kill one. Otherwise, the bystander would not be able to obey both duties and so there *would* be a conflict of duties.[20] Rather, it is possible to interpret the trolley situation, with Kant, in two ways:

(i) The bystander has to choose between obeying two different wide duties: saving the five and saving the one. Given the latitude of wide duties, both actions are permissible; given their permissibility, no conflict is involved (I call this the *wide/wide interpretation*).

(ii) The bystander has to choose between obeying a wide duty and a narrow duty: saving (the five) and not killing (the one). Given the latitude of the wide duty (to save others) and the narrow and negative character of the other duty (not to kill), it is morally obligatory to obey the latter, i. e., not to kill the one. Given the latitude of the wide duty, no conflict of duties arises. For even though it is, generally speaking, a duty to help others, there is no obligation to save the five in this particular situation, given the narrow duty not to kill the one (*wide/narrow interpretation*).[21]

---

20 With regard to the possibly conflicting "*grounds* of obligation" (MS: 224) already mentioned, one might wonder whether one could indeed interpret the trolley situation as a choice between not killing the five and not killing the one. Although there is no conflict of duties (for the general duty not to kill as such does not conflict with any other duty), there could be different *grounds of obligation* concerning this duty not to kill, i. e., the five, as one such ground, and the one as the other. – I will not pursue this line of argumentation. Firstly, because it is not clear at all what those *grounds of obligation* are. This interpretative problem, however, is no reason to worry. In fact, secondly and for reasons that will become clear below, it is not sensible to claim that the bystander *kills* the five by doing nothing (see below, 200–202). Thirdly, within Kantian ethics, it is never possible to interpret a choice as one between *killing* and *killing*. Since to kill innocent persons is strictly forbidden, one has to accept one's own death before killing someone else (I will get back to this point in detail; cf. also the gallows man example in KpV: 30).

21 Formally speaking, there is one further possible interpretation of the situation, namely the *narrow/wide interpretation* (rather than *wide/narrow*): The bystander would then have to choose between not killing the five (narrow) and saving the one (wide). Since this interpretation is highly implausible, I will leave it aside.

Option (i), the *wide/wide interpretation*, is not very promising. The bystander's two possible actions would be described as follows. Either the bystander *does* flip the switch in order to obey the wide duty to save the five or the bystander *does not* flip the switch in order to obey the wide duty to save the one. Note that it is quite correct to describe the bystander's action to pull the switch in order *to save the five* as an action obeying a wide duty. However, to say that the bystander *saves* the one on the track by not flipping the switch is implausible, for the one, at least in a strict sense, is not in danger at all before the bystander enters the scene.[22] It is not that the one on the track somehow is in danger of losing his life, and *then* the bystander shows up and has the option of doing away with that danger. If there is a danger at all, it arises *because* of the bystander's possible thought of actually pulling the switch; but there is, as it were, no danger *ante cogitationem*.[23] Also note that it would be of no help (even if it might be correct) to say that there are not *two* wide duties in this situation but only *one*, i. e. the general wide duty to help others. For if this is correct, this one wide duty allows the bystander to choose freely between flipping the switch or not. If he pulls the switch he chooses to help the five; if he does not pull the switch, he chooses to help the one. However, the problem remains even under this interpretation: It makes no sense to say that the bystander *helps* the one by not flipping the switch because the one person is not in need of help, to begin with. To conclude, it is not the case that the bystander has to choose between helping one and helping five.[24]

---

22 According to Kleingeld (2020, 219 f.), the agent has a choice between *saving* and *saving*. However, her line of argument goes into another direction (cf. below, 205–206).

23 For the reasons just given, it makes little sense to argue that all six people, the five and the one, together make up *one* endangered group. (Also note that German law rules out the possibility of singling individuals out to die for the sake of the others even in cases of a "Gefahrgemeinschaft" – in which without intervention all will die, cf. Wörner 2019, 48). Of course, *in some sense*, everybody on the tracks is in *some* danger even when no trolley is near. But this general kind of danger is different from the concrete danger the five are in or the concrete danger the one is in *after the bystander comes around*.

24 Joerden (1997, 45ff.) describes the following case: A father has to choose between saving his drowning son A and saving his drowning son B; he cannot save both, and if he does nothing, both will die. In this case, Joerden argues, the father is only faced with one duty indeed, namely the wide duty to help his children (or, generally speaking, to help others). Since he cannot save both, to save both cannot be a duty. According to Joerden (1997, 47), the father is obliged by one duty, but two "grounds of obligation". – For the reason mentioned above, we cannot interpret the bystander's situation as similar to this kind of situation. Rather, cases similar to that described by Joerden are so-called *Taurek cases* (in which only duties to help others are relevant); I will get back to these later.

Thus, from a Kantian point of view, option (ii), the *wide/narrow interpretation*, is the most sensible reconstruction of the bystander's situation. Since the latitude of the wide duty (to help others) allows one to refrain from carrying out the wide duty in this particular case, the narrow duty overrides the wide duty. Therefore, there is no conflict of duties and it is *morally obligatory not to flip the switch and therefore not to kill the one*. Put another way: According to option (ii), it is not permissible for the bystander to pull the switch in order to save the five. And of course, this answer to the trolley problem indeed looks very Kantian. Even if we might not like this result from a systematic, non-Kantian ethical point of view, it is the result Kantian ethics leads to.

This is the basic outline of the Kantian solution to the preceding trolley problem. I will now reject three objections and then adduce three additional arguments supporting this interpretation. In the course of this, the Kantian solution will further be unfolded.

4 The Wide/Narrow Interpretation: Three Objections

All three objections aim to show that the *wide/narrow interpretation* of the bystander's situation is wrong. The first two do so by denying the wideness of the duty concerning the five, although with different arguments. The third objection argues that the duty concerning the one is not a narrow duty. I will rebut all three objections.

Objection 1) It is not a wide duty to save the five because there is no latitude. Since the bystander has no latitude in helping the five, as posited by the objection, there is no wide duty to help but only a narrow one. The bystander cannot choose between helping the five now or tomorrow, to a greater or smaller extent, in this way or another. Given the typical trolley situation, there simply is no latitude in obeying the (allegedly wide) duty to help the five; if the bystander does not flip the switch, the five will die. Since wide duties require latitude and here there is no latitude, there can be no wide duty to help in this case, and therefore the *wide/narrow interpretation* cannot be correct. – This objection overlooks the difference between the *general* wide duty to help others and the alleged *specific* obligation to save the five on the track. Even though the bystander has the wide duty to help others in general, he is not obliged to save the five in the trolley situation.[25] Hence, there *is* latitude in obeying the general wide duty to help others – it is the latitude of the wide duty that indeed does make it morally permissible and even necessary to refrain from helping the five. Since a wide duty does not command specific actions but only maxims, it is not obligatory for the bystander to help the five. Once again: The point is not that there is no wide duty; there *is*, as there always is the wide duty to help others in need, but this duty does not apply given the specific situation. Thus, the bystander's situation includes both a wide as well as a narrow duty; they do not conflict, but the narrow duty trumps the wide duty.[26] (Furthermore, saving someone's life certainly cannot be a narrow duty in principle, for then we would be required to constantly save whosoever's life.)

However, matters do get more complicated when we dig a little deeper into Kant's distinction of duties. There are at least two problems: First, although Kant claims that all ethical duties (which the *Doctrine of Virtue* allegedly consists of) are wide duties that come with latitude,[27] we do find negative duties (*perfect* duties) in the *Doctrine of Virtue* as well, such as the prohibition of suicide or lying, for instance, and as negative duties, they seem to lack any latitude. Given the rather strong and repeated claim of Kant's that ethical duties are wide duties, there has to be a way to think of those negative duties in the *Doctrine of Virtue* as wide duties, too – or else Kant's distinction between wide and narrow duties on the one hand and between the duties of the *Doctrine of Right* and the *Doctrine of Virtue* on the other would make no sense whatsoever. Therefore, we must argue that *not all negative duties are narrow duties.*[28] Very briefly: There is (i) not only a *casuistry* for duties of commission (*imperfect* duties), but also for negative duties[29] – and since casuistry, if taken seriously, requires latitude, negative duties that allow for a casuistry seem to be wide. (ii) Kant repeatedly stresses that ethical duties as such, *i. e. including negative or imperfect duties*, only command maxims, which also implies that they are wide

---

25 For the distinction between *duty* and *obligation*, cf. also Timmermann (2013, 42 f.) and McCarty (1991, 68). *Duty* refers to the general duty before its application, *obligation* means the duty applied to a specific situation.

26 I will sometimes speak of the *wide duty concerning the five* even if there is no duty concerning *the five* in the strict sense but only the general duty to help others.

27 Cf. Kant's *Doctrine of Virtue*, MS: 390.

28 It is tempting to understand all legal duties as narrow duties and thereby as negative duties (cf. Mieth/Bambauer 2018, 116). However, with regard to the *Ulpian formulas* (MS: 236 f.), things might be more complicated. The third of these formulas, for instance, is not a negative one: "(If you cannot help associating with others), *enter* into a society with them in which each can keep what is his (*suum cuique tribue*)."

29 Kant speaks of "*casuistry*" (MS: 411) as well as of "*casuistic questions*" (MS: 423). For *casuistic questions* regarding the duty not to commit suicide, cf. MS: 423 f.

duties with latitude.[30] (iii) Kant at least at one point puts emphasis on his claim that negative duties can indeed be of a "wide obligation".[31] – In light of these distinctions, I take the duty not to kill other persons (which applies regarding the one on the track) to be a narrow duty, that is, as a legal duty of omission. Given that all legal duties are also "indirectly ethical" duties (MS: 221), one can also consider it as a negative, ethical duty (parallel to the duty not to kill oneself).

The second problem with Kant's system of duties is the following. One might think that even for Kant wide duties must be able to be *narrowed down*, so to speak. For instance, someone who has the general wide duty to help others *has to* help a drowning child if nothing else speaks against the act of helping; there is no latitude. The crucial point, however, is that wide duties remain wide even if in a specific situation there is only one action that is to be carried out. The fact that the wide duty, in a specific situation, must be realized through a specific act does not dispute its wideness, because the wide duty remains open to other acts in other situations.[32] In any case, the trolley situation is by no means similar to that of the drowning child. For there is a reason *not* to save the five (to wit, the one on the track), whereas there is no reason whatsoever not to save the drowning child.[33] To save someone's life is to fulfill a wide duty, and this is also true in the bystander's situation. The *wide/narrow interpretation* remains undefeated.

Objection 2) Not flipping the switch really is killing the five. According to the second objection, the *wide/narrow interpretation* is wrong since not to pull the switch is tantamount to *killing* the five, and since killing is strictly prohibited, it cannot be a

---

30 Cf. Kant's *Doctrine of Virtue*, MS: 410, for instance.

31 Cf. Kant's *Doctrine of Virtue*, MS: 394.

32 Perhaps, one could say, as Mieth/Bambauer (2018, 122, my own translation) suggest, that a wide duty "articulates both an imperfect and a perfect duty, depending on the specific context: It is a perfect duty only if the life of the other is at stake, but otherwise meritorious in the sense of morally desirable".

33 With regard to situations in which someone could save a child's life by committing a minor crime such as stealing something from a supermarket, for instance, Mieth/Bambauer (2018, 117) maintain the following: One can either argue that the wide (ethical) duty to help others turns into a narrow (legal) duty, or that the wide ethical duty trumps the legal duty. I would submit, however, that both options seem to run afoul of Kant's system of duties. As opposed to supermarket situations, it seems quite obvious that killing the one cannot be considered a *minor* crime; also, Kant would not even allow minor crimes to be committed in order to bring about something good. The question of whether minor crimes could be exculpatory on Kantian grounds is difficult to answer. Kant holds: "Yet there could be no necessity that would make what is wrong conform the law." (MS: 236) *Unpunishable actions* (cf. MS: 236,1 f.) are to be distinguished from actions that might be exculpatory. I cannot get into this here.

wide duty to save the five. – This objection is not convincing either. Not flipping the switch is not tantamount to killing the five, at least not in a morally relevant sense. I shall argue that this is not only true for the bystander but also for the driver of the trolley. Although most philosophers like Foot or Thomson typically assume – and do so without much ado – that the driver *kills* the five by not pulling the switch because he *started* the trolley (and here *killing* is supposed to be morally relevant killing, i. e., killing which violates negative duties),[34] this assumption is flawed or by no means indisputable. Rather, the fact that the driver started the trolley is irrelevant.[35] Let me draw an analogy: Think of someone who starts his non-autonomous car and drives up to the main road with regular speed. Suddenly, a young boy riding his bike crosses the street out of the blue, leaving the driver no chance whatsoever to swerve; the boy dies from the crash. Did the driver *kill* the boy? Given that the driver wasn't speeding, that he wasn't under the influence, given that he drove his car cautiously and so on, we would not say that he *killed* the boy, at least not in a morally relevant way. Of course, the boy is dead (he surely *got* killed), and of course there is a causal relation between the driver and the boy's death; the boy would not be dead if the driver had not gotten out of bed that morning. But the driver neither killed the boy intentionally or deliberately (he did not *want* to see the boy dead) nor acted negligently. So even if on occasion legal scholars or philosophers indeed say that A *killed* B although it was in no way A's intention or fault,[36] such a killing is not a *morally relevant* killing. (As a matter of fact, it seems to me that we should not say that the driver *killed* the boy even if we mean this in a morally neutral way; rather, we should say that the boy died in an accident.) And so just like the driver of the car, the driver of the trolley also does

---

34 See above, footnote 11. Thomson (1985, 1398) states the following: "[. . .] we might well wish to ask ourselves what exactly is the difference between what the driver would be doing if he failed to turn the trolley and what the bystander would be doing if he failed to throw the switch. As I said, the driver would be driving a trolley into the five; but what exactly would his driving the trolley into the five consist in? Why, just sitting there, doing nothing! If the driver does just sit there, doing nothing, then that will have been how come he drove his trolley into the five. [paragraph] I do not mean to make much of that fact about what the driver's driving his trolley into the five would consist in, for it seems to me to be right to say that if he does not turn the trolley, he does drive his trolley into them, and does thereby kill them." Yet it is obvious that this is not really an answer to the question posed by Thomson herself. She does not account for the *difference* between the driver and the bystander; she simply assumes that the driver commits an act of killing whereas the bystander does not.

35 A similar proposal is made, albeit very sketchily, by Mannino/Mukerji (2020, 106).

36 I am grateful to Reinhard Merkel for helpful comments regarding the legal context. – Thomson (1991, 289) holds: "[. . .] if an event that consists in the fall of Y on X kills X, then it follows that Y killed X, whatever Y may be".

not kill the five in a morally relevant way by doing nothing; he neither wants to kill the five nor is it his fault that something went wrong with the trolley. At first sight, the difference between the driver of the car and the driver of the trolley appears to be that the latter has an alternative, i. e. he could turn the trolley, whereas the former has no alternative (or so we assumed). But it is important to see that the driver of the trolley has, on second thought, no alternative either. For the only thing he *could* do is something which violates a narrow duty. Within Kantian ethics, to violate a narrow duty is not an option one may consider if one wants to do what is morally right. It is not permissible for the driver to turn the trolley; instead, he is obliged *not* to turn the trolley in order not to kill the one. Unlike the driver of the car, who is not even in a position to carry out an action that would save the boy, the driver of the trolley is (physically, as it were) in a position to carry out an action that would save the five; but this action is prohibited. It is important to stress that this is exactly what he is doing: he does not turn the trolley in order to fulfill his duty not to kill the one. Since he is not morally free to do otherwise, what he does cannot be described as killing the five (for again, a duty can only be neglected when the person who acts has a permissible alternative to choose). Note, too, that if there were no switch to be pulled in the first place, so that the five would inevitably die, neither the driver nor the bystander would kill the five (in a morally relevant way). Differently from what Foot assumes, the driver of the trolley does not have a choice between killing and killing; by not turning the trolley, he does not kill the five in a morally relevant way. Since this is true concerning the driver, it is all the more true that the bystander does not kill the five by doing nothing. This leads to an important point: *There is no morally relevant difference between the driver of the trolley and the bystander*. Neither has a choice between killing and killing: rather, both must choose between *saving* and killing.[37] Thus, to come back to the role of the programmer, it does *not* make any relevant difference whether we parallel the programmer of an autonomous vehicle with the driver of the trolley or the bystander. In Section 2, I pointed out that this question of whether the programmer is to be identified with the driver or the bystander is a question that deserves serious attention, for it *could* have made a difference. We now see, however, that the difference is actually irrelevant. Both driver and bystander have a choice between saving the five and killing the one. Not saving the five is not tantamount to killing the five. The *wide/narrow interpretation* remains undefeated.

---

37 Kamm (2016, 58), for instance, also holds that the question of *how* the trolley was turned is more important than the question of *who* turned the trolley.

Objection 3) It is not a narrow duty not to flip the switch because flipping the switch does not mean to kill the one. Given that whoever pulls the switch does not *want* to see the one dead but save the five (and would, if possible, do the latter without doing the former) – the objection goes – to flip the switch is not tantamount to killing the one (again, in a morally relevant way). So after all, it might as well be permissible to pull the switch because pulling the switch does not violate the narrow duty not to kill (since it does not mean to kill the one). – However, the opposite is true: To flip the switch does indeed mean to kill the one. One alternative to saying that one has a narrow duty not to kill the one would be to say that one has a wide duty to *save* the one. However, this option is null since the one on the track is, as described above, not in danger in a strict sense before someone thinks about turning the trolley; therefore, *saving* does not fit the situation. Now, and most importantly, the most obvious way to reinforce the thesis that flipping the switch is not tantamount to killing the one is the *Doctrine of Double Effect* (*DDE*). Suppose someone argues the following: Since we are confronted with a situation in which, firstly, the act itself (flipping the switch) is permissible, secondly, the negative effect (the death of the one) is not directly intended, thirdly, the death of the one is not a means to saving the five, and, finally, the negative effect stands in an adequate relation to the positive effect, the *DDE* applies and therefore it is permissible to flip the switch to save the five even though it will lead to the death of the one.[38] – However, there is no room for the *DDE* in Kant's ethics. Even if we ignore the severe systematic problems of the *DDE*,[39] it is not possible to deploy the principle in accordance with Kantian theory for two reasons. (i) As far as I can see, there is no direct reference to the *DDE* in Kant's (published) writings; if it did play any substantial role in Kant's ethics, one would expect it to show up at least in his main works. While self-defense is a classical Aquinian example for implementing the *DDE*, Kant does not refer to the *DDE* when he discusses that topic (according to Kant, self-defense leading to the aggressor's death is only permissible when someone is confronted with an unjust aggressor; it is not permissible to kill an innocent person to save one's own life –

---

38 For this classical version of the *DDE*, cf. Mangan (1949, 43). – Note that the *DDE*, strictly speaking, is not meant to show that *the killing of a person* can be permissible. Rather, if at all, the *DDE* is supposed to show that it can be permissible to carry out an otherwise morally neutral action (in this case, flipping the switch) leading to the death of a person.

39 Among other things, it seems impossible to determine what exactly the so-called *act in itself* is (since every act must have an end, according to Kant, this problem might especially arise for Kantian ethics). Furthermore, the relevance of the underlying distinction of intended and merely foreseen harm can be questioned, of course. For the last point, cf. for instance Thomson (1991, 292–296).

I shall come back to this below).[40] (ii) The *DDE* is in contrast with the very spirit of Kantian ethics; the fourth condition is especially unsuited to Kant's thoughts. There never can be an adequate relation between good and bad effects when persons, i. e. human beings endowed with dignity are concerned. One cannot weigh the worth of five persons against the worth of one person (I shall elaborate on this thought below). All in all, pulling the switch does indeed violate the narrow duty not to kill the one. The *wide/narrow interpretation* remains undefeated.

Excursus: The loop case. Thomson (1985, 1401–1403) created the *loop case* to show that the trolley problem cannot be solved by referring to the Kantian principle *not to use another person merely as a means*. In the loop case, Thomson says, it is permissible to flip the switch although the one on the other track, the large man who gets killed as a consequence of pulling the switch, is used as a means to save the five (because the track with the one and the track with the five circle back in a loop so that the five would be killed regardless of the switch's position, were it not for the large man whose body could stop the trolley). – Let me take up three points here: First, it is important to see that in debates initiated by the loop case, two elements are somehow intertwined: the *DDE* and the Kantian principle *not to use another person merely as a means*. As we have seen above, the Kantian principle is, at least in some sense, one element of the *DDE*, to wit, that the bad consequence (the death of the one) must not be a means to save the five. Given this conjunction of the *DDE* and the Kantian principle, the following is true: To hold that it is *permissible* to flip the switch in the loop case (even though the death of the one is a means to save the five) implies that the Kantian principle *not to use another person merely as means* is violated or rather refuted – and *a fortiori* so is the *DDE*.[41] Yet the fact that the Kantian principle is indeed (in some sense) part of the *DDE* does *not* show that Kant embraces the *DDE*.

---

40 There is no consensus concerning the question of whether the *DDE* does go back to Thomas Aquinas (cf. again Mangan 1949). For the Aquinian example of self-defense, cf. his *Summa Theologica* (II–II, Qu. 64, Art. 7). Cf. Kant, MS: 235 f., TP: 300. – According to Byrd, Kant refers at one point (MS: 336) to the so-called "*actio invita* (the *reluctant act*)" (Byrd, 2015, 2299, my own translation) which, he says, is discussed by Achenwall and goes back to Aristotle's thought on mixed acts. However, since Byrd only refers to this single passage of Kant's, this linkage seems to require some more evidence. Also, the context of this utterance of Kant's is the topic of duels, that is, a context in which the person to be killed is not innocent but has harmed the other. The agent's innocence in moral relations is crucial here; I will get back to this shortly.

41 Thomson does not refer to the *DDE* in her discussion of the loop case. However, she does reject the *DDE* (see Thomson 1991, 292–296). – Kamm (2007, 91–129) famously tried to save the *DDE* at least in some sense with the introduction of the *Principle of Triple Effect* and her distinction between *doing something in order to* and *because of* (which others were quick to

For, as mentioned above, the *DDE* contains other elements which Kant indeed rejects.[42]

Second, Pauline Kleingeld recently argued that, as a matter of fact, turning the trolley in the loop case does *not* necessarily go along with using the one merely as a means even on Kantian normative grounds. It all depends, she argues, on how the bystander relates to the one in his thinking about how to act. Unlike the case with the large man and the bridge, in which pulling the switch clearly implies using the one merely as a means, in the loop case – she says – it is only *possible* but *not necessary* to use the one merely as a means. Rather, the bystander could set himself the end of saving the five, but not by using the one as a means, although he knows that the one would ultimately stop the trolley. From this perspective, the one does not "enter into her [the bystander's] reasoning *as a means*" (Kleingeld 2020, 220). However, Kleingeld's argument seems flawed. For one thing, she describes the decision at stake as one between *saving* and *saving* and not as one between *killing* and *killing* (as Foot and Thomson do) or *saving* and *killing* (as Kant does, or so I claim).[43] For another, and most importantly, it is quite hard to see what her argument actually is. She admits that the bystander knows that it is the one who will stop the trolley. But simply saying that this functional role of the one does not enter into the bystander's reasoning does not prove that this way of reasoning is sensible. If the agent knows the one is, objectively speaking, the means to save the five (if he were not on the track, switching the track would not make any sense), just saying that nonetheless and somewhat mysteriously, the one does not enter into the bystander's reasoning as a means is neither a good account of what actually happens nor a good representation of what goes on in the bystander's mind. Kleingeld describes what she thinks is the morally permissible maxim of the bystander in the loop case as follows: "[. . .] either I let the trolley continue towards the five, which will save one life, or I divert it towards the heavy man, which will kill him but save five lives" (2020, 220). Since there is no mention of the large man as a means, he is not used as a means from the

---

criticize). However, Kamm does not fully embrace the principle herself. For a critique of Kamm's position, cf. Otsuka (2008). Otsuka (2008, 107–110), by the way, is one of few philosophers that entertain doubts about the question of whether it really is permissible to flip the switch in the loop case.

42 Here I concur with Parfit (2017, 382 f.), who makes exactly the same point; he also shares the opinion that the *DDE* is of no relevance for Kant. In discussions about the *DDE*, Kant is rarely mentioned and only with regard to the principle *not to use another person merely as means*. For instance, in his recent book on the *DDE*, Černý (2020, 99) mentions Kant once, but only to refer to the prohibition of using someone merely as a means.

43 Kleingeld (2020, 219 f.).

agent's perspective, she says. However, it is not clear why we should not be able to describe the bystander's maxim in the case with the large man and the bridge in a similar way. For we could very well describe the bystander's maxim in the footbridge case as follows: *either I let the trolley continue towards the five, which will save one life, or I throw the large man down the bridge, which will kill him but save five lives.* Here, too, there is no mention of the large man *as a means*, but from this it does not follow that it makes sense to say that from an internal perspective, he is not used as such. Put another way: It is not, at least not generally speaking, up to an agent's reasoning whether he does use someone (merely) as a means or not. Without there being a man on the loop's tracks, pulling the switch would not make any sense.

Third, even though loop discussions are, of course, quite enlightening, they are irrelevant for the question to be answered in this paper. For reasons that have been already laid out and will be further developed in due course, Kant would not permit flipping the switch, neither in the original trolley case (both for the driver and for the bystander) nor in the loop case. Indeed, it looks as if, for Kant, there is a short-cut answer to what I have called the prevalent trolley problem (the question of why turning the switch is permissible in some cases but not in others): this problem does not arise to begin with, given Kant's answer to what I have called the preceding trolley problem (the question of whether it is permissible to turn the trolley in the original case). One may not and never pull the switch; therefore, the question of why one may pull the switch in some cases but not in others simply does not arise.

5 Unfolding Kant's Solution: Three Additional Arguments

Having cleared these three objections out of the way, it seems not only possible but quite plausible to interpret the trolley situation in terms of the *wide/narrow interpretation*, which implies that whoever is in charge of the switch is obliged not to turn the trolley. I will now present three additional arguments to support this view. This will also help to further unfold the Kantian solution to the preceding trolley problem.

Additional argument 1) The maxim not to turn the trolley is universalizable on the basis of the principle of universalization. The categorical imperative (CI) is the central tool of Kantian ethics and supposed to be a procedure for testing the universalizability of maxims (if a certain maxim is universalizable, the action in question is at least morally permissible). I shall now show that the maxim not to pull the switch is universalizable. Since testing a maxim presupposes having phrased an appropriate maxim in the first place, we have to ask: What maxim adequately describes the act of not flipping the switch? Of course, this is a question that touches on a lot of subjects and further questions, so I have to focus on some well-chosen aspects.

Let me begin with two questions, one rather basic and one somewhat specific: What is Kant's account of *acts*? And since the act in question is *not* to pull the switch: Are omissions acts?[44] Very briefly, the answer to both questions is this: According to Kant, a "*deed*" (MS: 223) is a free and accountable act under the moral law which as such can only be performed by free, autonomous subjects capable of active and passive moral obligation (persons). A person acting in this sense is the author of a deed's results and therefore accountable for them.[45] Since the CI is supposed to be (also) a procedure showing which duties we have to fulfill, and since a duty can be positive (a duty of commission, i. e. a duty to do something) as well as negative (a duty of omission, i. e. a duty *not* to do something), omissions can also be *deeds*, at least when it comes to negative duties.[46] So to refrain from doing something that is prohibited by the moral law is a deed: "All moral omissions are negative actions and therefore not a lack of actions: but real actions realiter opposed to the positive actions" (PPH: 9). This understanding of omissions fits quite well with Kant's concept of what it means to obey the moral law. To act from duty means to act as our noumenal self tells us to and thus to resist our selfish inclinations. Not to perform an act we feel inclined to carry out means *doing* something, to wit, actively resisting these inclinations out of respect for the moral law.[47] If someone feels the strong need to lie to his

---

44 Cf. in more detail, Schmidt/Schönecker (2017, 136–148).

45 "An action is called a *deed* insofar as it comes under obligatory laws and hence insofar as the subject, in doing it, is considered in terms of the freedom of his choice. By such an action the agent is regarded as the *author* of its effect, and this, together with the action itself, can be *imputed* to him, if one is previously acquainted with the law by virtue of which an obligation rests on these" (MS: 223).

46 As stated above, Kant distinguishes between wide and narrow duties. Wide duties can be either positive duties (as the duty to be benevolent; cf. §§ 29–31 of the *Doctrine of Virtue*) or negative duties (as the duty not to kill oneself, for instance; cf. § 6). We have only duties to persons, either to oneself or to other persons (Kant also speaks of duties with regard to nature, animals and God which are really duties to oneself; cf. §§ 16–18 of the *Doctrine of Virtue*).

47 Cf.: "By contrast, imagine a human being who fails to help someone whom he sees in distress and whom he could easily help. There is a positive law to be found in the heart of every human being, and it is a law which is present in this man's heart as well; it commands that we

spouse but decides not to lie because it would be the wrong thing to do, he acts out of respect for the moral law. Thus, omissions *are* or at least *can be* deeds, and not to flip the switch clearly is an omission, and as such a deed.

To formulate an adequate maxim we must clarify what exactly the deed under consideration, understood as an omission, consists in: Is it (a) simply not pulling the switch without further qualification? Is it (b) not flipping the switch *and* thus *letting five die* (we already ruled out that whoever does or does not turn the trolley kills the five in a morally relevant way by not pulling the switch)? Or is it (c) not flipping the switch *and* thus *not killing the one* (recall that pulling the switch is tantamount to killing the one)? It is undisputed that deeds cannot only consist in the physically (not) carried out movement, and since every deed, according to Kant (MS: 385), has an end which essentially constitutes the deed by the maxim the subject is determined through, it cannot be option (a). Thus we are left with options (b) and (c), and then the question is: What is the end of a person who does not turn the switch? Of course, that depends precisely on which end she sets. Given the typical trolley situation, it is taken for granted that it is nobody's *end* to let the five die (they are nobody's enemies, or whatever). Therefore, option (b) is eliminated as well and option (c) is the correct specification of the maxim: "I do not flip the switch in order not to kill the one".[48] Again, as an act of omission, the end is to prevent something from happening (killing the one); killing the five is not part of the deed. Of course, the maxim just formulated looks quite unproblematic. But what about the maxim "I do not pull the switch in order not to kill the one *knowing that five will die*"? Is this maxim also universalizable? Or, to put it another way: Even if it is, *generally speaking*, true that not to kill someone is a narrow duty, could it be permissible or even morally obligatory to kill someone in a very specific situation in which the act of not killing elsewise would lead to even more harm (the death of five)?

---

love our neighbour. In the present example, the law must be outweighed. For this omission to be possible, it is necessary that there should be actual inner action arising from motives.' This zero is the consequence of a real opposition. And it really does initially cost some people a noticeable effort to omit performing some good, to the performance of which they detect within themselves positive impulses. Habit facilitates everything, and this action is in the end scarcely noticed any longer" (NG: 183). And: "Both omission and commission are actus of freedom. In the moral sense, they are both called acts, although omission is not an act in the psychological sense. In the moral sense, everything that has a motive [Bewegungsgrund] is an act. Omitting something for a moral motive [Bewegungsgrund] is just as much an action as doing something; for example, not taking revenge on someone who has offended us is really more difficult than taking revenge" (PPH: 128).

48 From another perspective, we already came to the same result above; see p. 202.

This leads to a notorious allegation that has often been brought up against Kant's ethics – his deontological rules were too rigorous. Let us have a look at the prohibition of lying and a well-known example related to it. Suppose Peter, who lives in Germany in 1942, harbors ten Jews and lets them hide in his attic. One night, some SS-men ring the bell, searching and asking about Jews. Is it permissible for Peter to lie to the SS-men, telling them he does not know any Jews at all? Since for Kant lying is prohibited in each and every case, the answer seems to be *no*. But this, the critics say, cannot be right; it cannot be right to let the Jews die if the only thing to do to avoid it is to lie to evil Nazis. But regardless of the question of whether it is *indeed* morally obligatory to lie or not, it is true that *for Kant* the answer is indeed that we must never lie, *without exception*. This holds both from a legal as well as from an ethical point of view.[49] As stated in the *Doctrine of Virtue*, not to lie is an ethical duty to oneself since lying (to others or to oneself) involves "an end that is directly opposed to the natural purposiveness of the speaker's capacity to communicate his thoughts, and is thus a renunciation by the speaker of his personality" (MS: 429); as famously stated in *On a Supposed Right to Lie from Philanthropy*, not to lie is "a duty of right" (VRML: 427 fn.) since lying "makes the source of right unusable" (VRML: 426). It is crucial for both the moral and the legal context that the wrongness of lying is independent of the harm to others that might be caused by a lie. With regard to another example, Kant concedes in *On a Supposed Right to Lie from Philanthropy*:

> [. . .] if you have *by a lie* prevented someone just now bent on murder from committing the deed, then you are legally accountable for all the consequences that might arise from it. But if you have kept strictly to the truth, then public justice can hold nothing against you, whatever the unforeseen consequences might be. It is still possible that, after you have honestly answered "yes" to the murderer's question as to whether his enemy is at home, the latter has nevertheless gone out unnoticed, so that he would not meet the murderer and the deed would not be done; but if you had lied and said that he is not at home, and he has actually gone out (though you are not aware of it), so that the murderer encounters him while going away and perpetrates his deed on him, then you can by right be prosecuted as the author of his death. For if you had told the truth to the best of your knowledge, then neighbors might have come and apprehended the murderer while he was searching the house for his enemy and the deed would have been prevented. Thus one *who tells a lie*, however well disposed he may be, must be responsible for its consequences even before a civil court and must pay the penalty for them, however unforeseen they may have been [. . .].   (VRML: 427)

---

49 However, given that ethical duties are supposed to have latitude (cf. MS: 390), that the prohibition of lying *is* an ethical duty, and that there is a casuistry concerning lying, things could be more complicated.

Someone who tells the truth is not responsible for bad consequences that possibly might occur; for it *might* be the case that these consequences change or vanish. On the contrary, someone who does not tell the truth *is* responsible for all consequences. Again, things *could* change and his lie could also cause harm:[50] "It was merely an *accident* (*casus*) that the truthfulness of the statement harmed the resident of the house, not a free *deed* (in the juridical sense)" (VRML: 428).[51] Lying is wrong – regardless of the consequences.

Can the same be said about killing? Unfortunately, neither the *Doctrine of Right* nor the *Doctrine of Virtue* explicitly contain a specific duty not to kill other persons (there is only the prohibition of suicide in § 6 of the *Doctrine of Virtue*). Here we do not have to address the question of why Kant does not explicitly treat homicide as such. In any event, the moral demerit of killing other persons is not as far-reaching as the demerit of lying. For it is beyond doubt that, on Kantian grounds, murderers have to be punished and even be sentenced to death.[52] Although it is always prohibited to kill innocent persons, this is not true for persons who have committed a severe crime.[53] Since all legal duties are ethical duties, too, to kill innocent persons is always wrong, both legally and ethically. As a matter of fact, Kant explicitly states that it is wrong to kill another innocent person even when one's own life is at stake: Discussing the famous *Plank of Carneades*, Kant holds that it is not permissible to push another innocent person off the swimming plank in a situation in which the only way to survive is to stick to the plank.[54] While such behavior is "*unpunishable*" (*unstrafbar*), it is "not [. . .] *inculpable*" (*nicht unsträflich*; MS: 236) – it is *wrong* to push an innocent person down the plank thereby causing his death

---

50 To some extent, this line of reasoning runs contrary to the trolley cases because in these it is assumed that the five (or the one) will undoubtedly die.

51 This is also what Kant says in the *casuistry* of the *Doctrine of Virtue* regarding a slightly different, but similar case: "For example, a householder has ordered his servant to say 'not at home' if a certain human being asks for him. The servant does this and, as a result, the master slips away and commits a serious crime, which would otherwise have been prevented by the guard sent to arrest him. Who (in accordance with ethical principles) is guilty in this case? Surely the servant, too, who violated a duty to himself by his lie, the results of which his own conscience imputes to him." (MS: 431).

52 Cf. Kant's *Doctrine of Right*, MS: 332–337.

53 Kant also discusses at least two further cases of killing in this regard. Both concern "the feeling of honor" (MS: 336), firstly in the case of a mother killing her illegitimate child and secondly in the case of duels. These cases are difficult to understand. Nevertheless, Kant seems to say that these acts of killing are wrong and must be punished under ideal legal conditions. The only question that arises is whether the state has reached a level of justice that is close enough to these conditions so that capital punishment is justified.

54 Cf. MS: 235 f., TP: 300. Cf. Hruschka (1991, 8 ff.).

(note that in a case of self-defense, the situation is different since the other person is not innocent). This is why Kant writes: "[. . .] not to take the life of another who is committing no offense against me and does not even *lead* me into the danger of losing my life is an unconditional duty" (TP: 300, fn.).

Now let us go back to the trolley case. Since it is presupposed that there are no relevant differences between the persons involved in the trolley case, it is crucial that the one on the track is an *innocent* person. Also, the life of the person flipping the switch is not at stake, so it is no case of *"right of necessity"* (MS: 235). This leads to the inevitable conclusion that pulling the switch and thus killing the one cannot be permissible. To kill the one person on the track is wrong, regardless of the consequences.

So far, so good. But we still have to test the maxim not to flip the switch in a strict sense. As we know, there are different formulas of the CI. I will concentrate here on the *principle of universalization* (*"act only in accordance with that maxim through which you can at the same time will that it become a universal law"*, GMS: 421).[55] The universalization of the maxim under consideration leads to the following formulation:

> It is a universal law that all rational beings in a trolley situation decide not to flip the switch in order not to kill one innocent person, despite knowing that five other innocent persons will die.

As Kant holds in GMS: 424, we have to check for so-called contradictions in *conception* or contradictions in *willing* to see whether a maxim is universalizable or not, whereby those different contradictions are said to somehow correspond with *perfect and imperfect duties.*[56] Can I will without contradiction that it is a universal law that all rational beings must decide not to kill one innocent person even though doing so would save five others? Well, as opposed to the case concerning potential suicide out of selflove and also different from the cases concerning false promises or lying in general, there seems to be no obvious contradiction here.[57] Of course, this answer is not as satisfying as it could be,

---

55 For a discussion of the different formulas of the CI, cf. Allison (2011, 176–236) and Schönecker/Wood (2015, 122–172).

56 I shall not discuss the question of whether the distinction between perfect and imperfect duties is on all fours with the one between narrow and wide duties or the one between negative and positive duties.

57 Cf. GMS: 421 ff. and 429 f.

but that is due to the fact that the whole procedure of testing maxims is problematic and often said to be malfunctioning.[58]

Let us think for a moment about the universalizability of the alternative maxim "I do flip the switch in order to save the five, knowing that I will thereby kill one innocent person". There appears to be a contradiction between killing and the general prohibition of killing innocent persons as described above (which would be circular), or between killing and the required respect for beings with dignity, but I submit that this is not fully convincing either. As we worked out above, to kill innocent persons is forbidden, according to Kant; but that is one thing to say. Another thing to say would be to point to a specific contradiction, where this contradiction is supposed to be the reason for the prohibition in the first place. This too shows that Kant's idea of testing maxims is burdened with difficulties. However, there is no *obvious* problem with the universalizability of the maxim not to flip the switch.

Additional argument 2) The maxim not to turn the trolley is universalizable on the basis of the principle of humanity. Kant's principle of humanity (*"So act that you use humanity, whether in your own person or in the person of any other, always at the same time as an end, never merely as a means"*; GMS: 429) commands not to use a person merely as a means. At first sight, it is quite obvious that the death of the five is in no way a means not to kill the one and *a fortiori* the five are not used merely as a means (by the same token, the death of the one is not a means to save the five since the five would also be saved by flipping the switch without there being anyone on the other track). However, things get more complicated once two different interpretations or rather aspects of the formula of humanity are distinguished. First, it is not permissible to use someone only as a means in a direct way (it is not permissible to throw the large man down on the tracks to stop the trolley). In this sense, *no one* is used as a mere means in the original trolley case, regardless of whether the switch is flipped or not.[59] Second, it is not only not permissible to use someone as a means, but it is also not permissible to carry out actions that do not do justice to a person's unconditional worth, that is, to his or her dignity. In this (second) sense, someone is also used as a mere means when he is not treated with the appropriate

---

58 For a critique of the procedure of universalization and testing maxims, cf. Schönecker/ Wood (2015, 125–141).

59 However, according to Welzel (1951, 51 f.), the bystander has to pull the switch although he thereby does something wrong ("[. . .] the perpetrator must inescapably accept lesser moral guilt in order to escape greater guilt"). Welzel refers to Kant's formula of humanity to show that the bystander uses the people on the track as means when he pulls the switch (but still, he claims, it is the right thing to do).

respect he deserves.[60] In the *Groundwork*, after having presented the formula of humanity, Kant discusses four examples, the last two of which undergird this interpretation: It is neither permissible not to cultivate one's own talents nor is it permissible to refrain from promoting other people's happiness; in the context of these examples, it is striking that Kant does not speak of not using anyone merely as a means. Rather, he states: "[. . .] with respect to contingent (meritorious) duty to oneself, it is not enough that the action does not conflict with humanity in our person as an end in itself; it must also *harmonize with it*" (GMS: 430). Recall that saving or helping others is only a wide duty with certain restrictions: It is not permissible to promote another person's happiness when the other person's ends are immoral[61] or when the promotion of the other person's happiness is, or involves, a violation of a narrow duty. Flipping the switch, however, means violating the duty to respect the dignity of the one, for not to kill is a narrow duty. Therefore, not pulling the switch does not violate the formula of humanity interpreted in that second way either. The respect one owes to the dignity of the five is not neglected if one decides not to flip the switch. (Furthermore, one violates the formula of humanity by attributing a greater worth to the five than to the one; I will discuss this argument below.) The maxim not to pull the switch remains morally permissible.

Additional argument 3) Numbers are irrelevant: dignity and deontology. Let us now imagine the trolley situation with different numbers. Suppose there is a choice between watching the trolley hit just *one* (rather than five) by driving straight on and flipping the switch, leading to the death of *one* other person. Would Kant concur with pulling the switch in this case? It seems clear to me that he would not, and the reason for this is Kant's concept of dignity as an absolute value and his deontological approach to ethics. In light of this deontology, it is not possible to offset beings that possess dignity against other such beings.[62] As

---

60 Cf. for this distinction Mieth (2014, 17) and, with reference to Thomas Hill (1980), Mieth (2018, 118–122).

61 Cf. MS: 388 where Kant says that one must only promote the happiness of other beings by making their ends one's own, provided that their ends are "permitted".

62 Incidentally, this is also what the German jurisdiction says with a strong reference to Kant, cf. Wörner (2019, 43 f.; my own translation) with regard to a slightly different case: "The justification [of pulling the switch] fails, however, because the good to be preserved [*Erhaltungsgut*] (life of the persons on the train) does not substantially outweigh the good to be intruded [*Eingriffsgut*] (life of the three workers). According to the prevailing opinion, human lives cannot be weighed against each other, neither according to their quality (track workers against train passengers) nor according to their quantity (50 against 3); rather, each individual human life stands on its own."

famously stated in GMS: 428, beings that possess dignity have an absolute value and no prize.[63] One can weigh them neither against other things, nor against other beings with value; there is no "scale" of dignity.[64] One cannot sacrifice one person for another, and this is also why one cannot sacrifice one person for five others – *numbers do not count*. Otherwise, the distinction between deontology and consequentialism would blur at least to some extent.[65]

The impossibility of weighing a certain number of beings with dignity against another number is further illuminated by taking into account so-called *Taurek cases*.[66] These are cases in which a subject has to choose between saving a relatively small number of people (or even just one person) *or* saving a larger number of people; it is presupposed that both options only differ by their numbers. Importantly, such cases are different from trolley cases because the subject has to choose between *helping* and *helping*; as opposed to the one in the trolley case, all persons in Taurek cases are already endangered independently of the subject that has to make a decision. For instance, imagine you are at high seas with your yacht and you are informed about five people in distress fifty miles away from you to the north and ten people in distress fifty miles away to the south; you cannot save both the five and the ten. Are you obliged to save the ten *because they are more than five*? John Taurek argues – though against the background of a subjectivist metaethical system very different from Kant's – that you are *not* obliged to save the ten. Thus, he says, it is permissible, though of course not obligatory, to save the five rather than the ten; as a matter of fact, you should flip a coin to choose which way to go so that everyone involved has "an equal chance to

---

63 Cf. also GMS: 436 and MS: 434. For Kant's concept of dignity, cf. Schmidt/Schönecker (2018).

64 Hill (1980, 92 f.) discusses the question of whether the worth of several beings possessing dignity can be compared with each other although it cannot be compared with things possessing no dignity. He discriminates the following interpretations (laid out in questions): "Is his [Kant's] view, for example, that there are two scales of value, price and dignity, such that things can be ranked comparatively on each scale even though nothing on the scale of dignity can be overweighed by any amount of value on the scale of price?" And: "[I]s Kant's view that dignity is something that cannot be quantified, so that it does not make sense to say that dignity of humanity in one person can fairly and reasonably be exchanged for the sake of a greater amount of dignity elsewhere?" As I see it (but here cannot really argue for), Kant's ground-thesis (cf. Schmidt/Schönecker 2018) implies that there can be no scale of dignity.

65 For the question of whether counting numbers can be reconciled with deontological positions, cf. Hevelke/Nida-Rümelin (2015); for the question of whether consequentialism really implies that one ought to kill the one, cf. Howard (2021).

66 Cf. Taurek (1977).

survive" (Taurek 1977, 303).[67] At first glance, this position might seem outlandish (or counterintuitive, if you will), but on second thought, it is worth considering. Although it is not undisputed what Kant's response to Taurek cases would be,[68] I submit it would be the following: Given that a group of ten beings that possess dignity is by no means of greater worth than a group of five such beings because there is no *scale* of dignity, there is no moral reason to save the larger group rather than the smaller one. With Kant, it is certainly permissible to save the ten, but it is not obligatory: it is also permissible to save the five. On Kantian grounds, therefore, Foot's rule 2 cannot be correct; it is not true that numbers count in situations involving the same kind of duties (helping ten vs. helping five).[69] A fortiori, we have good reason to argue that in a trolley situation (which, again, is different from a Taurek case) the numbers are *completely* irrelevant; yet not only, *nota bene*, because of the equal worth of five vs. ten persons, but also because the set of duties at stake is different (helping vs. killing). Even if Kant *did* accept the obligation to save the ten and not the five when it comes to Taurek cases, this would not imply the obligation to save the five and kill the one in the trolley situation.

---

67 In recent literature, different kinds of Taurekian positions are discussed. Dufner/Schöne-Seifert (2019, 27) distinguish between a *strong* version (as explained above) and a *weighted* version (according to which the ten people should have a chance of rescue twice as big as that of the five because the group is twice the size). Additionally, they discuss the *Tie Breaker* position (stemming from Scanlon) and their own. However, only the first, strong version is the Taurekian version in a strict sense. For the discussion concerning Taurek and the question of whether saving the greater number is required, cf., amongst others, Timmermann (2004) and Meyer (2006).

68 Cf. Dufner/Schöne-Seifert (2019, 29).

69 Timmermann (2004, 110) shares the opinion that from a Kantian perspective numbers do not count. However, he suggests another quite enlightening method to determine whom to save which he calls *individualist lottery* (he describes a situation in which you can save A on one island or B and C on another island): "To give the claims of A, B and C equal weight, a coin will not do. We need a wheel of fortune with three sectors, each of which bears the name of one islander. The person whose sector comes up is saved. If this person is A, both B and C perish. If B's sector is selected, B is saved. Having reached the island, the rescuer then incurs an obligation to save C. Similarly, if C wins B is also saved. We neither count, nor aggregate, nor quantify; nor do we arbitrarily assign roles to individual islander." – On a different note, stressing the impossibility of counting numbers when it comes to beings that possess dignity, it might seem impossible to say that the death of ten (either through murder or a natural disaster, for instance) is worse than the death of a single person (cf. Dufner/Schöne-Seifert 2019, 26). I am not sure whether this is true (and I am not sure if it posed a problem if it were true), but I cannot get into this discussion at this point.

6 Conclusion. Kant and the Programmer

How should autonomous vehicles be programmed with regard to trolley-like situations against the background of Kantian ethics? As we have seen, there is no normative difference between the bystander and the driver of the trolley because by not intervening neither of them *kills* the five in a morally relevant way. Instead, whoever turns the trolley must choose between the wide duty to help (the five) and the narrow duty not to kill the one. Since the narrow duty trumps the wide duty, and because the general wide duty to help others (that allows for a certain amount of latitude) is different from a specific obligation to help the five, it is not permissible to flip the switch – no conflict of duties is involved. Hence, it is also not permissible for the Kantian programmer of an autonomous vehicle to make his algorithm steer the car around a group of people if doing so results in hitting a smaller group or a single person. I do not claim that *indeed* it is morally obligatory not to flip the switch – my only aim was to show what a Kantian position looks like.

The Kantian solution to the trolley problem differs considerably from Foot's. Although both Foot and Kant take narrow duties to trump wide duties (Foot's rule 1),[70] there is no Kantian way to interpret the situation as one only concerning negative duties; whoever has to pull the switch is not to choose between killing the five and killing the one. Furthermore, Kant presumably would not have accepted Foot's rule 2, i. e., the rule that the number of victims is to be minimized, neither in a case involving the same kind of duties (Taurek cases) nor in a situation in which one would have to kill one person to save others (trolley). Kant's concept of dignity as an absolute value forbids weighing one life against another, regardless of the numbers.

Now let us take a step back. We moved from highly abstract trolley cases and thus from philosophical thought experiments to ethical puzzles in quite mundane situations concerning autonomous driving. One might wonder whether this is a good idea at all. There are at least two possible objections here. First, it might be argued that the whole endeavor of trolleyology is misguided, or at least misguided in the way it is actually done. Philosophers take their intuitions about whether it is permissible to flip the switch as their irrefutable and so in some sense axiomatic starting points of argumentation, searching for theories why it is permissible – according to their intuitions – to pull the switch in one case but not in another. Whilst doing so, they do not question these intuitions – which they

---

[70] Foot (1978 [1967], 27) actually speaks of *negative* and *positive* duties but, at least roughly speaking, she means narrow and wide duties.

should, according to the first critique.[71] For there are reasonable doubts concerning the epistemic reliability of our intuitions, both in general and with regard to trolley cases in particular. Thus, Joshua Greene (2016, 176; Greene et. al 2009) argues that our intuitions concerning trolley cases might correlate with factors which are not morally relevant at all but whose significance for us is rather due to other circumstances. For example, people seem to be more critical about actions that harm other people when carried out through *personal strength* (pushing the large man down the bridge with my own hands as opposed to pushing a button which initiates a causal reaction leading to the fall of the large man). This could explain why people tend to say it is permissible to flip the switch in the loop case but not in the large man case. Also, our intuitions might at least partly depend, as Di Nucci (2014) argues, on the order of the cases presented. While most participants in his study judge it to be permissible to pull the switch in the original bystander's case when confronted first or only with this case, judgements change a great deal when people are presented first with Thomson's three options case (in which the bystander has a choice between the death of the five, the death of the one, and his own death) and only afterwards with the bystander's original case; then the majority indeed opts *not* to flip the switch in the bystander's case. All this might lead us to think, as Peter Singer (2005) argues, that we should not use arbitrary intuitions to refute ethical theories but use ethical theories to refute our intuitions.[72]

Secondly, from an application-oriented point of view, there are serious doubts about the reasonableness of comparing hypothetical trolley situations with situations that autonomous vehicles might get into. For several reasons, trolley cases, it is argued, are unlikely to be of any help in real life. I concentrate here on three aspects.[73] (i) Trolley cases do not occur in reality. A rather specific variant of this critique was put forward by Johannes Himmelreich (2018, 674): For technical reasons, he says, "there seems to be a tension between having a meaningful choice and a collision being unavoidable", which is to say that it is unlikely that one can steer a trolley if the brakes have completely failed. (ii) In reality, we cannot be sure whether endangered persons really do have no chance of survival at all. Rather, there are only different probabilities for different situations (we usually cannot be sure whether a person hit by a car will certainly die, nor can we be sure

---

71 For this general position, but not only concerning trolleys, cf. Kagan (2001).

72 According to Singer (2005, 350), such a revisionist approach to intuitions leads us to the conclusion that throwing the large man down the bridge is indeed the right thing to do.

73 For the following aspects of critique and further aspects, cf. Goodall (2016), Nyholm/Smids (2016), Himmelreich (2018), and Keeling (2020, though he ultimately defends the advantages of discussing trolley problems for autonomous driving).

whether the car will hit the person at all). (iii) Trolley problems get much more complicated when more details are known, for instance, the age of the persons involved, their gender, their health conditions, their role in society, their criminal record, their social and familial status, or their role or responsibility in the given situation. – Since there are these differences between trolley and real-world situations, critics say, it does not make any sense to talk about trolleys when what one really wants to talk about are real-world situations.

How can these charges be addressed? To begin with the objection of applicability: It is crucial to see that from a Kantian point of view, quite a number of those real-life aspects mentioned above are irrelevant. Human beings possess dignity no matter how old or healthy they are, for instance, and thus the relevance of the objection is dependent on the ethical outlook one has. Furthermore, although it is certainly true that real-life situations are more complicated, thinking about trolley cases makes us see essential aspects of the ethical problem to be solved and this asset is not undermined by the fact that in reality *more* features of the situation have to be taken into account.[74] Also, it is of course true that to consider risks and probabilities in the trolley scenario would make the analysis *much* more complicated.[75] Nevertheless, solving the trolley problem in a merely theoretical manner is indeed a sensible thing to do since exploring the theoretical framework of a practical problem does help to solve the practical problem. This is true even if trolley situations in the real world are somewhat more rocky.

A final word on intuitions. The question of what intuitions are and what epistemic role they play in the game of justification has been disputed ever since the very idea of something like intuition or maybe self-evidence came up; more recently, experimental philosophy has shed new doubts on the reliability of intuitions. What we can learn indeed from a Kantian analysis is that although intuitions cannot (and should not) be banned completely from practical philosophy, we should not rely on them blindly. Rather, we should be ready to dismiss some of them, and this is exactly what a Kantian analysis of the trolley problem brings home. Although it certainly appears to many intuitively clear that flipping the switch in the original trolley cases is permissible, it came to light that on Kantian grounds flipping the switch really is not permissible – or at least Kant's approach is capable of shaking our intuition that it is. In many respects, if one wants to sustain Kantian theory, it would be more sensible to give up the intuition that it

---

74 Cf. Keeling (2020, 296–300).
75 From a Kantian perspective, such an analysis is provided by Bjorndahl/London/Zollmann (2017).

is permissible to flip the switch and try to make our judgements fit our theories rather than to try desperately to make Kantian theory fit our intuitions. This is not to say, however, that Kant's ethics does not rely on some kind of intuition itself.

References

I use the following abbreviations for Kant's writings:

GMS	*Groundwork of the Metaphysics of Morals*
KpV	*Critique of Practical Reason*
MS	*The Metaphysics of Morals*
NG	*Attempt to Introduce the Concept of Negative Magnitudes into Philosophy* (AA 2)
PPH	*Practical Philosophy Herder*
TP	*On the Common Saying: That may be Correct in Theory, But it is of no Use in Practice*
VRML	*On a Supposed Right to Lie from Philanthropy*

GMS, KpV, MS, TP, and VRML are quoted according to the edition by Mary J. Gregor, *Practical Philosophy*, general introduction by Allen W. Wood, New York 1996.
NG is quoted according to the edition by David Waldorf/Ralf Meerbote, *Theoretical Philosophy, 1755–1770*, New York 1992.
PPH, my own translation.

Adkins, Brent (1999): "Kant and the *Antigone*: The Possibility of Conflicting Duties," in: *International Philosophical Quarterly* 39/4, pp. 455–466.
Allison, Henry E. (2011): *Kant's "Groundwork for the Metaphysics of Morals." A Commentary*, Oxford.
Bjorndahl, Adam/London, Alex J./Zollmann, Kevin J. S. (2017): "Kantian Decision Making under Uncertainty: Dignity, Price, and Consistency," in: *Philosophers' Imprint* 17/7, pp. 1–22.
Bruers, Stijn/Braeckman, Johan (2014): "A Review and Systematization of the Trolley Problem," in: *Philosophia* 42/2, 251–269.
Bykvist, Krister (2017): "Moral uncertainty," in: *Philosophy Compass* 12/3, pp. 1–8.
Byrd, B. Sharon (2015): "Todesstrafe," in: Willaschek, Marcus/Stolzenberg, Jürgen/Mohr, Georg/Bacin, Stefano (eds.), *Kant-Lexikon*, volume 3, Berlin/Boston, pp. 2298–2300.
Černý, David (2020): *The Principle of Double Effect. A History and Philosophical Defense*, New York.
Di Nucci, Ezio (2014): "Trolleys and Double Effect in Experimental Ethics," in: Christoph Lange/Hannes Rusch/Matthias Uhl (eds.): *Experimental Ethics: Towards an Empirical Moral Philosophy*, London, pp. 80–93.
Dufner, Annette/Schöne-Seifert, Bettina (2019): "Die Rettung der größeren Anzahl: Eine Debatte um Grundbausteine ethischer Normenbegründung," in: *Zeitschrift für Praktische Philosophie* 6/2, pp. 15–41.
Engisch, Karl (1930): *Untersuchungen über Vorsatz und Fahrlässigkeit im Strafrecht*, Berlin.

Esser, Andrea (2008): "Kant on Solving Moral Conflicts," in: Monika Betzler (ed.), *Kant's Ethics of Virtue*, Berlin/New York, pp. 279–302.

Foot, Philippa 1978 [1967]: "The Problem of Abortion and the Doctrine of the Double Effect," in: Philippa Foot, *Virtue and Vices and Other Essays in Moral Philosophy*, Oxford 1978, pp. 19–32 [first published in *Oxford Review* 5, 5–15, 1967].

Goodall, Noah (2016): "Away from Trolley Problems and Toward Risk Management," in: *Applied Artificial Intelligence*, 30/8, pp. 810–821.

Greene, Joshua D. (2016): "Solving the Trolley Problem," in: Justin Sytsma/Wesley Buckwalter (eds.): *A Companion to Experimental Philosophy*, Hoboken, pp. 175–177.

Greene, Joshua D./Cushman, Fiery A./Nystrom, Leigh E./Stewart, Lisa E./Lowenberg, Kelly/ Cohen, Jonathan D. (2009): "Pushing Moral Buttons: The Interaction between Personal Force and Intention in Moral Judgement," in: *Cognition* 111/3, pp. 364–371.

Hevelke, Alexander/Nida-Rümelin, Julian (2015): "Selbstfahrende Autos und Trolley-Probleme: Zum Aufrechnen von Menschenleben im Falle unausweichlicher Unfälle," in: *Jahrbuch für Wissenschaft und Ethik* 19, pp. 5–23.

Hill, Thomas E. (1980): "Humanity as an End in Itself," in: *Ethics* 91/1, pp. 84–99.

Hill, Thomas E. (2002): "Moral Dilemmas, Gaps, and Residues," in: Thomas E. Hill, *Human Welfare and Moral Worth. Kantian Perspectives*, Oxford, pp. 362–402.

Himmelreich, Johannes (2018): "Never Mind the Trolley: The Ethics of Autonomous Vehicles in Mundane Situations," in: *Ethical Theory and Moral Practice* 21, pp. 669–684.

Howard, Christopher (2021): "Consequentialists Must Kill," in: *Ethics* 131, pp. 727–753.

Hruschka, Joachim (1991): "Rechtfertigungs- und Entschuldigungsgründe: Das Brett des Karneades bei Gentz und bei Kant, " in: *Goltdammer's Archiv für Strafrecht* 138, pp. 1–10.

Joerden, Jan C. (1997): "Der Widerstreit zweier Gründe der Verbindlichkeit. Konsequenzen einer These Kants für die strafrechtliche Lehre von der 'Pflichtenkollision," in: *Jahrbuch für Recht und Ethik* 5, pp. 43–52.

Kagan, Shelly (2001): "Thinking about Cases," in: *Social Philosophy and Policy* 18/2, pp. 44–63.

Kamm, Frances M. (2007): *Intricate Ethics: Rights, Responsibilities, and Permissible Harm*, Oxford.

Kamm, Frances M. (2016): "Who Turned the Trolley" & "How Was the Trolley Turned?," in: Frances M. Kamm/Eric Rakowski (ed.): *The Trolley Problem Mysteries*, Oxford, pp. 11–109.

Keeling, Geoff (2020): "Why Trolley Problems Matter for the Ethics of Automated Vehicles," in: *Science and Engineering Ethics* 26, pp. 293–307.

Kleingeld, Pauline (2020): "A Kantian Solution to the Trolley Problem," in: *Oxford Studies in Normative Ethics* 10, pp. 204–228.

Mangan, Joseph T. (1949): "An Historical Analysis of the Principle of Double Effect," in: *Theological Studies* 10, pp. 41–61.

Mannino, Adriano/Mukerji, Nikil (2020): "Nachwort: Das Trolley-Problem: Ein mehrgleisiger Lösungsversuch," in: *Judith Jarvis Thomson. The Trolley Problem/Das Trolley-Problem*, übersetzt und herausgegebnen von Adriano Mannino/Nikil Mukerji, Stuttgart, pp. 99–164.

McCarty, Richard (1991): "Moral Conflicts in Kantian Ethics," in: *History of Philosophy Quarterly* 8/1, pp. 65–79.

Meyer, Kirsten (2006): "How to be Consistent without Saving the Greater Number," in: *Philosophy & Public Affairs* 34/2, pp. 136–146.

Mieth, Corinna (2014): "The Double Foundation of Human Rights in Human Nature," in: Marion Albers/Thomas Hoffmann/Jörn Reinhardt (eds.), *Human Rights and Human Nature*, Dordrecht et al., pp. 11–22.

Mieth, Corinna/Bambauer, Christoph (2018): "Kant, soziale Menschenrechte und korrespondierende Pflichten," in: Reza Mosayebi (ed.), *Kant und Menschenrechte*, Berlin, pp. 101–129.

Nyholm, Sven/Smids, Jilles (2016): "The Ethics of Accident-Algorithms for Self-Driving Cars: an Applied Trolley Problem?," in: *Ethical Theory and Moral Practice*, 19, pp. 1275–1289.

Otsuka, Michael (2008): "Double Effect, Triple Effect and the Trolley Problem: Squaring the Circle in Looping Cases," in: *Utilitas* 20/1, pp. 92–110.

Parfit, Derek (2017): *On What Matters*, volume 3, Oxford.

Schmidt, Elke E./Schönecker, Dieter (2017): "Kant über Tun, Lassen und lebensbeendende Handlungen," in: F.-J. Bormann (ed.), *Lebensbeendende Handlungen. Ethik, Medizin und Recht zur Grenze von "Töten" und "Sterbenlassen"*, Berlin/Boston, pp. 135–168.

Schmidt, Elke E./Schönecker, Dieter (2018): "Kant's Ground-Thesis. On Dignity and Value in the Groundwork," in: *The Journal of Value Inquiry*, 52, pp. 81–95.

Schönecker, Dieter/Wood, Allen W. (2015): *Immanuel Kant's "Groundwork for the Metaphysic of Morals." A Commentary*, Cambridge/London.

Singer, Peter (2005): "Ethics and Intuitions," in: *The Journal of Ethics* 9/3–4, pp. 331–352.

Taurek, John M. (1977): "Should the Numbers Count?," in: *Philosophy and Public Affairs* 6/4, pp. 293–316.

Timmermann, Jens (2004): "The individualist lottery: how people count, but not their numbers," in: *Analysis* 64/2, pp. 106–112.

Timmermann, Jens (2013): "Kantian Dilemmas? Moral Conflict in Kant's Ethical Theory," in: *Archiv für Geschichte der Philosophie* 95/1, pp. 36–64.

Thomson, Judith Jarvis (1985): "The Trolley Problem," in: *The Yale Law Journal* 94/6, pp. 1395–1415.

Thomson, Judith Jarvis (1991): "Self-Defense," in: *Philosophy and Public Affairs* 20/4, pp. 283–310.

Thomson, Judith Jarvis (2008): "Turning the Trolley," in: *Philosophy & Public Affairs* 36/4, pp. 359–374.

Thomson, Judith Jarvis (2016): "Kamm on the Trolley Problems," in: Frances M. Kamm/Eric Rakowski (ed.): *The Trolley Problem Mysteries*, Oxford, pp. 113–134.

Welzel, Hans (1951): "Zum Notstandsproblem," in: *Zeitschrift für die gesamte Strafwissenschaft* 63, pp. 47–56.

Wörner, Liane (2019): "Der Weichensteller 4.0. Zur strafrechtlichen Verantwortlichkeit des Programmierers im Notstand für Vorgaben an autonome Fahrzeuge," in: *Zeitschrift für Internationale Strafrechtsdogmatik* 14/1, pp. 41–48.

Ava Thomas Wright

8 Rightful Machines

Abstract: In this paper, I set out a new Kantian approach to resolving conflicts between moral obligations for highly autonomous machine agents. First, I argue that efforts to build explicitly moral autonomous machine agents should focus on what Kant refers to as *duties of right*, which are duties that everyone could accept, rather than on duties of virtue (or "ethics"), which are subject to dispute in particular cases. "Moral" machines must first be *rightful* machines, I argue. I then show how this shift in focus from ethics to a standard of public right resolves the conflicts in what is known as the "trolley problem" for autonomous machine agents. Finally, I consider how a deontic logic suitable for capturing duties of right might meet Kant's requirement that rightfully enforceable obligations be consistent in a system of equal freedom under universal law.

1 Introduction: (Im)moral machines

In a massive experiment conducted online (the "Moral Machine Experiment"), millions of subjects were asked what a self-driving car whose brakes have failed should do when its only choices were to swerve or stay on course under various accident conditions (Awad, et al., 2018). Should the car swerve and kill one person in order to avoid killing five people on the road ahead? Most subjects agreed that it should. Most subjects also agreed, however, that the car should generally spare younger people (especially children) over older people, females over males, those of higher status over those of lower status, and the fit over the overweight, with some variations in preferences correlated with subjects' cultural backgrounds.[1] But while such results may be interesting, they seem to me at best irrelevant to the question of what a self-driving car faced with such a dilemma should do. Ethical preferences to spare more rather than fewer lives, or to spare humans over animals, are for the most part morally banal, while

---

[1] These results are ceteris paribus preferences derived by aggregating individual decisions made by subjects across many different variations of the basic swerve-or-stay-on-course accident scenario (see Awad, et al. 2018, p. 60). They should not be understood to indicate absolute or overriding ethical preferences.

Ava Thomas Wright, California Polytechnic State University

ethical preferences to spare those of higher over lower status, or those of one gender or body type over another, are morally problematic. The latter preferences raise the strong moral intuition that choices guided by them would fail to respect the moral *equality* of persons. Self-driving cars programmed to enact such preferences would therefore be immoral machines.

According to Immanuel Kant, there are two kinds of moral duties: 1) *duties of right* ("legal" duties), which are duties that are rightfully enforceable by others, and 2) *duties of virtue* ("ethical" duties), which are not rightfully enforceable by others because their application in particular cases is subject to dispute.[2] Kant accordingly divides the *Metaphysics of Morals* into the *Doctrine of Right* and the *Doctrine of Virtue* (see TL, AA 06: 379). In this paper, I argue that efforts to build explicitly moral autonomous machine agents should focus on duties of right, rather than on duties of virtue, when resolving conflicts between obligations or rights. While dilemmas such as those in the (in)famous "trolley problem" – which inspired the experiment above – have received enormous attention in "machine ethics," there will likely never be a consensus as to their correct resolution.[3] What matters morally in such controversial cases is whether machine agents charged with making decisions that affect human beings act *rightfully*, that is, in ways that respect real persons' equal rights of freedom and principles of public right and law. The point is not merely that conflict cases like those in the trolley problem likely will, as a practical matter, be resolved by the law rather than by ethical principles (Casey 2017). The point is, rather, that the resolution of such disputes between equals morally should be determined by principles of right and public law before controversial ethical principles may be applied. A "moral machine" must first be a *rightful machine*, I argue.

This paper has three main sections. In the first two sections, I set out some basic elements of Kant's theory of justice and then apply them to resolve the conflicts between duties in the trolley problem. An action is right, Kant says,

---

2 Following Kant, I will refer to duties of right as "legal," "rightful," or also "juridical," and reserve the term "ethical" to refer to duties of virtue (see MS, AA 06:219). I will use the term "moral" to refer broadly to any duty or power, whether legal or ethical or both. Kant occasionally appears to disregard his own distinction and use the term "ethics" to refer to morality generally, but I avoid this usage. For some critical discussion of Kant's distinctions, see O'Neill 2016, pp. 114–117.

3 The field of "machine ethics" is primarily concerned with building autonomous machine agents that can take moral considerations into account in their decision-making. Machine "ethics" therefore should not be understood as limited to what Kant would refer to as "ethics" (i.e., virtue).

when it "can coexist with the freedom of every other under universal law;" therefore, the rightfulness of an action is specified explicitly in terms of its consistency within a system of equal rights of freedom under universal law (RL, AA 06:230). I interpret this consistency not descriptively but normatively as a moral requirement that public right imposes upon any system of rightfully enforceable duties and rights. Without such consistency, the enforcement of either conflicting obligation in a disputed case would be arbitrary, and arbitrary enforcement is tantamount to coercion. Hence when dilemmas between duties of right such as in the trolley problem arise, we should not conceive them as cases where we are forced to violate one or another of our inconsistent duties of right but, instead, as cases where a legitimate public authority must precisely *specify* our duties and rights in order to meet the requirement of consistency in a system. The legislative, executive and judicial institutions of the civil state are necessary, Kant argues, to construct and maintain a system of equal freedom under universal law for human beings inevitably engaged in social interactions.

Finally, in the third section, I consider how a deontic logic suitable for governing explicitly rightful machines might meet the normative requirement of consistency in the system of equal rights of freedom under universal law. I suggest that a non-monotonic deontic logic can meet the consistency requirement, though with certain reservations, and that a logic of belief revision may be preferred.

2 Rightful Machines

2.1 Kantian Right and the Innate Right of Freedom

In the *Doctrine of Right*, Kant defines the "Universal Principle of Right" as follows:

> Any action is *right* if it can coexist with the freedom of every other under universal law; or if on its maxim the freedom of choice of each can coexist with everyone's freedom in accordance with a universal law.   (RL, AA 06:230)

Kant thus defines the legal permissibility (rightfulness) of any action in terms of its systematic consistency with everyone's equal freedom under universal law. If the act is consistent with everyone's equal right of freedom, then it is permissible. While Kant defines legal permissibility here, permissions, duties and (claim-) rights are logically interdefinable by taking any one as a primary operator (see Hohfeld 1919, pp. 35–50).[4]

Kant reiterates justice as systematic freedom under universal law when defining the innate right of freedom:

> *Freedom* (independence from being constrained by another's choice), insofar as it can co-exist with the freedom of every other in accordance with a universal law, is the only original right belonging to every [person] by virtue of [his or her] humanity.   (RL, AA 06:237)

Hence while freedom is "'independence from being constrained by another's choice," according to Kant, the *right* of freedom is that freedom systematically limited by everyone else's equal freedom under universal law. The right of freedom lacks definition outside a system of equal rights of freedom under universal law.

2.2 The Priority of Right

According to Kant, reason alone cannot specify a priori what our rights and duties, and powers and liabilities, with respect to each other are in particular cases (RL, AA 06:312). Since everyone is innately *equal*, each person has her "own [natural] right to do *what seems right and good to [her]* and not to be dependent on another's opinion about this," Kant says (RL, AA 06:312). No one individual or group has the innate moral authority to unilaterally define everyone's rights and duties with respect to others (i.e., legislate them), or to enforce them (i.e., execute them), or to resolve disputes (i.e., determine them) in particular cases. Intractable disputes over our rights and powers with respect to each other in particular cases are thus inevitable in a "state of nature" lacking public institutions to resolve them. While the state of nature is not necessarily a state of injustice, Kant says, "it would be a state *devoid of justice (status justitia vacuus),* in which when rights are in *dispute (ius controversum),* there would be no judge competent to render a verdict having rightful force" (RL, AA 06:312). Hence even if everyone were committed to acting perfectly ethically, according to Kant, rightful relations with others are impossible in a state of nature (RL, AA 06:312).

---

4 For example, if legal *duty* is taken as basic, then: person x has a *permission* to perform action P iff x has no duty not to P with respect to y; x has a (claim-) *right* that P iff person y has a duty to perform P for x; and x has what Hohfeld calls a "*no-right*" that P with respect to y iff y has no duty to not-P with respect to x.

What is needed, Kant says, is to construct

> *a system of laws for a people. . .which because they affect one another, need a rightful con-*
> *dition under a will uniting them, a constitution (constituto),* so that they may enjoy what is
> laid down as right.   (RL, AA 06:311)

Kant refers to this system of public laws and institutions as "public right," and a society existing under such a system as one existing in a "rightful" or "civil" condition. The coercive enforcement of public law is rightful under such a system, Kant says, because

> when someone makes arrangements about another, it is always possible for him to do the
> other wrong; but he can never do wrong in what he decides upon with regard to himself
> (for *volenti non fit iniuria*). Therefore only the concurring and united will of all, insofar as
> each decides the same thing for all and all for each, and so only the general united will of
> the people, can be legislative.   (RL, AA 06:313–14)

It is only by constituting a general or united will to authoritatively define, enforce, and adjudicate our rights and duties with respect to each other that we can avoid wronging one another in cases of dispute over our rights, Kant argues.

Hence determinations made in the system of public laws regarding what our rights or duties are take moral *priority* over individual ethical judgments in cases where those rights or duties are in dispute. To reject public authority and use one's own private judgment in such disputed cases is to act wrongfully, indeed, to do "wrong in the highest degree," Kant says (RL, AA 06:308n). Resolving such disputes in order to enable rightful relations with others is the very purpose of the system of public laws.

2.3 Duties of Rightful Machines

Duties of right concern only the public, outward aspects of one's actions and, according to Kant, are thus completely specifiable without reference to the agent's motive or "maxim" of the end of action (TL, AA 06:390). For example, while one has a moral duty to keep one's promises, one has a (legal) duty of right to keep only those promises that meet the outward, public criteria that legitimate public authority has defined as a contract such as offer, acceptance, consideration, etc. Whether I perform on the contract in order to honor my promise or solely because I fear a civil suit, I meet my legal obligation just the same (see RL, AA 06:230). Similarly, I meet my legal obligations to avoid criminal acts such as theft and murder even if I avoid them solely because I fear punishment. Corresponding ethical duties, by contrast, require me to avoid such crimes because they are wrong.[5]

The rightful enforceability and precise specifiability of duties of right have important implications for builders of explicitly moral machine agents. First, the precision required in the specification of duties of right should make conformity with those duties somewhat easier to achieve in a machine agent, since determining whether duties of right apply and what action they require should demand considerably less moral judgment in particular cases. It is much more difficult to determine what the duty of virtue to help others requires in particular cases than to determine what a positive legal duty to render assistance at the scene of an automobile accident requires (see, e.g., Minn Sec. 604A.01). Second, shifting the focus of machine ethics to conformity with duties of right sidesteps objections related to the machine agent's potential capacity for freedom. If a machine cannot act according to a principle that it freely chooses, then the machine cannot act ethically and can at best produce only a simulacrum of ethical action (Guarini 2012). On the other hand, if advanced machines of the future do become capable of genuine ethical agency (i.e., true Kantian "autonomy"), then installing a coercive, explicitly ethical control system would violate the *machine's* right of freedom (see Tonkens 2009). By contrast, duties of right require no particular subjective incentive for action; hence, mere conformity with the outward aspects of such duties is sufficient to act rightfully. And since duties of right are rightfully enforceable, a coercive control system might not violate even a truly "autonomous" machine's rights.

Finally, and perhaps most importantly, explicitly *ethical* machines that acted on preferences such as those collected in the Moral Machine Experiment might often violate rights of equality and freedom, and it is not difficult to imagine dystopias where such machine agents paternalistically manage human affairs in the service of partial ethical ideals. By contrast, machines that conform to duties of right will by definition respect real human persons' equal rights of freedom and avoid paternalistic ethical meddling.

Self-driving cars and other machine agents programmed to act in accordance with popular ethical preferences would be immoral machines and seem to me to pose a threat to civil society. The goal of machine ethics should be *rightful machines*.

---

5 Kant also holds that one has a general ethical duty to obey legitimate law, which implies that all legal duties are therefore also indirectly ethical duties (see TL, AA 06:390–91). This indirect ethical duty to obey the law out of the incentive of duty is not my concern here, however, and the priority of public right does not depend upon it. For a perspicuous account of the relation between right and ethics in Kant's moral philosophy, see Guyer 2016.

3 Solving the Trolley Problem

3.1 The Original Trolley Problem: Driver versus Footbridge

Consider one ("Driver") variation of the "trolley problem" (Foot 1967, p. 3): Imagine you are driving a trolley whose brakes have failed. The runaway trolley, gaining speed, approaches a fork in the tracks, and you must choose which track the trolley will take. On the main track are five people who will be struck and killed if you stay on course, while on the side track is one person who will be struck and killed if you switch tracks. What are you obligated to do? In polls and experiments, most people (about 90%) say they would turn the trolley (see, e.g., Mikhail 2007).

Now contrast Driver with the following variation ("Footbridge") (Thomson 1976, pp. 207–8): Imagine that instead of driving the trolley, you are standing on a footbridge overlooking the tracks. The five are still in jeopardy in the path of the runaway trolley, but now there is no side track. Standing next to you on the footbridge is a large man leaning over the footbridge railing. You could stop the trolley and save five people if you pushed the large man off the footbridge. He would be struck and killed, but the collision would block the forward momentum of the trolley, saving the five. Should you push the large man over? Most people (again, about 90%) say they would *not* do so, in a reverse mirror image of the intuitions in Driver (Mikhail 2007).

The trolley "problem," originally raised by Phillipa Foot, is the problem of how to rationally reconcile moral intuitions in Driver with those in cases like Footbridge, since most people are willing to kill one to spare five in the former but not in the latter case (Foot 1967, p. 3). Foot suggests that the answer is that "negative" duties such as to avoid injuring or killing others are qualitatively more important than "positive" duties such as to render aid to them (Foot 1967, pp. 5–6). In Driver, you are faced with an unavoidable conflict between negative duties not to kill five and not to kill one, Foot says, and since you must violate a negative duty not to kill someone no matter what you do, it is only rational to turn the trolley so as to inflict the least injury (Foot 1967, p. 5). By contrast, in cases like Footbridge, you are faced with a conflict between a negative duty not to kill one (the large man) and a positive duty to protect the five from harm, Foot says, and in such cases, the negative duty takes priority over the positive duty (Foot 1967, p. 6). One therefore should kill one to spare five in Driver but avoid doing so in Footbridge, according to Foot.

3.2 The Priority of Right Solves the Original Trolley Problem

Foot's analysis is roughly correct but incomplete. To complete the analysis Foot needs to provide some account of why and in what sense "negative" duties to avoid acts such as killing others should take normative priority over "positive" duties to perform acts such as protecting others from harm (Thomson 2008, p. 372). I argue that duties not to kill in the trolley problem take such normative priority not because they are negative duties but because they are *duties of right*, whereas conflicting positive duties to aid others in cases like Footbridge are *ethical* duties. Duties of right determined authoritatively in public law take normative priority over conflicting ethical reasons for action. Foot's distinction between negative and positive duties roughly tracks the distinction between legal and ethical duties, since most legal duties are negative and most ethical duties are positive duties. But the relevant distinction is between duties of right and those of virtue.

Perhaps you are one of the 10% who think it might not be unethical for you to push the large man because that minimizes lives lost. But the large man's right to life in such a case of conflict has already been authoritatively determined in the system of public laws, and you have a moral duty to respect that determination rather than substituting your own individual ethical judgment for it in the case, even if you disagree. The large man's right to his life includes at least the right not to be coerced to die in order to aid others. Indeed, this much of his right to life likely must be present in any legitimate system of equal freedom under public laws to which everyone could possibly consent (see ZeF, AA 08:349–50). Hence the large man's right to life in such a case has already been authoritatively determined in public law, and you therefore have a moral duty to respect it, whatever your ethical preference in the case may be. To do otherwise is to act lawlessly, Kant says, to commit wrong "in the highest degree" (RL, AA 06: 308n). This is the priority of right.

In the Driver variation, by contrast, there is a conflict between a duty of right not to kill the one and duties of right not to kill each of the five. Some may object that by not turning the trolley, the driver avoids taking action and so avoids violating any legal duty of right not to kill the five. But this objection fails because as the driver of the trolley you are subject to a prior legal duty to drive the trolley safely, and failing to fulfill this duty therefore constitutes an action by omission. To see this prior legal duty more clearly, compare an analogous case where you are driving a car: if there are five people stranded in the lane ahead (let us assume, through no fault of their own), and you could safely change lanes to avoid killing them, then choosing to nevertheless maintain your lane and kill them would violate a prior legal duty to drive the car safely (see Thomson, 2008, p. 369). There is, therefore, a conflict between (legal) duties of right in Driver. In cases of conflict between legal duties, the priority of right does not control, and this is what distinguishes Driver from Footbridge. Since the resolution of the conflict between legal duties in Driver is unclear, it seems only rational to minimize rights violations as a fallback ethical principle in the case.

Distinguishing right from ethics and observing the priority of right thus solves Foot's original trolley "problem." In Footbridge, one has a duty of right determined authoritatively in public law not to kill the large man that therefore takes priority over one's ethical duty to save the five from harm. In Driver, by contrast, there is a conflict between duties of right that the priority of right cannot resolve and so rational moral intuition falls back on minimizing harm. Prevailing intuitions to kill one to spare five in Driver but not to do so in Footbridge are thus both rational. This solves Foot's trolley problem.[6]

3.3 The Real Trolley "Problem:" Driver

Foot takes it for granted that it is better to violate only one rather than five negative duties not to kill and that this is why you should turn the trolley in Driver. But since principles of justice characteristically bar the violation of one person's rights to achieve a greater good such as to save many people, it is not clear why justice should allow the violation of one person's rights to achieve the greater good of avoiding violating five people's rights. The one whose rights are violated may complain of being wronged in either case.

I propose the following approach to understanding the dilemma between duties of right in Driver. First, let us stipulate that the conflict is indeed a dilemma in which one is subject to contradictory strict legal obligations not to wrong another by intentionally killing her (i.e., 'OBa $\land$ OB~a', where 'OB' is obligation and 'a' is an action). That is, there is no other legally relevant factor,

---

6 Another trolley "problem" that has attracted some attention is the Bystander variation, which is like Driver except that instead of being the driver of the trolley, you are a bystander with access to a switch that can turn the trolley. This variation is a bad thought experiment because, unlike the Driver or Footbridge variations, the Bystander variation is subject to framing and ordering effects (see, e.g., Liao et al. 2012). These effects likely arise because intuitions about what one should do in Bystander will shift depending upon whether subjects take the control the bystander exercises over the trolley to be sufficient to make an analogy with the control the driver exercises in Driver, or not. Hence experimental results obtained by polling in the Bystander variation will be equivocal.

such as the act-omission distinction, or a superior right on one side or the other due to fault, that would eliminate or prioritize one of the obligations. Now recall Kant's requirement that the prescriptive system of public laws specifying strict legal obligations must be consistent. What does this normative requirement of consistency imply in such a dilemma case?

The first implication is that *neither obligation in the dilemma can be rightfully enforced.* It is not possible to consent to be subject to the enforcement of contradictory narrow legal obligations, as this is tantamount to consenting to arbitrary acts of coercion. But this requirement of consistency in the system of legal duties is a second-order principle of justice. Normative consistency is a constraining property of the system of enforceable public laws; hence a lack of consistency with other legal duties in the system cannot be the reason that a duty is not rightfully enforceable. A legal duty that contradicts another is simply inadmissible into the prescriptive system of legal duties, and the implication of a dilemma in the system is, rather, that the enforcement of either obligation is both rightful and wrongful, i.e., that its rightfulness *cannot be determined.*

The second implication of the normative consistency requirement is that public right requires that *the dilemma must be resolved* (i.e., either by legislative action or judicial verdict). It does not matter how it is resolved, so long as the procedural and substantive requirements of the universal principle of right are met when resolving it. What matters is that the conflict is resolved; and moreover, its resolution may vary by jurisdiction. Legitimate variation in the law by jurisdiction is in fact a common feature of most legal systems: in some U.S. states, for example, contributory negligence will completely bar recovery by injured plaintiffs, while in other states, fault might play no or a very limited role. Yet in each state, the law that resolves the conflict is rightfully enforceable.

From the point of view of justice, then, dilemmas like that in Driver are little different from other conflicts between obligations. The main difference appears to be that in the dilemma case we assume that there is no rational resolution of the conflict at issue, whereas in ordinary cases of conflict, we may assume that some rational resolution of the conflict exists. Regardless, public law must resolve the dilemma, just as it must resolve other cases of conflict between moral equals. I do not mean to imply that civil institutions are authorized to resolve such conflicts irrationally or arbitrarily; rationality will still impose bounds upon acceptable resolutions and their public justifications. It is just that in the dilemma case there will be no decisive reason to resolve the conflict one way or the other.

4 Normative Consistency and Deontic Logic

4.1 Standard Deontic Logic and Non-Monotonic Reasoning Systems

One might think that the standard system of deontic logic would best reflect Kant's normative consistency requirement, since no-conflicts (i.e., '~(OBa & OB~a)') is a theorem of Standard Deontic Logic (SDL). But there seems no reason to think that even a rational public authority might not inadvertently create legal obligations that contradict in situations that authority did not foresee. For example, suppose a municipal authority passes a traffic law that requires stopping at stop signs and another that forbids stopping in front of military bases. It is not inconceivable that a local government agency might then erect a stop sign in front of a military base, creating a conflict of legal obligations under applicable enforceable laws for drivers unfortunate enough to encounter the situation (Navarro/Rodriguez 2014, p. 179). The possibility of such conflicts seems a mundane fact about any actual system of laws, and while one might be tempted to assert that the ordinances in question cannot be held to conflict in the case because the driver can have only one true legal obligation, this assertion seems clearly normative rather than descriptive.

Formal systems should be able to represent the conflict between obligations in such a case *descriptively* while maintaining some mechanism to resolve the conflict at the *prescriptive* level. The logic should not make it impossible to describe such conflicts, as SDL does. Efforts to strategically weaken the axioms or rules of inference of SDL in order to admit contradictions without generating a deontic explosion of inferences appear to merely quarantine rather than resolve contradictions, since the logic provides no mechanism for resolving the contradiction (see, e.g., Goble 2005). They therefore fail to meet the demand that contradictions be resolved at the level of prescriptive obligations.

At the other extreme from SDL are deontic logics that accept contradictions between norms and then attempt to draw reasonable inferences despite them. Semi-classical logics and some paraconsistent logics abandon classical semantics with its two truth values (true, false) and replace it with a semantics of many values (e.g., null, just true, just false, and both true and false). Such systems are often regarded as too weak to be very useful, but the problem with them in the present context is that their very purpose is to tolerate contradictions. Such logics thus appear to accept contradictions not only descriptively but *prescriptively* as well. What the normative demand for consistency requires, however, is a deontic logical system that admits the presence of contradictions descriptively but whose semantics insists that they be resolved at the level of prescriptive obligations.

Non-monotonic reasoning systems (NMRs) with a classical base can describe contradictions while meeting the normative consistency requirement at the prescriptive level, though perhaps not as explicitly as might be desired. NMRs are able to admit contradictions descriptively because they reject monotonicity (i.e., "if K' $\vdash$ p and K' $\subseteq$ K, then K $\vdash$ p"). What monotonicity means is that some inferences might no longer be drawn when new premises are introduced; for example, one might introduce a new fact that directly contradicts some fact upon which an inference depends, so defeating that inference. NMRs therefore can describe contradictions while avoiding the deontic explosion of inferences from a contradiction that plagues SDL. NMRs with a classical (rather than paraconsistent) base meet the normative consistency requirement at the prescriptive level because, semantically, they require an explicit preference or choice relation between possible worlds that are maximally consistent in order to continue to draw defeasible inferences. Each possible world of obligations is thus one that meets the normative consistency requirement at the prescriptive level. NMRs also seem promising for purposes of programming autonomous machine agents because they have known efficient implementations such as answer set programming (Gelfond 2008).

4.2 Logics of Belief Revision

Carlos Alchourrón rejects non-monotonic deontic legal logics, however, on the grounds that such systems obscure the distinction between descriptive and prescriptive activity in the law (Maranhao 2006). Alchourrón is a legal positivist who looks outside any formal property of positive law for sources of that law's moral authority. By contrast, Kant understood there to be a necessary connection between law and the moral obligation to obey it. For Kant, a public law that conforms to the Universal Principle of Right will be morally obligatory because of the law's formal structure (universality, consistency, etc.) as well as, to some degree, its substantive content (respect for the constitutional rights of equality, freedom, etc., that the UPR generates for social human beings).

Yet for Kant a number of diverse but internally consistent bodies of legitimate positive public law are possible. Hence like Alchourrón Kant may have some reason to prefer a deontic legal logic that shows the explicit evolution of such a body of law toward the strongest and most coherent system realizing equal freedom under universal law. Logics of belief revision such as Alchourrón's

"AGM" (named after Alchourrón, Gardenfors, Makinson 1985) may thus provide the best approach to implementing Kant's normative requirement of consistency. AGM has robust formalisms for various operations such as expansion, contraction or revision of the normative system, and all refinements to legal rules are made as explicit as possible (Alchourrón, Gardenfors, Makinson 1985). Rules are not described as defeasible defaults, although they may still achieve appropriately defeasible inferences by Alchourrón's use of a revision operator on the antecedents of conditional obligations (Alchourrón 1991). The ultimate goal of a system like AGM is to completely and consistently and *explicitly* represent the full specification of all legal rules. Defeasible logics, on the other hand, may never eliminate rules that appear to be in conflict but do not generate contradictions because of a preference ordering found elsewhere in the logic. While formally such logics are equivalent to AGM when supplemented by Alchourrón's "f" revision operator (Aqvist 2008), a logic such as AGM may better reflect the normatively consistent system of equal freedom under universal laws constructed by a civil community.

It is important to note that while a deontic logic like AGM may be necessary to capture and reason about duties of right, conformity with those duties might be engineered in a machine agent in a number of different ways (e.g., by symbolic or by statistical, machine-learning techniques, or by some hybrid). The problem of what the *right-making properties* of action are is not the same as the engineering problem of *how to implement right action* in accordance with those properties (see Keeling 2020).

5 Conclusion

I have argued that efforts to build explicitly moral machine agents should focus on public right rather than ethics. *Rightful machines* that respect the priority of right will avoid acting in ways that paternalistically interfere with equal rights of freedom, whereas "ethical" machines that act on popular ethical preferences such as those collected in the Moral Machine Experiment may not. I then showed how shifting the focus from ethics to a standard of public right provides a new approach to resolving deontic conflicts such as those in the trolley problem for autonomous machine agents. Finally, I argued that this shift has important implications for how a deontic logic should handle conflicts between duties or rights.

References

All references to Kant's works follow the German original, *Gesammelte Schriften*, ed. by the Königliche Preussische Akademie der Wissenschaften, 29 Volumes. De Gruyter et al. 1902. English citations follow *The Cambridge Edition of the Works of Immanuel Kant.* Cambridge: Cambridge University Press (1992).

GMS   Grundlegung zur Metaphysik der Sitten/*Groundwork of the Metaphysics of Morals*
MS   Metaphysik der Sitten/*Metaphysics of Morals*
RL   Rechtslehre/*The Doctrine of Right*
TL   Tugendlehre/*The Doctrine of Virtue*
ZeW   Zum ewigen Frieden/*Toward Perceptual Peace*

Alchourrón, Carlos E. (1991): "Conflicts of Norms and the Revision of Normative Systems". In: *Law and Philosophy* 10, pp. 413–425.
Alchourrón, Carlos E./Gärdenfors, Peter/Makinson, David (1985): "On the logic of theory change". In: *Journal of Symbolic Logic* 50. Nr. 2, pp. 510–530.
Åqvist, Lennart (2008): "Alchourron and Bulygin on deontic logic and the logic of norm-propositions, axiomatization, and representability results". In: *Logique & Analyse* 203. pp. 225–261.
Awad, Edmond/Dsouza, Sohan/Kim, Richard/Schulz, Jonathan/Heinrich, Jospeh/Shariff, Azim Bonnefon, Jean-Francois/ Rahwan, Iyad (2018): "The Moral Machine experiment". In: *Nature* 563. pp. 59–64.
Casey, Bryan (2017): "Amoral Machines, Or: How Roboticists Can Learn to Stop Worrying and Love the Law". In: 111 *Nw. U. L. Rev.* 1347.
Foot, Phillippa (1967): "The problem of abortion and the doctrine of double effect". In: *Oxford Review* 5. pp. 5–15.
Gelfond, Michael (2008): "Chapter 7: Answer Sets". In: *Foundations of Artificial Intelligence* 3. pp. 285–316.
Goble, Lou (2005): "A logic for deontic dilemmas". In: *Journal of Applied Logic* 3. pp. 461–483.
Guarini, Marcello (2012): "Conative Dimensions of Machine Ethics: A Defense of Duty". In: *IEEE Transactions on Affective Computing* 3. Nr. 4, pp. 434–442.
Guyer, Paul (2016): "The Twofold Morality of Recht: Once More Unto the Breach". In: *Kant-Studien* 107. Nr. 1, pp. 34–63.
Hohfeld, Weasley (1919): *Fundamental Legal Conceptions as Applied in Judicial Reasoning.* New Haven, CT: Yale University Press.
Keeling, Geoff (2020): "Why Trolley Problems Matter for the Ethics of Automated Vehicles". In: *Science and Engineering Ethics* 26. Nr. 1, pp. 293–307.
Maranhao, Juliano S. A. (2006): "Why was Alcourron afraid of snakes?". In: *Analisis Filosofico* XXVI. Nr. 1, pp. 162–92.
Liao, S. Matthew/Wiegmann, Alex/Alexander, Joshua/Vong, Gerard (2012): "Putting the trolley in order: Experimental philosophy and the loop case". In: *Philosophical Psychology* 25. Nr. 5, pp. 661–671.
Mikhail, John (2007): "Universal moral grammar: Theory, evidence, and the future". In: *Trends in Cognitive Sciences* 11. Nr. 4, pp. 143–152.

Navarro, P. E., & Rodríguez, J. L. (2014): *Deontic Logic and Legal Systems*. Cambridge University Press.

O'Neill, Onora (2016): "Enactable and Enforceable: Kant's Criteria for Right and Virtue". In: *Kant-Studien* 107. Nr. 1, pp. 111–124.

Thomson, Judith (1976): "Killing, Letting Die, and the Trolley Problem". In: *The Monist* 59. Nr. 2, pp. 204–17.

Thomson, Judith (2008): "Turning the Trolley". In: *Philosophy & Public Affairs* 36. Nr. 4, pp. 359–374.

Tonkens, Ryan (2009): "A Challenge for Machine Ethics". In: *Minds & Machines* 19. Nr. 3, pp. 421–438.

Claus Dierksmeier

9 Partners, Not Parts. Enhanced Autonomy Through Artificial Intelligence? A Kantian Perspective

Abstract: While providing an extensive legal and moral philosophy, Kant never worked out his social philosophy in great depths. Gleaning cues from how, in the *Critique of Judgment,* he employed organic notions analogically in regard to societal institutions, one can, however, arrive at a reasonably clear conception of the normative contours for social organizations within the overall framework of his practical philosophy. Central to these reflections is the notion that social institutions should treat individuals in accord with their personal autonomy. Individuals must not be submerged as mere *parts* in a whole which disregards their moral nature as ends-in-themselves but should rather be integrated as *members* whose purposes become co-constitutive for the respective organization. The self-same notion of a societal organization respectful of and conducive to the purposes of its members can offer guidance when it comes to evaluate recent technological advances in the field of artificial intelligence, namely virtual organizations whose social functions are executed by algorithms unconstrained by local contexts or geographical confines. This article aims to showcase the critical potential of a Kantian concept of autonomy-enhancing institutions by discussing how it provides normative orientation for assessing two extant applications in the field of professional matchmaking.

1 Introduction

In the literature on artificial intelligence, a common distinction runs between a 'weaker' version of AI, mimicking human behavior or accomplishing tasks defined by their programmers, and a 'stronger' one which centers on artificially generated entities, setting their aims free from and, potentially, opposed to human interests likewise (Russell/Norvig 2010). This essay does not engage in reflections about systems with autonomous goal-setting capacities, nor in speculations about their technical feasibility or moral desirability. Instead, in what follows, the focus is squarely on the 'weaker' version of AI, i.e. on algorithmic systems pursuing goals

Claus Dierksmeier, University of Tübingen

dictated by their human designers, employing techniques of machine-learning within clearly confined realms whose contours are set by way of conventional programming (Weber/Zoglauer 2019). Instead of a foray into the future, this paper thus takes aim at technologies already shaping and reshaping our present situation, trying to glean criteria for their normative evaluation.

First, I will try to work out Kant's concept of social organizations (1), guided by how Kant, in his *Critique of Judgment,* pondered on whether and how an analogy could legitimately be drawn between *natural organisms* and *social organizations*. I am retracing these arguments in order to see where, in the wide spectrum between a *mechanic* and a *teleological* conception of causality, one would have to locate the specific nature of decisions based on machine-learning. This reconstruction of Kant's positions serves at once as a reminder of the normative ideal guiding his conception of civil society institutions – as associations of and for free beings which are ends-in-themselves: An ideal social organization treats its members as co-constitutive partners rather than as expendable parts. From that normative angle, I will discuss (2) the chances and risks inherent to algorithms currently used by two professional matchmaking platforms. Last, I am closing with reflections on the added benefit that Kantian criteria proffer as compared to assessments based on neoclassical-economic or neoliberal-political analysis (3).[1]

2 Kant's Concept of Social Organizations

In his legal philosophy, Kant provides contours for how individuals and institutions are (not) to act (Willaschek 2002). Restraining the use of anyone's *outer* freedom so that it can coexist with the selfsame freedom of everyone else according to universal laws of freedom (Köhler 1992), his philosophy of law proffers a framework – of mostly 'negative' obligations – for personal or institutional agency (Pogge 1998). This indispensable legal foundation is then complemented as well as transcended by his ethics, supplying, via the categorical imperative, 'positive' duties for the *inner* freedom of any and all persons (Höffe 1983). These obligations direct the moral agent towards the 'highest good,' understood by Kant as a state of affairs where happiness come to those who morally deserve it (Dierksmeier 1998, Guyer 2000).

For *individual* agency, the dual imperatives of his legal and ethical doctrines can be unfolded into a comprehensive set of normative guideposts, as Kant himself

---

1 For helpful critique and instructive pointers I wish to thank Vanessa Schäffner, Peter Seele und Dieter Schönecker.

expounded at length within his "Metaphysics of Morals" through his "Rechtslehre" (*doctrine of right*) and his "Tugendlehre" (*doctrine of virtue*), respectively (Wood 1999, Ripstein 2010). Whereas the micro level of individual action and the macro level of state agency are extensively covered by these works, for the normatively appropriate design of social *institutions* on the meso level of analysis (e.g., firms, unions, associations, etc.), however, we find only scarce pointers. Certainly, the two pillars of legal and ethical orientation can offer a suitable scaffolding, as it were, for erecting social architectures within the field of civil society – but the conceptual space they leave open is quite considerable still and (especially, when compared to the social philosophy of Hegel) provides only scant guidance as to how social institutions should ideally be designed (Farneth 201, Brudner 2017). It is therefore helpful to turn one's glance to other aspects of Kant's work, in order to fill in this lacuna.

As is well-known, Kant always resisted *mechanical* doctrines of society (Bartuschat 1987). Instead, and especially since the "Groundworks of the Metaphysics of Morals," Kant advocates a theory of an ideal social community ('kingdom of ends') wherein no element is merely to be regarded and treated as a *means*, but each is at the same time to be respected as an *end* in itself; that is to say, Kant sought a social formation wherein the individuals do not merely exist for the sake of the whole, but the whole respects the dignity of the individuals (Guyer 2000).

Throughout Kant's works, the *terminus technicus* for this distinction is his differentiation between a "limb" (*Glied*) and a "part" (*Teil*) of a whole, with the *limb* denoting an element which serves itself as an end for the whole – as opposed to the mere *part*, an element integrated solely for the sake of an external purpose (Korsgaard 1992). Mapping this nomenclature onto society, the 'whole' constituted by a social institution should not mechanically force its elements into a merely external union. Instead, it should emerge as a unity arising from and indicative of their genuine purposes (Velkley 1989). Or, in more current parlance, institutions ought to treat their members never as expendable parts but always as essential partners.

Yet before employing organic terminology in the context of social philosophy, we need to consider whether it is permissible at all to apply biological metaphors to a theory of social phenomena (Krieken 1873, Ahrens 1855, Dierksmeier 2001). What are the conditions which must be met in order that a theory of *social organizations* can aptly be informed by theories concerning *corporeal organisms*?

Kant considers this question in the *Critique of Judgment* and highlights that "strictly speaking" we must admit that "the organization of nature has nothing analogous with any causality that we know" (KU, AA 05: B 294). We 'know' adequately only two types of causality: *mechanical* causality – situated, so to speak, 'below' the "forming force" (KU, AA 05: B 293) of nature – and *purposeful* causality (teleological finality) – 'above' the formative causality of nature. The auto-formation and auto-determination of natural organisms seems to be distinct from either: a causality *sui generis* – purposive in its results, yet not emanating from a process of a reflective pursuit of purposes (Bartuschat 1972, Fulda and Horstmann 1990, Hartmann 1951).

Since it is through conscious goal-setting that we form and transform social institutions, we can by no means *identify* the formative-but-irreflexive causality of nature with societal formations that humanity brings about intentionally. If, nonetheless, in Kant's telling, it seems "very appropriate" that in a contemporary transformation of a large people into a state "the word organization was often used for the establishment of magistrates etc. and even of the whole body of the state", then this prods us to ask: How can one at all, as Kant suggests, "by an *analogy* with the aforementioned direct natural purposes" give more "light" to the essential nature of social organizations (KU AA 05:B 295, note; italics C.D.)? Beholding the aforementioned difference between the formative powers of biology and consciously wrought social formations, we must ask, what is it exactly that said analogy is supposed to illuminate?

The gist of Kant's answer is this: Since already in nature an entity's parts are neither functioning nor treated merely as dead, replaceable elements, but as living, indispensable members of a whole, acting and being acted towards within the respective organism in accord with their internal principles, free human beings should all the more be integrated into their respective organizations according to their essential autonomy (Dierksmeier 2003, 2002). That is to say, although nature does not form states, associations, or any other social institutions, if these were designed in analogy to how nature itself structures living organisms, the purposes of their members must become, consequently, as decisive for the whole as the purpose of the whole is to be for its members (Köhler 2017). Social organizations, in other words, should conform to the fact that individuals are ends-for-themselves (KU, AA 05: B 382) and consequently to be subjected only to rules in accord with their moral autonomy (KU, AA 05: B 391).

Put this way, the analogy between natural organism and social organizations is indeed shining an important 'light' on how, through and within institutions, people should act collectively in the realm left open by Kant's legal philosophy and ethics. Whereas Kant's legal philosophy, notwithstanding a few positive legal duties against oneself and others, leaves largely unsettled the question to which *purposes* to direct oneself (Byrd/Hruschka 2010) and whereas Kant's ethical philosophy focuses on *individual* conduct (Dierksmeier 2013), we now do get some pointers as to the positive *purposes of institutions* (DiCenso 2019).

Like natural organizations, constrained but not completely determined by the laws of physics, social organizations are regulated but not enlivened by juridical laws. There is an overarching component in either. Kant points to this supervening dimension when he notes that, although being part of nature, the final purpose of human sociability "lies outside of it" and requires for its attainment more than biology can offer, namely "culture" (KU, AA 05:B 392). Social organizations, while being part of the legally constituted landscape of societal life, transcend legal regulations both in regard to purposes they define for themselves and how they achieve them. The law certainly can set up normative constraints for social institutions, but it cannot itself accomplish that social organizations go beyond what the law demands in order to, say, harmonize the freedoms of their members amongst themselves as well as of their members and of society at large. In other words, if people did nothing beyond what the law commands, societal life would suffer: both individually and collectively people must *voluntarily* do more for society to thrive.

This brings us to another aspect of the analogy. What, ideally, social organizations accomplish, i.e., the harmonization of personal freedoms through a shared culture and its attendant features, can be said to realize important aspirations of Kant's ethics, expressed as they are through the metaphor of the "kingdom of ends" (AA 4: 434) which directs humanity to align their diverse projects via shared purposes. Therein, too, social organizations are akin to what nature brings forth in biological organisms: entities which, without having been designed for a set purpose, feature internal as well as external functions of a purposive kind. Likewise, social organizations can and will be brought about for the pursuit of certain, specific goals which neither need to, nor typically will, be garnered, *directly*, from ethics, while frequently still, *indirectly*, serving an ethical agenda.

After all, if a given social organization wants to harness to the fullest potential the energies of its members, it must not thwart their energies; a goal best accomplished by enhancing rather than suppressing the personal autonomy of its members. As a result, social institutions which in effect protect and promote individual freedoms and capabilities, may come about simply because people are eager to organize for certain shared purposes in the most effective and efficient way; corporations are an oft-cited point in case (Aßländer/Curbach 2014). Thus, the world of business can be a possible realm for the application of Kantian principles, in particular with a view to analyzing whether firms in their strategic decision-making opt for procedures which assure that all concerned by their decisions are – directly or by way of representation – also involved in bringing them about. The potential, and oftentimes real, upshot – a freedom-conducive institution – may be thus but a byproduct of amoral (albeit not immoral) ends intelligently and consistently pursued.

Now, to repeat, other than Hegel, Kant does not go into detail as to which social organizations are particularly good at supporting human autonomy, and how. In his legal philosophy, Kant does give an affirmative nod here and there to traditional institutions of bourgeois society such as the family. Yet, by and large, we must glean the information as to which type of social institutions to favor from pointers elsewhere in his philosophical oeuvre. Within this wider scope, though, we can say that, on Kant's view, humanity will reach its destination only guided by reason, governing wisely over the manifold impulses and inspirations proffered by internal inclinations as well as external constellations. The "culture" and "cultivation" Kant looked for in human affairs is in good part one where social institutions buttress the work of moral reason – beyond the requirements of the law (Städtler, Berger, Vollmann 2005).

As much as individuals (on the micro level of analysis) form habits in order to solidify patterns of trialed and tested behavior and as much as states (at the macro level) sanction certain laws in order to stabilize peaceful forms of co-existence, civil society institutions (on the meso level) can also help to express and support activities which align the otherwise oftentimes disparate purposive agency of people. Institutions can assist individuals, especially in moments of personal weakness or disorientation, to stay on the straight and narrow by promoting, incentivizing, training, and rewarding apt behaviors (Moore 2002, Etzioni 1995, Wood 1990). The normative mettle of social institutions can thus be gauged as to whether they are helping people making decisions that are at once morally sound, socially acceptable, and in their own long-term interest. The schooling in worldly affairs along with the training of pro-social attitudes and aptitudes that social institutions provide – a point much dwelled upon by Hegel (Wood 1990) –, can assume an *indirect* moral quality inasmuch as it instructs people to find ways to pursue their own personal interest in ways and manners acceptable to, respectful of, and, ideally also, conducive to the interests of others. Through their internal culture and the resultant cultivation of their members, social institutions can thus be a formidable force of moral education and exert a formative influence within society to boot.

To put the same idea in a more abstract and sociological manner, institutions are congealed forms of interpersonal decision-making and cooperation bent on solving societal coordination problems (Nielsen 2009). Not incidentally, this sounds almost as if social institutions were but algorithms for societal problem-solving: a bespoke technology to cope with the challenges of inevitable coexistence and requisite collaboration (Esquith/Gifford 2010). For it does not, looked at from this angle, demarcate a difference in principle whether the social institution in question is offline or online, physically manifested in Euclidian space or virtually organized in cyberspace (Kasper-Fuehrer/Ashkanasy

2001). What does matter is rather whether a given social institution approximates the Kantian ideal of a social organization as an institution negatively protecting and positively promoting the autonomy of its members. From this perspective we shall now inspect two recent online platforms employing AI algorithms that expressly endorse said normative ideal of autonomy-enhancement as part and parcel of their strategic value proposition.

3 Algorithms and Autonomy

In what follows, I am side-stepping the discussion on what constitutes genuinely 'artificial' intelligence (Floridi/Sanders 2004, Misselhorn 2019). According to the most demanding definitions, only technological systems independently setting their goals or having autarky over their energy and existence, can truly be called 'artificially intelligent' (Russel/Norvig 2010). With a standard so demanding, however, one probably must also concede that, at present, such systems can nowhere be found (Anderson/Anderson 2011, Wallach/Allen 2009). Yet thus one would gainsay the potential of the term 'artificial intelligence' to help us discern between software-based technology of yesteryear, programmed as rigid if-then-conditionals, and far more advanced applications of the present which, through advanced algorithms and pattern-recognition technologies, display an undisputed capacity for machine-learning (Etzioni/Etzioni 2017, pp. 408f.).

After all, not only do many present applications pass the Turing-test of producing results which, to the uninitiated observer, are *equivalent* to outputs generated by human operators (Turing 1950). What is more, machine-learning can produce outcomes that, in some respects, *surpass* what, during comparable time intervals, humans could generate (Deng 2015, p. 26). Moreover, when in 1955, in the context of a funding proposal to the Rockefeller Foundation, John McCarthy used the term 'artificial intelligence' for the first time (McCarthy et al. 1955), the notion of 'machine learning' was not at all on the horizon. Consequently, the concept of artificial intelligence (AI) was designed to suggest that, sometime in the future, machines, if programmed adequately, might be able to solve problems of a far higher order than possible with the hitherto available technology. McCarthy and colleagues agreed that the real challenge in devising arithmetic operations which mimic human problem-solving capacity would soon be no longer due to a "lack of machine capacity, but our inability to write programs taking full advantage of what we have" (McCarthy et al. 1955, p. 2). It seems thus apt to name as 'artificially intelligent' all such algorithm-based systems today that have overcome this erstwhile problem, since, although the software they run on at present was written by human programmers, their outputs are generated independently of further human influence – and can be regarded in *that* sense as 'artificially' autonomous (Etzioni/Etzioni 2017).

For our present purpose, this weaker definition of artificial intelligence can suffice, or so I would argue, in order to examine extant applications whether they can reasonably be called 'social institutions' in a Kantian sense. As candidates for such a probe, two start-ups are selected here which both, drawing each on machine-learning as well as on blockchain technology, have established online platforms running a matching software for professional collaboration. Not their technical commonalities were what motivated their selection, however, but the fact that each company in its own way aims to realize aspirations akin to the Kantian ideal of autonomy-enhancing social institutions. Both applications cater to the global job market and intend to change the way people collaborate all around the world. The goal of either is, more specifically, to bring more autonomy to workers and to help people worldwide find employment that suits their talents and aspirations (for a broader discussion of both firms within the context of blockchain technology, see Dierksmeier/Seele 2019).

The first firm I wish to introduce is "TiiQu" (the name is emblematic of the 'trust quotient,' one of the firm's unique selling points) which aims to lower the costs of and reduce the bias involved in recruiting processes, especially but not only in the gig economy. TiiQu wants to make hiring decisions more merito-cratic by cutting out conventional middlemen such as headhunters, replacing them with algorithms that establish the professional trustworthiness of job candi-dates based on certified competences, recorded in a globally accessible and tamper-proof blockchain. The matching algorithms employed are deliberately de-signed so as to prevent the impact of stereotypes in hiring decisions (based on gender, ethnicity, age, etc.) and to hinder corruption (for their code of ethics, see http://anyflip.com/keby/zdgj/).

Not always, certainly, is such disintermediation tantamount to an unam-biguous gain in moral quality, since there may well be circumstances where personal intermediation is preferable for sound judgment as compared to the generalization and standardization inherent to algorithmic decision-making. At times, however, and to the extent that tasks and profiles are already standard-ized so as to allow for meritocratic matchings, such algorithms may prove in-valuable (Bhatia et al. 2018). While previous digital technologies had already been used to dissociate capacity sets and personal identifiers in digitized appli-cation processes (Barron et al. 1985), they were hitherto hampered by a single point of failure: If the central node in the respective network was corrupted, so might be the matchings between prospective employers and employees. It is to this problem that the decentralized approach of blockchain technology, as employed by TiiQu, promises a solution (Dierksmeier/Seele 2019).

What makes TiiQu a candidate for the label of a social institution in the Kantian sense is the fact that it aims to strengthen the autonomy of its members both substantially and procedurally. On a *substantial* level, we can appreciate the fact that here is a hiring platform whose matchmaking is expressly geared to functional benchmarks alone. Its technology enforces that prospective employers cannot circumvent the very criteria they define for job applicants through the influence of biases, stereotypes, nepotism, favoritism, and so on. TiiQu's software assures that any and all hiring on this platform is based on professional criteria alone which first must be made explicit and then have to be abided by on part of the employer. Likewise, TiiQu eliminates the opportunity for misrepresentation on part of the would-be employee. Through independently verifying their claims to expertise, TiiQu ensures that employers committing to hire based on said explicated criteria are secure against imposters who try to game the system in their favor.

TiiQu's matching and hiring process is anonymized and standardized which is in the interest of both trustworthy employers and honest employees. As a result, the career chances – i.e. the professional autonomy – of people who truthfully represent the qualities they have and for firms that sincerely wish to hire without bias to find one another are decisively augmented. Especially with a view to a global, multicultural marketplace which puts up countless obstacles to such matches, this is no small feat. Due to either the offline character of job interviews (hampered by national borders and spatial distance) or the online filters used by conventional headhunters (who have a vested interest in the eventual pairing of openings and candidates, but less so in a truthful representation of both parties *per se*), the quantity and quality of the hindrances to meritocratic hiring overcome by TiiQu are notable. The upshot is a tangible empowerment for job candidates from all around the world who, under default conditions, would have a disadvantage on the global job market as against locally embedded and 'better connected' candidates or might suffer from discrimination based on gender, ethnicity, etc.

This is matched on the *procedural* level by TiiQu inviting all the participants of its platform to become part of its governance. Through a model that allots the ability to introduce changes to the platforms standards and policies in proportion to one's collaboration (as opposed to, say, to one's stake in venture capital or one's shareholdings), TiiQu deliberately democratizes what in most firms is a plutocratic affair: the nexus between membership and control. No one is barred from driving the kind of change he or she wishes to see in TiiQu's parameters and processes. In this way, the firm allows platform participants to be 'limbs' of the institution quite in a Kantian sense, i.e. by affecting what affects them and by becoming part of a whole whose direction they themselves influence.

Even more ambitious in terms of self-governance 'from below' is "YourCompany" (https://www.your.company). This start-up sets out not only to bring would-be employees and extant employers together but also aspires to overhaul entirely how entrepreneurial ideas are being realized. Assuming that many more people would cultivate their creative inspirations and dare to become entrepreneurs, if only the administrative, bureaucratic, logistical, and financial burdens of setting up a firm could be lowered, YourCompany promises to semi-automate the process of incorporation. The operative idea is to offer a blockchain-based default structure for a (financial, logistic, legal) support network so that aspirant entrepreneurs may focus on their innovative ideas and products.

Anyone with spare resources (time, knowledge, expertise, etc.) on their hands can enter this network freely and peruse the projects on display. By self-selecting which business idea or corporate infrastructure people want to support through their services, individuals commit their labor, not unlike a vote, to those projects that they find most deserving. Money is thus not the main draw, although also conventional forms of crowdfunding and remuneration are on offer; what attracts collaborators is mainly the perceived worthiness and overall appeal of the projects themselves. As a result, this online cooperation platform promises to be more egalitarian than others: Whereas capital is unequally distributed, everyone has 24 hours/day at their disposal.

Moreover, by bringing people from all corners of the world together to engage in transactions that not only replace offline interactions but also, absent the opportunities offered by these platforms, might never take place at all, either platform increases the overall amount of cooperative engagements between global citizens for presumed mutual benefit; a result a Kantian might applaud as a welcome enhancement of the professional autonomy of all involved parties. In fact, where, as in the case of YourCompany, some such professional communities are built solely for the reason of seeing through a certain social innovation or transformation, one could go as far as to regard the resultant businesses as social entrepeneurships (Pate/Wankel 2014) or as quasi-public enterprises (Franz/Hochgerner/Howaldt 2012). At any rate, YourCompany represents and intensifies an ongoing process where inter-firm, firm/market, and firm/society boundaries become increasingly blurred, leading to entirely new constellations at the business-society interface (Catalini 2017).

The governance of these two platforms-*cum*-networks is meant to be as democratic as their organizational structure is decentralized. In YourCompany, too, people gain influence over the network and its ecosystem in proportion to their active contributions. The typical bifurcation between management or owners on one hand and the creative class or those putting in 'sweat equity' on the other yields to a governance structure where influence ensues involvement – bolstering personal autonomy. If TiiQu and YourCompany succeed, they stand not only to broaden access to the global economy quantitatively. Over time, they might also qualitatively alter the power matrix of job markets. The professional opportunities of workers and independent creators could grow, while the rents for conventional gatekeepers such as capital owners might dwindle. This requires, however, a broad adoption and hence approval of their respective activities, itself depending on utter transparency about their processes and procedures. Last, not least, this would indirectly satisfy a key Kantian condition for public decision-making: strict *publicity* – as a precondition for the active involvement of, ideally, all passively affected individuals (Habermas 1995).

4 Kantian Conclusions

From the perspective of neoclassical economics, the aforementioned developments towards collaboration based on algorithmic matchmaking appear as net-positive: To succeed, such platforms need to reach economies of scale by satisfying the wants of numerous customers; and where many voluntarily agree to transact, one can, assuming rationally operating economic agents, infer that aggregate utility is increased. An assessment from a market-liberal angle comes to the same conclusion: Where uncoerced contracts come to fruition, the voluntary nature of these transactions alone signals that the freedom of the involved parties was respected and enacted: Given a plurality and, consequently, a healthy competition of such online employment brokers, their offers appear to advance the liberty of each and all to find forms of gainful employment and meaningful cooperation.

From a Kantian perspective, the assessment is a bit more complicated, as we need to discern between an indirect and a direct assessment of these business models. The *indirect* perspective refers to the Kantian notion that purposiveness in outcome need not result from intentional purposes. The same holds for social institutions in that they can realize moral ends without necessarily being set up to do so. From this angle, it seems that the firms here investigated have chosen to democratize their governance structures in order to offer the best possible service to their members. Treating them, not as mere parts, but as partners, they are in matter of fact realizing a Kantian goal – participatory governance via procedural autonomy – without this being their *raison d'être*. While both TiiQu and YourCompany do explicitly endorse said goal also as part and parcel of their respective mission statements, they were not created in the first place to realize this objective; rather, in spite of their appreciation of professional autonomy as an *intrinsic* good, either pursues this end as *instrumental* and, in fact, crucial for the success of their overall corporate agenda.

Their agenda must also be scrutinized *directly*. At first glance, one will surely feel inclined to applaud anything that promises to promote individuals' freedom to contract voluntarily for legitimate purposes and, especially, to open up professional opportunities otherwise foreclosed or inaccessible. Whatever lowers the threshold for people from all corners of the world to engage one another in economic freedom for their reciprocal benefit, is justly an auspicious candidate for moral approval from a Kantian vantage point, not in the least because it raises the number and strengthens the nature of cosmopolitan exchanges. Yet, while the commitment of these online platforms to contribute to a just and fair commercial order for all global citizens is certainly laudable, at the same time, a Kantian should be chary of economic structures that put quasi-public powers into private hands alone. Firms brokering deals essential for the livelihood of the involved parties assume enormous power over people's lives and, in keeping with Kant's legal and political philosophy, should be subject to public scrutiny.

The invisible operative standards ('white norms') that regulate the encounters on such platforms are not of a merely technological nature but also expressive of certain value standards – or their absence. A Kantian might take recourse in this regard to something akin to the slogan 'no regulation without representation;' that is, from a Kantian perspective one should insist on the public oversight of the quasi-public powers of such platforms instead of letting them use these simply at their discretion. After all, customs and conventions in the offline world have typically stood the test of time and thus may merit the benefit of the doubt as to their appropriateness. Yet what qualifies, one has to ask, the programmers of the algorithms governing online platforms to make – via default settings – the right choices for others? How open are such systems for inside and outside criticism as well as the implementation of the moral lessons thus learned? In keeping with other semi-autonomous societal organizations – like universities, for instance – the participatory self-governance of such platforms must remain subject to public supervision and, where necessary, revision.

Also noteworthy are the risks posed by the facelessness of these systems. We should assume that the very fact which advocates for these platforms adduce in their favor – i.e. an anonymous matching of persons to tasks – implies not only benefits but risks as well: Whereas in socially embedded and culturally framed markets, transactions are, for better or worse, permeated by the social norms immanent to the respective social realm, the same does not hold for algorithmic decision-making. The latter requires the explication – and subsequent operationalization – of implicit normative standards lest ethical lacunas arise. It seems, consequently, that from a Kantian perspective the morality of AI-applications can never be assessed in bulk. Rather, one must evaluate their moral mettle on a case-by-case basis and in direct comparison with the conventional alternatives they aim to replace.

In sum, from a Kantian perspective, one would need to demand, *first*, as a mandate of *legal* philosophy, that AI-products be regulated by law so as to rule out egregious impropriety. Paraphrasing, for this purpose, Kant's demand for publicity in the political realm, the public should have an effect on whatever affects it. *Second*, on the level of *social* philosophy, such platforms should demonstrably manage the leeway left open by the law in ways that assure that stakeholder criticism is afforded the appropriate scrutiny and has concomitant chances to induce changes. The more such platforms enable stakeholder governance through participatory design and procedural malleability, the likelier is their eventual endorsement from a Kantian perspective.

References

All references to Kant's works are to *Kant's Gesammelte Schriften, Ausgabe der Preußischen Akademie der Wissenschaften* (Berlin: de Gruyter, 1902 ff.). The following abbreviation is used:

KU   Kritik der Urteilskraft/*Critique of the Power of Judgement*

Ahrens, Heinrich. (1855): *Juristische Encyclopädie, oder, Organische Darstellung der Rechts- und Staatswissenschaft, auf Grundlage einer ethischen Rechtsphilosophie.* Wien: C. Gerold & Sohn.
Anderson, Michael/Anderson, Leigh Susan. (2011): *Machine ethics.* Cambridge: Cambridge University Press.
André, Quentin, et al. (2018): "Consumer choice and autonomy in the age of artificial intelligence and big data". In: *Customer Needs and Solutions* 5. Nr. 1–2, pp. 28–37.
Aßländer, S. Michael/Curbach, Janina. (2014): "The Corporation as Citoyen? Towards a New Understanding of Corporate Citizenship". In: *Journal of Business Ethics* 120. Nr. 4, pp. 541–554. DOI: 10.1007/s10551-013-2004-8.
Barron, M. John/Bishop, John/Dunkelberg, C. William. (1985): "Employer search: The interviewing and hiring of new employees". In: *The Review of Economics and Statistics.* pp. 43–52.
Bartuschat, Wolfgang. (1972): „Zum systematischen Ort von Kants Kritik der Urteilskraft". In: *Philosophische Abhandlungen* 43.
Bartuschat, Wolfgang. (1987): „Praktische Philosophie und Rechtsphilosophie bei Kant". In: *Philosophisches Jahrbuch* 94. Nr.1, pp. 24–41.

Bhatia, G. K./Kumaraguru, P./Dubey, A./Buduru, A. B./Kaulgud, V. (2018): *WorkerRep: building trust on crowdsourcing platform using blockchain* (Doctoral dissertation, IIIT-Delhi).

Brudner, Alan. (2017): *The owl and the rooster: Hegel's transformative political science.* Cambridge, United Kingdom, New York, NY: Cambridge University Press.

Byrd, B. Sharon/Hruschka, Joachim. (2010): *Kant's Doctrine of right a commentary.* Cambridge: Cambridge University Press.

Catalini, C. (2017): "How blockchain technology will impact the digital economy". Oxford Business Law Blog. www.law.ox.ac.uk/business-law-blog/blog/2017/04/how-blockchain-technology-willimpact-digital-economy. Retrieved 02/10/2018.

Deng, Boer. (2015): "Machine ethics: The robot's dilemma". In: *Nature News* 523. Nr.7558, pp. 24–26.

DiCenso, James J. (2019): "Kant on Ethical Institutions". In: *The Southern Journal of Philosophy* 57. Nr.1, pp. 30–55.

Dierksmeier, Claus. (1998): *Das Noumenon Religion: Eine Untersuchung zur Stellung der Religion im System der praktischen Philosophie Kants, Kantstudien- Ergänzungshefte.* Berlin, New York: Walter de Gruyter.

Dierksmeier, Claus. (2001): "Mechanischer oder organischer Rechtsbegriff?". In: Christian, Danz/Claus, Dierksmeier/Christian, Seysen (Eds.): *System als Wirklichkeit.* pp. 57–69.

Dierksmeier, Claus. (2002): "Absolute Konstruktion des Rechts?: Zum Rechtsbegriff in Hegels Naturrechtsaufsatz". In: Klaus, Vieweg (Ed.): *Gegen das ‚unphilosophische Unwesen'.* pp.157–166.

Dierksmeier, Claus. (2003): *Der absolute Grund des Rechts: Karl Christian Friedrich Krause in Auseinandersetzung mit Fichte und Schelling, Spekulation und Erfahrung. Abteilung II, Untersuchungen.* Stuttgart-Bad Cannstatt: Frommann-Holzboog.

Dierksmeier, Claus. (2013): "Kant on Virtue". In: *Journal of Business Ethics* 113. Nr 4, pp. 597–609. DOI: doi: 10.1007/s10551-013-1683-5.

Dierksmeier, Claus/Seele, Peter (2019): "Blockchain and business ethics". in: *Business Ethics: A European Review* 29. Nr. 2, pp. 348–359.

Esquith, Stephen L./Gifford, Fred. (2010): *Capabilities, power, and institutions: toward a more critical development ethics.* University Park, Pa.: Pennsylvania State University Press.

Etzioni, Amitai/Etzioni, Oren. (2017): "Incorporating Ethics into Artificial Intelligence". In: *The Journal of Ethics* 21. Nr.4, pp. 403–418.

Etzioni, Amitai. (1995): *New communitarian thinking: persons, virtues, institutions, and communities, Constitutionalism and democracy.* Charlottesville: University Press of Virginia.

Farneth, Molly B. (2017): *Hegel's social ethics: religion, conflict, and rituals of reconciliation.* Princeton, New Jersey: Princeton University Press.

Floridi, Luciano/Sanders, W. Jeff. (2004): "On the Morality of Artificial Agents". In: *Minds and Machines* 14. Nr. 3, pp. 349–379.

Franz, Hans-Werner/Hochgerner, Josef/Howaldt, Jürgen. (2012): *Challenge social innovation: potentials for business, social entrepreneurship, welfare and civil society.* Heidelberg, New York: Springer.

Fulda, Hans Friedrich/Horstmann, Peter Rolf. (1990): *Hegel und die "Kritik der Urteilskraft". 1. Aufl. ed, Veröffentlichungen der Internationalen Hegel-Vereinigung.* Stuttgart: Klett-Cotta.

Guyer, Paul. (2000*): Kant on Freedom, Law, and Happiness.* New York.

Habermas, Jürgen. (1995): *Strukturwandel der Öffentlichkeit Untersuchungen zu einer Kategorie der bürgerlichen Gesellschaft.*, Suhrkamp Taschenbuch Verlag.

Hartmann, Nicolai. (1951): *Teleologisches Denken.* Berlin: W. de Gruyter.

Höffe, Otfried. (1983): *Immanuel Kant.* München: C.H. Beck.

Kasper-Fuehrer, Eva C./Ashkanasy, M. Neal. (2001): "Communicating trustworthiness and building trust in interorganizational virtual organizations". In: *Journal of Management.* Elsevier Science Publishing Company.

Köhler, Michael. (1992): „Zur Begründung des Rechtszwangs im Anschluss an Kant und Fichte". In: Michael, Kahlo/Ernst A., Wolff/Rainer, Zaczyk (Eds.): *Fichtes Lehre vom Rechtsverhältnis: Die Deduktion der §§ 1–4 der Grundlage des Naturrechts und ihre Stellung in der Rechtsphilosophie.* pp. 93–125.

Köhler, Michael (2017): *Recht und Gerechtigkeit. Grundzüge einer Rechtsphilosophie der verwirklichten Freiheit.* Tübingen: Mohr-Siebeck.

Korsgaard, Christine M. (1992): "Creating the Kingdom of Ends: Reciprocity and Responsibility in Personal Relations." In: *Philosophical Perspectives* 6. pp. 305–332.

Krieken, Albert Th. van. (1873): *Ueber die sogenannte organische Staatstheorie: Ein Beitrag zur Geschichte des Staatsbegriffs.* Leipzig: Duncker & Humblot.

McCarthy, John/Minsky, Marvin/Rochester, Nathanael/Shannon, E. Claude (1955): *A Proposal for the Dartmouth Summer Research Project on Artificial Intelligence.* http://jmc.stanford.edu/articles/dartmouth/dartmouth.pdf, visited on 4/6/2021.

Misselhorn, Catrin. (2019): "Maschinenethik und Philosophie". In: Oliver, Bendel (Eds.): *Handbuch Maschinenethik.* Wiesbaden: Springer, pp. 33–56.

Moore, Geoff. (2002): "On the implications of the practice-institution distinction: MacIntyre and the application of modern virtue ethics to business. (Abstract)." In: *Business Ethics Quarterly* 12. Nr.1, p. 19.

Nielsen, Helle. (2009): *Bounded rationality in decision-making: how cognitive shortcuts and professional values may interfere with market-based regulation, Issues in environmental politics.* Manchester, New York: Manchester University Press.

Pate, E. Larry/Wankel, Charles. (2014): *Emerging Research Directions in Social Entrepreneurship, Advances in Business Ethics Research.* Dordrecht: Springer.

Pogge, Thomas Winfried Menko. (1998): "Is Kant's Rechtslehre Comprehensive?". In: *The Southern Journal of Philosophy* 36, pp. 161–187.

Ripstein, Arthur (2010): *Force and freedom.* Cambridge, MA.: Harvard University Press.

Russell, Stuart/Norvig, Peter. (2010): *Artificial Intelligence. A Modern Approach.* New Jersey: Pearson.

Städtler, Michael/Berger, Maxi/Vollmann, Heiko. (2005): *Kants "Ethisches Gemeinwesen": die Religionsschrift zwischen Vernunftkritik und praktischer Philosophie.* Berlin: Akademie Verlag.

Stuart, J. A. Susan/Dobbyn, Chris. (2002): *A Kantian Prescription for Artificial Conscious Experience.* In: Leonardo 35. Nr. 2, pp. 407–411.

Turing, Alan. (1950): "Computing machinery and intelligence". In: *Mind* 59. pp. 433–460.

Ulgen, Ozlem (2017): "Kantian Ethics in the Age of Artificial Intelligence and Robotics". In: *QIL* 43. pp. 59–83.

Velkley, L. Richard. (1989): *Freedom and the end of reason: on the moral foundation of Kant's critical philosophy.* Chicago: University of Chicago Press.

Wallach, Wendell/Allen, Colin. (2009): *Moral Machines. Teaching Robots Right From Wrong.* New York: Oxford University Press.

Weber, Karsten/Zoglauer, Thomas. (2019): „Maschinenethik und Technikethik". In: Oliver, Bendel (Hrsg.): *Handbuch Maschinenethik.* pp. 145–163.

Willaschek, Marcus. (2002): "Which Imperatives for Right? On the Non-Prescriptive Character of Juridicial Laws in Kant's Metaphysics of Morals." In: *Kant's Metaphysics of Morals: Interpretative Essays.*

Wood, Allen W. (1990): *Hegel's Ethical Thought.* Cambridge England, New York: Cambridge University Press.

Wood, Allen W. (1999): *Kant's Ethical Thought.* Cambridge: Cambridge University Press.

Aesthetics

Larissa Berger

10 On the Subjective, Beauty and Artificial Intelligence: A Kantian Approach

Abstract: The subjective or phenomenal character of experience has been famously captured by Thomas Nagel's question "What is it like to be an x?". At first glance, Kant seems to care little about such 'what is it like' questions. His philosophy does not seem to be concerned with phenomenal character. However, I will argue that this picture falls short of Kant's account of beauty. For Kant, an adequate account of pleasure in general and pleasure in the beautiful in particular must refer to phenomenal character. Pleasure cannot be understood but needs to be *felt*. Since beauty is constituted by a specific feeling of pleasure, beauty can only be grasped by creatures with the ability to *feel*. Despite new achievements in affective computing, AI is not able to *feel*. Hence, the realm of beauty is foreclosed to AI.

In 1974, Thomas Nagel introduced the famous question "What is it like to be an x?" into philosophy of mind. Nagel argues that there is a subjective point of view, which is inaccessible from the perspective of physics or natural science. The existence of a subjective point of view, together with the phenomenal character of experience that goes along with it, provides a promising argument against the existence of strong Artificial Intelligence (AI): AI cannot occupy a subjective point of view, let alone the human-specific point of view. One crucial thing AI is missing is the ability to have mental states with phenomenal character, where the latter is essential to human experiences.

All of this might seem rather detached from Kant's philosophy. At first glance, Kant seems to care little about what Nagel calls the subjective point of view, or 'what-it-is-likeness.' I will, however, show that a closer look at Kant's aesthetics reveals that at least one part of Kant's philosophy relies and depends on 'what-it-is-likeness:' his account of beauty. More precisely, I will argue that Kant's argument in the *Analytic of the Beautiful* depends on the aesthetic pleasure's phenomenal character of disinterestedness. This will be the basis to argue that the realm of beauty, understood in Kantian terms, is foreclosed to AI.

I will proceed as follows: First, I will briefly sketch Kant's understanding of the subjective. Second, I will introduce Nagel's notion of the subjective, which is quite distinct from Kant's usage of this term. Third, I will argue that, nonetheless,

Larissa Berger, MIT

not only Kant's understanding of pleasure in general, but also his notion of the pleasure in the beautiful, depend on the phenomenal character of pleasure. Finally, I will put forward an argument for the thesis that AI is foreclosed from the Kantian realm of beauty.

1 Kant's Notion of the Subjective

The term 'subjective' has come to carry with it a certain flavor of arbitrariness. What is subjective is merely valid for the individual subject and bound to her idiosyncratic point of view. Although something along these lines can be found in Kant, his usage of this term is multifaceted. For our present purposes, I submit to distinguish four different meanings of 'subjective': origins in the subject (S_1), merely private validity (S_2), validity for all judging subjects (S_3), and uselessness for cognition (S_4).[1]

In its first and broadest meaning (S_1) the term 'subjective' signifies that something originates in, or relates to, the subject. For instance, Kant says that the "merely subjective in the representation of an object" is that which "constitutes its relation to the subject" (KU, AA 05: 188). Thus, "space and time are nothing but subjective forms of our sensory intuition" (Progress, AA 20: 268).[2]

S_1 Something is subjective iff it relates to, or originates in, the subject.

In this broad sense, the term 'subjective' is applied to transcendental notions, such as space and time, as well as empirical notions, such as sensations (*Empfindungen*).[3]

A second sense of the subjective (S_2) refers to the validity of judgments or representations. Whereas objective validity is coextensive with universal validity – "[o]bjective validity and necessary universal validity (for everyone) are [. . .] interchangeable concepts" (Prol., AA 04: 209) –, (merely) subjective validity signifies

---

1 As a matter of fact, there are further aspects of the meaning of 'subjective.' For instance, in the context of the *third Critique* one might think of the subjective principle of reflective judgment. In the ethical context, the "incentive [*Triebfeder*]" by which "is understood the subjective determining ground of the will" (KpV, AA 05: 72) comes to mind, but also maxims being "the subjective principle of volition" (GMS, AA 04: 400 fn.) and "the subjective principle of acting" (GMS, AA 04: 420 fn.).

2 See also Progress, AA 20: 267; KU, AA 05: 188 f.

3 See: "Sensation (in this case external) likewise expresses the merely subjective aspect of our representations of things outside us" (KU, AA 05: 189).

'private validity.'[4] It is this notion of the subjective in Kant which comes closest to the contemporary meaning in terms of arbitrariness.

S_2 Judgments (or representations) are merely subjectively valid iff they have only private validity.

In the *Prolegomena* Kant applies this sense of 'subjective' to judgments of perception: "Empirical judgments, insofar as they have objective validity, are judgments of experience; those, however, that are only subjectively valid I call mere judgments of perception." (Prol., AA 04: 298) Judgments of experience are universally valid because they refer to the object as an intersubjectively accessible reference point.[5] On the contrary, judgments that have a reference point within the judging subject are merely subjectively valid, i.e., they have merely private validity. This latter claim, however, is abandoned in the *third Critique,* where Kant introduces the differentiation between objective and *subjective universality* of judgments.[6] With this notion of subjective universality he establishes a third sense of 'subjective' (S_3). In this context, objective universality concerns the sphere of objects to be judged – objectively universal judgments have the form "All S are P". Instead, subjective universality concerns the "sphere of those who judge" (KU, AA 05: 215) – subjectively universal judgments are valid for every judging subject (every human being). Hence, this is a third sense of 'subjective' in Kant:

S_3 A judgment has subjective universality iff it is valid for all judging subjects.

Note that S_3 (subjective universality) is incompatible with S_2 (merely private validity). Thus, these two senses of 'subjective' mark off a shift in thought between the *Prolegomena* and the *third Critique.*

S_3 is not the only sense of the subjective that we find in the *third Critique*. It is in this work that Kant uses this term most frequently. For instance, Kant also

---

4 See for instance KrV: A820/B 849; KU, AA 05: 217 & 338. – See also Kant's remarks in *On Having an Opinion, Knowing, and Believing,* for instance: "Subjective sufficiency is called conviction (for myself), objective sufficiency, certainty (for everyone)." (KrV: A 822/B850).
5 See: "for there would be no reason why other judgments necessarily would have to agree with mine, if there were not the unity of the object – an object to which they all refer, with which they all agree, and, for that reason, also must all harmonize among themselves." (Prol., AA 04: 298).
6 See KU, AA 05: 214 f.

employs 'subjective' (S_4) to signify that something "does not serve for any cognition at all" (KU, AA 05: 206). Thus, the feeling of pleasure is merely subjective, whereas sensations (*Empfindungen*), which provide the material for cognition, are "objective representation[s] of the senses" (KU, AA 05: 206).[7]

S_4 A representation is subjective iff it cannot serve for cognition.[8]

Indeed, according to this definition, the feelings of pleasure and displeasure are the only subjective representations of which Kant conceives. As Kant puts it: "the subjective aspect [*dasjenige Subjektive*] in a representation which cannot become an element of cognition at all is the pleasure or displeasure connected with it; for through this I cognize nothing in the object of the representation, although it can well be the effect of some cognition or other" (KU, AA 05: 189).

The common core of S_{1-4} is that the subjective refers to the subject or, more precisely, the human being. Note that one and the same thing can be subjective in one sense and objective in another. For instance, the *a priori* forms of intuition are subjective in that they originate in the subject (S_1), but they are objective in that they serve for the cognition of objects (S_4); in addition, they have objective validity (S_2). Sensations are subjective in that they have merely private validity (S_2), but they are objective in that they can serve for cognition (S_4). For our purposes, it is important to see that none of Kant's notions of the subjective explicitly refers to the phenomenal character of experience.

2 Nagel's Notion of the Subjective

A seminal contemporary conception of the subjective was famously suggested by Thomas Nagel in his paper '*What is It Like to Be a Bat?*'. It is a fundamental critique both of reductionism (in its different variants) and functionalism or, at least, it calls attention to the limits of these positions. Nagel's argument is based on the notion of the *subjective*, which is contrasted with the *objective* as associated with the realm of physics. Nagel links the subjective to the notion of

---

7 In *Progress* Kant makes use of a broader sense of the subjective. Here, everything that "can provide no knowledge of the object" and "cannot even be counted as knowledge of objects at all" is subjective (Progress, AA 20: 268 f.). Since sensations "e.g. of bodies in light as color, in sound as tones, or in taste as sour" alone do not amount to knowledge of the object, they "remain merely subjective" (Progress, AA 20: 268 f.).

8 This sense of the subjective is also contained in Kant's notion of the aesthetic judgment's subjective determining ground (see KU, AA 05: 203 f.).

experience and defines the "subjective character of experience" (Nagel 1974, pp. 436 & 441) in terms of 'what-it-is-likeness' or phenomenal character:

> the fact that an organism has conscious experience *at all* means, basically, that there is something it is like to *be* that organism. [. . .] But fundamentally an organism has conscious mental states if and only if there is something that it is like to *be* that organism – something it is like *for* the organism. We may call this the subjective character of experience.
>
> (Nagel 1974, p. 436)

Consciousness is inextricably ('if and only if') linked to 'what-it-is-likeness': There is no conscious mental state without something it is like to be in that state, and no 'what-it-is-likeness' without some kind of consciousness. Because of their 'what-it-is-likeness' conscious mental states are subjective or, more precisely, 'what-it-is-likeness' is nothing but the 'subjective character of experience.' Although Nagel himself does not employ the term 'qualia,' we may use it, understood as "the introspectively accessible, phenomenal aspects of our mental lives" (Tye 2017, par. 1), to refer to 'what-it-is-likeness.'[9]

Nagel holds that experiences with phenomenal features or 'what-it-is-likeness' are connected with "a single point of view" (Nagel 1974, p. 437), viz., a subject-specific point of view. The latter is not true for what is objective.[10] This does not mean that an objective, physical theory is free from any point of view whatsoever. Whereas the subjective character of experience is bound to the "internal view" or view from inside, the objective is connected to (or aims at) an "external view" or view from outside (Nagel 1979, p. 207). The view from outside is constituted by a transcendence of all particular points of view (of individuals as well as species) – it is a view "from nowhere in particular" (Nagel 1979, p. 208).

One could suspect that the subjective or internal point of view is intimate to each individual and, therefore, not accessible to other individuals. And it seems reasonable that our first grasp of the phenomenal character of experience is bound to this first-person or individual point of view. To have any idea of what it is like to see red, I need to see something red myself in the first place. In this respect, there is a certain *priority of the individual point of view*. Yet,

---

9 See also Chalmers: "A number of alternative terms and phrases pick out approximately the same class of phenomena as 'consciousness' in its central sense. These include 'experience,' 'qualia,' 'phenomenology,' 'phenomenal,' 'subjective experience,' and 'what it is like.'" (Chalmers 1996, p. 6). Nagel himself uses a number of different terms to denote 'what-it-is-likeness,' including "phenomenological facts" (Nagel 1974, p. 442), "phenomenal features of experience" (Nagel 1974, p. 437), and "quality" of "experience" (Nagel 1974, p 442).

10 Nagel states: "every subjective phenomenon is essentially connected with a single point of view, and it seems inevitable that an objective, physical theory will abandon that point of view" (Nagel 1974, p. 437).

when Nagel refers to the subjective as opposed to the objective, he refers to the broader human point of view or, more generally, to "species-specific points of view" (Nagel 1974, p. 444). As Nagel writes: "I am not adverting here to the alleged privacy of experience to its possessor. The point of view in question is not one accessible only to a single individual. Rather it is a *type*." (Nagel 1974, p. 441) In this respect, Nagel's subjective point of view is intersubjective (in terms of the members of a certain species) and yet not objective. For, what is objective must be available not only to the members of a certain species but must be accessible from a point of view beyond the boundaries of any species whatsoever (presupposing an adequate level of intelligence).[11] Negatively speaking, the objective point of view is characterized by "externality or detachment" (Nagel 1979, p. 208).

The question arises of how an individual can occupy this broader human-specific though subjective point of view. Two things are required: First, one can only occupy the point of view of creatures sufficiently similar to oneself. To have an idea of what it is like for humans to see red, one needs to have the visual system of humans or, at least, a visual system that is sufficiently similar.[12] Conversely, I cannot occupy the point of view of someone whose visual system is not sufficiently similar to mine (e.g., a deaf and blind person).[13] The second requirement to occupy the broader human-specific point of view is *imagination*. By *imagining* what it is like to see red for other people, I leave my individual point of view behind in favor of a species-specific, but still experiential point of view. Such imagining could proceed in either of two ways:[14]

> To imagine something perceptually, we put ourselves in a conscious state resembling the state we would be in if we perceived it. To imagine something sympathetically, we put ourselves in a conscious state resembling the thing itself. (This method can be used only to imagine mental events and states – our own or another's.)   (Nagel 1974, p. 446 fn. 11)

We can imagine what it is like to *perceive* and what it is like to *feel* for somebody else. In both cases, "[o]ur own experience provides the basic material for our imagination" (Nagel 1974, p. 439). This confirms our assumed *priority of the individual point of view*. Note that the subjective standpoint is "beyond the reach of

---

11 See the following example: "A Martian scientist with no understanding of visual perception could understand the rainbow, or lightning, or clouds as physical phenomena, though he would never be able to understand the human concepts of rainbow, lightning, or cloud, or the place these things occupy in our phenomenal world." (Nagel 1974, 443).

12 See Nagel 1974, p. 442 & Nagel 1979, p. 207.

13 See Nagel 1974, p. 440.

14 Nagel mentions a third kind of imagination, viz., "symbolic imagination" (Nagel 1974, p. 446 fn. 11), but does not expand on this notion.

human concepts" (Nagel 1974, p. 441). It cannot be put into propositions which could be true or false.[15] Thus, the subjective standpoint cannot be occupied by applying rules but only by the power of our imagination.

Two clarifications are called for. First, Nagel's distinction between the subjective and the objective point of view might suggest that both are strictly separated categories. Yet, the two are connected via a continuum between the individual point of view on one side and the 'view from nowhere in particular' on the other.[16] Second, one might be tempted to think that the individual first-person point of view falls short in Nagel's account. As Kriegel and Zahavi have emphasized, "[w]hat-it-is-like-ness is properly speaking what-it-is-like-*for-me*-ness" (Zahavi/Kriegel 2016, p. 36). On their account, "experiential for-me-ness is [. . .] an experiential feature of all phenomenal episodes that remains constant across them and constitutes the subjectivity of experience" (Zahavi/Kriegel 2016, p. 39).[17] As I see it, Nagel is forced to deny neither such 'for-me-ness' nor its supposed constitutional function for experience. It is simply not his focus.

We can now formulate Nagel's notion of the subjective (S_N) as follows:

S_N A mental state is subjective iff it is endowed with phenomenal character ('what-it-is-likeness') and bound to a particular (individual or species-specific) point of view.

This formulation suggests that 'having phenomenal character' and 'being bound to the individual or species-specific point of view' amount to separate conditions. Nagel writes that "every subjective phenomenon is essentially *connected* with a single point of view" (Nagel 1974, p. 437, my emphasis). So, 'having a phenomenal character', at least, *implies* 'being bound to a single point of view.' But is there a more precise determination of this relation? We shall have a look at the following quote:

> the concepts and ideas we employ in thinking about the external world are initially applied from a point of view that involves our perceptual apparatus, they are used by us to refer to things beyond themselves – toward which we *have* the phenomenal point of view.
> (Nagel 1974, p. 444)

---

15 See Nagel 1974, p. 441. See also Walter 2006, p. 13 fn. 4.

16 See Nagel 1974, p. 442 f. & Nagel 1979, p. 206.

17 For a similar claim see Rinofner-Kreidl 2004. Rinofner-Kreidl differentiates between two kinds of subjectivity: subjectivity in terms of the phenomenal first-person perspective, which is a constituent of experience, and subjectivity in terms of a particular perspective on certain contents or objects. Only the latter can be overcome to reach the more objective perspective of physics; the former is in principle invincible.

The first possibility to understand the subjective point of view is in terms of the human-specific basis of the different phenomenal experiences, e.g., our perceptual capacities. For, as Nagel notes, the human-specific 'point of view . . . involves our perceptual apparatus.' A second possibility would be that the subjective point of view is nothing but the total of experiences with phenomenal character. Therefore, one might argue, Nagel calls this viewpoint the '*phenomenal* point of view.' In other words, in this reading the species-specific point of view consists in the "phenomenal world" of a certain species (Nagel 1974, p. 443). There might be a third possibility. Here, the subjective point of view would encompass more than phenomenal character – namely, for instance, "the narrow range of a human *scale* in space, time, and quantity" (Nagel 1979, p. 206), intersubjective values etc. Thus, the species-specific point of view would refer to everything that is somehow endowed with intersubjectivity but cannot be extended to other species. I am not sure which of these pictures best captures Nagel's conception of the subjective point of view since his own formulations remain ambiguous. In what follows, I will ask separately whether the Kantian conceptions of pleasure and beauty refer to a phenomenal character *and* the subjective point of view. Whereas for Nagel both might amount to the same thing or be inextricably linked, this might not be the case with Kant.

3 Kant, the Subjective and Pleasure in the Beautiful

Is the pleasure in the beautiful subjective in Nagel's sense (S_N)?[18] In other words: Is the Kantian pleasure in the beautiful endowed with a phenomenal character, and is it bound to the subjective (individual or species-specific) point of view? To answer these questions, we shall first have a look at Kant's general notion of pleasure.

---

18 Nagel's question 'What is it like to be an x?' has been transferred to Kant's conception of rational beings by Birgit Recki (2004). Recki also focuses on Kant's theory of feelings (*Gefühle*). Her concern, however, is with the 'what' in 'what it is like.' My concern is rather with the question of whether Kant's notion of pleasure comprises 'what-it-is-likeness' in the first place.

3.1 Pleasure in General

Pleasure, for Kant, is subjective in the S_4-sense: it cannot serve for cognition. This does not imply, however, that all kinds of pleasure are merely private or have merely private validity (S_2). Rather, the pleasure in the beautiful and the pleasure in the good are intersubjectively valid and, at least, the former can serve as the determining ground for subjectively universal judgments (S_3). From a contemporary point of view, it might seem obvious that feelings are paradigmatic cases of phenomenal states.[19] It is by no means obvious, however, that for Kant, too, the feeling of pleasure is endowed with phenomenal character (S_N).

One might assume that Kant had a *functional understanding of pleasure*. Following Levin, "functionalist theories take the identity of a mental state to be determined by its causal relations to sensory stimulations, other mental states, and behavior" (Levin 2018, par. 3).[20] At first glance, Kant's definition of pleasure in § 10 of the *third Critique* seems to fit well with such a functionalist picture:

> The consciousness of the causality of a representation with respect to the state of the subject, for maintaining it in that state, can here designate in general what is called pleasure; in contrast to which displeasure is that representation that contains the ground for determining the state of the representations to their own opposite (hindering or getting rid of them).
> (KU, AA 05: 220)

A similar picture of pleasure is evoked in the following passage of the *First Introduction*:

> Pleasure is a state of the mind in which a representation is in agreement with itself, as a ground, either merely for preserving this state itself (for the state of the powers of the mind reciprocally promoting each other in a representation preserves itself), or for producing its object.
> (EEKU, AA 20: 230 f.)

These two passages allow for the following definition of 'pleasure': *A mental state counts as pleasure iff it has a representation as its causal input and either*

---

19 See for instance Walter 2006, p. 14.

20 Nagel emphasizes that the subjective character of experience "is not analyzable in terms of any explanatory system of functional states, or intentional states, since these could be ascribed to robots or automata that behaved like people though they experienced nothing" (Nagel 1974, p. 436). Still, a functionalist account of pleasure could be complemented by a phenomenal understanding of the latter. So, even if Kant defined pleasure in functionalist terms, he could also hold that pleasure has a subjective character.

its own preservation or the production of its object as its causal output. If this functional definition were complete, pleasure would be objective in Nagel's understanding: It could be fully understood from a vast variety of standpoints or, rather, from nowhere in particular.

It is striking that both definitions cited above do not include phenomenal character or something along these lines. With regard to the definition from § 10, Guyer emphasizes:[21]

> there is no suggestion here [in KU, AA 05: 220] that there is a specific way that it always feels to be in one of these states or the other, that there is a specific, always identical way the disposition to continue in one's current state feels and a particular, likewise always identical way the disposition to alter one's state feels.[22] (Guyer 2018, p. 157)

This diagnosis leads Guyer to abandon the "phenomenological account of pleasure and pain" in favor of a "dispositional [. . .] account of pleasure and pain" (Guyer 2018, p. 162). On that account, which is quite in line with the functional definition sketched above, "pleasure just consists in the disposition to remain in the state one finds pleasing" (Guyer 2018, p. 149). But is such a functionalist interpretation of the Kantian concept of pleasure adequate? Does Kant really deny any phenomenal understanding of pleasure? I do not think so. On the contrary, I submit, Kant is well aware that pleasure has a phenomenal character and that it is, first and foremost, characterized by the latter.

The most explicit evidence for this thesis is found in a remark from the *First Introduction*. It follows right after the definition of pleasure:

> It can be readily seen here that pleasure or displeasure, since they are not kinds of cognition, cannot be explained by themselves at all, and *are felt*, not understood; hence they can be only inadequately explained through the influence that a representation has on the activity of the powers of the mind by means of this feeling.
>
> (EEKU, AA 20: 231 f., my emphasis)

---

21 See also Zinkin: "Kant's definition of pleasure is also not phenomenological. [. . .] he does not define pleasure in terms of how it feels, but rather as a certain kind of consciousness." (Zinkin 2012, p. 435).

22 Here, it seems as if Guyer would merely deny that there was a 'specific, always identical way' pleasure would always feel. But, indeed, he is committed to the much stronger thesis that, unlike objective sensations [*Empfindungen*], pleasure does not have any phenomenal character at all: "To be sure, some cases of pleasure must involve distinctive sensations, for there is a characteristic way or range of ways that a good Bordeaux tastes, and a different way that a good Burgundy tastes, and each is enjoyable; but it is less plausible that there is a distinctive feeling of pleasure, whether always the same or not, *in addition* to the characteristic Bordeaux taste and Burgundy taste." (Guyer 2018, p. 163) Guyer is more hesitant on this point when it comes to displeasure.

The contrast between feeling and understanding Kant avails himself of – pleasure and displeasure '*are felt*, not understood' – must refer to the *phenomenal character* of pleasure, i.e., to the way pleasure feels. What else should this contrast refer to? Thus, to properly grasp what pleasure is, one must *feel* pleasure oneself.[23] Recall that, for Nagel, the subjective point of view associated with the phenomenal character of experience is "beyond the reach of human concepts." (Nagel 1974, p. 441) Kant's remark that pleasure is *not understood* and, thus, *ineffable* is much in line with this specific trait of experience's phenomenal character.

The thesis that, for Kant, pleasure is subjective in Nagel's sense (S_N) finds further support in the structure of the *Analytic of Beautiful*.[24] Obviously, 'pleasure' is one of the key concepts in Kant's theory of beauty. As early as in § 1, this notion is at the center of Kant's argument; for he claims that "[t]he judgment of taste is aesthetic" (KU, AA 05: 203), which basically means that judgments of taste can only be justified by the *feeling* of pleasure. In § 2, Kant goes on by claiming that the pleasure in the beautiful is disinterested.[25] In § 5, he claims that the pleasure in the beautiful is free;[26] and in § 6, this pleasure is described as non-conceptual (and yet universal).[27] However, it is only in § 10 that Kant puts forward a definition of pleasure, to wit, the one quoted above: "The consciousness of the causality of a representation with respect to the state of the subject, for maintaining it in that state, can here designate in general what is called pleasure" (KU, AA 05: 220). This procedure makes good sense once we acknowledge that pleasure is something which is '*felt*, not understood.' If pleasure is primarily characterized by a certain 'what-it-is-likeness,' Kant does not need to define 'pleasure' in the first place, because qua being a feeling everyone has an implicit grasp on what pleasure is and, most importantly, what pleasure feels like.

Let me emphasize that this phenomenological understanding of pleasure does not contradict the functional (or dispositional) picture sketched above. It

---

23 In the *Observations on the Feeling of the Beautiful and the Sublime* Kant already notes: "To be sure, we do one another an injustice when we dismiss one who does not see the value or the beauty of what moves or charms us by saying that he does not understand it. In this case it is not so much a matter of what the understanding sees but of what the feeling is sensitive to." (Observations, AA 02: 225) See also Kant's remark in the *Metaphysics of Morals* that "pleasure and displeasure cannot be explained for themselves" (MS, AA 06: 212).

24 For a comprehensive reconstruction of the *Analytic of the Beautiful* see Berger (2022).

25 See KU, AA 05: 204 f.

26 See KU, AA 05: 210.

27 See KU, AA 05: 211.

is undeniable that Kant's official definitions of 'pleasure' refer to something like a disposition or a functional role to remain in a current state. Yet, as Kant himself points out, this does not provide an adequate understanding of pleasure: "they [pleasure and displeasure] can be only *inadequately* explained through the influence that a representation has on the activity of the powers of the mind by means of this feeling" – the influence of 'preserving this state itself . . . or for producing its object' (EEKU, AA 20: 232, my emphasis).[28] Hence, Kant himself argues that the functional or dispositional picture is inadequate and, thus, incomplete. Nagel, too, holds that it is incomplete, and in this sense inadequate: "I do not deny that conscious mental states and events cause behavior, nor that they may be given functional characterizations. I deny only that this kind of thing exhausts their analysis." (Nagel 1974, p. 437)[29]

As outlined above, Nagel's understanding of the subjective includes essentially the individual or species-specific point of view. For Kant, pleasure must be *felt*, and therefore it seems reasonable that pleasure is, in the first place, experienced from the first-person point of view (*priority of the individual point of view*). But what about the species-specific point of view which, according to Nagel, can be occupied using one's imagination? In general, Kant holds that every creature endowed with sensibility is able to feel pleasure. Therefore, "[a]greeableness is also valid for nonrational animals" (KU, AA 05: 210). However, I am hesitant to assume that we, as human beings, could properly imagine what it is like for a bat to feel pleasure. I am not aware of any passage in Kant which would clarify whether the phenomenal character of pleasure is bound to certain species or is the same for every feeling creature, so I will not pursue this point further. We will see that things are much clearer when it comes to pleasure in the beautiful.

---

28 Therefore, the following argument put forward by Guyer is at odds with the passage from the *First Introduction*: "on Kant's account of definition, according to which a proper definition must include everything essential to its concept and indeed everything essential to recognize an instance of its concept, anything left out of the definition would only be accidentally connected to its object. Thus, if there were a distinctive way in which pleasure or pain always feel, that would be an additional, synthetic claim, which would have to be based on empirical evidence – and Kant makes no attempt to provide such evidence" (Guyer 2018, p. 158).

29 See also Chalmers' distinction between the "*phenomenal* concept of mind" and the "*psychological* concept of mind": "On the phenomenal concept, mind is characterized by the way it *feels*; on the psychological concept, mind is characterized by what it *does*." (Chalmers 1996, p. 11) Chalmers relates the latter to functionalism. Moreover, he argues that both can co-occur in one mental state. Unlike Kant, he leaves it an open question of whether emotions are *primarily* phenomenal states: "It is not quite obvious whether the phenomenal aspect is *essential* for a state to be an emotion, however; there is clearly a strong associated psychological property as well." (Chalmers 1996, p. 19).

3.2 Pleasure in the Beautiful

If pleasure in general is endowed with phenomenal character, this will also hold true for pleasure in the beautiful. This phenomenality, however, does not imply that pleasure in the beautiful is characterized by a *specific* phenomenal character which makes it distinguishable from any other kind of pleasure. Still, a phenomenological understanding of pleasure in general will open up the way for attributing such a specific phenomenal character to the pleasure in the beautiful.[30] In what follows, I will argue for this latter thesis by focusing on the disinterested character of the pleasure in the beautiful.

3.2.1 Disinterestedness and Phenomenal Character

There is no explicit textual support for an interpretation of disinterestedness in terms of phenomenal character. There is, however, a strong structural reason for this interpretation that draws on the overall argument of the *Analytic of the Beautiful*. In § 2, Kant claims that the pleasure or "satisfaction that determines the judgment of taste is without any interest" (KU, AA 05: 204). The pleasure in the beautiful is not a pleasure in the existence of an object and it is not connected to any desire; this is the starting point of Kant's overall argument in the *Analytic*. All other major claims and arguments are derived directly or indirectly from this *thesis of disinterestedness* (TD). In § 6, Kant argues that "[t]he beautiful is that which, without concepts, is represented as the object of a universal satisfaction" (KU, AA 05: 211); and he claims that "[t]his explanation of the beautiful can be deduced from the previous explanation of it as an object of satisfaction without any interest" (KU, AA 05: 211). In § 9, Kant refers to the thesis that the pleasure is non-conceptual and universal to argue for the free and harmonious play of the faculties;[31] since the non-conceptuality and universality of the pleasure in the beautiful was 'deduced' from TD, Kant must indirectly draw on the latter to argue for the free and harmonious play. In § 11, Kant goes on to argue that the judgment of taste is grounded on a subjective purposiveness without a

---

30 In my understanding, the different kinds of pleasure in Kant all have a distinct phenomenology. Thus, one can distinguish the feelings in the agreeable, the beautiful and the good merely by relying on their phenomenal character. For a characterization of the phenomenal character of respect [*Achtung*] see Kriegel & Timmons (2021). – Note that if the functional account of pleasure was complete, pleasure in the beautiful could only be identified as such by reflecting on its causes or consequences.
31 See KU, AA 05: 216 f.

purpose; and again, he presupposes TD in his argument.[32] Because of its function as the starting point and crucial reference point of the overall argument, one would assume that Kant would offer a good argument to firmly establish TD in the first place. But in fact, Kant never offers any such argument, and only on pain of circularity could he rely on any thesis introduced later in the text (e.g., the free play of the faculties) to argue for disinterestedness.[33] Rather, and quite strikingly, Kant seems to be confident that he can just presuppose TD as a brute matter of fact. This impression is primarily evoked by the following formulations of TD:

> But if the question is whether something is beautiful, *one does not want to know* whether there is anything that is or that could be at stake, for us or for someone else, in the existence of the thing, but rather how we judge it in mere contemplation (intuition or reflection).　　　　　　　　　　　　　　　　　　　　　(KU, AA 05: 204, my emphasis)

> *One only wants to know* whether the mere representation of the object is accompanied with satisfaction in me, however indifferent I might be with regard to the existence of the object of the representation.　　　　　　　　　　(KU, AA 05: 205, my emphasis)

> *One can easily see* that to say that it is beautiful and to prove that I have taste what matters is what I make of this representation in myself, not how I depend on the existence of the object.　　　　　　　　　　　(KU, AA 05: 205, translation altered, my emphasis)

> *One must not be* in the least biased in favor of the existence of the thing, but must be entirely indifferent in this respect in order to play the judge in matters of taste.
> 　　　　　　　　　　　　　　　　　　　　　(KU, AA 05: 205, my emphasis)

Note Kant's frequent usage of 'one' (in German: '*man*'). My suggestion is that '*one can easily see*' that the pleasure in the beautiful is disinterested because disinterestedness is an integral part of the phenomenal character of the pleasure in the beautiful. In other words, one can easily see or, rather, feel that the pleasure is disinterested simply because this is *what the pleasure feels like*.

There is further support for such a phenomenological understanding of TD. We have already seen that TD, broadly speaking, means that pleasure in the beautiful is not taken in the existence of an object and is not connected to any desire. This meaning can be inferred from Kant's definition of 'interest' put forward in § 2:

---

32 See KU, AA 05: 221.

33 For such a strategy see the following remark of Guyer: "the fact that the disinterestedness of aesthetic response is a consequence of its explanation as due to the harmony of imagination and understanding, rather than *vice versa*" (Guyer 1979, p. 169; see also p. 178).

> The satisfaction that we combine with the representation of the existence of an object is called interest. Hence such a satisfaction always has at the same time a relation to the faculty of desire, either as its determining ground or else as necessarily interconnected with its determining ground.
> (KU, AA 05: 204)

What it means that a pleasure is not taken in the existence of an object and is not connected to any desire is far from obvious, especially as matters stand argumentatively in § 2. To really understand what TD means, one would have to draw on the notions of the free play of the faculties and the formal purposiveness of the beautiful object's form. Thus, one aspect of the meaning of TD is that pleasure in the beautiful is not taken in the existence of an object, but in an inner activity of the subject (the free play of the faculties) which is not an activity of the faculty of desire. Another aspect is that pleasure in the beautiful is not taken in the "matter of the representations" (KU, AA 05: 224), i.e., in a mere sensation, by which something existing is given to us, but in the object's form. Moreover, it is based on a purposiveness without any purpose, where the latter could determine the will. However, these different aspects of the meaning of TD are not yet present or let alone in any sense argued for in § 2; for, again, it is much later that the notions of the free play of the faculties, the beautiful object's form and the purposiveness without a purpose are introduced. Hence, TD must have a basic meaning which *is already available and comprehensible* in § 2. And this meaning, I suppose, is phenomenological.[34] From this point of view, TD is grounded in everyone's experience of what it is like to feel pleasure in the beautiful.

Is it linguistically possible to explain what the pleasure in the beautiful feels like? Recall that pleasure 'is felt, not understood.' So, strictly speaking, we cannot understand or put into words what it is like to feel a disinterested pleasure. We can only try to describe this phenomenal experience further by making use of other phenomenological terms. Thus, we could say that the pleasure is detached from any wanting or desiring, where the latter is also characterized by a specific phenomenal character.

Was Kant himself aware of how much his argument in the *Analytic of the Beautiful* depends on the specific phenomenal character of the pleasure in the beautiful? As the remark from the *First Introduction* shows, he certainly concurred that pleasure is essentially characterized by its phenomenal character. However, he does not make explicit that pleasure in the beautiful has a distinct phenomenal character, to wit, the character of disinterestedness. Why not?

---

34 Thereby, I do not deny that TD also has those other meanings or aspects of meaning. I merely deny that these are already available to the reader in § 2.

Three possible reasons are maybe not far to seek: First, Kant was unaware of how much his argument depends on the phenomenal character of disinterestedness; he only *unconsciously* used it in his argument. Secondly, the distinct phenomenal character of the pleasure in the beautiful was so obvious to Kant that he did not consider it necessary to put any emphasis on it. Thirdly, Kant was aware of the distinct phenomenal character of the pleasure in the beautiful and its role for his argument, but he did not address it more explicitly in the text because that might have arisen the suspicion that his argument would not properly fit within the framework of transcendental philosophy.[35] Any decision on this matter would be merely speculative. For our current purposes, suffice it to say that Kant's argument will only work if we take into account that pleasure in the beautiful has a specific phenomenal character: the character of disinterestedness.

So far, we have seen that pleasure in the beautiful has the phenomenal character of disinterestedness. Thus, we already have good reason to assume that pleasure in the beautiful is subjective in Nagel's sense (S_N). In what follows, I will ask how pleasure in the beautiful relates to the individual and the species-specific points of view.

3.2.2 Pleasure in the Beautiful and the Subjective Point of View

Nagel's notion of the subjective (S_N) is inextricably linked to his conception of points of view: What is subjective is merely accessible from the individual or species-specific point of view. Is this aspect of the subjective also an essential part of Kant's conception of the pleasure in the beautiful?

First and foremost, pleasure in the beautiful is bound to the individual or first-person point of view. Surely, I must have felt pleasure in the beautiful myself to have any grasp on what it is like to feel such a pleasure. This is the *priority of the individual point of view* that we also find in Nagel. But for Kant, the individual point of view is important in another respect, that is, with regard to specific manifestations of beauty. To decide whether a given object (e.g., a certain flower) is beautiful, I need to behold that object *myself* and feel pleasure in the beautiful *myself*. As Kant puts it:

---

35 For a discussion of why a phenomenological starting point of the *Analytic* does in fact not contradict Kant's transcendental approach see Berger 2022, pp. 193–202.

> Whether a garment, a house, a flower is beautiful: no one allows himself to be talked into his judgment about that by means of any grounds or fundamental principles. One wants to submit the object to his own eyes, just as if his satisfaction depended on sensation; [. . .].
>
> (KU, AA 05: 215 f.)

This second role of the individual point of view constitutes a difference to other judgments about experiences with phenomenal character. To make the judgment that Jim's house is red I can rely on Joanne's report that Jim's house is red. But to make the judgment that Jim's house is beautiful I need to submit his house to my own eyes and feel pleasure in the beautiful myself.

The species-specific point of view is important for Kant's theory of beauty in two respects. First, pleasure in the beautiful is bound to the human nature being sensuous as well as rational. Therefore, only human beings can experience pleasure in the beautiful. As Kant puts it: "beauty is valid only for human beings, i.e., animal but also rational beings, but not merely as the latter (e.g., spirits), rather as beings who are at the same time animal" (KU, AA 05: 210). Pleasure in the beautiful can only be felt by creatures endowed with sense organs (for the sensory input) as well as the faculties of imagination and understanding (to enter into a free play of the faculties). In that way, pleasure in the beautiful can only be felt by human beings and is, thus, bound to the human-specific point of view. Considering Nagel once more, it seems reasonable that we can imagine (sympathetically) what it is like for other human beings to feel pleasure in the beautiful, because they are sufficiently similar to us (they have sense organs, imagination and understanding). In that way, the Kantian pleasure in the beautiful seems to be accessible from the human-specific point of view. The second respect in which the species-specific point of view is important refers to Kant's thesis that the pleasure in the beautiful is universally valid.[36] When I feel pleasure in the beautiful on the occasion of a certain object, this pleasure is not only valid for me but for every human being. In that way, each manifestation of the pleasure in the beautiful includes the human-specific point of view. Importantly, a beholder who feels pleasure in the beautiful is aware that her pleasure extends to all human beings. For Kant explicitly speaks of "the universal validity of this pleasure *perceived in the mind* as connected with the mere judging of an object" (KU, AA 05: 289, my italics).[37] When I feel

---

36 See for instance: "The beautiful is that which, without concepts, is represented as the object of a universal satisfaction." (KU, AA 05: 211).

37 One might suspect that it is not the 'universal validity of the pleasure' but merely the pleasure which is 'perceived in the mind as connected with the mere judging of an object.' However, Kant's original formulation strongly suggests the reading above: "Also ist es nicht die Lust, sondern die Allgemeingültigkeit dieser Lust, die mit der bloßen Beurteilung eines

pleasure in the beautiful, I *perceive* the universal validity of this pleasure 'as connected with the mere judging of an object.' This presupposes that I perceive the universal validity of this pleasure in the first place and, thus, that I am immediately aware of the pleasure's universal validity. I have argued elsewhere that this awareness is included in the phenomenal character of the pleasure: It is part of the pleasure's 'what-it-is-likeness' that we feel connected to our fellow human beings.[38] In that spirit, Kant speaks of "the confluence of the feeling of everyone with that of each" (KU, AA 05: 240). Now, the immediate awareness of the pleasure's universality has an interesting consequence for the human-specific point of view: The first-person experience of the pleasure already includes a transcending of the individual point of view in favor of the human-specific point of view. When compared to Nagel's approach, this leads to an interesting result: On Kant's account of the pleasure in the beautiful we do not need to *imaginatively* take up the point of view of other human beings. Rather, we already occupy this point of view whenever we feel pleasure in the beautiful.

In sum, the individual point of view (IP) and the human-specific point of view (HP) each have a twofold relevance for Kant's theory of aesthetic pleasure:

IP_1 To have a grasp on what pleasure in the beautiful feels like in the first place, I need to feel this pleasure myself.

IP_2 To decide whether a given object is beautiful, I need to behold that object and feel pleasure in the beautiful myself.

HP_1 The pleasure in the beautiful is bound to the sensuous and rational nature of human beings. Thus, human beings can imaginatively take a grasp on what it is like to experience pleasure in the beautiful from the human-specific point of view.

HP_2 The first-person experience of the pleasure in the beautiful already includes a transcending of the individual point of view in favor of the human-specific point of view.

The pleasure in the beautiful has a phenomenal character, and it is also bound to the individual and human-specific point of view. The Kantian pleasure in the beautiful is subjective in Nagel's sense of the subjective (S_N).

Gegenstandes im Gemüte als verbunden wahrgenommen wird, welche a priori als allgemeine Regel für die Urteilskraft, für jedermann gültig, in einem Geschmacksurteile vorgestellt wird." (KU, AA 05: 289).

38 See Berger 2022, pp. 186–188.

4 AI, Pleasure and Beauty

What does all of this teach us about AI? A functionalist account of pleasure along the lines presented above could possibly attribute to AI (computers) the ability to have pleasure. As a matter of fact, Nagel remarks that "functional states, or intentional states, [. . .] could be ascribed to robots or automata that behaved like people though they experienced nothing" (Nagel 1974, p. 436). For the sake of argument, we shall assume that AI could have representations (something which I actually doubt). If a computer received a representation as an input and either preserved its current state or produced the corresponding object as an output, we could, on the functionalist picture drawn from Kant's definition of pleasure, ascribe pleasure to this computer. Yet I have argued that, for Kant, an *adequate* understanding of pleasure is not functional, but phenomenological. My argument for the claim that AI cannot experience pleasure is straightforward: AI (at the current stage of development) is determined and at least in principle completely describable by the laws of physics. The laws of physics are bound to the objective point of view. They do not reveal what-it-is-likeness, otherwise we would know what it is like to be a bat if we knew everything there is to know about bats in terms of physics.[39] Since pleasure, for Kant, is primarily characterized by the way it feels – its phenomenal character –, AI cannot experience pleasure. As Schönecker puts it: "There is no *what it is like to be a computer*, and therefore, unlike beings for whom there is a certain phenomenal inner life, to be in a computational state is not to be in a mental state." (Schönecker 2018, pp. 78 f.) Since there is no 'what it is like to be a computer,' there is no 'what it is like to feel pleasure' for a computer.

What is true for pleasure in general applies to pleasure in the beautiful as well. We have seen that the pleasure in the beautiful has the specific phenomenal character of disinterestedness. Recall, once more, that for Kant pleasure is primarily *'felt*, not understood.' Thus, pleasure in the beautiful is primarily felt as being disinterested. Since AI *cannot feel anything*, it cannot feel disinterested pleasure. There is no 'what it is like to feel disinterested pleasure' for a computer.

Computers are bound to the objective point of view, the point of view of physics. Conversely, there is no subjective point of view for computers. There are no first-person experiences for computers and, thus, no individual point of view. Therefore, there is also no species-specific (i.e., no computer-specific) point of view. In addition, it is dubitable that computers have the ability to *imagine* (sympathetically) and, thus, to *imaginatively* take up others' points of

---

39 See also Jackson's famous Mary-case (Jackson 1986).

view. Moreover, since computers cannot experience pleasure in the beautiful, they cannot experience the transcending of the individual point of view which is included in that pleasure's phenomenal character.

The fact that AI cannot experience pleasure in the beautiful has an important consequence for *beauty*. For Kant, beauty is constituted by the feeling of disinterested pleasure, experienced from the first-person perspective. Moreover, there is no grasp on beauty by applying rules. As Kant puts it: "there can be no objective rule of taste that would determine what is beautiful through concepts" (KU, AA 05: 231). Since AI cannot feel pleasure but can only apply rules (based on algorithms), AI has no adequate grasp on beauty.[40] Although AI might be able to identify beautiful objects, it is not able to experience beauty as such. Like Mary who knows everything about colors in terms of physics but has never *seen* the color red,[41] AI could know many things about beauty (e.g., facts about art history, empirical facts about proportions or color arrangements people tend to find beautiful) but could not feel disinterested pleasure and, thus, could not experience beauty.

Two objections could be raised, both related to empirical issues in the development of AI. The first concerns AI's ability to have emotions. Don't we have affective computing yet and, therefore, evidence that AI can have emotions *such as pleasure*? When in 1997 Rosalind Picard introduced the term 'affective computing,' she put forward the following rather broad definition: Affective computing is "computing that relates to, arises from, or deliberately influences emotions" (Picard 1997, p. 3). In what follows, we shall have a brief look at current achievements in the realm of affective computing.

Affective computing has made some progress when it comes to the recognition of emotions (*affect recognition*). For instance, there has been some

---

40 For this argument see Berger 2018.
41 See Jackson 1986, p. 291. – For a Mary-case concerning emotion see the following example by Goldie: "Irene is an icy-cool ice-scientist. Being an ice-scientist, she knows all the properties of ice. In particular, she has complete knowledge of the dangers that can arise from walking on ice; show her any icy pond or lake and she will know where the dangers lie. Yet she is icy-cool, and has never felt fear (far-fetched perhaps, but no more than Mary and her black and white world; imagine that Irene has been brought up in an incredibly coddled manner). Nevertheless, in spite of this lack, she not only has a theoretical concept of dangerousness; she also has a theoretical concept of fear, as being a sort of state that, roughly, plays a causal role: People are typically afraid when they perceive dangerous things, and they respond to fear by behaving in certain typical ways. Then, one day, Irene goes out onto the ice, falls, and for the first time feels fear – fear towards the dangerous ice. She now knows, 'from the inside', what it is like to *feel* fear, so she has gained a new concept – a phenomenal concept." (Goldie 2002, pp. 244 f.)

success in implementing the capacity to identify emotions by detecting and processing facial expressions (e.g., by making use of Paul Ekman's *Facial Action Coding System FACS*).[42] Other approaches focus on voice analysis (e.g., emotion detection via the tone of voice), sentiment analysis (i.e., emotion detection in the content or meaning of verbal expressions), or biosensors (i.e., emotion detection via the detection of bodily changes); in addition, there are also multimodal-approaches.[43] However, affect recognition so far has often led to inaccurate results, since, for instance, the context of the emotion is not considered and cultural variances are ignored. Thus, the authors of the *AI Now 2019 Report* claim: "There remains little to no evidence that these new affect-recognition products have any scientific validity." (AI Now 2019 Report, p. 51) In any case, it should be clear that the mere recognition of emotions does not include or presuppose the ability to *feel* emotions. Human beings often recognize others' emotions by means of empathy, and at least affective or emotional empathy includes 'what-it-is-likeness.' But surely, such emotional empathy is not experienced by a computer that makes use of affect recognition in the way just outlined.[44]

AI, at the current stage of development, can also "give the impression of emotionality. This is likely to be possible in various manifestations in robots, in avatars and in embodied conversational agents (ECAs), through speech, appearance, behaviour and in other ways." (Goldie, Döring & Cowie 2011, p. 728) Still, none of these abilities amounts to the ability to have or, rather, *feel* emotions. For, again, it is the phenomenal character of the emotion which is lacking.

We have seen that, according to Picard's definition, affective computing also pursues 'computing that . . . *arises from* . . . emotions.' There have been some attempts to make AI feel emotions. However, such attempts generally focus on the *functional role* of emotions for cognition and behavior.[45] For instance, Kuehn and Haddadin recently introduced "the artificial Robot Nervous System aRNS as a new way of integrating tactile sensation and according reflex

---

42 See Bösel 2019, p. 223; Misselhorn 2021, pp. 20 f.
43 For an overview see Misselhorn 2021, pp. 20–42.
44 See also the following definition of 'affect recognition': "Affect recognition is an AI-driven technology that claims to be able to detect an individual's emotional state based on the use of computer-vision algorithms to analyze their facial microexpressions, tone of voice, or even their gait." (AI Now 2019 Report, p. 50) Notably, in his suggestion for a developmental approach to artificial empathy, Asada (2015) differentiates between emotional and cognitive empathy; but, concerning the application to affective developmental robotics, he does not mention the phenomenal character of emotional empathy.
45 See Misselhorn 2018, pp. 42 f.

reactions into robot control based on the concept of *robot pain sensation"* (Kuehn/Haddadin 2017, p. 2). aRNS is explicitly designed to achieve a certain robot behavior. As Asada puts it, "[t]heir motivation was to apply the idea of ensuring safety in human-robot collaborations, and the main focus was the generation of avoidance behavior" (Asada 2019, p. 5).[46] Strikingly, the authors explicitly do not claim to have created *emotional experiences* in robots. They explain:

> Obviously, pain is also strongly an emotional experience, not only influenced by the signals coming from the nociceptors. Thus, one distinguishes between the emotional experience of pain and the nociceptive signals that may lead to pain experiences. In this paper, we focus on the latter. (Kuehn/Haddadin 2017, p. 1)

Hence, the authors are not concerned with the phenomenal character of pain or other emotions.

Another approach to affective computing, proposed by Man and Damasio, focuses on "the design and construction of a new class of machines organized according to the principles of life regulation, or homeostasis" (Man/Damasio 2019, p. 446). Man and Damasio suggest a combination of soft robotics and machine learning to "produce machines with an artificial equivalent of feeling" (Man/Damasio 2019, p. 446). As compared to hard materials such as metal, soft materials may add vulnerability to robots.[47] Moreover, the authors suggest combining soft material with deep neural networks to build "correspondences between inner space and outer space, between internal homeostatic data and external sense data" (Man/Damasio 2019, p. 450). However, the authors are very clear that soft matter is "not sufficient to generate feeling on its own"; it is merely "more likely to naturally create the kind of relationship that, we expect, admits of an approximation to feeling" (Man/Damasio 2019, p. 448). As with aRNS, their homeostatic approach pursues a functional goal. The authors explain: "The initial goal of the introduction of physical vulnerability and self-determined self-regulation is not *to create robots with authentic feeling*, but rather *to improve their functionality* across a wide range of environments." (Man/Damasio 2019, p. 451, my emphasis)

---

46 See also: "The overall behavior allows the robot to sensitively interact with its environment at nominal pain level, while mitigating potential risks by activating human inspired reflex strategies if the pain level increases." (Kuehn/Haddadin 2017, p. 2).

47 The authors give the following example: "Markvicka et al. fabricated a soft electronic 'skin' that localizes and can trigger responses to damage. They impregnated an elastomer base with droplets of liquid metal that, on rupture, cause changes in electrical conductivity across the damaged surface." (Man/Damasio 2019, p. 448).

In sum: At the current stage of development, we cannot ascribe experiences with phenomenal character and a subjective point of view to AI. Affective computing has not succeeded yet in creating computers that *feel* emotions.[48] As Man and Damasio put it: "Today's robots lack feelings. They are not designed to represent the internal state of their operations in a way that would permit them to experience that state in a mental space. They also lack selfhood and 'aboutness.'" (Man/Damasio 2019, p. 446)[49]

The second objection focuses on the thesis that, on the assumption of some kind of naturalistic evolutionary theory, consciousness along with 'what-it-is-likeness' has evolved from unconscious matter.[50] Thus, we cannot foreclose the option that conscious computers will evolve from a complex arrangement of unconscious matter. Although we cannot completely deny this possibility, it is very unlikely. As Schönecker puts it: "Just a single biological cell already is *extremely* complex, let alone the brain. By comparison, a computer is a very primitive object; there is no more reason to think that it has a mind than to think a sewing machine has one." (Schönecker 2018, p. 86)

5 Conclusion

Unlike Nagel, Kant does not use the term 'subjective' to refer to the phenomenal character of experience. Nonetheless, what is signified by Nagel's notion of the subjective, to wit, 'what-it-is-likeness' and the subjective point of view, can be found in Kant's works, most prominently when it comes to his notion of pleasure. Not only does an adequate account of pleasure, for Kant, rely on its phenomenal character, but different kinds of pleasure can also be distinguished by their different phenomenal characters. I have argued that the phenomenal character of the pleasure in the beautiful can be characterized by disinterestedness. Moreover, the pleasure in the beautiful is bound to the individual point of

---

48 See similarly Goldie, Döring & Cowie 2011, p. 727.
49 It has been argued by quite a few authors that pleasure, for Kant, is an *intentional* mental state (see for instance Allison 2001, pp. 53 f. & 122 f.; Aquila 1982; Ginsborg 2015, pp. 94–110; Zuckert 2002). In different variants of this intentionality-thesis, pleasure in the beautiful is directed towards either another mental state (the free play of the faculties) or the representation of the beautiful object. If pleasure in the beautiful is intentional, one could draw on John Searle's Chinese Room thought-experiment and argue that intentionality cannot be caused by "formal structure[s]" (Searle 1980, p. 420) or "computational processes" (Searle 1980, p. 422). I leave it for another day to follow this line of argument.
50 See Schönecker 2018, p. 86.

view: to have a grasp on what pleasure in the beautiful feels like I must feel this pleasure myself, and to judge whether a given object is beautiful I must feel disinterested pleasure myself while beholding this object. Although one can possibly occupy the human-specific point of view by sympathetically imagining what it is like to feel disinterested pleasure for other people, there is no need for such a procedure. In fact, a transcending of the individual point of view in favor of the human-specific (universal) point of view is already contained in the feeling of disinterested pleasure itself, to wit, in its phenomenal character.

I have, finally, argued that the Kantian realm of beauty is foreclosed to AI. Beauty, for Kant, is constituted by the feeling of disinterested pleasure, which must be experienced by each beholder herself when being confronted with a given object. Since computers or AI cannot have mental states with phenomenal character and, thus, cannot *experience* pleasure, AI cannot experience beauty. Therefore, AI does not have a proper grasp on beauty.

References

Apart from the *Critique of Pure Reason*, all references to Kant's works are to *Kant's Gesammelte Schriften, Ausgabe der Preußischen Akademie der Wissenschaften* (Berlin: De Gruyter, 1902 ff.). References to the *Critique of Pure Reason* are to the standard A and B pagination of the first and second editions. Translations are from *The Cambridge Edition of the Works of Immanuel Kant*; translations are altered when considered necessary.

The following abbreviations of individual works are used:

EEKU	Erste Einleitung in die Kritik der Urteilskraft/*First Introduction to the Critique of Judgment*
GMS	Grundlegung zur Metaphysik der Sitten/*Groundwork of the Metaphysics of Morals*
KpV	Kritik der praktischen Vernunft/*Critique of Practical Reason*
KrV	Kritik der reinen Vernunft/*Critique of Pure Reason*
KU	Kritik der Urteilskraft/*Critique of Judgment*
MS	Die Metaphysik der Sitten/*Metaphysics of Morals*
Observations	*Observations on the Feeling of the Beautiful and the Sublime*
Progress	*What Real Progress Has Metaphysics Made in Germany Since the Time of Leibniz and Wolff?*
Prol	Prolegomena zu einer jeden künftigen Metaphysik/*Prolegomena to Any Future Metaphysics*

AI Now 2019 Report. New York 2019. https://ainowinstitute.org/AI_Now_2019_Report.pdf, last visit 4 February 2022.

Allison, Henry (2001): *Kant's Theory of Taste*. Cambridge: Cambridge University Press.

Aquila, Richard (1982): "A New Look at Kant's Aesthetic Judgments". In: Ted Cohen/Paul Guyer (eds.): *Essays in Kant's Aesthetics*. Chicago & London: The University of Chicago Press. pp. 87–114.

Asada, Minoru (2015): "Development of Artificial Empathy". In: *Neuroscience Research* 90. pp. 41–50.

Asada, Minoru (2019): "Artificial Pain May Induce Empathy, Morality, and Ethics in the Conscious Mind of Robots". In: *Philosophies* 4. Nr. 3. pp. 1–10.

Berger, Larissa (2018): "Can Artificial Intelligence Know about Beauty? – A Kantian Approach". In: *Journal of Artificial Intelligence Humanities* 2. pp. 119–143.

Berger, Larissa (2022): *Kants Philosophie des Schönen. Eine kommentarische Interpretation zu den §§ 1–22 der Kritik der Urteilskraft*. Freiburg: Alber Verlag.

Bösel, Bernd (2019): "Affective Computing". In: Kevin Liggieri/Oliver Müller (eds.): *Mensch – Maschine – Interaktion. Handbuch zu Geschichte – Kultur – Ethik*. Berlin: Metzler. pp. 223–225

Chalmers, David J. (1996): *The Conscious Mind. In Search of a Fundamental Theory*. Oxford: Oxford University Press.

Ginsborg, Hannah (2015): *The Normativity of Nature. Essays on Kant's Critique of Judgment*. Oxford: Oxford University Press.

Goldie, Peter/Döring, Sabine/Cowie, Roddy (2011): "The Ethical Distinctiveness of Emotion-Oriented Technology: Four Long-Term Issues". In: Paolo Petta/Catherine Pelachaud/Roddy Cowie (eds.): *Emotion-Oriented Systems. The Humaine Handbook*. Berlin, Heidelberg: Springer Verlag. pp. 725–733.

Goldie, Peter (2002): "Emotions, Feelings and Intentionality". In: *Phenomenology and Cognitive Sciences* 1. pp. 235–254.

Guyer, Paul (1979): *Kant and the Claims of Taste*. Cambridge MA: Harvard University Press.

Guyer, Paul (2018): "What Is It Like to Experience the Beautiful and the Sublime?". In: Kelly Sorensen/Diane Williamson (eds.): *Kant and the Faculty of Feeling*. Cambridge: Cambridge University Press. pp. 147–165.

Jackson, Frank (1986): "What Mary Didn't Know". In: *The Journal of Philosophy* 83. Nr.5. pp. 291–295.

Kriegel, Uriah/Timmons, Mark (2021): "The Phenomenology of Kantian Respect and Persons". In: Richard Dean/Oliver Sensen (eds.): *Respect. Philosophical Essays*. Oxford: Oxford University Press.

Kuehn, Johannes/Haddadin, Sami (2017): "An Artificial Robot Nervous System to Teach Robots How to Feel Pain and Reflexively React to Potentially Damaging Contacts". In: *IEEE Robotics and Automation Letters* 2. Nr. 1. pp. 72–79.

Levin, Janet (2018): "Functionalism". In: Edward N. Zalta (ed.): *Stanford Encyclopedia of Philosophy*. https://plato.stanford.edu/entries/functionalism/, last visit 9 July 2021.

Man, Kingson/Damasio, Antonio (2019): "Homeostatsis and Soft Robotics in the Design of Feeling Machines". In: *Nature Machine Intelligence* 1. Nr.10. pp. 446–452.

Misselhorn, Catrin (2018): *Grundfragen der Maschinenethik*. Stuttgart: Reclam.

Misselhorn, Catrin (2021): *Künstliche Intelligenz und Empathie. Vom Leben mit Emotionserkennung, Sexrobotern & Co*. Stuttgart: Reclam.

Nagel, Thomas (1974): "What Is It Like to Be a Bat?". In: *The Philosophical Review* 83. Nr.4. pp. 435–50.

Nagel, Thomas (1979): *Mortal Questions*. Cambridge: Cambridge University Press.

Picard, Rosalind (1997): *Affective Computing*. Cambridge MA: MIT Press.

Recki, Birgit (2004): "Wie fühlt man sich als vernünftiges Wesen? Immanuel Kant über ästhetische und moralische Gefühle". In: Klaus Herding/Bernhard Stumpfhaus (eds.): *Pathos, Affekt, Gefühl: die Emotionen in den Künsten*. Berlin, New York: De Gruyter. pp. 274–294.

Rinofner-Kreidl, Sonja (2004): "Das ‚Gehirn-Selbst'. Ist die Erste-Person-Perspektive naturalisierbar?". In: *Phänomenologische Forschungen*. pp. 219–252.

Schönecker, Dieter (2018): "Can Practical Reason Be Artificial". In: *Journal of Artificial Intelligence Humanities* 2. pp. 67–91.

Searle, John (1980): "Minds, Brains, and Programs". In: *The Behavioral and Brain Sciences* 3. pp. 417–457.

Tye, Michael (2017): "Qualia". In: Edward N. Zalta (ed.): *Stanford Encyclopedia of Philosophy*. https://plato.stanford.edu/entries/qualia/, last visit 9 July 2021.

Walter, Sven (2006): "Allgemeine Einleitung: Phänomenales Bewusstsein: Unlösbares Mysterium oder seriöses wissenschaftliches Problem?". In: Heinz-Dieter Heckmann/Sven Walter (eds.): *Qualia – Ausgewählte Beiträge*. Paderborn: mentis. pp. 11–60.

Zahavi, Dan/Kriegel, Uriah (2016): "For-me-ness: What it is and what it is not". In: Daniel O. Dahlstrohm/Andreas Elpidorou/Walter Hopp (eds.): *Philosophy of Mind and Phenomenology: Conceptual and Empirical Approaches*. New York: Routledge. pp. 36–54

Zinkin, Melissa (2012): "Kant and the Pleasure of 'Mere Reflection". In: *Inquiry* 55. Nr. 5. pp. 433–453.

Zuckert, Rachel (2002): "A New Look at Kant's Theory of Pleasure". In: *The Journal of Aesthetics and Art Criticism* 60. Nr. 3. pp. 239–252.

Name Index

Subject Index